First Published in Britai
Author: Gill McGregor NDSF CBA Cert Ed.
Designs by: Gill McGregor

Published by: Gill McGregor College Publishers
ISBN 978-0-9929332-6-5
Volume 1
Printed in the UK
Layout design: www.sosbusyweb.co.uk

Introduction

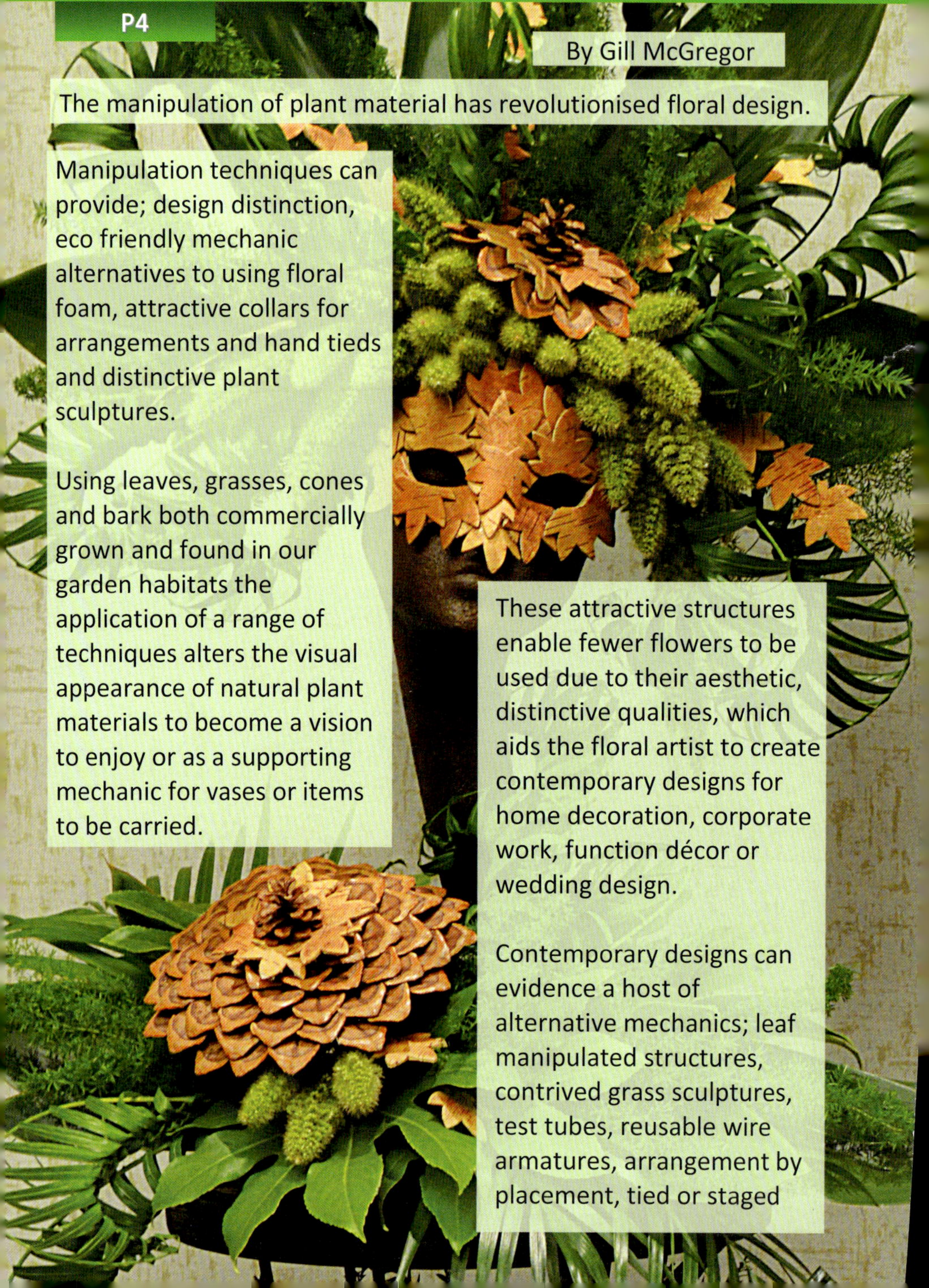

By Gill McGregor

The manipulation of plant material has revolutionised floral design.

Manipulation techniques can provide; design distinction, eco friendly mechanic alternatives to using floral foam, attractive collars for arrangements and hand tieds and distinctive plant sculptures.

Using leaves, grasses, cones and bark both commercially grown and found in our garden habitats the application of a range of techniques alters the visual appearance of natural plant materials to become a vision to enjoy or as a supporting mechanic for vases or items to be carried.

These attractive structures enable fewer flowers to be used due to their aesthetic, distinctive qualities, which aids the floral artist to create contemporary designs for home decoration, corporate work, function décor or wedding design.

Contemporary designs can evidence a host of alternative mechanics; leaf manipulated structures, contrived grass sculptures, test tubes, reusable wire armatures, arrangement by placement, tied or staged

Introduction

with the use of minimal floral foam.

Sculptures from cones and bark also echo that "Go green" ethos. As they can be reused, recycled and reborn to be hand made to provide elements of art to incorporate in our contemporary floral designs.

This book is the first in a series of "Go Greener Flower Arranging" publications, which evidence different design concepts using natural plant materials in their different forms to develop design styles for the floral artist and florist.

I hope this book gives you joy and inspiration.

Inverted woven obelisk sculpture using Typha grass

P6

Typha latifolia (typha grass, bulrush or reedmace) is sold in bunches of 20 and each is a straight, flat, strap-shaped, smooth, strong blade of grass.

Take 8 typha grass blades and place 4 in a row with their tips all facing the same way. Weave the remaining 4 blades through the row to create a central woven square; woven tips to face the same way. Manoeuvre the tips and blade ends which extend beyond the woven square to all measure the same length.

Place a ruler so its straight edge is just beyond one of the sides of the woven square and bend each blade upwards at a 90 degree angle. Repeat the process until all 4 sides (16 tips and ends of blades) are bent.

Spiral the 16 tips and ends of the typha blades to form neat, slightly overlapping sides by selecting one blade and placing each adjacent blade in turn to slightly overlap the blade before.

Inverted woven obelisk sculpture using Typha grass

By pushing the woven square with your hand whilst holding the spiralled blades' tips and ends together you can face the woven square diagonally or horizontally to suit your design. Once you have achieved your desired angle of this inverted obelisk, tightly bind the blade tips and ends together with paper covered wire.

The spaces between the woven square will allow for plant materials to be inserted through the sculpture if desired.

To create a larger inverted obelisk use 10 typha blades and make in the same manner to make a 5 x 5 woven square.

Composite Sugar pine cone Glamelia

P8

A glamelia is a composite bouquet. It is normally made from the petals of many flowers to form one large "flower". So I thought, can I make a glamelia (5) from a large sugar pine cone? (4)

Wire securely a small fir cone (1) with a 1.20mm x 40cm green lacquered wire between its scales at the base of the cone. Bend the remaining wire to mould around the cone's base to the centre and then bend the wire at a 90 degree angle to form a handle.

Using a large (Pinus lambertiana) (4) sugar pine cone, twist one scale until it breaks off from the cone's central axis. Repeat until you have a large number of individual scales and grade them according to size. This effective glamelia requires concentric rings of like sized scales to be hot glued into position to create uniform rings.

Composite Sugar pine cone Glamelia

To ensure you achieve visual balance, it is best to have a trial run positioning the scales to form the first concentric ring at the base of the wired fir cone before they are individually hot glued to the underside of the cone (2).

Allow to set before adding additional hot glue to the scales' base fibres at the back of the glamelia to achieve greater strength and integrity to support further concentric rings. Once set, continue to attach concentric rings of like sized scales as described (3), until you have created your desired size glamelia (5).

China grass petals

P10

Liriope muscari (China grass) is sold in bunches of 50 and has off white longitudinal striped blades.

Take 13 Liriope muscari (China grass) blades and secure tightly at the base with an elastic band. Clamp the bunch between your knees and commence plaiting 3 blades from the outer edge. Fold plait the blades uniformly to make it even for 10cms.

It is now that you will need to include additional blades from the bunch into the plait.

So every time you fold plait into the middle away from the bunch you then lay a China grass blade right side up, from the bunch nearest to the plait, on top of the blade you have just plaited. Continue fold plaiting using the same method and tension for uniformity of spacing. The 3 "braids" will be getting thicker as the blades pile up on top of each braid. Carry on until there are no blades left in the bunch. Continue to plait the "3 braids" until you reach the tips and secure into position with bound metallic wire. Do not bind the wire too tightly or you will damage the grass.

Undo the elastic band making sure that the original 3 plaited blades do not unravel. Hold the plait and then "spiral" the blades each in turn as they

China grass petals

were added into the plait to now cross over each other and are all the “right” side up.

Ease the grasses to form a petal shape with the plait on the outside and with even spaced grass blades within the structure. Cut the ends as appropriate and bind into position with metallic wire.

Repeat until you have made 5 China grass petals in order to construct a “flower” with a concentric ring of round headed flowers with a central flower. A distinctive idea for a coffee table design.

Eucalyptus bark collar

P12

Select a 31cm (12 inch) flat copper wreath ring. Take 4 x 1.20mm x 40cm green lacquered wires, bend each wire 5cms from the tip at a 90 degree angle. Secure each bent wire with pot tape to the inner ring of the copper ring equidistant apart to act as supports or as a handle.
Cut out a cardboard template slightly larger than the ring.
Using a pair of hanging basket liners, cut out the equivalent of 2 rings - you may need to make the rings from segments to be economic. Place the copper ring on top of one of the liner ring shapes and hot glue together.
Place the second liner on top of the glued copper ring to form a sandwiched copper ring foundation and hot glue. You may need to stitch the liners together strategically, with metallic wire, if you feel the glue has not adhered properly.
Using dried Eucalyptus bark fallen from a tree, hot glue different sized rolls of bark

attractively to cover the liner foundation. Do not cut the bark to size but physically break it with your fingers as it will look more natural. Add a few additional rolled bark placements diagonally on top of the collar for effect.

The completed Eucalyptus bark collar can be used to frame a hand tied; by bringing the wire arms together at the centre and brought down to form a handle. Alternatively, the wire arms are inserted into a container to form a collar, to enhance a design with or without floral foam as the mechanic.

Cycas palm - sculptured, threaded, embellished, ...

P14

Cycas revoluta (Japanese sago palm) is sold in bunches of 10 at varying centimetre lengths. The fronds have dark green, leathery, pinnate leaves. The Cycas palm can be dried either in its natural or manipulated form, especially in the summer, when laid in the extreme sun, it will dry a beautiful yellow colour.

1

(1) **Sculptured**, cut the frond to create angular patterns either side of the leaf. The pinnate leaves will seal and not bruise.

2

(2) **Threaded**, strategically thread beads and glue to secure into position with a rubber glue to add a decorative feature.

3

(3) **Embellished**, stitch a string of beads to the midrib vein for enhancement secured with complementary coloured metallic wire.

4

(4) **Manipulated ring,** ease the stem to curve. Calculate the length of pinnate leaves that need to be removed from one side in order to make a round form with enclosed space and secure into position with metallic wire.

(5) **Manipulated Lobe,**
ease the stem to curve and securely attach a length of metallic wire 5cms from the tip. Continue to curve the stem to make a single lobe shape and bring the wire diagonally towards the frond's base and wind between the pinnate leaves to secure, before trimming the wire.

Sugar pine mini cone flower

P16

Using a saw, cut through a Pinus lambertiana (sugar pine) cone to provide a quantity of sections which look like flower shapes. You may have sections of one, two or three rings of scales.

With a fine drill, or a bradawl,

make a small, central hole on the underside of a section and hot glue a 1.8mm x 50cm black wire in the hole to form a stem and tape with brown stem tape.

Decorate with different cones or dried materials hot glued in the centre for effect.

To add Betula pendula (birch) bark star shaped "petal" extensions. Make a cardboard template of your desired star shape and draw round on flat silver birch bark sheets.

Cut to create the desired star shape petal extension and make a hole with a bradawl in the centre of each. Thread the birch extensions onto the sugar pine flower wire and hot glue into position. Stagger the points to make effective layers.

Monstera leaves sculptured, rolled and laced

Monstera deliciosa – (Swiss cheese plant) has heart-shaped, pinnatisect and often perforated, glossy deep green leaves which in their own right are very distinctive, yet a bunch of ten in one design can look over powering.

There are a variety of different ways the leaves can be manipulated to create further distinction:

1. **Sculptured**, by cutting the leaf into an alternative shape. The leaf does not bruise but seals where it has been cut.

1

2

3. **Rolled**, roll the leaf, upper surface facing you, to form a tube and secure in position by binding string, wool or wire in a pattern formation to hold the tube in place. Thus evidencing the underside of the leaf's lighter green colour.

3

2. **Laced**, select a leaf which mirrors the same number of perforations either side of the midrib vein. Attach the string or wool to the leaf's stem and lace in a diagonal fashion to create crossing lines for enhanced distinction.

Eucalyptus threaded and layered with ...

P18

Eucalyptus gunni (cider gum) is sold by the weight and has round silver/ blue, blue/ green, round to sickle-shaped leaves arranged in pairs.

This Eucalyptus can be manipulated to aid distinction and is especially useful as the manipulated structures will air dry for reuse.

1. **Threaded**, the individual leaves are threaded onto a piece of metallic wire. The sizes can be graded or random. Air dry for reuse.

1

2. **Layered polystyrene spheres,** can be based with layered concentric rings of Eucalyptus leaves pinned on with steel pins to provide overall, neat coverage. A pick wire is added for easy insertion. Start by pinning a pattern of leaves at the top, for effect. Complete by pinning concentric layers on to the sphere ensuring the leaves are positioned to hide the pins from the layer before. Air dry for reuse.

2

3. **This alternative reusable mechanic,** is useful for a design of air dried plant materials. Take 10 x green lacquered 0.90mm x 50cm wires to form a bundled spine. Using the same gauge wire, bind a wire twice around the spine 8cms up from the base and pull the wires in opposite directions and cut down to between 4 and 7cms.

Repeat binding the wires in close order up the spine whilst pulling them at different angles and cutting them to different lengths for effect. When you reach near the tip you can cut the wires shorter for a tapered look and the wire mechanic can be curved for additional effect.

3

It is not advisable to use this type of mechanic near, for example, young children or pets.

This collection of dried flowers had originally been arranged as fresh plant materials in a posy ring design.

The flowers were left to air dry before being reused and impaled onto the green lacquered wire mechanic which is so suitable for an elegant vase with a very narrow aperture.

Kentia Palm Plaited

P20

Howea forsteriana (kentia palm) is sold in 10s at a variety of different centimetre lengths. It has triangular shaped, widespread fronds with evenly spaced lance-shaped leaflets. I have used a 120cm palm to demonstrate the plaiting technique. Clamp the stem between your knees, underside of the leaf facing you.

The secret is to achieve a firm, uniform plait parallel to the stem and treat the leaflets like paper and not like wool or hair, so you fold as you plait and crease to make it hold in position.

1) The tip will either be forked, if so, fold flat to make "braid 1" or if there are a quantity of fine leaflets - squash together to form "braid 1". As a * right hander, take the top right hand leaflet and fold/ plait into the middle and crease and lay the next right hand leaflet on top of what you have just plaited "braid 2". Swap hands without letting go of the braids. Fold/ plait the top left hand leaflet into the middle and crease and lay the next left hand leaflet on top of what you have just plaited "braid 3".

2) Now that you have "3 braids" continue plaiting as stated above by fold plaiting into the middle, and crease and then lay the next leaflet on top of what you have just plaited from the same side and swap hands. *Make sure you keep hold of the braids at all times. You will find the "braids" will become thicker as more leaflets pile up on top of each other.*

Kentia Palm Plaited

3) As you fold plait and crease, you must gradually extend the length of the leaflet that you position on top of what you have just plaited to increase the dimension of the curving 3 dimensional structure.

4) Continue fold plaiting, creasing and extending the length of the leaflet that you have laid on top of what you have just plaited into the middle to achieve your required width.

Try to make pairs of leaflets either side of the stem identical in length for visual balance.

Having achieved the required width you will need to plait as before but gradually decrease the length of the leaflet that you lay on top of what you have just plaited to achieve a tapered look.

Kentia Palm Plaited

P22

5) Just keep fold plaiting, creasing and laying shorter leaflet lengths each time you lay one on top of what you have just plaited until you achieve a virtual point.

6) When you have no more leaflets left to use, continue plaiting so the plait can lay against the stem. With metallic or paper covered wire, secure the plait to the stem. After a week your wiring will feel loose as the stem and leaflets have dehydrated and have therefore shrunk in size, so just add another binding wire just above your initial wiring to secure the plait.

The plaited palm can be air dried for reuse.

Fine leaflet tips may stick out, but these can be ripped off once complete.

** Please note I as a left hander would start from the left side and plait and then continue as described, but thought as there is a higher percentage of right handers I would talk in right hand terms.*

Plaited Kentia Palm as a Mechanic

Using the plaited palm as a mechanic, flowers can be threaded through the structure to enable them to be arranged into position.

Once happy with their placement the stems can be tied at the base of the plait before being arranged in the vase as desired. The rolled, stacked Dracaena fragrans leaves helps to evidence a contrast of lines whilst the hint of Mimosa provides textural contrast.

For greater distinction spray the underside of the palm with floral spray paint before plaiting.

Spruce pine cone flower

P24

The cones of the Picea pungens (spruce) have wonderful gold shaded scales when dried. Often when they fall off the tree they are closed as damp, but when placed on top of a radiator they open to reveal their delicate, frilly edged scales.

This simple flower requires each cone to be wired at the base, between the scales, using a green lacquered 0.71mm x 50cm wire. Dependent upon the size of the cones, five, six or seven wired cones of the same size are arranged around a central wired cone to form a 'flower'. When happy with their positioning secure with 0.38mm green lacquered reel wire. The wire "stem" is then taped with brown stem tape.

Feature bark with threaded conkers

Lengths of bark can be torn to allow for a piece of the bark to become the support pick in a vase. Always tear don't cut as it looks far more natural.

(Aesculus hippocastanum) horse chestnut conkers, drilled with a fine drill are ideal for threading with aluminium wire to create interesting lines of movement. Using aluminium wire is the best material as over time the conkers will shrink and the end of the wire can be further manipulated to shorten; thus keeping the string of conkers close together.

China grass heart

P26

This heart is plaited in a similar way (page 10) to the Liriope muscari (China grass) flower. Instead of using 13 blades per "petal" each of the two lobed structures use 17 blades of China grass.

The plaiting is the same method but each half has to be plaited so that the plait is on the outside of the shape. You therefore have to plait as a right handed person and then as a left handed person; to get the lobes to be mirror image. To create a curved lobe secure tightly, 17 blades of China grass at the base and clamp the bunch between your knees.

Plait 3 grasses which are positioned on the outside edge of the bunch for 10cms. You then need to add grasses from the bunch to create the "ribs". Every time you fold plait into the middle away from the bunch you then lay a China grass blade right side up, from the bunch nearest to the plait, on top of the blade you have just plaited. Every two full plaits, release the bunch which is between your knees and twist the bunch slightly away from you, clamp with your knees and resume plaiting to help create a curve.

Once all the grasses are plaited continue to plait the 3 "braids" for around 3cms and secure the plait with paper covered wire. Undo the elastic band and spiral the leaf blades in consecutive order as to how they were added in to the plait and manipulate into a heart shaped lobe form with even spaced grasses before securing with paper covered wire.

China grass heart

Repeat to make the opposite lobe. Make sure the outline plait is mirror image (opposite) to the previously made structure.

By using aluminium wire woven through the underside of each lobe (A) and secured at both the base and the tip, the aluminium wire was shaped to make the heart form more rigid.

Equisetum disc and bespoke sculpturing

P28

Equisetum hyemale (snake grass) is sold in bunches of 20 and has tall, hollow, dark green stems with black ringed nodes.

Equisetum requires internal support wiring as the stems bend at the nodes easily. Insert from the tip down a green lacquered 0.71mm x 50cm wire (1) and then insert from the stem end upwards an additional 0.71mm x 50cm wire. To create a disc, internally support the Equisetum and using one stem at the tip coil tightly to form a flat, spiralled circle. Insert a pin, horizontally, through the coil to hold its position. Take a second internally supported stem and insert its tip into the base (2) of the coiled stem. Continue to wind the snake grass tightly and continue pinning the coil strategically, with black headed pins, to hold it together whilst making sure the pin points do not stick out from the disc. Ensure you pin where the tip goes into the base of the previous stem for stability (3). Repeat winding and pinning to secure until you have made the disc to the required size.

Bespoke Equisetum Sculptures

To create bespoke Equisetum sculptures, internally support the snake grass stems as before.

Equisetum disc and bespoke sculpturing

Pin the stems strategically together like a fence secured with black headed pins, until you have sufficient to cut out your desired shape using a template as a guide. Additional pins can be used to ensure stability after cutting.

To stabilise and preserve, Equisetum sculptures.

Apply a mixture of one part PVA glue to one part water to all sides and place on a plastic surface.

Allow to dry before use.

Wood slice and sugar pine cone flower

P30

Using a saw, cut through a Pinus lambertiana (sugar pine) cone to provide a quantity of sections which look like flower shapes. You may have sections of one, two or three rings of scales.

With a fine drill, or a bradawl make a small central hole in the underside of the section and hot glue a 1.8mm x 50cm black wire in the hole to form a stem.

Select sufficient oblong pre cut wood slices which can either be slotted in-between 2 rings of scales or be glued underneath a scale ring to form a uniform "flower". Hot glue into position.

Decorate with dried acorn nuts and cupules (cups) for effect. To disguise the wire stem, insert the wire into an Equisetum hyemale (snake grass) stem which will eventually dry.

*To make a **fir cone ribbed unit strand**, use a 1.8mm x 50cm black stay wire and wire the cones to the stay wire, in close order, with black metallic wire. The metallic wire is securely wound around the base scales of a cone before winding the metallic wire tightly around the black stay wire. Repeat the technique making sure the cones are locked into each other. The ribbed unit can be bent to your desired shape.

Wood slice and sugar pine cone flower

P31

Birch Masquerade masks

P32

The use of pre cut Betula pendula (birch) bark shapes to cover manufactured plastic shapes, such as masks, provides the ability for a composition to evidence the predominance of plant material in a design. The plastic masks, removed of their fabric decoration, were sanded with sand paper to create a rough surface for the hot glue to adhere to. The birch shapes were used to base the plastic mask foundation to form a bonded, layered coverage. Some bark shapes were cut to facilitate the outline of the eyes.

Textured Polystyrene Forms

Polystyrene shapes are useful for incorporation in a design due to their light weight.

It is advisable that you do not cut polystyrene with a heated wire cutter or heated knife as this action is extremely hazardous. If you wish to have straight edges you will need to cut with a saw as required and then seal the polystyrene with a thick layer of PVA glue. Allow to dry and then fill with an over the counter filler.

Small containers can then be attached by drilling holes in the container and then screwing it into position with a small amount of PVA on the screw to help secure. Place an identical container on top to house your mechanics.

Textured polystyrene forms

P33

To achieve a textured look, I mixed the PVA glue with paprika and painted it on and allowed it to dry. The dry surface was red and lightly textured to hide the polystyrene "cells".
* I then sprayed the polystyrene form with a floral spray paint primer before adding my required colour.

Painting *
If you wish to spray paint polystyrene, you will also need to seal the surface with a thick layer of painted on PVA glue and allow to dry, before spraying with a floral spray paint.

Remember to spray in a well ventilated area.

Typha precision cut Herringbone

P34 Select a suitable shallow, oblong container and cut floral foam to size, do <u>not</u> soak or place in the container at this stage.
Pin, with pearl headed pins, through the midrib vein Prunus laurocerasus (common laurel, cherry laurel) around the foam's edges so the tips of the laurel are level. For neatness, make sure the outer edge of each leaf buffs up against the midrib vein of the previous leaf attached. You can then trim the base of the laurel leaves to make sure they are level with the bottom of the floral foam. Place the laurel edged foam in the oblong dish; <u>do not</u> wet the floral foam at this stage.

Cut a small piece of floral foam (1) to the size of your required spray bump. Mark its desired position on the floral foam.

Cut a quantity of typha grass blades to a length of 15cms. Do not use the very woody base of the blade as it does not bend uniformly.

Commence arranging row one of the typha herringbone by inserting each 15cm cut blade to be at the same diagonal angle, to the same desired length to create a uniform loop. Do not place loops where the floral foam spray bump will be.

Typha precision cut Herringbone

Space each typha loop to be 2 fingers apart for effect.

Row 2 requires the typha loops to be positioned diagonally in the opposite direction. Each blade must be inserted uniformly and with even spacing for effect as previously described.

You can now wet the floral foam with the herringbone pattern and secure the wet spray bump with cut down kebab sticks.

Continue arranging rows 3 and 4 in opposing directions or until the foam is covered with typha herringbone as desired.

Finish with a small, complementary flower and foliage spray.

Rhapis palm sculptured and rolled

P36

Rhapis excelsa (finger palm, lady palm) is sold in bunches of 10 and have shiny, dark green, fan shaped, lance-shaped, furrowed lobed leaves on a slender stem. Their pointed tips are often blunt cut before they arrive at the wholesalers.

1

1. **Sculptured**, by cutting the leaf into an alternative shape. The leaf does not bruise but seals where it has been cut.

2

Rhapis palm sculptured and rolled

2. **Rolled**, by adhering a good quality double sided tape to either the upper or lower surface of the "finger's" blunt tip and creating different sized rolls. In turn roll each finger to your desired size and secure with the tape. By rolling in opposing directions you will achieve greater visual interest and variety.

Flexigrass Cobra head structure

P38

Take 9 blades of Ficinea fascicularis (flexigrass) and bind tightly together at the base of the blades. Divide into 3 sets of 3 and plait uniformly to create a braid. Carefully curve the braid and secure to form a loop.

Thread 5 individual blades through the gaps between the plait on one side of the loop, evenly spaced and continue to thread through the plait on the opposite side. Pull the grasses through until the blades are the same length either side.

Carefully bring down each length of grass to form an even, Cobra head shape and bind to secure.

This structure can be used in a design to achieve distinction or be used as a manipulated mechanic by threading flowers and foliage through the Cobra head structure for support. A distinctive structure for bridal or contract vase work.

Calla lilies are threaded through this flexigrass Cobra head structure. The stems are disguised by a handle of Aspidistra secured with decorative pins.

Flexigrass Swan's Neck

This Ficinea fascicularis (flexigrass) Swan's neck is made from 18 grasses. Bind to secure, with paper covered wire, to create the bunch of grasses level at the base. Continue to bind, now with even spacing, upwards for 15 cms. Carefully move 2 blades away, without damaging the blades, from the original bundle and bind the remaining bundle 4 times uniformly. Repeat this process by removing each time 2 grasses away from the bundle and bind 4 times to create even spacing. When there are only 2 grasses left in the bundle, bind to the tips and cut the wire to measure a 15cm residue.

To create the Swan's neck shape, spiral the pairs of grasses at their tips in the order they were moved away from the bundle to create an even spaced structure. When happy with their positioning secure with the residue wire.

This Swan's neck structure provides a distinctive form to interconnect 2 designs or as a distinctive feature.

Cedar rose and silver birch bark flower

P40

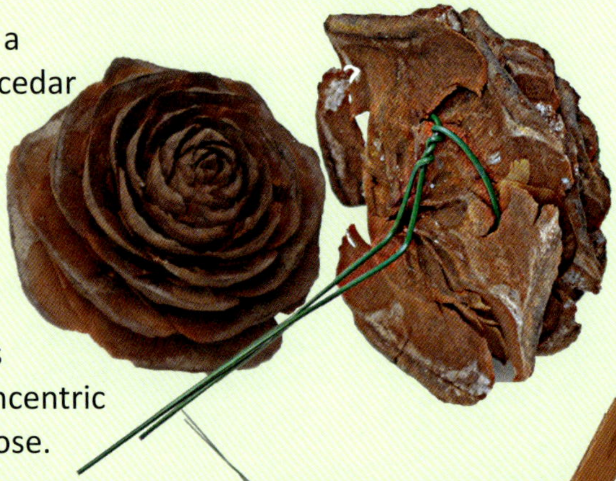

This design requires the use of a Cedrus deodara (deodar pine) cedar rose cone as the centre of this attractive birch flower. Wire a cedar rose cone using a green lacquered 0.71mm x 50cm wire. For effect make a Glamelia with additional scales hot glued on to the cone in concentric rings to create a larger cedar rose.

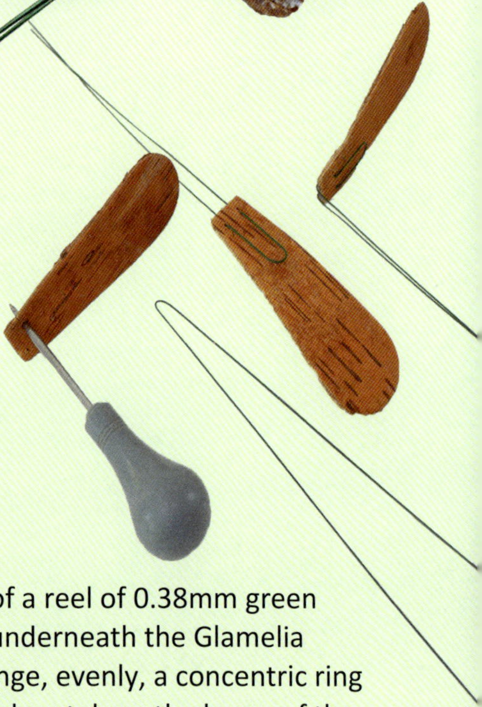

Using pre cut petal shaped Betula pendula (birch) bark, make 2 bradawl holes 5mm from the base of each birch "petal". Bend a green lacquered 0.71mm x 50cm wire in the middle to form a long hair pin and insert the hair pin through the holes from the back of the "petal" and pull the wires through until there is a 1cm loop at the back. Bend the wires at the base of the "petal" at a 90 degree angle. Repeat until you have a quantity of wired Birch "petals".

Secure the end of a reel of 0.38mm green lacquered wire underneath the Glamelia cedar rose. Arrange, evenly, a concentric ring of birch petals so the bases of the "petals" are underneath the rose and meet up with each other. When happy with their placement bind together tightly using the reel wire until secure.

Do not cut the reel wire.

Cedar rose and silver birch bark flower

P41

Arrange a second concentric ring of petals to your desired effect and secure into position by binding tightly with the reel wire. Repeat as desired.

Finish by taping the wires together tightly with brown stem tape and add hot glue around the binding point area to further strengthen the stability of the birch "flower". The glued back of the flower can be disguised with sisal or brown fibres from a hanging basket liner.

Rolled Aspidistra

P42

Aspidistra elatior (common Aspidistra, cast iron plant) are sold in bunches of 10 in varying centimetre lengths. Their dark green leaves are upright, leathery, elliptic (oval, with a short or no point) or lance-shaped.

Rolling Aspidistra leaves is a simple yet effective manipulation technique. To start the roll have the upper surface of the leaf facing the ceiling and roll down from the tip, ensuring the midrib vein stays in line and the roll is large enough for 2 fingers to be inserted each side. Roll and turn the leaf over to see the back and pin with a 0.71mm hair pin wire where you believe there are 3 thicknesses of leaf. Insert the hairpin at a diagonal angle either side of the midrib vein and push the wires inside the roll to cross over, like folded arms, to lay flat against the leaf. Alternatively the roll can be stapled, either side of the midrib vein, into position.

Rolled Aspidistra leaves can be dried when left out of water in a warm, dry place and after 3-4 months will be copper in colour.

Tree Fern Sculptured

Asparagus pyramidalis (tree fern) is sold by the weight and has a wonderful conical shape with a soft fluffy texture which lends itself to being sculptured.

Place a few stems together (1) to create a 3 dimensional conical shape and using either bullion or metallic wire commence binding the stems together with uniform spacing (2). Continue binding up the stems to the tip, so the fern itself becomes bound to create a thin, solid conical shape.

Once at the tip, start to bind down the sculptured fern to achieve a cross wire pattern and bind down to the base of the stems. The closer the bind the more it will bend. The thicker the wire the more it will bend (3).

To create a ring at the tip, manipulate the sculptured materials to the desired shape and secure into position with a piece of complementary wire (4).

This sculptured tree fern, moulded to create repetition of line to complement the vase, is arranged in a thick bunch of Alchemilla mollis as the mechanic to support the Agapanthus.

Rhapis palm Single Puff and Double Puff

P44

Double Looped Puff. Select 2 x blunt tipped Rhapis palms which have identical number of fingers. Stick the tips of all “fingers” together using squares of good quality double sided tape, so the front sides face each other. Carefully turn the Double Looped Puff inside out to create a much fuller puff for larger designs.

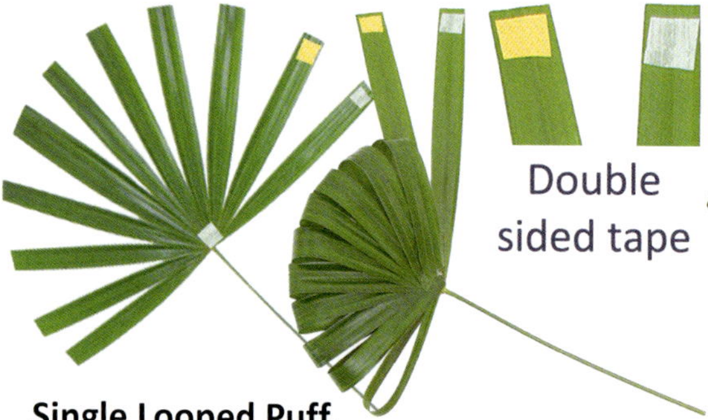

Single Looped Puff.

Start by taking a blunt cut tipped Rhapis leaf and apply a square of good quality double sided tape to the centre of the reverse of the leaf where all the “fingers” radiate from. In turn, from right to left, a “finger” tip is adhered with a square of double sided tape to the leaf base, without squashing the “puff”, so the puff echoes the shape of the original leaf.

Use a decorative pin or a staple to ensure the Single Looped Puff is held in position.

Rhapis palm Single Puff and Double Puff

P45

This floral composition evidences the use of repetition to create distinction with the design of the herons echoing the leaf manipulated Rhapis palm single and double puffs. The double puff fills a vast area enabling fewer materials to be used as the stems are spaced widely apart. The shadowed, vertical typha (bulrushes) are arranged to provide a vertical line of movement whilst contrasting with the forms of the Cymbidium orchids.

Preserved and coloured Masquerade masks

P46

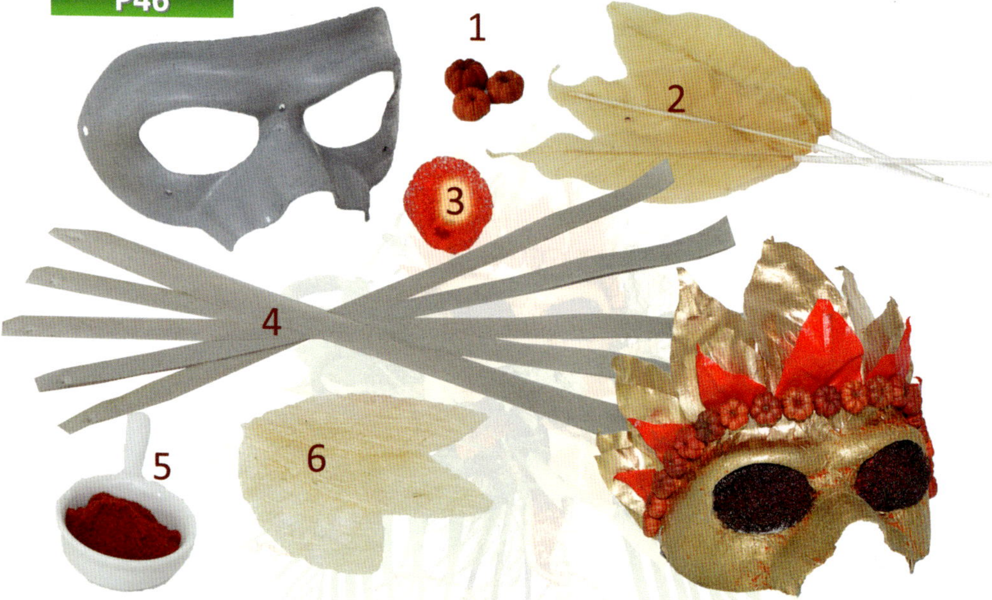

Preserved and glycerined plant materials, natural or coloured make striking adornments to plastic masks to evidence distinctive use of plant material.

The masks were sanded with sand paper to create a rough finish to aid adherence, before being covered with strips of newspaper glued with PVA glue. Once dry they were either spray painted or covered with a layer of saw dust and paint sprayed. A few holes were drilled each side of the mask to allow wires to go through for support insertion.

Stapled assemblies of graduated, layered leaves were attached with hot glue for effect, before adding the final elements of adornment.

1) Glochidion ferdinandi (Putka Pods - mini pumpkins),
2) Glycerined Magnolia grandifolia, 3) Luffa aegyptiaca,
4) Strips of newspaper, 5) Paprika, 6) Sculptured sisal sheeting,
7) Sculptured bamboo leaf structure.

Preserved and coloured Masquerade masks

P47

To provide the eerie atmosphere, the eyes were made from Luffa aegyptiaca (sponge gourd) sprayed black.

Flexigrass bound circle and loops

P48

Using 40 stems of Ficinea fascicularis (flexigrass), secure tightly at the base with an elastic band. Thread an end of green paper covered wire through the band and twist to secure. Place the bunch between your knees and select 3 adjacent blades of flexigrass from the outside of the bunch and bind the 3 blades uniformly upwards for 15cms.

Loosen your grip to turn the bunch slightly away from you before clamping the bunch between your knees and select 2 more blades adjacent to the 3 bound blades and bind together, uniformly, 4 times.

Again, loosen your grip and turn the bunch away from you, before adding 2 more adjacent, outside blades to the 5 bound blades, binding uniformly 4 more times. Try to create a curve as you bind. The bound grasses will get thicker the more sets of 2 x flexigrass are added.

Flexigrass bound circle and loops

Continue to repeat the process, turning the bunch each time, selecting 2 more adjacent, outside blades and binding, evenly 4 times, to the growing number of bound blades; to develop a transparent, even structure with a curved, bound rim.

Leave the last 3 blades to stand out of the bunch and continue to bind, uniformly, the bundle of grasses so that when curved they will overlap where you started. Secure with the paper covered wire to make a round shape.

Flexigrass bound circle and loops

P50

Loop the remaining 3 blades and secure at the base of the bunch. The nook of the structure acts as a mechanic to support flowers and foliage for bridal work, hand tieds or as a vase design.

Flexigrass bound circle and loops

This flexigrass structure is a very easy mechanic to use as flowers can be threaded through the grasses as well as nestling in the nook with stems parallel. The stems can be disguised with a pinned Aspidistra leaf or left natural. Fewer flowers are needed as the enclosed space is a wonderful secondary focal area.

Plaited Edged Kentia Palm

P52

1

2

5

3

A 120cm Howea forsteriana (kentia palm) has been used for this plaited edged technique. Place the palm on a large work surface, upper surface of the leaf facing the ceiling and commence plaiting at the base of the one side you feel most comfortable plaiting.

It does not matter which side you start from.

(1) Commence plaiting with the first 3 leaflets. Plait so that each time you plait away from the leaf you lay the next leaflet on top of what you have just plaited.

4

(2 to 5) Continue plaiting so that each time you plait away from the leaf you lay the next leaflet on top of what you have just plaited. Slightly extend the length of the leaflets when added to allow the plait to become curved in shape - thus gradually getting wider towards the middle of the palm frond. Once at the widest point you continue to plait using the same method but this time you are making sure the outside plait curves inwards by shortening the length of the leaflets added until you reach about 8cms from the tip and secure the plait with metallic or paper covered wire.

(6 to 13) Turn the leaf over, so the under surface of the leaf is now facing the ceiling and plait the same way, in the same direction to obtain the outline plait to represent the curve of an oval leaf and bind to hold the side plaits into position.

(12) Rip off any tips protruding from the plaits.

I find it is easier to plait the opposite side by turning the leaf over and plaiting from the same side - this does mean the plaits are not identical in look.

Plaited Edged Kentia Palm

P54

10-a

10-b

11

12

13

Pandanus woven throughout the palm leaflets

Woven Pandanus

through a plaited edge palm as a manipulated mechanic

To use an edge plaited kentia palm as an alternative mechanic to floral foam, weave 3 x Pandanus veitchii (screw pine) by threading through the kentia palms leaflets in a random zig zag pattern.
Arrange 5 Rosa (roses) by threading each stem through the screw pine for support to create a vertical line demonstrating variation. Finish with 3 looped screw pines leaves, cut the stems to the required length and bind to secure with string before disguising with 12mm green pot tape. This arrangement can now be placed in a vase.

Looped Typha

P56

with Strelitizia leaf used as the mechanic

A fresh Strelitzia reginae (bird-of-paradise) leaf can withstand not being in water for many days before it starts to split and curve inwards.

With that in mind I have selected a container which holds water to sit underneath the leaf. The Strelitizia leaf sits on the rim as a mechanic.

By making slits in the leaf with a knife it can support graduated typha loops threaded through to gain water. Additional holes were made with a bradawl through the midrib vein to support stems of the roses and Rudbeckia.

Mexican fan palm plaited

P57

I study the foliage wherever I am and found this wonderful Washingtonia robusta (Mexican fan palm) in Estepona whilst teaching and demonstrating. Hence the strange background of the table which was in our apartment. To plait the points of this plicate (arranged in folds like those of a fan) leaf, commence plaiting from the base, upper surface of the leaf facing you. Work towards the tip of the palm, and every time you plait away from the leaf you lay the next point on top of what you have just plaited. Continue, easing the plait to echo the central shape of the palm until you plait to the tip and then turn the leaf to continue to plait downwards towards the leaf base. Once plaited, tie off using the fan palm's pointed base tips.

Flexigrass Angel Wing Heart

P58

Ficinea fascicularis (flexigrass) is a flexible, nodeless, cylindrical grass.
As with the China grass heart (page 26) you will need to plait two opposite lobes of a heart, with the plait always being on the outside of the structure.

Divide one bunch of flexigrass in half and secure each half with an elastic band at the base of the grasses. Hold one half bunch with the elastic band at the top and commence plaiting downwards with 3 flexigrass blades for 15cms.

Now turn the bunch upside down and clamp the base between your knees. Continue plaiting and every time you plait into the middle of the plait away from the bunch you then lay a flexigrass blade on top of what you have just plaited. Every two full plaits, release the half bunch which is between your knees and turn the bunch slightly away from you; this helps to create the plaited curve. Then clamp and continue plaiting as described until you have no flexigrass left to add to the structure. Continue to plait the grasses to create a long plaited length and secure tightly with wire.

Undo the rubber band making sure the 3 strands you originally plaited do not come undone and spiral the leaf blades in consecutive order as to how they were added in to the plait and manipulate into a heart shaped lobe with even spaced grasses before securing with wire.

Fan palm, plaited and woven

“finger” on top of what you have just plaited. Continue to the tip of the leaf and glue the plait into position with a permanent glue dot. Repeat plaiting the other side to the tip using the same method. To finish place the more attractive plaited tip over the other plait and securely glue dot into position and then trim off the excess to create a spade shaped leaf.

(4) **Woven**, commence weaving a “finger” from one side of the leaf’s base to flow around its solid centre. Intermittently you will need to fold over the “finger” you are weaving to curve it round in order to be able to weave around the

leaf’s solid centre. Weave each “finger” in turn until you have completed one side. Repeat weaving the other side. Finish by neatening the top by gluing the tips with permanent glue dots to achieve an attractive look.

Fan palm, plaited and woven

P64

Fan palm, plaited and woven

P65

This composition incorporates manipulated fan palms which have been inserted into clean, recycled, water-filled, plastic test tubes before being arranged amongst a collection of textured containers together with threaded twigs and cedar rose cones for effect.

Knotted Aspidistra

P66

Clean both sides of an Aspidistra elatior leaf with a wet wipe to remove any residue.

Cut lengthwise the leaf blade equally in half until you feel the midrib vein (central vein) is too woody to bend. You will find the midrib vein is not central so one half of the leaf will have the midrib vein present.

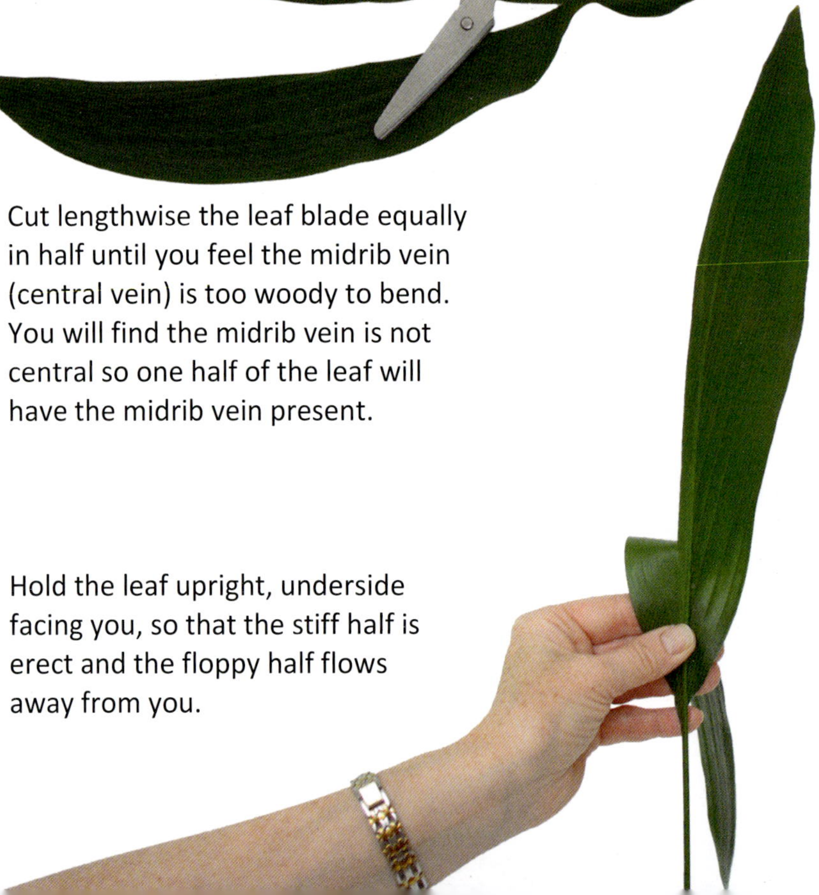

Hold the leaf upright, underside facing you, so that the stiff half is erect and the floppy half flows away from you.

Knotted Aspidistra

P67

Whilst holding the stem in one hand, hold the tip of the stiff half leaf and bring towards you

before manoeuvring it so it goes underneath the floppy leaf and is eventually positioned to be at right angles to the stem

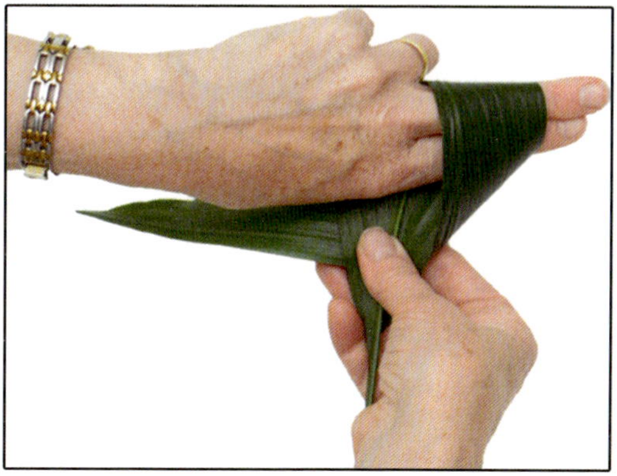

to make a loop that has a hole through which two fingers can pass.

Knotted Aspidistra

Insert the tip half way up through the loop and pull the tip through the hole

to be sufficiently long

in order that you can bring the tip downwards and towards you; to the leaf base to form what looks like a slightly puffed arrow head. Constantly hold in position and turn the leaf structure round to the other side.

You will need to make sure the floppy half leaf is not twisted. Place 2 fingers through what looks like the “knot of a tie” to loosen it sufficiently so that you can insert the tip of the floppy half up through the “tie knot”.

Knotted Aspidistra

Catch hold of it's tip and ease it up through the "tie knot" until the length is long enough to be brought down to the leaf base towards you; in order to make a puffed shape. Secure the manipulated knot structure with paper covered wire.

Grouped Aspidistra knots can be incorporated in a design for distinction or can be used as a mechanic. Flower stems can be threaded through the knots which hold them into position.

Knotted Aspidistra

P70

This line arrangement uses Aspidistra knots as the mechanic. The large Dracaena acts as the back bone. Each Gerbera is threaded through a knot which when arranged in the hand forms a graduated, vertical style arrangement. Asparagus pyramidalis provides the textural contrast with looped Aspidistra completing the design to aid the profile.

Knotted Aspidistra

P71

When placed in a vase this design looks like an arrangement.

This Asymmetrical hand tied uses the Aspidistra knots as the mechanic to support the Anthuriums. The Aspidistra 'mechanic' makes it so much easier to make this design.

Foam Free Competitions

P72

As floral artists and florists seek to utilise more eco-friendly mechanics to improve sustainability when planning designs, competitors too are encouraged to explore alternative methods in their staging and to minimise the use of non-biodegradable materials and use only enhanced-degradable foam if truly necessary.

So I decided to use one pin holder in a rectangular, shallow, glass dish and the remaining three glass globe vases each had a posy of 6 knotted Aspidistra tied with jute string to act as the mechanics to

support and control the Typha grass inverted obelisks, together with the Anthuriums, Craspedia globosa and complementary foliage.

From the Author

Exploring the dynamics of natures' products to best showcase their diversity has been an inspiring and educational experience. It has allowed the design aspect of leaf manipulation in flower arrangement to be further developed as now not only can plant materials be transformed through manipulation into exciting sculptures but these structures can often be used as the mechanic to control and support flower and foliage enhancements to create very pleasing designs. The addition of cones and bark to a design has also been further developed to enable their final configuration through the application of mixed natural ingredients to become the focal point which can be reused in a host of design concepts.

The beauty of nature shines through with each pleasing technique. I hope Volume 1 of the "Go greener Flower Arranging" books has given you inspiration and will help to develop your artistic skills.
Happy flower arranging.

Rolled aspidistra leaves

This Autumnal design highlights the rolled aspidistra leaves' wonderful copper colour after they have been dried with threaded conkers to provide interesting lines of movement.

Rolled Aspidistra provide rhythmic movement in this asymmetrical design.

A compendium of designs . . .

evidencing some of the techniques covered in Volume 1

Glamelia

This fresh flower Glamelia is made from the Camellia and framed with a collar of Camellia leaves for effect.

This design to interpret World Book Day evidences the use of paper to create a Glamelia flower. The paper coils adhered to the vase are made in the same way as the Equisetum disc.

A compendium of designs . . .

evidencing some of the techniques covered in Volume 1

A fun way to incorporate plaited palms in this exotic design.

The Equisetum disc acts as the base to plaited palms and Equisetum spheres arranged in a shallow dish with a pin holder.

Contemporary designs: Designs which reflect current fashion trends in style and product, which push the boundaries and often include Contemporary techniques which alter the natural look of the plant materials and products used.

Distinction: The use of plant materials/ components through placement, manipulation or technique to achieve a distinctive or "attention grabbing" design whilst adhering to the Elements and Principles to interpret a specific design brief/ show schedule to a pre set budget.

Hand tied: A design made in the hand, stems spiralling or parallel, secured by a binding point which does not travel. Stems are clean below the binding point for ease of carrying and to prevent water festering when placed in a vase.

Index - Structures

 This Index is listed in the order of the different structures you can make and then in the order of which plant materials you can make them from.

Index - Structures

Index - Plant Materials

 This Index is in the order of plant materials and then in the order of the different structures you can make from them.

Index - Plant Materials

Flower Arranging Books written by Gill McGregor include:

- '50 Techniques Used in Contemporary Floral Designs'
  ISBN 978-0-9929332-0-3
- 'How to.. Contemporary Floral Design - Wire Manipulation'
  ISBN 978-0-9929332-1-0
- 'How to - Festive Winter Floral Designs'
  ISBN 978-0-9929332-2-7
- 'How to .. Make—Living Vases, Screens & Structures for Contemporary Floral Designs'
  ISBN 978-0-9929332-3-4
- 'How to .. Apply The Elements & Principles of Floral Design ' - My Little Black Book
  ISBN 978-0-9929332-4-1

Further information on flower arranging books by Gill McGregor can be found at

www.gillmcgregor.com/books

Gill also provides free flower arranging video lessons when you visit

www.gillmcgregor.com/free

Coming Soon

P82

It was during the design process of this book, 'How to.. Go Greener Flower Arranging: Leaf Manipulation & Bark and Cone Structures - Volume 1', that I found myself exploring new ways to arrange our flowers and foliage without the use of floral foam and especially without turning back to an earlier method that had its own many drawbacks for which floral foam was seen as the solution to the problems chicken wire caused.

In my next book - 'How to .. Go Greener - Floral Foam Free - Volume 1' I introduce a number of exciting mechanics for floral designers, that are recyclable, can be given away and are cost effective.

A useful resource for;

Flower Arrangers
Floral Art Demonstrators
Commercial Florists &
Floral Artists

Publish date: August 2019

Designs do not use:
Chicken Wire or
Test Tubes.

De boomgrens

Ben Rawlence

De boomgrens

Het laatste bos en de toekomst van de planeet

Vertaling Huub Stegeman

th ten have

Oorspronkelijk verschenen onder de titel *The Treeline; The Last Forest and the Future of Life on Earth* bij Jonathan Cape, een imprint van Vintage, onderdeel van Penguin Random House.

Postbus 13288
3507 LG Utrecht
www.uitgeverijtenhave.nl

Vertaald uit het Engels door Huub Stegeman
Omslag Bij Barbara
ISBN 978 90 259 1041 9
ISBN e-book: 978 90 259 1042 6
ISBN audiobook: 978 90 259 1069 3
NUR 130

Uitgeverij Ten Have vindt het belangrijk om op milieuvriendelijke en verantwoorde wijze met natuurlijke bronnen om te gaan. Bij de productie van het papieren boek van deze titel is daarom gebruikgemaakt van papier waarvan het zeker is dat de productie niet tot bosvernietiging heeft geleid.

Opgedragen aan de bomen en al het leven dat in het bos thuis is.

Inhoud

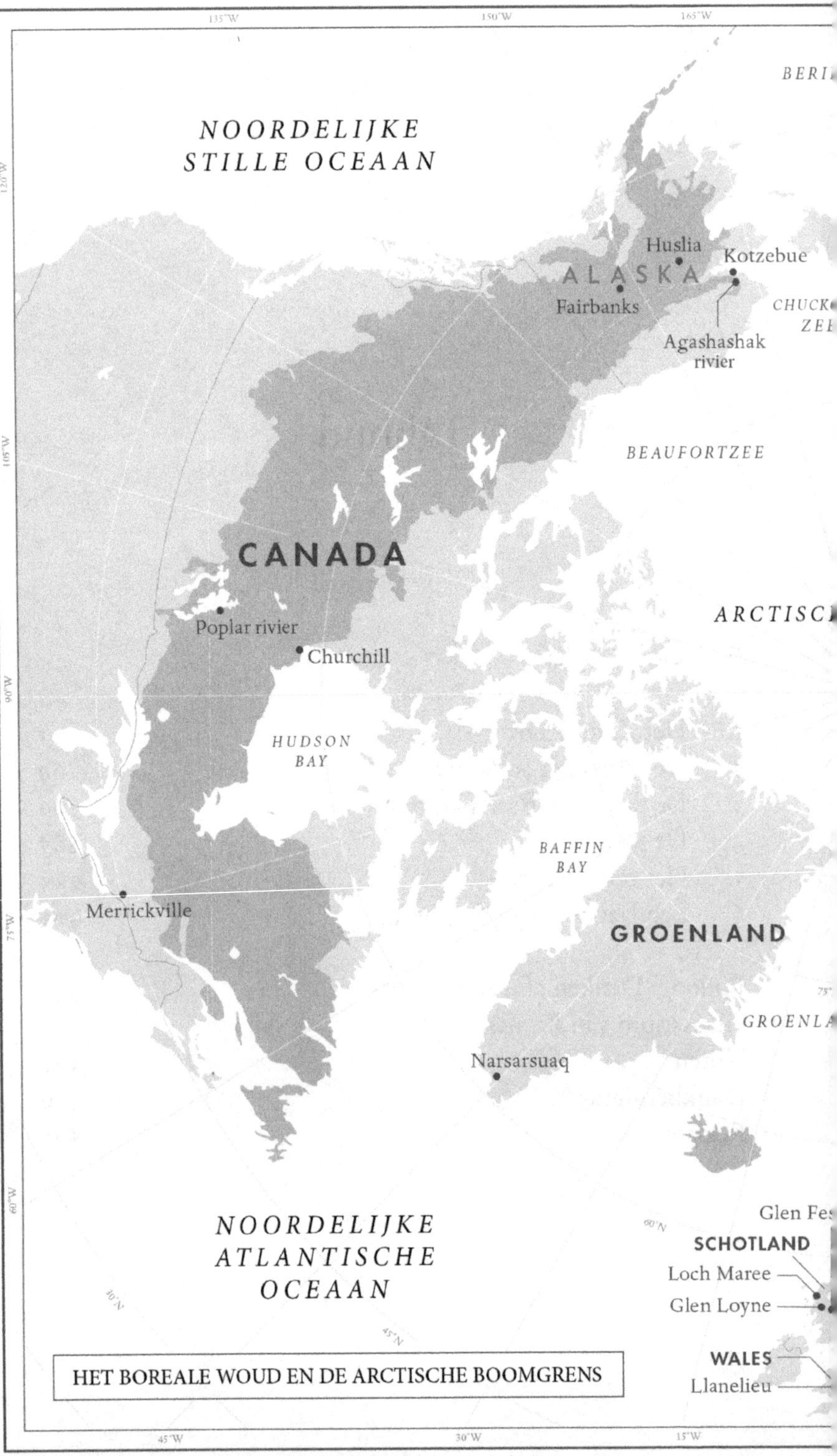

HET BOREALE WOUD EN DE ARCTISCHE BOOMGRENS

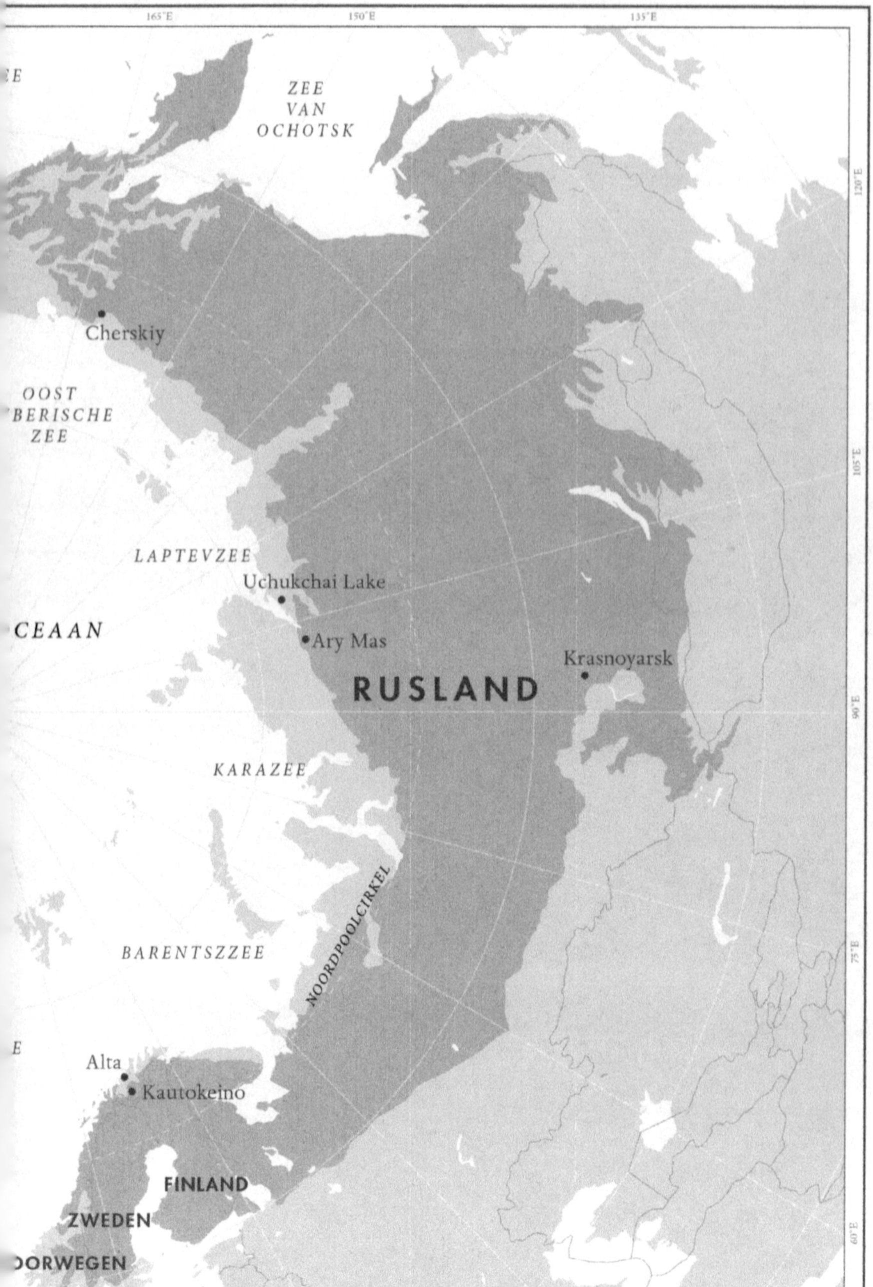
165°E
150°E
135°E
120°E
105°E
90°E
75°E
60°E
15°E
30°E
45°E
ZEE
VAN
OCHOTSK
Cherskiy
OOST
BERISCHE
ZEE
LAPTEVZEE
Uchukchai Lake
Ary Mas
CEAAN
Krasnoyarsk
RUSLAND
KARAZEE
NOORDPOOLCIRKEL
BARENTSZZEE
Alta
Kautokeino
FINLAND
ZWEDEN
ORWEGEN
Boreaal woud

Proloog

Taxus, *Taxus baccata*

Llanelieu, Wales
52° 00' 01" N

Achter mijn huis staat een enorme, oeroude boom. Het is zo'n typische, alledaagse, knoestige oude boom op een kerkhof, typisch Welsh, en ik had er nooit veel aandacht aan besteed. Maar de laatste tijd heb ik meer aandacht voor bomen, merk ik.

De boom in kwestie is een taxus, *Taxus baccata*. Hij staat op een heuvel enkele meters boven de weg, de wortels dicht opeengepakt onder de grond, als een spierbundel onder de huid. De tere wintergroene naalden van de taxus lijken op fijn haar en ze hangen aan grote gebogen takken als een slordige franje die een gezicht verbergt – een verlegen Groene Man misschien. Om de stam te benaderen, moet je het hoofd buigen onder de afhangende franje en de takken opzij duwen als de zware gordijnen voor een heiligdom – alsof je je achter het altaar waagt. Het is een mysterieus toevluchtsoord op een steenworp afstand van het pad, met de sterke kenmerkende geur van altijdgroen, van het leven.

Aan de overkant van het pad staat een andere taxus, iets kleiner maar met dezelfde gladde rozige schors, op sommige plaatsen harig en kleverig. Ik volg de blootgelegde wortels die uit de grond barsten, zich een weg banen langs en onder het pad, zich verstrengelen met die van de grotere buurman en één levende structuur vormen. Bij nader inzien heeft de kleinere boom helderrode besjes en is vrouwelijk en de grotere, zonder vruchten, blijkt mannelijk. Het is een knap paar. Wat ik echter ook probeer, ik kan niemand vinden die weet hoe oud deze oude geliefden zijn en hoe zijn ze hier zijn terechtgekomen.

Taxusbomen dateren is altijd een probleem. Dat komt deels doordat ze geen maximumleeftijd kennen. Wanneer ze nog jong zijn groeien ze snel, op middelbare leeftijd houden ze een stabiel tempo aan, en hun senescentie lijkt eeuwig te kunnen duren. Soms kan de groei stilvallen en kan de boom lange tijd, mogelijk eeuwenlang, slapend blijven staan. Het tellen van boomringen heeft geen zin bij de taxus. Net als ceders kunnen ze groeien uit een laaghangende tak die wortel heeft geschoten in de grond, en uit stronken kunnen scheuten ontspruiten: een taxus die met rust wordt gelaten zou in staat moeten zijn om zichzelf tot in het eeuwige te regenereren. Dit was een van de redenen waarom ze heilig waren voor de Kelten. Die vereerden de taxus met zijn giftige rode bessen, roze vlees en overvloedig sap juist om zijn goddelijke eigenschappen, zijn vermogen om leven en dood te schenken en om zijn aanspraak op onsterfelijkheid. Het kerkhof is cirkelvormig, een aanwijzing dat er een *llan* – een voorchristelijke heilige plaats is voorafgegaan aan de kleine Normandische kerk. Taxusbomen worden vaak gevonden op llans. Het oude stel dat rustig boven de steencirkel staat en al eeuwen, zo niet millennia, elkaar vasthoudt onder het pad, is misschien de reden dat het dorp Llanelieu er überhaupt is.

Oude bomen zijn een bron van verwondering. Als vluchtelingen uit een ander tijdperk, met een levenscyclus die zoveel langer is dan de menselijke tijdschaal. Hun verspreiding en vestigingsgebied is het resultaat van onvoorstelbaar lange planetaire cycli van geologie, klimaat en evolutie. De merkwaardige verspreiding van de taxus bijvoorbeeld, die alleen voorkomt in het hooggebergte van Centraal-Azië en in verspreide bolwerken in Noord-Europa, doet vermoeden dat hij ooit wijder verbreid moet zijn geweest en nu een relict is – de resterende exemplaren zijn uitlopers uit een ander tijdperk. Dat kan misschien een troost zijn tijdens crises: ze herinneren ons eraan dat onze zorgen slechts stipjes zijn in de diepe, aangegroeide tijd van duizenden en duizenden boomringen. Nu de mensheid echter het planetaire systeem van oceanen, wouden, winden en stromingen, het evenwicht van gassen in water en lucht waaruit onze soort is ontstaan, heeft verstoord, is het nog maar de vraag welke troost ze bieden. Bomen bieden niet langer troost, ze waarschuwen ons.

Onze zelfgenoegzame houding tegenover de tijd is het eerste slachtoffer van de opwarming van de aarde: millennia zijn momenten geworden. Vandaag de dag kan ik niet naar de berg, het bos of het veld kijken zonder de grond te voelen beven in angstige afwachting of bij een herinnering. Onze beste gids voor de onzekere toekomst is de geschiedenis: geologie, glaciologie en dendrochronologie – de studies van gesteente, ijs en bomen. Zo zijn verleden en toekomst immanent gemaakt, is de tijd glibberig geworden en kan een wandeling in de heuvels je duizelig maken. Plotseling zie ik overal bomen: waar ze niet zijn, waar ze geweest zijn, waar ze zouden moeten zijn. Het is een manier om buiten de tijd naar het landschap te kijken, zoals de mensen die dichter bij de aarde stonden dat altijd hebben gedaan. En vanuit dat perspectief ziet het er niet best uit. De duidelijke, groene contouren van de Black Mountains die boven de kerk en het dorp uitsteken, lijken me nu een tragische woestijn: een monument voor een geologisch tijdperk van collectieve menselijke dwaasheid.

Deze heuvels vormen de grens tussen Engeland en Wales. Het overschrijden van deze lijn, eerst door de Romeinen, later door de Denen en vervolgens door de middeleeuwse koningen van Engeland, markeerde het begin van een beweging die uiteindelijk in haar eindspel komt met de laatste grote resten oerwoud op de planeet: het tropische Amazonegebied en de subarctische boreale wouden. De Romeinen, Denen en de edelen van Engeland waren op zoek naar natuurlijke rijkdommen, voornamelijk hout. De kolonisatie van Wales was de eerste uiting van een economisch systeem dat op roofbouw was gebaseerd: nadat de grenzen van wat hun eigen leefomgeving kon dragen waren overschreden, gebruikten de vroege mercantilisten geweld om elders tribuut en hulpbronnen te verwerven. Het imperium, of het nu Brits, Viking, Romeins of anderszins is, gaat per definitie te ver. En kolonialisme, kapitalisme en wit superioriteitsdenken delen een gemeenschappelijke, perverse filosofie: beperkingen van de handelingsvrijheid van de individuele mens worden gezien als een aantasting van het beginsel van de vrijheid zelf. Dat is precies het tegenovergestelde van de co-evolutionaire dynamiek van het bos.

Ooit waren deze heuvels bedekt met bomen. Wat er nu nog rest is een fragmentarisch ecosysteem dat *ffridd* of *coedcae* wordt genoemd – haagdoorn, struikgewas en varens, gemengd met loofbomen, een overgangszone: het raakvlak tussen de leefgebieden van laag- en hoogland. Het veen op de top getuigt van het bos dat er ooit heeft gestaan. Maar dat was vóór onze neolithische voorouders het bos rooiden voor weidegrond en brandstof, en vóór onze latere voorliefde voor herten, korhoenders en natuurlijk schapen. Daarvoor, vóór er ook maar iets het gesteente bedekte, was er het ijs.

De laatste ijstijd eindigde tienduizend jaar geleden, nog maar enkele seconden geleden op de planetaire klok. De oude taxussen van Llanelieu zouden de kleinkinderen of zelfs kinderen kunnen zijn van een van de eerste bomen die wortel schoot toen het ijs zich terugtrok. Naaldbomen zoals de taxus hebben zich nadrukkelijk ontwikkeld in relatie tot de cycli van het ijs. Ze gedijen in marginale omgevingen, in harde grond met weinig voedingsstoffen. Hier zien we de boomgrens aan het werk. De boomgrens is namelijk niet echt een grens.

Het feit dat de term 'boomgrens' in het moderne taalgebruik een vaste lijn op een kaart is gaan betekenen die de uiterste grens aangeeft tot waar bomen groeien, getuigt enkel van de zeer beperkte tijdshorizon van de mens en van hoezeer wij onze huidige habitat als vanzelfsprekend zijn gaan beschouwen. In feite zijn de groeiomstandigheden voor bomen, of ze nu beperkt worden door de hoogte (op een berghelling) of door de breedtegraad (in de richting van de Noordpool), slechts zo zeker als de omgeving die ze voortbrengt: de beschikbaarheid van grond, voedingsstoffen, licht, kooldioxide en warmte. Gedurende enkele millennia zijn deze klimatologische omstandigheden opmerkelijk constant gebleven, maar over langere tijdschalen hebben minieme veranderingen in de temperatuur op aarde ervoor gezorgd dat de boomgrens altijd in beweging is gebleven.

Het ijs is zo vaak gekomen en weer gegaan, en steeds begon de natuur opnieuw en koloniseerde het land langzaam weer. Eerst komt korstmos, dan mos, dan grassen, struiken en de pioniers onder de bomen, zoals de berk en de hazelaar die de bodem verbeteren en tonnen bladafval storten voor de trager bewegende groten die volgen: de den, de wintereik en de taxus. In de meeste leefgebieden op aarde neigt het natuurlijke evenwicht, tenzij het wordt beperkt door koude of droogte, naar de uiteindelijke productie van bos. En zo bewoog, terwijl het ijs zich naar het noorden verplaatste, de boomgrens langzaam mee, wortelde in schrale grond, bedreef fotosynthese, schudde zijn naalden af en stierf om de rijke vruchtbare korst van de aarde te vormen, de grondvesten leggend voor de leefgebieden van al het andere aardse leven. Er is nauwelijks een plek op het noordelijk halfrond waar de boomgrens niet is gepasseerd.

Sinds het Plioceen, drie miljoen jaar geleden, toen de explosieve groei van planten de atmosfeer afkoelde tot het huidige evenwicht, hebben ijstijden onze planeet getekend met intervallen van zo'n honderdduizend jaar. Die treden op omdat de aarde niet gelijkmatig draait, maar wiebelt als een tol. Die wiebel wordt de Milankovitch-cyclus genoemd. Hierdoor kantelt de planeet elke honderdduizend jaar een beetje weg van de zon, waardoor ze iets afkoelt en het ijs aan de polen uitzet en zich weer terugtrekt in een duizendjarige versie van onze jaarlijkse seizoenen. De zuidpool is een eiland en gletsjers zijn zeldzaam op het zuidelijk halfrond, behalve op Nieuw-Zeeland en in Patagonië. Het noordelijk halfrond is ondertussen steeds weer opnieuw bebost en ontbost. Een time-lapsefilm van de geologische tijd op de planeet aarde zou een ijskap laten zien die in een ritmisch patroon afdaalt en zich weer terugtrekt, en een groene bosmassa die naar de Noordpool opklimt en dan vervolgens weer terugzakt, als een ademhaling.

Nu is de planeet echter aan het hyperventileren. Deze heldergroene halo beweegt zich onnatuurlijk snel en bekroont de planeet met een lauwerkrans van naalden en bladeren, waardoor de witte Noordpool groen kleurt. De migratie van de boomgrens naar het noorden gaat niet langer met enkele centimeters per eeuw, maar met honderden meters per jaar. De bomen zijn in beweging, en dat zouden ze niet moeten zijn. En dit onheilspellende feit heeft enorme gevolgen voor al het leven op aarde.

Ik weet niet meer waar of wanneer ik voor het eerst hoorde over het oprukken van de bomen. Het beeld is me echter nog jaren bijgebleven tot ik de moeite nam om te onderzoeken wat er werkelijk aan de hand was. Ik ging ervan uit dat wetenschappers kleine veranderingen hadden waargenomen, misschien als reactie op de recente opwarmingstrajecten in de afgelopen decennia, en was totaal niet voorbereid op wat ik vervolgens vond.

Ik las dat de Arctische toendra struikachtiger wordt, en groener. Het is echter geen simpel verhaal van bomen die zich volvreten met koolstofdioxide en naar het noorden racen. Het is een beeld van een planeet in flux, van ecosystemen die zich aan enorme veranderingen aanpassen en hun evenwicht proberen te vinden. Van wouden ter grootte van een land die elk jaar worden vernietigd door brand, parasieten en mensen, terwijl elders kostbare toendra's worden gekoloniseerd door bomen die nu als invasieve soorten worden beschouwd. Bossen veranderen hun soortengemeenschappen of duiken op waar ze niet zouden moeten zijn, hetgeen verwarring veroorzaakt onder de dieren en de mensen die er voor hun overlevingsstrategie afhankelijk van waren dat de bossen bleven waar ze waren.

Onze kaarten zijn verouderd. De positie van de Arctische boomgrens was een van de definities van de noordpoolcirkel. Die komt bijna precies overeen met een andere, de 10°C-juli-isotherm – de lijn rond de top van de wereld die een gemiddelde zomertemperatuur van tien graden Celsius aangeeft. Deze golvende lijn raakt kort de toppen van het Cairngormgebergte in Schotland alvorens weer aan land te gaan in de binnenlanden van Scandinavië, weg van de gematigde beboste fjorden. Vanaf de hoogvlakte van Finnmark loopt hij dan in een ononderbroken lijn van de Witte Zee bij Rusland bovenin Siberië naar de Beringstraat. In Alaska ligt de boomgrens tegen de Brooks Range alvorens een diagonale duik te nemen dwars door Canada om bij de Hudson Bay opnieuw op de zee te stuiten. Aan de andere kant van die binnenzee baant hij zich een weg door Quebec en het bergachtige Labrador en maakt dan de sprong naar zuidelijk Groenland.

Dit is de route van de reis die in dit boek wordt beschreven, maar het concept van een lijn is op zich misleidend. Wanneer we inzoomen blijkt de boomgrens helemaal geen lijn te zijn, maar een overgangszone tussen ecosystemen, wat wetenschappers de Forest-Tundra-Ecotone (FTE) noemen, in sommige gevallen honderden kilometers breed, en in andere slechts een paar meter. Door de opwarming van het klimaat ondergaan de zone en de enorme ecosystemen van toendra en bos aan weerszijden ervan verschillende, onverwachte veranderingen. Bovendien klopt de lijn niet. De 10°C-juli-isotherm is niet langer een stabiel gegeven waarop cartografen kunnen vertrouwen: hij is overal wild in beweging, zoals blijkt uit de zomertemperaturen in Siberië, Groenland, Alaska en Canada. Waar bomen in staat zijn te groeien en waar ze feitelijk staan, heeft steeds minder met elkaar te maken. Dit maakt het hele gebied tot een zone van mogelijkheden, en gevaren.

Op mijn reis door die zone heb ik veel geleerd over de fundamentele rol die de noordelijke wouden spelen bij het reguleren van het huidige klimaat op aarde. Sterker nog dan het regenwoud van de Amazone is het boreale woud echt de long van de wereld.

Met een oppervlakte van een vijfde van de wereldbol en een derde van alle bomen op aarde is de boreale zone het op één na grootste bioom, of leefsysteem, na de oceaan. Planetaire systemen: cycli van water en zuurstof, atmosferische circulatie, het albedo-effect, oceaanstromingen en poolwinden worden gevormd en gestuurd door de positie van de boomgrens en het functioneren van het bos.

Ik heb geleerd hoe weinig we weten over de veranderende werking van deze systemen onder invloed van de opwarming. We weten dat de wereld gevaarlijk heter wordt, maar we weten nog niet wat dat voor ons zal betekenen, of voor de andere levensvormen van het woud. Naarmate ze warmer worden, verliezen bossen hun vermogen om kooldioxide te absorberen en op te slaan. Hoewel het boreale gebied de grootste zuurstofbron op aarde is, betekenen meer bomen daar niet noodzakelijkerwijs dat er meer koolstof uit de atmosfeer wordt gehaald. Wanneer bomen bevroren toendra's binnendringen, versnellen ze het smelten van permafrost, bevroren grond die genoeg broeikasgassen bevat om de opwarming van de aarde te versnellen, meer dan wetenschappers in hun modellen hebben berekend. Er gebeuren veel tegenstrijdige dingen tegelijk.

De aarde is uit evenwicht en de boomgrenszone is een gebied dat in de greep is van grote geologische veranderingen, waardoor onze ideeën over verleden, heden en toekomst overhoop worden gehaald en op de proef worden gesteld. 'We zitten tussen twee verhalen in. Het oude verhaal, het verhaal van hoe de wereld is ontstaan en hoe wij daarin passen, klopt niet langer. Toch kennen we de nieuwe verhalen nog niet,' aldus cultuurhistoricus Thomas Berry.[1] Ik vond de kiemen van die nieuwe verhalen geworteld in oudere ordeningen in het boreale gebied. Voor het grootste deel zijn bossen plaatsen waar menselijke manieren om op voet van gelijkheid samen te leven met de natuur nog steeds bestaan.

Het gebied is echter, zowel in wetenschappelijk als geografisch opzicht, enorm, en de reikwijdte van waar het boreale gebied voor staat is zo enorm dat het onmogelijk leek om het in één enkel boek te beschrijven. Pas toen ik ontdekte dat een handjevol boomsoorten de boomgrens vormt, begon ik in te zien dat een poging tot beschrijving mogelijk zou moeten zijn. De zes hier getoonde soorten, een eliteclubje, zijn bekende verschijningen in de noordelijke gebieden: drie naaldbomen en drie loofbomen die zijn geëvolueerd om de kou te overleven. Bovendien heeft elk van deze boomsoorten zich een deel van de boomgrens eigengemaakt en daarbij andere soorten verdrongen en unieke ecosystemen verankerd: de grove den in Schotland, de berk in Scandinavië, de lariks in Siberië, de spar in Alaska en in mindere mate de populier in Canada en de lijsterbes op Groenland. Ik besloot elke boom in zijn thuisland te bezoeken om te zien hoe het de verschillende soorten vergaat in reactie op de opwarming en wat hun verhalen zouden kunnen betekenen voor de andere bewoners van het bos, waaronder wijzelf. Mijn bezoeken aan de verschillende plaatsen vonden plaats tussen 2018 en 2020, op verschillende tijdstippen van het jaar om de seizoensgebonden werking van het bos te kunnen vastleggen, maar de hoofdstukken zijn geografisch gerangschikt, waarbij ik de boomgrens in oostelijke richting volg, de opkomende zon tegemoet.

Deze noordelijke soorten zijn met weinigen, maar ze zijn taai. In het lange spel van geologische natuurlijke selectie overleven alleen de meest creatieve op deze breedtegraden met hun extreme koude. Terwijl de tere tropische regenwouden met hun grote biodiversiteit al miljoenen jaren een vertrouwde soortenrijkdom in stand houden, zijn de noordelijker gelegen gebieden als een lei die steeds opnieuw werd schoongeveegd. Dit is de plaats om te zoeken naar een glimp van wat er, na de grote transformatie die zich momenteel op aarde voltrekt, zal overblijven. Over duizenden of misschien miljoenen jaren, wanneer de planeet weer afkoelt, zouden de soorten die tevoorschijn komen om de aarde opnieuw te bevolken wel eens die kunnen zijn die endemisch zijn voor het boreale gebied. Zij zijn op unieke wijze aangepast aan de klimaatverandering, want ze hebben duizenden jaren lang de getijden van het ijs gevolgd. De ontbossing en de huidige emissies in de atmosfeer hebben reeds een groot deel van het regenwoud in de wereld tot savanne gedoemd. Mijn buren, de oude groene man en vrouw van Llanelieu, halen het misschien, afhankelijk van hoe heet en droog het eiland Groot-Brittannië wordt, en afhankelijk van de omvang en het succes van de menselijke inspanningen om de schade te beperken, maar het laatste woud zal de boreale zone zijn. Wanneer van de mensheid niet meer dan fossielen resten, zullen deze winterharde noordelijke soorten nog overeind staan.

1.

Het Zombiebos

Grove den, *Pinus sylvestris*

Glen Loyne, Scotland
57° 04' 60" N

Toen het ijs zich aan het begin van de huidige interglaciale periode naar hoger gelegen gebieden terugtrok, zette het boreale woud de achtervolging in. Planten die al duizenden jaren niet meer op de Britse eilanden waren gezien, begonnen geleidelijk terug te keren. Op de hoogvlakten van Noord-Wales en de Schotse hooglanden bleef het ijs nog liggen, maar in de valleien en de vlakten vormden korstmossen een korst op de blootgelegde rotsen. Toen kwamen de mossen met hun kruipende vacht die de bodem voorbereidden voor grassen en zegge, spoedig gevolgd door de eerste pioniersstruiken hazelaar, berk, wilg, jeneverbes en esp. Dit boreale systeem zocht zich een weg naar het noorden, over de landbrug waar het Kanaal nu is, een vloed van groen die het ijs op de hielen volgde, de cocktail van vroege zaden, verspreid volgens de natuurlijke cycli van wind, regen en de migratiepatronen van dieren, waaronder ook de mens.

Tienduizend jaar later volg ik dezelfde weg. Ik rijd vanuit Wales in noordelijk richting, naar de plaats waar volgens de kaart de boomgrens op zijn huidige positie tot stilstand is gekomen: Schotland. Op weg naar Fort William, door de spectaculaire diepe valleien aan de westkust van Schotland, lijken de rotsen van de bergtoppen stil te staan, als het dak van een kathedraal dat overgaat in de hemel. De overvloedig groene hellingen rollen heen en weer bij elke bocht in de weg, steenslag tuimelt in lange stromen als watervallen uit verborgen meren van steen hoog boven ons. Het zonlicht tekent scherp het uitzicht, het ene moment verblindend, het andere een beloofd land onthullend.

Pas wanneer ik op mijn bestemming ben aangekomen, dringt de tegenstrijdigheid tot me door: Ik ben op zoek naar de noordelijkste grens van het bos, maar waar is het bos? De onverbiddelijke Schotse heuvels, rij na rij van beschaduwde hellingen die uit de mist oprijzen, zijn zo'n vertrouwd beeld in het collectieve geheugen en de cultuur, dat het bijna onmogelijk is om ze ons anders voor te stellen, en toch was Groot-Brittannië ooit, gedurende korte tijd, een eiland van bomen. Caledonia, zoals de Romeinen het noemden, betekent 'beboste hoogten', maar dat grootse woud is iets van de mythen geworden. De kale heuvels van Schotland zijn zowel grafschrift als waarschuwing: dit is waar het commodificeren van de natuur toe leidt.

De vraag 'wat gebeurt er met de boomgrens?' is in een dergelijk verwoest landschap een uiterst politieke. Op papier wordt Schotland beschouwd als de zuidelijke en westelijke grens van de Arctische boomgrens in Europa. Schattingen op basis van temperatuur en groeiseizoenen suggereren dat deze hier op 700 tot 750 meter zou moeten liggen.[1] Op 790 meter hoogte zijn stronken opgegraven die dateren uit een iets warmer tijdperk, 4000 jaar geleden.[2] Maar hoe de boomgrens nu op de opwarming reageert, is moeilijk te zeggen omdat bijna alle bomen al zijn gekapt. Er wordt gewerkt aan het herstel van het grote bos van Schotland, waarbij de heuvels worden 'herbebost' en bomen worden geplant, gedeeltelijk om ze in staat te stellen hun niveau te vinden en een natuurlijke overgangszone tussen het bos en de heide te herstellen. Maar dergelijke veranderingen zijn controversieel. Hoe wij het heden en de toekomst zien, hangt vaak af van ons begrip van het verleden: Wat is natuurlijk? Wat wordt er hersteld? Terwijl de mens debatteert over de ecologiegeschiedenis, wordt de opwarming van de aarde steeds sterker en dreigt zelfs onze zwakke reactie er niet meer toe te doen.

De eerste of primaire golf, die van de vegetatieve bedekking van de boomgrens na de ijstijd, resulteerde in een fragmentarisch bos dat de belangrijkste historicus van het Britse landschap, Oliver Rackham, het *wildwood* noemt.[3] Dit was een dynamische, zich verplaatsende plantengemeenschap – aan de zuidkant verbonden met het vasteland van Europa door de landbrug en aan de noordgrens uitlopend in de veentoendra van het 'stroomland' in het uiterste noorden van Schotland en de verspreide rotsen van de Hebriden, waar de droge koude van de Arctische polaire vortex met de Golfstroom om voorrang vecht.

Dit wildwood tierde welig, maar was ook kwetsbaar. De berk vestigde zich snel, maar was van voorbijgaande aard en maakte plaats voor andere, grotere en doortastender bomen. Naarmate de zich ontwikkelende samenleving van het woud haar eigen logica uitwerkte, zou er een 'stabiele toestand' ontstaan waarin één of enkele specifieke bomen domineren. In een groot deel van Zuid-Engeland was dit de linde, in het noorden en in Wales was het een mengeling van hazelaar en eik. In de Schotse hooglanden was de belangrijkste boom oorspronkelijk de eik. Maar de stabiele toestand van het wildwood kan ook weer worden verstoord en in een andere cyclus overgaan door de instroom van een nieuwe soort of een weersverandering. De introductie van de den is daarvan een voorbeeld.

Uit pollendata blijkt dat rond 8500 v.Chr. de grove den (*Pinus sylvestris*) plotseling in Groot-Brittannië opdook, een corridor langs de westkust van de Britse eilanden koloniseerde, zich een weg baande naar de inhammen en fjorden van Schotland en vervolgens over de dalen en valleien en omhoog de bergen in. Dennen verdrongen de berken en eiken die royaal voor meer bodem hadden gezorgd zodat de den er kon gedijen. De den was zo succesvol dat de berk duizenden jaren lang bijna volledig was verdwenen en alleen overleefde in de overgebleven zone in het moerasland ten noorden van wat nu de stad Inverness is.

Dit dennenbos verspreidde zich over Schotland en bereikte volgens Rackham rond 4500 v.Chr., met ongeveer 80 procent van het landoppervlak zijn hoogtepunt. Recente archeologische vondsten, pollenanalyses en zelfs de 7000 jaar oude skeletten van dennenbomen die in moerassen bewaard zijn gebleven, hebben het debat gevoed over de omvang en het lot van het ooit zo prachtige wildwood van Schotland.[4] Natuurbeschermers zijn op zoek naar feiten om hun pogingen tot 'ecologisch herstel' op te baseren. De tegenstanders willen bewijzen dat de bomen door natuurlijke oorzaken zijn verdwenen en dat de huidige status quo van korhoenderjachtgebieden en hertenparken evenzeer het predicaat 'natuurlijk' verdient. Het meningsverschil lijkt er een te zijn tussen twee visies op de natuur die geen van beide erg geneigd zijn te erkennen hoe groot de rol van de mens is geweest bij de totstandkoming van dit landschap, en toch zijn de geschiedenis van mens en woud ten diepste met elkaar verstrengeld.

Voordat ik naar het noorden reed, las ik een wetenschappelijk artikel van Litouwse onderzoekers die aantoonden dat het DNA van de grove den in de oostelijke helft van Schotland afkomstig is van een refugium – een plaats waar soorten standhielden tijdens de laatste ijstijd en zo overleefden – in de buurt van Moskou rond 9000 tot 8000 v.Chr.[5] Uit eerder DNA-onderzoek is gebleken dat de overgebleven dennen in het westen van Schotland afkomstig zijn van het Iberisch schiereiland, het huidige Portugal en Spanje. In beide gevallen is het zaad naar Schotland gemigreerd op een tijdschaal die honderden malen sneller is dan via natuurlijke successie mogelijk is. Het meest waarschijnlijke vehikel voor zo'n snelle migratie was de mens.

Er bestaat een mythe in de Keltische folklore – een die een kern van waarheid bevat – dat toen de Kelten Schotland koloniseerden, zij op Oekraïners stuitten die van de andere kant kwamen. Voor de Kelten was de den een heilige boom met een groot aantal toepassingen. De dennenboom was een *ailm* in het Keltische alfabet, het Ogham-schrift, en het is zeer waarschijnlijk dat ze hem uit Ierland en Wales hebben meegebracht. Hij was misschien ook heilig voor de mysterieuze Oekraïners die deel uitmaakten van het Keltische koninkrijk, 'de mensen van de Donau' in het oud-Iers, de enige anderen met rood haar. Voor mensen die zo sterk verbonden zijn met de natuur en afhankelijk zijn van planten, zou het logisch zijn om met de eigen habitat mee te reizen. Dat is iets waar eenentwintigste-eeuwers maar al te snel naar zullen gaan verlangen.

Het gevolg is dat er nu in Schotland twee verschillende genetische gemeenschappen van de grove den zijn, van elkaar gescheiden door de Hooglanden. Er heeft nog geen kruisbestuiving plaatsgevonden en natuurbeschermers zijn erop gebrand dat dit niet gebeurt, aangezien het genetische en chemische onderscheid gevolgen heeft voor andere soorten die afhankelijk zijn van de den die de hoeksteen van hun habitat vormt. Insecten zoals houtmieren, bijvoorbeeld, kunnen verschillende soorten hars proeven en zullen bepaalde bomen uitkiezen. Bladchemie, bloeitijden en groeivormen zijn allemaal verschillend. De kuifmees blijft ten oosten van de Cairngorms, ingebed als hij is in zijn omgeving. De natuurbeschermers hoeven zich echter nog geen zorgen te maken. Het risico van kruisingen is minimaal, aangezien de overgebleven bosfragmenten verspreid liggen en zeer klein zijn. Er is minder dan 1 procent van de oude dennenbossen in Schotland over.

Rackham beweert dat het dennenbos zich nooit van kust tot kust heeft uitgestrekt, maar het heeft zeker het grootste deel van Schotland bedekt totdat de Mesolithische mens het bos begon te rooien voor landbouw, jacht en bouw. Bosbeheer door middel van kappen, rooien of platbranden voor wild speelde een rol bij het creëren van biodiverse habitats van heide en veen, maar vormde ook de basis voor het kruipende hoogveen dat het kenmerkende landschap van het Britse hoogland is geworden. Het hoogveen is in zekere zin een verwoest ecosysteem, omdat door het kappen van bomen mineralen en ijzer naar de onderste lagen van de bodem zijn gespoeld, waardoor een oerbank is ontstaan die ondoordringbaar is voor water. Het toendralandschap kan zijn water niet kwijt, raakt verzadigd en planten verteren niet volledig, zodat er turf wordt gevormd.

De inheemse *crofters*, de keuterboeren die tot de *clearances*, de ontruimingen in de achttiende en negentiende eeuw, de Hooglanden bewerkten, verplaatsten hun vee van oudsher tussen het laaglandbos en de heide. De ontbossing van de Hooglanden wordt vaak geweten aan de ontruimingen en de daaropvolgende uitbreiding van de Victoriaanse jachtvelden voor korhoenders en herten, maar hoewel heideverbranding en overbegrazing door herten bij afwezigheid van roofdieren als wolven, lynxen en beren inderdaad hebben voorkomen dat de bomen terugkwamen, was een groot deel van het open landschap in de Hooglanden al ontstaan door het rooien van alle bomen.

Traditionele gebruiken en gewoonten, geërfd van de Kelten, respecteerden het bos. Dennenhout was een hernieuwbare bron van bouwmaterialen, dennenkaarsen voor licht, teer en hars voor het looien en waterdicht maken, vezels voor touwen en schors voor aanmaakhout, meel en medicijnen. Tot ver in de jaren 1960 leverde dennenhars kaarsvet, het hout werd gebruikt voor spoorbielzen en boten, en buizen werden gemaakt van uitgeholde boomstammen. Inheemse systemen kenden een hele reeks rechten toe op goederen die door het bos werden geleverd – hazelaartwijgen, brandhout, hout, paddenstoelen en veevoeder – en er waren strenge morele en financiële straffen voor het verkwisten van hakhout, voor het illegaal laten grazen van dieren in gemeenschappelijke bossen, enzovoort. Zoals vele andere, meer recente gevallen van tropische ontbossing aantonen, is het gebruik van het bos door de inheemse bevolking vaak de meest betrouwbare manier om het in stand te houden. De zogenaamde 'tragedie van de meent' (dat men er niet op kan vertrouwen dat de mens een gemeenschappelijke hulpbron verstandig beheert) kan een probleem zijn voor individualistische samenlevingen die niet in staat zijn vervuiling en overexploitatie te beteugelen, maar als historische verklaring voor het Britse landschap gaat ze niet op.

Behalve misschien als een ideologische rechtvaardiging achteraf voor de echte tragedie die zou volgen: de *enclosure*, de omheining van gemeenschappelijk land.[6]

Eigendomsrecht op land was oorspronkelijk een Romeins idee, waartegen zowel Grieken als Kelten zich verzetten. Zij bleven erbij dat de natuur nooit het eigendom van de mens kon zijn, maar alleen gebruikt kon worden. Honderden jaren nadat de Romeinen Groot-Brittannië hadden verlaten, maakte dit begrip de weg vrij voor buitenlandse landheren en de extreme concentratie van het grondbezit in Schotland nu.[7] Het woud werd gebruikt door de clans. Zij hadden het bos nodig. Het woord *forest*, 'bos' of 'woud', dat ondanks het ontbreken van bomen op kaarten blijft staan, is een echo van zijn vroegere betekenis als een niet omheind gebied dat beschermd was voor de jacht en voor gemeenschappelijk gebruik, meer recentelijk door de Kroon. De verschuiving van gebruiksrechten naar eigendomsrechten, gezien als de handelsgeest van Noord-Europa die de wereld binnendrong of zich eraan opdrong, was, zo lijkt het, een cruciale, aangezien bossen niet langer werden gezien als heilige plaatsen van wonderen, mysterie en voedsel, maar als een gewas op stam met een waarde, uitgedrukt in ponden, shillings en pence, berekend per hectare en per ton.

Schotland en Ierland en hun natuurlijke rijkdommen, waaronder in de eerste plaats wat er nog restte aan hout, vormden de frontlinie van dat vroege kapitalistische verlangen dat zich uitte in kolonialisme. Engelse koningen die vanaf de middeleeuwen schepen, huizen, karren en kathedralen nodig hadden – lang voordat Henry Hudson en John Davis droomden van de noordwestelijke doorvaart en sir Walter Raleigh van de Orinoco – keken eerst naar Wales en daarna naar hun kolonie Ierland. Toen de Schotse en Engelse kronen verenigd waren en de bossen van Ierland verdwenen waren, richtten ze de blik op Schotland.

Langs Loch Linnhe schuiven laaghangende wolken tussen de toppen van de Ardgour over het water. Op het schiereiland bevindt zich het meest zuidwestelijke overgebleven relict van het dennenbos, dat deel uitmaakt van het landgoed Conaglen, dat is gereserveerd voor de hertenjacht. In een holte tussen heuvels ligt het laatste stukje bos waar vroegere generaties zoveel van hun rijkdom aan te danken hadden. Een waarnemer die commentaar gaf op de enorme hoeveelheden hout die vanuit Schotland in Ierland werden ingevoerd, schreef in 1686: 'er kwamen daar altijd veel schepen aan uit Ardgoure, beladen met timmerhout, masten en hakhout van sparren. Deze vallei is zeer winstgevend voor de Heer.'[8]

De groene heuvels gaan over in de zwarte diepten van het loch. Een trein ratelt langs het water op weg naar het einde van de lijn. De rijkdom van het bos heeft zelfs de geografie van Schotland gevormd. De rivier de Spey werd afgedamd en aangepast om het mogelijk te maken dat boomstammen naar de zagerijen en scheepsbouwers van Speyside dreven, totdat de stoomtreinen de houtvlotters met hun specifieke vocabulaire en hun *currachs* – een lichte frameboot bedekt met huiden voor de terugreis stroomopwaarts – wegconcurreerden. Aan de westkust kwam het hout uit de binnenlanden langs de militaire weg van generaal Wade en vervolgens de spoorweg die eindigt in Fort William aan de kop van Loch Linnhe.

Voorbij Fort William begint de beroemde Road to the Isles. De majestueuze, weidse dalen en blauwe pieken wijken bij Knoydart om zicht te bieden op de overkant van de zee, op Skye. In plaats van tijdloos komt dit landschap me nu apocalyptisch voor: het slachtoffer van een catastrofe. Het is eigenlijk een wonder dat er überhaupt nog oerbossen zijn overgebleven. Door toedoen van een verlichte *laird*, een vooruitziende bosbouwambtenaar of gewoon doordat ze zo afgelegen waren, zijn er echter nog 84 stukken inheems Caledonisch dennenbos overgebleven. Dit zijn de *granny pines*, dennen als knoestige en schijnbaar halfdode oude omaatjes die het anders zo lege canvas van sommige Schotse hellingen animeren. Het oudst bekende exemplaar is 540 jaar oud en groeit in een afgelegen moerassige vallei, Glen Loyne genaamd. Dit zijn de enige bomen die groot genoeg waren om te ontsnappen aan de afgrazing nadat de wolven waren uitgeroeid en de herten en schapen hun gang konden gaan.

Er is iets grondig mis met een eenzame den. Dennen zijn sociale wezens en ze zijn afhankelijk van andere bomen voor het delen van hulpbronnen via schimmelnetwerken. Wanneer dennen volwassen zijn, transporteren ze koolstof onder de grond om jonge boompjes te ondersteunen, en op oudere leeftijd reizen koolstof en voedingsstoffen in omgekeerde richting, waarbij de jonge bomen de oudere helpen. De natuurlijke levensduur van een grove den kan tot zes- of zevenhonderd jaar bedragen binnen het gezonde netwerk van een bos. De overgebleven oude omaatjesdennen van Schotland zijn meestal jonger dan vierhonderd jaar. Grote afnames in het pollenbestand suggereren dat dit het gevolg is van de massale kap van bomen tussen 1690 en 1812. Volgens dendrochronoloog Rob Wilson 'kun je de gevolgen van de Napoleontische oorlogen nog steeds zien in de structuur van het bos.' Er is echter nog een factor.

Eenzame bomen lopen een groter risico om plotseling te sterven vóór het einde van hun normale levensverwachting. Zou het kunnen dat deze matriarchen van onze oudste bossen, deze rentmeesters van onze oeroude ecosystemen en vroedvrouwen van zoveel industriële rijkdom, op hun oude dag eenzaam zijn? Inheemse Amerikaanse verhalen vertellen over eenzame bomen die tot mensen 'spreken' over hun eenzaamheid, en de mensen vragen om buren te planten. Missen de oude dennen misschien het gezelschap en het tafeltje-dek-je van hun kinderen? Rouwen ze om de geest van het bos?

Ik laat de auto achter bij een parkeerplaats op de doodlopende, eenbaansweg, niet meer dan één auto breed. In de vallei die zich beneden ontvouwt, is het verhaal te zien van de laatste keer dat Schotland te maken kreeg met het industrieel kapitalisme, een panorama van de verwoesting. De heuvel ertegenover ziet er gecamoufleerd uit met zijn *muir-burn* – ongelijke bruine en vaalbruine strepen die zijn ontstaan doordat heide is verbrand om korhoenders aan te trekken voor de jacht. Dit zou anders regenereren in bos en lijkt nu op een ruw geschoren hoofdhuid. Verder naar beneden zien we de littekens van een monocultuur van sparren, een woestijn zonder biodiversiteit. De donkere, militair-groene bomen staan te dicht op elkaar geplant om ander leven toe te laten. De heuvels zijn verwoest doordat machines bomen hebben geveld voordat ze volgroeid waren, waardoor grote bruine groeven zijn ontstaan waarlangs de kostbare toplaag in kolkende linten naar het loch stroomt. Verderop is een verlaten lariksplantage die iemand vergeten is uit te dunnen. De stammen zijn takloos, de helft van de bomen is omgevallen en hangt tegen elkaar, door de wind omver gewaaid omdat ze geen kracht in hun wortels hebben. Op het loch dobberen pontons, en daartussen is het wateroppervlak doorweven met de drijvers van een intensieve zalmkwekerij. Plastic vaten met voer staan zes meter hoog opgestapeld op de oever. Daarboven staan stalen masten die gonzen met 66 kilovolt in marsorde langs de oever tot aan de waterkrachtcentrale van Kingie, een knalrood-geel zuurtje boven op een betonnen dam. Zelfs het loch is kunstmatig: het landschap als de ultieme hulpbron, slechts gezien door de bloedeloze ogen van een boekhouder. Er is niets natuurlijks te zien, behalve een groepje wilgen bij de beek op de voorgrond.

Een wegwijzer voor een voetpad wijst naar het noorden, bergopwaarts. Eronder staat een waarschuwing:

> OPGELET: U betreedt afgelegen, dunbevolkt, potentieel gevaarlijk berglandschap. Zorg ervoor dat u voldoende ervaring en uitrusting hebt om uw reis zonder hulp te kunnen voltooien.

Aan de andere kant van de vallei begint een van de meest afgelegen stukken wildernis in Groot-Brittannië. Je kunt drie dagen lopen naar Knoydart zonder een weg of huis te zien. Daarom staan de oude dennenbomen van Glen Loyne er nog. Het was zo moeilijk om ze uit de vallei te krijgen, dat ze tot het laatst werden overgelaten en vervolgens waarschijnlijk vergeten.

Het modderige pad zoekt slingerend een weg tussen een beekje en een hertenkamp. Er staat nog een stel laarsafdrukken in de modder. Die staan er al wat langer. Binnen de omheining lijken de zaailingen van berken, wilgen en dennen het goed te doen. Het ziet er vreemd uit, een omheind gebied dat drie keer zo dicht begroeid is als de rest van de heuvel, maar buiten de omheining lopen schapen en herten. Dit is de frontlijn van het ecologisch herstel in Schotland, de scheidslijn tussen degenen die investeren in een economie en een landschap, gebaseerd op commerciële bosbouw en jacht, en de natuurbeschermers die zich inzetten om te voorkomen dat de bomen worden opgevreten. De strijd heeft de passie – en het prikkeldraad – van een oorlog.

Al gauw klauter ik over opstapjes en stenen. Pinguicula met zijn venusvliegvallen groeit er op de rotsen en een reusachtig Lycopsida van vijftien centimeter dik, als een berenmuts, waaruit alpenplanten, grassen en andere mossen groeien met fijne piekhaartjes als de baard van een oude man, bekleedt er een grote zwerfkei.

De zwerfkei is als een miniatuurvoorstelling van wat de boomgrens doet: een toekomstige zogenaamde *hummock*, een klein heuveltje. Een blootliggende steen wordt eerst gekoloniseerd door korstmossen die er mineralen uithalen en met 0,1 millimeter per jaar groeien. Om de mineralen te verkrijgen, scheiden de korstmossen een zuur af dat het gesteente afbreekt. Andere foliose korstmossen, met meer bladachtige structuren, profiteren van deze gebroken laag, net als de mossen, die vervolgens nog meer organisch materiaal in hun bladeren vastleggen en het proces van de bodemvorming versnellen. Wanneer deze toplaag uiteindelijk een boomstronk of een rotsblok overwint en zich met de oppervlaktegrond verbindt, vormt ze een hummock. Dicht op elkaar staande hummocks van regelmatige grootte zijn vaak overblijfselen van oude bossen waar de bodem zich over boomstronken heeft opgehoopt. Het ontstaan kan tientallen, zo niet honderden jaren duren. Hoeveel seizoenen heeft dit doorweekte huishouden gekend?

Tegen de tijd dat ik de bergkam bereik, heb ik een verschrikkelijke dorst. Ik had verwacht overal beekjes te vinden en vond het dus niet nodig water mee te nemen, maar had geen rekening gehouden met het veenmoeras. In Groot-Brittannië is 13 procent van al het turf in de wereld te vinden, en een groot deel ervan is aangetast en snel aan het uitdrogen. Het veen hoopt zich op als een soort kruipend lavaveld, maar dan nat, met een paar millimeter per jaar. Als de bomen eenmaal uit een landschap als dit zijn verdwenen, kunnen ze moeilijk terugkeren, en dus kan ik, vanaf de top van de bergkam, genieten van een ononderbroken uitzicht in alle richtingen op een schrale groene vallei vanaf de kop van Loch Loyne. In noordwestelijke richting rijst berg na berg op in een golvend vergezicht van graniet en gras. Er is geen geluid, behalve de wind die aan mijn haar rukt, geen vogels, geen kabbelend water. Het is gemakkelijk te begrijpen waarom de Britse ecoloog sir Frank Fraser Darling de Schotse hooglanden een 'natte woestijn' noemde.

Op zoek naar water, stak ik mijn arm bijna tot aan mijn schouder in een geultje in het veen, diep onder de huid van de heuvel om een schamel kopje bruingelooide vloeistof omhoog te halen. Die smaakt bitter, maar het is goed zo. Denk toch eens aan al die vezels bos die de grondwaterspiegel filteren tot een heerlijk heldere drank!

Wanneer ik de wind van Glen Loyne achterlaat en afdaal, klinkt het geluid van ruisend water me tegemoet. Dit is het zwakke gebrul van de stroomversnellingen, die ik de rivier ver beneden mij kan zien tekenen, terwijl zij zich een duizend jaar oude weg door de kom van de vallei baant. Het geluid herinnert me eraan hoe alleen ik ben. Het uitzicht is een verrassing, alsof je op een verborgen Afrikaanse savanne achter een vertrouwde heuvel stuit. Een eenzame lijsterbes rijst op uit een spleet in een rotsblok, buiten het bereik van herten. Verderop is er de vage lijn van een kapot hek tegen de herten, en dan opent de hele vallei zich. Een tapijt van groen, helemaal tot de grillige bergkam op 600 meter hoogte. En op de voorgrond, als het goed is beschermd door het hek, strekken honderden wijd uit elkaar staande eeuwenoude dennen zich uit tot in de verte.

Het is alsof ik de eerste ben die op de nasleep van een veldslag stuit. Er zijn vooral grijs-witte stammen, zogenaamde *snags*, die er bijstaan als skeletten. Andere oeroude bomen zijn halfgroen met naaldachtige ledematen die naar de lucht grijpen, ontdaan van hun vlees, als zombies die uit een graftombe omhoog strompelen.

De oudste binnen de omheining is niet de hoogste. Ik beschouw haar als een zij, hoewel dennenbomen eenhuizig zijn, met mannelijke en vrouwelijke delen in hun bloemen. Er groeit een bosbes in de holte van een van haar takken, en varens ontspruiten over de hele lengte van een andere. Rood, oranje en zwart gevlekt korstmos bedekt haar afbladderende rozige schors, en slierten groene Bryoria hangen als spinnenwebben aan haar uitsteeksels. In een gezond bos zouden ze ooit dichte zeilen gevormd hebben die het vocht vast houden. Haar takken hangen en wuiven weg van de heersende wind, taps toelopend tot korte stekelige groene naalden, elke vinger eindigend in een dikke stoffige bruine 'kaars' ongeveer ter grootte van een sigaret – het groeiende uiteinde van de tak. Hogerop in haar stam zitten donkere gaten, sommige bevlekt met recente uitwerpselen: de nesten van uilen of spechten.

Het heeft een zeker pathos dat deze reusachtige boom een habitat biedt aan anderen om hun jongen groot te brengen en zich voort te planten, terwijl haar eigen nakomelingen jaarlijks worden opgeofferd. De overblijfselen van zaailingen liggen versnipperd aan de lijzijde van de boom, verwoest door herten die door de omheining zijn gebroken. Herten zijn bosdieren die essentieel zijn voor het gezond functioneren van een dennenbos – ze maken grond vrij door te grazen en bemesten de bosbodem met hun uitwerpselen – maar als ze te lang blijven of te talrijk worden, kunnen ze een ravage aanrichten. Herten eten van bijna elke boom zo hoog als ze kunnen komen, en ze zullen zaailingen aanvallen met hun gewei om dat te krabben en daarbij jonge stengels breken. De Schotse natuurschrijver Jim Crumley noemt de wolf de 'schilder van de bergen' omdat hij de hertenpopulatie in toom houdt.[9]

Hertenkeutels liggen overal onder het uitgestrekte bladerdak, en wanneer ik over het omheinde land loop, ook overal tussen de heide. De afgekloven takken van jonge berken, lijsterbessen en dennen liggen als strepen over de helling. 540 jaar lang heeft deze den zaad verspreid in de hoop op nageslacht. In de beginjaren van de omheining hebben zich hier misschien zaailingen kunnen vestigen, maar ik betwijfel of die nu nog een winter zullen overleven.

De naaste buur van de den is een enkele stam, zo wit als gebeente, die er bijstaat als een totempaal. Op een verbleekt blauw label dat op zijn lichaam is genageld, staat '50a'. Een vreselijk gevoel hangt over het land. De dennen zijn als gewonde soldaten, bevroren in het moment waarop ze sneuvelden. De oude den heeft de pels van een lynx gevoeld of de natte neus van een wolf, heeft gezien hoe haar buren werden geveld voor schepen in de strijd tegen Napoleon. Een machtige boom die het ergste weer en de ergste ziekte kan weerstaan, maar haar nageslacht niet kan beschermen tegen de vreetlust van herten.

Ze weet wat er gebeurt. Monoterpenen zijn vluchtige organische chemische stoffen die door dennen worden geproduceerd en die de bomen gebruiken om signalen naar elkaar uit te zenden – om planteneters of insecten af te schrikken of om het vrijkomen van zaden te coördineren. Monoterpenen zijn uiterst kleine moleculen die de dennengeur verspreiden en zonlicht terug de ruimte in kaatsen. Wanneer dennenbomen in het zonlicht metaboliseren, kunnen er zich wel duizend tot tweeduizend deeltjes per kubieke centimeter in de lucht rond de boom bevinden, waardoor de hoeveelheid zonnestraling die de aarde treft, wordt verminderd. Via de dichtheid van het chemische signaal en de beschikbaarheid van licht, kunnen ze de aanwezigheid van andere bomen detecteren. In feite zien ze de ruimte in veelhoeken terwijl ze weg van hun buren en naar het licht toe groeien, zodat er een vijfzijdige vlakvulling in het bladerdak ontstaat die de basis vormt van de zelforganisatie in het bos.[10] Door de structuur van hun cellen kunnen bomen galm opvangen en geluiden om zich heen 'horen', maar ook ultrasone klanken van ver weg.[11] Dennen kunnen de vertrouwde aanwezigheid van ritselende naalden of het kraken van een vallende boom waarnemen, en natuurlijk communiceren en zorgen zij voor elkaar via het rijke mycorrhizanetwerk onder de grond. De grove den heeft een van de sterkst ontwikkelde schimmelnetwerken in de bodem, met meer dan negentien bekende ectomycorrhizale relaties voor het delen van koolstof, stikstof, essentiële zuren en andere voedingsstoffen.

En inderdaad, overal om mij heen, opdoemend uit het moeras, vormen reusachtige vruchtbare paddenstoelen ringen rond dode stronken – het genoom van het bos blijft bestaan onder de grond, wachtend. De bomen moeten misschien nog een paar jaar wachten, maar zal daar tijd voor zijn? Met de legioenen doden aan de kop van de vallei, het aantal oudere bomen met één verdorde arm, magere naalden en een kleine oogst aan onvolgroeide kegels, kan ik me moeilijk aan het gevoel onttrekken dat de oude dennen op het punt staan om het op te geven. Ik kan me voorstellen dat ze op hun eenzame heuvel hun knoestige schouders ophalen en zeggen: 'Wat heeft het nog voor een zin?' De kans die de oudste dennen van Groot-Brittannië hebben om hun genen door te geven aan de volgende generatie is maar zo reëel als de vastberadenheid van de mensen om de omheining te onderhouden.

Loch Maree, Schotland
57° 42' 37" N

Er zijn maar weinig plekken in Schotland waar herten niet kunnen komen. De eilanden in Loch Maree zijn zo'n plek. Vanaf Glen Loyne is het een lange, slingerende rit naar het noorden door dunbevolkte valleien langs verschillende andere fragmenten Caledonisch dennenbos: Attadale, Taodail, Achnashellach. Maar zelfs hier is sprake geweest van houtkap en verstoring. De eilanden van Loch Maree zijn uniek omdat ze al bijna achtduizend jaar ononderbroken bebost zijn en slechts af en toe bewoond werden door mystici of monniken – op één ervan staan de ruïnes van een priorij. Herten kunnen natuurlijk zwemmen, maar de eilanden liggen ver van de oever en hoewel er herten op de eilanden zijn geweest, heeft geen enkel hert er noemenswaardige schade aangericht.

Het is bijna midzomer en een warme avond met 19 graden Celsius. De zon staat nog steeds hoog aan een blauwe hemel en is zo helder als papier. Het loch is glinsterend zwart. De veelhoekige toren van Bein Eighe doemt op boven het donkere water als een uitschieter van de Alpen of de Himalaya. De dramatische puinhellingen hangen er onder onmogelijke hoeken bij. Bein Eighe is de Eiger van de Britse eilanden, omringd door een coterie van intimiderende Munro's, stuk voor stuk ook indrukwekkende toppen. Vanaf de uitlopers van de bergen tuimelen eeuwenoude dennenbossen helemaal tot aan de oever, waardoor een van de mooiste waterkanten van Schotland ontstaat. Loch Maree strekt zich uit als een lange slanke vinger die naar het zuidoosten wijst en aan het noordelijke uiteinde uitwaaiert als een palm alvorens naar het noordwesten in zee uit te monden, een palm die een waaier van juwelen bevat: zijn smaragdgroene eilanden.

Vanaf het strand van Slattadale werpt de zon een bleek vuur over het meer dat de stammen van de dennen op de beboste eilanden in lichterlaaie zet. We zien dichte rijen bomen in een verleidelijk, ongerept paradijs, een natuurreservaat waar kamperen en motorboten verboden zijn. Ik sta op het kiezelstrand, mijn tenen gekoeld door de bruine rimpels van turfachtige golven, mijmerend over de eilanden die gloeien in het gouden licht. Ik kwam hier voor de beboste eilanden, maar ik had er niet over nagedacht hoe ik ze ging bereiken. Behalve een paar picknickbanken en een parkeerplaats van de Forestry Commission zijn er in de wijde omtrek geen noemenswaardige voorzieningen. Geen kanoverhuur, geen veerboot. Maar ik moet en zal voet zetten op de ongerepte eilanden. Ik moet de geur inademen van het oudste overlevende bos, misschien wel het enige dat er nog is in Groot-Brittannië.

De dunne lijn van het altijd groene bladerdak bovenop de oranje stammen is op een kilometer afstand nog net zichtbaar. De bomen wenken, ze dagen me uit. Ik zie maar één oplossing.

Het kost me half uur om de moed op te brengen om te zwemmen en nog eens een half uur om de oversteek ook echt te maken. De afstand is niet het probleem, maar mijn geest. Juist die begint me halverwege parten te spelen. Wat als ik kramp krijg? Of moe word? Als dat midden op Loch Maree gebeurt, zal niemand ooit weten wat er is gebeurd. Onder me driehonderd meter van het allerzwartste water. Vijfhonderd meter in elke richting. Het is 1027 slagen zwemmen naar de overkant. Ik haal het. Het water aan de overkant klotst tegen granieten platen die in de diepte verdwijnen. Ik ga op de hete steen liggen om op adem te komen. Dan kijk ik rond.

Het bos loopt door tot aan de oever van het meer. Bomen zijn in het water gevallen en liggen met hun turf-oranje schachten onder water, daarboven stammen die zijn uitgewassen tot de kleur van beenderen. Het is niet eenvoudig om door het kreupelhout te komen. Enorme wortelplaten van omgevallen stammen steken uit het kreupelhout, zo hoog als huizen, druipend van leven: mossen, gaspeldoorn, wilgen, lijsterbessen, varens en bessen groeien in de krater die de boom heeft vrijgemaakt. Ik loop op mijn tenen langs de oever, over een strand van fijn rood zand dat geen sporen vertoont, afgezien van een heel zwakke afdruk van een drietenige waadvogel. Dit is een eiland zonder mensen, maar waar veertien libellensoorten leven, en het is een beetje beangstigend, een wilde natuur die bijna spookachtig is in haar onverschilligheid.

De vogels vieren feest, hun gezang is rijk, gevarieerd en druk. Vogels in verschillende grootte en kleuren hippen en dartelen door het bladerdak. Een bruine steltloper kijkt me argwanend aan vanaf zijn veilige plek op een onder water liggende boomstam terwijl ik me een weg baan over de oever, langs de keien die begroeid zijn met roestrode en koraalgroene korstmossen. Xyleem en floëem, de vezels van bomen, zijn erg lang in oerbossen, waardoor de resonantie van geluid beter is. Het blijkt dat vogels het verschil kunnen horen en hun gezang letterlijk afstemmen op hun omgeving. Het bos weerkaatst geroep: ja, dit is een goede plek om voedsel te vinden, een nest te bouwen, jongen groot te brengen.

Onderzoek heeft aangetoond dat vogels sterkere, grotere eieren leggen in oudere bossen.

Kronkelige dennen groeien in de meest onwaarschijnlijke spleten in de rotsen. Overal dode bomen, staand en omgevallen. Dit is het kenmerkende van wildwood – dode bomen mogen rusten waar ze vallen. Dode bomen ondersteunen veel meer leven dan levende, vandaar dat er hier zoveel vogels zijn. Sommige soorten, zoals de boompieper en de roodstaart, zoeken alleen de oerbossen op vanwege de hoeveelheid en de soorten insecten. De grote bonte specht nestelt alleen in dode grove dennen. Nog uitzonderlijker is dat de dennenzweefvlieg uitsluitend broedt in natte holten van dode grove dennen. Geen wonder dat hij bijna uitgestorven is in Schotland.

In elke koolstofcyclus is de dood de motor van het leven. Wanneer een boom sterft, dringen houtborende kevers het spinthout binnen en beginnen het afbraakproces. Dan komen schimmels die ruimtes binnen, samen met wespen, spinnen en andere insecten, en nodigen andere schimmels uit. En in de laatste fase, de humificatiefase, zetten bodemorganismen de laatste ligninemoleculen van het hout om in grond. Daarmee is de cyclus voltooid. Door zijn hoge harsgehalte heeft een volwassen grove den veertig jaar nodig om te rotten, waarbij langzaam stikstof vrijkomt in de bodem, die de larven en bacteriën voedt die de onderste sport vormen van de voedselketen voor insecten en vogels.

De grond op het eiland is lichtbruin, bijna rood, en voelt vezelig aan. Onder het afbrokkelende dode hout lijkt zich haast wel een huid te hebben gevormd, een weefsel van wortels waar elke spade moeite mee zou hebben. Een levende boom bestaat voor 5 volumeprocent uit levende cellen, een dode voor 40 volumeprocent, en in een ongerept oerbos kan tot 40 volumeprocent van de totale biomassa dood zijn, hetgeen veel meer leven ondersteunt: de hoeveelheid insecten in ongerepte, onbeheerde bossen is exponentieel hoger. Totale regeneratie van oerbossen, het doel van veel van de huidige natuurbeschermingsinspanningen, is pas mogelijk als de huidige jonge bomen zijn afgestorven en weggerot. Voor veel van de fragmenten Caledonisch dennenbos die men pas onlangs toestond te regenereren, is dat over 400 of 500 jaar. Er is een subcategorie in de classificatie van beschermde soorten die verder gaat dan 'oerbos', namelijk 'waar oerbos'. Waar oerbos heeft een bodemstructuur en een complexe ondergroei (de vegetatielaag onder het bladerdak van een bos) die alleen kan voortkomen uit de opeenstapeling van sterfgevallen van generatie op generatie bomen. Dat is waarom de eilanden van Loch Maree zo belangrijk zijn.

Een enorme zwart-geel gestreepte libel inspecteert mijn gezicht voordat hij verdwijnt over het bronzen oppervlak van het meer. Verderop hangen slierten korstmossen van de soort *Bryoria fremontii* die er uitzien als paardenhaar, helder in de stille avondlucht, buiten bereik in het ondoordringbare bos. Wat ik ook probeer, op blote voeten kom ik niet ver in het struikgewas van het bos. De dennen verdringen zich voor elke centimeter ruimte op de rots. Het eiland ziet eruit alsof het zou kunnen zinken onder het gewicht van de bomen. Ik waad terug het loch in en watertrappel terwijl ik terugkijk op het eiland. De amberkleurige vloeistof vloeit rond mijn ledematen en in mijn mond. Hij smaakt zoet, de bomen hebben hem gefilterd. Waarom, vraag ik me af, zijn de zeeforel en de zalm de laatste drie jaar niet meer teruggekeerd naar Loch Maree – is het water te warm geworden?

Van een afstand lijkt het bladerdak van de dennen op een tapijt, één enkel organisme van vijfhoekige cellen. De schors is een caleidoscoop van kleuren, van grijs tot oranje tot scharlaken. Een stokoude den heeft een van de keien naast het meer met wortels omstrengeld, haar kromme armen strekken zich in kronkelige lijnen uit over het water.

Wanneer ik weer aankom op de oever, trekt het laatste zonlicht een streep over het bladerdak dat zich met gouden spatten achter me terugtrekt. Een parelduiker scheert laag over het water en flitst met zijn witte onderstel op korte afstand van mijn gezicht. Met klapperende tanden schud ik koperen druppels van me af op de kiezelstenen, terwijl de hemel langzaam haar kleur verliest en een koekoek roept in het bos. De roep van deze eens zo gewone en nu zo zeldzaam geworden vogel stemt niet tot vreugde. In plaats daarvan hoor ik een smeekbede. Oehoe! Kijk dan! Overal om je heen bedreigde diersoorten in een meer dat zijn vis kwijt is. Klimaatverandering vraagt dat we onze omgeving steeds opnieuw bekijken. Ik heb het gevoel dat de strijd om de kloof tussen ons wereldbeeld en de werkelijkheid te overbruggen de komende jaren bepalend zal zijn: onze verbeelding zal altijd druk zijn met een inhaalslag. Ik zie hoe het licht dieper wordt en het meer magenta opvlamt voordat het weer diepglanzend zwart wordt. Lange tijd weerkaatsen de wolken nog roze, haast als een verwijt, terwijl de blauwe nacht niet geheel wil vallen, zodat het oordeel wordt opgeschort.

Glen Feshie, Schotland
57° 11' 40" N

Als Loch Maree een versie van het verleden is, dan is Glen Feshie de toekomstige echo ervan. Om daar te komen rijd ik over de continentale kloof, de kloof van Loch Ness die de Hooglanden in tweeën snijdt, en klim ik over de weg van Inverness naar de Cairngorms naar het hart van de oostelijke populatie van dennenbossen die vanuit Oekraïne zijn uitgezaaid. Glen Feshie is een van de prachtige valleien aan de noordwestkant van het massief waar het bos is bevrijd van de tirannie van korhoenders en herten. Ik heb gehoord dat ik hier moet zijn voor de natuurlijke boomgrens in Schotland.

Ik kom er 's avonds aan op de dag voor midzomer en sla mijn tent op aan de rivier. Het bruine water is donker in de diepten onder de brug, en koud. Ik vind een vlakke plek bij een greppel die lijkt te zijn gegraven voor de afwatering, geen centimeter van deze legendarische vallei is ongepland. In het nog heldere zonlicht loop ik de vallei in en kom op een plek waar het pad breder wordt en een vergezicht van steile grijze heuvels zich ontvouwt. Dit was het decor voor The Monarch of the Glen, een beroemd schilderij door Landseer van een vorstelijk hert met een twaalfender-gewei, omlijst door de rotsen boven de vallei. Het beeld, bekend van whiskyflessen en Highlandkitsch, romantiseert een landschap zonder inheemse crofters of bomen, gewijd aan herten en de Victoriaanse liefde voor de jacht.

Het uitzicht is inmiddels flink veranderd. De rivier stroomt nog steeds door de ontvolkte vallei en wilde, ondiepe kanalen over bleekroze en gele granietbollen. De toppen van de hoogvenen zijn nog steeds bruin en paars gekleurd met heide, maar de valleibodem is een feest van altijdgroen, en dicht aangesloten rangen dennen bestormen de heuvels om hun natuurlijke grens te vinden. Ze zijn losgelaten. Glen Feshie is een poging tot een nieuwe aanpak van landbeheer: *rewilding*, herwildering.

De geschiedenis van dit land is aan de heuvels af te lezen. Ik zie de rechte lijnen en gelijkmatige hoogten van de vroegere aanplanting die langzaam zijn losgelaten, het zachtere, minder strakke bladerdak van de oude groepen bomen die zijn blijven staan en de stekelige toppen van de nieuwkomers, nakomelingen die zijn gekiemd sinds de herinvoering van het natuurlijke bos vijftien jaar geleden: soms alleen, soms in kluitjes, maar overal bloeiend in een reliëf van iriserend groen.

De grond naast het pad is zo diep en veerkrachtig als een matras, vol mos, heide, bosbes, grassen en kleine bloemetjes. Net buiten de dekking van hun bladerdak worden de oude dennen omringd door jongere bomen. Onder het bladerdak kunnen die niet terugkeren. Het Caledonische woud was daarom waarschijnlijk een dynamisch, beweeglijk bos dat met elke generatie bomen iets opschoof. Stroomopwaarts domineren enorme bomen van twintig, dertig, veertig meter de bochten in de rivier, aan alle kanten ondersteund door zaailingen van zo'n vijf meter hoog. Aan de kop van de vallei opent zich een spectaculair uitzicht met aan weerszijden een kom die door gletsjers is uitgeslepen.

Een haas steekt het pad over. Een kuifmees maakt herrie, en drie witte paarden grazen onbekommerd in de laatste avondzon.

Het is een indrukwekkend beeld van hoe de natuur het weer overneemt, een voorbeeld van wat er kan gebeuren wanneer bomen ongestoord hun gang kunnen gaan, of misschien toont het ons hoe het ooit was – maar dan zonder de inheemse keuterboeren, de crofters. Vliegen, motten, sap, honingdauw, parasieten en schimmels zwermen over de oude dode stammen die zijn blijven liggen waar ze vielen. Berken, lijsterbessen en elzen staan ertussen en werken samen met de dennen in wat een sociaal gebeuren lijkt. Alles straalt, bloeit, gonst. Het is alsof de natuur in gezang is uitgebarsten. Die ochtend word ik wakker met het geluid van een auerhoen dat roept in de mist – *ketuk, ketuk* – als de hoeven van een dravend paard. De Kelten noemden hem het 'paard van het bos'. Er is geen hert te zien. Die zijn weer eens hun typerende, ongrijpbare zelf.

'Herten zijn geen vijanden van het bos,' zegt Thomas MacDonnell, de houtfactor van Glen Feshie, als ik hem later ontmoet. Ze zijn de boswachters, houden het gras eronder en bevorderen de groei van kruiden. Vooral de auerhoen volgt in het voetspoor van herten die door het bos struinen – als er tenminste een bos is.

De etymologie van het woord wildernis in het Engels is te herleiden tot *wild deer place*, 'plaats van wilde herten', maar men heeft dit romantische ideaal uit de hand laten lopen toen de Highlands eenmaal van mensen waren ontdaan. In zekere zin heeft een overmaat aan herwildering ten gunste van herten het ecosysteem uit evenwicht gebracht. In de negentiende en de twintigste eeuw, het tijdperk van de hertenjacht, waren er in Glen Feshie vijftig herten per vierkante kilometer. Nu zijn er een of twee. En de met uitsterven bedreigde auerhoen is zich aan het herstellen. Haantjes die voor nieuwe aanwas zorgen hebben onlangs een nieuw territorium, een baltsplaats, gevestigd bij Glen Feshie, en alle betrokkenen zijn bijzonder trots. Een baltsplaats is als een soort arena voor gladiatoren op een open plek in het bos waar de haantjes hun vertoningen houden, maar kan alleen bestaan als er veel oud bos is. De auerhoen is afhankelijk van een dieet van bosbessen die alleen groeien in de halfschaduw van goed gestructureerde dennenbossen.

Glen Feshie is het juweel in de kroon van Wildland Ltd, het privé-vastgoedimperium van de Deense zakenman Anders Povlson, dat zich toelegt op herwildering. Wildland was een pionier in een beweging die nu terrein wint. Algemeen wordt erkend dat de industriële landbouw en de verstedelijking tijdens mijn leven (ik ben van 1974) hebben bijgedragen aan de vernietiging van meer dan 40 procent van de Britse wilde fauna en de bodem gevaarlijk ver hebben uitgeput. 'Natuurherstel' is in heel Europa een mantra geworden, zo niet een prioriteit van de regeringen, en politieke partijen doen nu hun best om meer bomen te planten dan hun rivalen. Herwildering is hip, maar roept ook sterke emoties op. Sommigen op het platteland pleiten er hartstochtelijk voor, anderen zien het als een dodelijke bedreiging voor hun cultuur en geschiedenis, voor een hele manier van leven.

Het lijkt wat vreemd dat bomen zulke extreme reacties oproepen, maar Glen Feshie stelt een fundamentele vraag over land aan de orde. Waar dient het land eigenlijk nog voor zonder inkomsten uit de jacht of productieve waarde als bosbouw of voor commerciele landbouw – zonder vooruitzicht op financieel rendement? Het simpele antwoord is: 'leven'. We hebben land nodig om voedsel te verbouwen, maar we moeten ook genoeg wild land met rust laten om de zuurstof en de biodiversiteit te produceren die we nodig hebben om te overleven. Er is genoeg land om iedereen te voeden als het goed wordt verdeeld en beheerd en als kwesties als levensstijl, consumptie, waarden, rechtvaardigheid en billijkheid, en het ontbreken van een zinnig verband tussen levensonderhoud en de levende wereld worden aangepakt. Als er niet genoeg diversiteit en overvloed is in de levende wereld, dan is er helemaal geen leven, menselijk noch niet-menselijk.

Thomas MacDonnell is een onwaarschijnlijke revolutionair. In zijn groene fleece en wandelbroek, met gladgeschoren wangen en kortgeknipt zilvergrijs haar, ziet hij eruit als een wandelaar die op het punt staat aan een tocht te beginnen, maar zijn doordringende zwarte ogen branden met een vuur dat ik tot nu toe alleen bij priesters en politici ben tegengekomen. Hij nestelt zich in een leunstoel met uitzicht over een woonwijk in Aviemore, waar Wildland zijn kantoren heeft, en kijkt me aan met zijn pokerface.

Thomas MacDonnell is waarschijnlijk verantwoordelijk voor de dood van meer herten dan wie dan ook in Schotland. Als manager natuurbehoud van Wildland is het al meer dan vijftien jaar zijn missie om de begrazingsniveaus in Glen Feshie terug te brengen tot een niveau waarop de bomen zich kunnen herstellen. Het bloeiende bos is een levend monument voor zijn inspanningen. Nu het succes van het programma eindelijk zichtbaar wordt op landschapsschaal, begint het tij in zijn voordeel te keren, maar het is niet eenvoudig gebleken om tot op dit punt te komen.

Goede jeugdvrienden beschuldigden hem ervan hun baan in gevaar te brengen. In volgepakte dorpshuizen werd hij weggehoond toen hij probeerde uit te leggen waarom hij de herten wilde afmaken en wat zijn visie voor de komende tweehonderd jaar in Glen Feshie is. Boeren, hertenjagers, *ghillies* (drijvers) en jachtopzieners waren bezorgd over de gevolgen die zijn plannen zouden hebben voor hun werk, hun cultuur. Wat Thomas betreft had het echter totaal geen emotionele dimensie. Hij was opgeleid als ingenieur. Hij heeft altijd willen begrijpen hoe iets werkt, analyseren wat er mis was en dan een oplossing bedenken.

'In zekere zin zaten ze nog steeds gevangen in een koloniale manier van denken,' zegt Thomas. Hij vormt een afstandelijk oordeel over de kritiek die hij te verduren kreeg. Het land, zegt hij, is letterlijk en figuurlijk 'afgebrand', en de gemeenschappen die afhankelijk zijn van patronen van Victoriaans landgebruik zijn 'vluchtelingen uit de negentiende eeuw'.

Toen hij twintig jaar geleden de factor – landbeheerder – van Glen Feshie Estate werd, was het hem duidelijk wat er mis was. Eigenlijk hadden de verschillende regeringen en landeigenaren dat al sinds de Tweede Wereldoorlog begrepen. De ene regeringscommissie na de andere heeft geprobeerd het aantal herten terug te brengen, maar slaagde er niet in de landeigenaren te overtuigen en was ook niet bereid hen ertoe te dwingen het bestand uit te dunnen, aangezien ze sterk afhankelijk zijn van de inkomsten uit de hertenjacht. Als jonge man had Thomas vele natte en koude dagen doorgebracht met het omheinen van houtplantages om herten buiten te houden. Hij was opgegroeid in Glen Feshie en de aangrenzende vallei. Hij begreep hoe het ecosysteem werkte en was benieuwd wat er zou gebeuren als de aanbevelingen van de hertencommissies daadwerkelijk zouden worden uitgevoerd. Toen het landgoed in andere handen overging, kreeg Thomas een nieuwe baas die openstond voor zijn ideeën om dingen anders aan te pakken. Dit was zijn kans om een experiment uit te voeren.

'Soms is het meest radicale en moedige wat je kunt doen juist niets doen,' stelt hij. Hoewel het afmaken van herten niet bepaald niets is, bedoelt hij dat het land niet actief wordt beheerd, en dat druist in tegen honderden, ja zelfs duizenden jaren praktijk als we ook het half-nomadisme van de crofters meerekenen, dat in zekere zin ook een vorm van beheer was. Er was moed voor nodig geweest. Er was een moment, een spiritueel moment, herinnert hij zich, in 2006. Hij had in de voorgaande drie jaar vijfduizend herten afgeschoten op het Glen Feshie Estate, ondanks hevige kritiek – herten worden niet door hekken op één bepaald landgoed gehouden, maar lopen vrij rond in de Hooglanden. Er was drie jaar verstreken met weinig herten, maar de dennen leken niet terug te willen komen.

'Dat waren duistere tijden. Verdorie, dacht ik, misschien heb ik het mis.'

In juni van het derde jaar wandelde Thomas in Glen Feshie en kwam hij langs een bekende den die hij al lang voor senescent hield. Overal rond de oude boom staken kleine groene vingers uit het gras omhoog – een ring van zaailingen. Hij keek omhoog in het bladerdak en zag het meest fantastische arsenaal aan zaden – dit oude dametje sliep helemaal niet.

'Het was alsof iemand een schakelaar had omgezet. Ze waren gewoon ineens verschenen. De tranen schoten me in de ogen! Misschien hadden ze door dat iemand hen probeerde te helpen.'

Grove dennen produceren niet elk jaar een goede oogst dennenappels. Op hogere breedtegraden zorgen strenge winters en korte groeiseizoenen ervoor dat een boom soms drie, vier of zelfs twaalf jaar lang niet bloeit en geen zaad produceert. De opeenvolging in het klimaat is belangrijk – wat het ene jaar gebeurt, beïnvloedt wat het volgende jaar gebeurt. Een warme, zonnige zomer leidt meestal tot een grote hoeveelheid bloemen in het jaar daarop, en dan draagt een boom in één seizoen voor drie jaar aan dennenappels.

De naaldenknop die in het voorjaar verschijnt, ontvouwt zich tot een harsachtig bruine tros bloemen langs de stengel. Deze dicht op elkaar gepakte bommen dragen de mannelijke gameet. Ze beginnen hun leven als miniatuur dennenappels, maar verkruimelen al gauw tot poeder en worden door de wind verspreid. In mei en juni zie je wolken gele pollen door een volgroeid dennenbos dwarrelen. In een gezond ecosysteem kan dit een schuimlaag vormen op het oppervlak van poelen en meren – het stuifmeel heeft twee luchtblazen die speciaal zijn ontworpen om het drijvend te houden. Niet alleen geven grove dennen hun stuifmeel de best mogelijke uitgangspositie in het leven, ze synchroniseren hun bloei bovendien met andere dennen om de kans op een succesvolle bevruchting te vergroten. Van grove dennen is aangetoond dat ze synchroon bloeien over afstanden tot 200 mijl. Hoe weten ze dat? Ecologen denken dat dit misschien werkt met hormonale communicatie in de wind en via ondergrondse schimmelnetwerken, maar het zou ook een dieperliggende genetische reactie kunnen zijn die door bepaalde klimatologische drempels op gang wordt gebracht. Maar niemand weet het echt, nog niet.

De vrouwelijke dennenappel begint als een klein paars gezwel op een jonge stengel. De stuifmeelkorrels komen terecht op het roodpaarse oppervlak van de schubben van de dennenappel. De suiker van het stuifmeel en het vocht van de hars van de kegel vormen samen een zoete bestuivingsdruppel die in de micropylebuis – in feite een kanaal in de cel – wordt gezogen, waar hij in contact komt met de nucellus. De dennenappels harden verder uit gedurende de zomer en worden net geen centimeter groot alvorens te overwinteren. Pas wanneer de stuifmeelbuizen in het volgende voorjaar weer gaan groeien, vindt de bevruchting plaats doordat de zich uitstrekkende buizen de nucellus binnendringen. Tegen het einde van de tweede zomer zijn ze volgroeid, maar ze zijn nog groen en kleverig en worden pas in de herfst en winter bruin en hard. In de derde lente barsten de kegels open als de schubben terugveren om de zaden te onthullen en ze los te schudden in de wind.

Een zaadje van een grove den lijkt een beetje op de vleugel van een insect, met een harde zaadhuls en een lange papierachtige vleugel die werkt als een zeil dat de wind vangt. Het endosperm van het zaad is een essentiële voedselbron voor kruisbekken, sijzen, mezen, spechten en rode eekhoorns. Rode eekhoorns verscheuren de schubben om bij de zaden te komen en eten tot wel tweehonderd dennenappels per dag. Er is een hectare bomen nodig om één eekhoorn de winter door te helpen.

De kruisbekken daarentegen wrikken de schubben open met hun gekruiste onderkaken voor ze hun hongerige tongen naar binnen laten glijden om het zaad eruit te trekken. Dankzij de richels in het gehemelte kan de vogel het zaad van zijn schil ontdoen terwijl hij het doorslikt. Knaagdieren en insecten zijn dol op dennenzaden, dus een bos moet een zaadoogst produceren die groter is dan de eetlust van de rest van de voedselketen als het wil dat zijn zaailingen een kans maken. Dit schijnt de reden te zijn voor synchrone mastjaren – wanneer alle bomen op hetzelfde ogenblik een spectaculaire zaadoogst produceren.

Mastjaren komen echter steeds vaker voor en de opwarming brengt de bomen in verwarring, waardoor de dennen hun zaden steeds vroeger gaan afgeven en de normale seizoenscycli van het bos dreigen te worden verstoord. Momenteel is er nog een overlapping van zaden in het ene cohort dennenappels en de beschikbaarheid van zaden in het volgende cohort dennenappels dat zich nog aan het ontwikkelen is. Maar als de generaties kegels op de boom volledig van elkaar worden losgekoppeld, zouden flink wat soorten die van het zaad afhankelijk zijn, honger kunnen lijden. En het zijn niet alleen de zaadeters die eronder zullen lijden. De nectarrijke dennenbloemen zijn belangrijke voedselbronnen voor tientallen soorten nachtvlinders, vlinders en andere gevleugelde insecten. De mottenlarven brengen de winter door in de beschermende plooien van de schors van de grove den, om in het voorjaar uit de pop te komen, klaar om zich met de bloemen te voeden. Als de boom echter al gebloeid heeft, zal een hele generatie motten sterven. En als de motten sterven, hebben de vogels minder te eten, enzovoort. Eenentwintig dagen is de maximale afwijking van de normale bloeidatum die de meeste soorten rupsen- en mottenlarven kunnen verdragen. In 2020 zitten we inmiddels op elf à twaalf dagen. Het meest verontrustende fenomeen voor de dennen zou een ontkoppeling zijn van de timing van de bloei en het vrijkomen van stuifmeel. Als synchrone bloei afhangt van aangeleerde genetische reacties op klimaatsignalen en niet van communicatie onder de grond of door de lucht, dan zou asymmetrische opwarming – ongelijkmatige weerpatronen waarbij sommige delen van het bos een ander klimaat ervaren dan andere – kunnen betekenen dat er helemaal geen zaden worden gevormd.

Zelfs als de zaden zich vormen en vervolgens aan ontdekking en consumptie door knaagdieren, vogels en kevers ontsnappen, is kiemen niet verzekerd. De zaden hebben grindrijke plaatsen nodig of gebieden met ondiep veen, zoals wegbermen en rivieroevers. Zwaar veen is te arm aan voedingsstoffen en houdt waarschijnlijk niet de mycorrhizaschimmels vast die dennen nodig hebben om toegang te krijgen tot fosfaten en nitraten in verder arme grond. Het opbouwen en uitbreiden van de mycorrhizale relaties van bestaande bossen is veruit de gemakkelijkste en meest betrouwbare manier om een succesvolle kieming te verzekeren. Zelfs waar generaties lang geen bos is geweest, zijn de mycorrhiza waarschijnlijk nog in een slapende vorm aanwezig.

De bodem geeft de belangrijkste indicatie waar het planten of aanmoedigen van bomen een kans maakt, aldus Thomas. Overal waar paddenstoelen, varens, korstmos en bepaalde soorten bosplanten zoals viooltjes te vinden zijn, was ooit bos. Ringen van paddenstoelen geven meestal de omtrek aan van het lang geleden gevormde grondwerk van een boomstronk. Er zijn tussen de vijftien en negentien ecto-mycorrhizaschimmels (schimmels die rond de wortels groeien) in een volgroeid dennenbos, en ze spelen een rol in alles, van koolstof- en voedingsstoffentransport tot de korstmosbedekking, waarbij ze suiker aan de boom onttrekken en deze in ruil daarvoor mineralen verschaffen. Bomen planten zonder rekening te houden met de essentiële symbiotische 'andere helft' van het bos onder de grond kan veel minder effectief zijn dan de grond in zijn eigen tempo tot bos te laten evolueren. Oliver Rackham beschrijft een aangeplant eikenbos in Essex dat zelfs na 750 jaar nog niet de orchideeën, planten en paddenstoelen heeft die je van een natuurlijk bos zou verwachten.[12]

Wildland beschikt nu over vijftien jaar basisgegevens om het toekomstige beheer te onderbouwen. Ecologen werken er samen met vrijwilligers om de bodem in kwadranten van zeven meter in kaart te brengen om te begrijpen hoe ecologische successie werkt. De ecologen tellen de mest om het aantal herten te bepalen, ze meten de hoogte van de heide om te zien of die andere planten in de schaduw stelt, en ze tellen de poppen van de kleine wintervlinder op de bladeren van de bosbessenplanten die de auerhoen in de winter aan zijn kuikens voert.

Thomas weet nog steeds niet wat er zal gebeuren, hoe de verschillende soorten zullen reageren – we hebben hierbij te maken met immense tijdschalen die moeilijk te bevatten zijn voor het menselijk verstand – maar hij geniet van het kijken naar en het meten van de verandering. Plotseling zijn er overal dennen, en niet alleen in Glen Feshie. In de beginjaren waren er tweehonderd stammen per hectare, nu zijn het er zesduizend. En de bomen worden sterker.

Het eerste doel is het herstel van habitats. Vervolgens zal Thomas proberen een maat te vinden voor wat een beheersbaar aantal herten is en zijn gewaagde visie zichzelf laten terugbetalen via toerisme en andere 'natuurlijk kapitaal'-initiatieven. Maar bij gebrek aan een roofdier als de wolf zal Thomas nog steeds herten moeten schieten en nog steeds moeten samenwerken met de buren van Glen Feshie, aangezien de herten wild zijn en de bergen onmogelijk in hun geheel kunnen worden omheind. Dat is ook het idee achter de oprichting van Cairngorms Connect – een samenwerkingsverband tussen Wildland en het naburige landgoed Abernethy, dat wordt beheerd door de Royal Society for the Protection of Birds (RSPB), de Forestry Commission Scotland, het Scottish Natural Heritage en het Cairngorms National Park, een adembenemend gebied van 600 vierkante kilometer dat nadrukkelijk niet wordt beheerd vanwege zijn potentieel als wildernis.

Wat Thomas me op het laatst vertelde, voordat hij me uitnodigde voor een midzomerse *ceilidh* – een avond vol Schots-Keltische zang en dans – in de *bothy*, de berghut van Glen Feshie die avond, geeft een idee van hoe groot zijn ambities zijn. De helft van alle landgoederen in Schotland staat te koop. En Wildland is bezig met de aankoop van verschillende ervan. Tegen eind 2020 zal Wildland 90.000 hectare bezitten, waardoor het de grootste grondbezitter van Schotland wordt. Glen Feshie, zo vertelt hij me, is 'maar' 17.400 hectare groot.

'Ik ben hier aan het tuinieren,' grinnikt hij ironisch. Het is de enige keer tijdens onze ontmoeting dat ik hem echt zie glimlachen.

Verder buiten Aviemore, in een omgebouwde loods naast de parkeerplaats van Scottish Natural Heritage, is het kantoor van Cairngorms Connect gevestigd. Die bescheiden locatie logenstraft de ambitie van het partnerschap als een buitenbeentje in een verder nog uiterst behoudende natuurbeschermingsindustrie. De crisis in de natuurlijke wereld vraagt dat we onze diepgewortelde veronderstellingen en gewoonten opnieuw overwegen, zelfs van diegenen die worden betaald om voor die wereld te zorgen.

Mark Hancock is als wetenschapper door de RSPB gedetacheerd bij Cairngorms Connect. Hij maakt een kop thee voor me die we mee naar buiten nemen, naar een boomstronk in de zon op een veld naast de kantoorhut. De volle breedte van het Cairngorms-massief – graniet en gneis tot een hoogte van meer dan 1200 meter – schittert aan de horizon, met Glen Feshie aan het westelijke uiteinde en Abernethy Forest aan het oostelijke. Cairngorms Connect wil een corridor van wildernis tussen de twee tot stand brengen.

Mark duwt zijn bril omhoog op de brug van zijn neus en kiest zijn woorden met wetenschappelijke voorzichtigheid en precisie. Ik heb het gevoel dat de omvang en de doelstellingen van het plan onbekend terrein zijn voor hem en anderen die gewend zijn aan de taal van de wetenschap, controle en management. Hij geeft grif toe dat Cairngorms Connect alle gewoonten op de kop heeft gezet, 'dwars tegen de stroom in van honderd jaar natuurbehoudsgeschiedenis, de praktijk van actief beheer.' Maar als het werkt, en Glen Feshie lijkt te suggereren dát het werkt, dan zou het de manier waarop de Britse natuurbescherming op nationale schaal denkt en handelt kunnen veranderen. Het zou onze manier van denken over de waarde van het land kunnen veranderen, en zelfs onze ideeën over het doel van nationale parken.

Groot-Brittannië probeert wanhopig de omvang van zijn bosgebieden te vergroten. Met 13 procent bosbedekking ligt het VK ver achter op het Europese gemiddelde van 37 procent en het wereldgemiddelde van 30 procent. Bovendien is een groot deel van die 13 procent plantage – één enkel gewas dat wordt geteeld voor hout – met heel weinig soortendiversiteit tussen en onder de bomen. Plantages zijn eigenlijk niet echt bossen.

Zweden en Finland zijn goed voor een derde van de bossen in de Europese Unie met respectievelijk 68 en 71 procent bebost grondgebied.[13] En zelfs dan absorberen de Finse bossen slechts ongeveer de helft van de Finse broeikasgasemissies. Als het VK zijn bosareaal zou willen verdrievoudigen tot het Europese gemiddelde zou dat revolutionair zijn, maar nog steeds niet genoeg. Bossen zouden een kwart tot een derde van de wereldwijde koolstofdioxideverontreiniging door de mens kunnen opvangen, maar de schaal waarop het landgebruik moet veranderen om een dergelijk doel te bereiken is verbijsterend. In studies wordt een gebied ter grootte van India gesuggereerd, gelijk aan al het land dat nu al wereldwijd voor landbouw wordt gebruikt, en dat nog zonder rekening te houden met de bomen die elk jaar verloren gaan. Vijftien miljard bomen – 30 miljoen hectare bos – worden elk jaar wereldwijd gekapt, en ongeveer evenveel gaan er verloren door bosbranden. Cairngorms Connect geeft maar een glimp van wat er zou kunnen gebeuren als koolstofvastlegging of de aanleg van bosgebieden nationale veiligheidskwesties zouden worden, hetgeen al snel het geval zou kunnen zijn. Bedrijven die hun uitstoot willen compenseren, drijven de prijs van grote Schotse landgoederen nu al op.

Op dit moment is Cairngorms Connect echter geen militaire operatie, maar een kwetsbaar experiment om de natuur te leren begrijpen als een dynamisch werk in uitvoering, om bossen te zien als mobiele gemeenschappen en land als voortdurend in beweging. Marks voornaamste interesse zijn de vogels en hun leefomgeving. In dat opzicht is hij niet zozeer minder bezorgd over het oppervlak van de grond die het partnerschap vertegenwoordigt, maar over de topografie ervan, over de diversiteit van de ecosystemen waaraan het plaats zou kunnen bieden. Zou het bos kunnen migreren als dat nodig was? Is er een beletsel om het tegen de helling op te laten groeien als het dat zou willen? En als het daar aankomt, is er dan nog genoeg koude berg over?

In een onverstoord systeem zouden de dennen op de natuurlijke boomgrens plaats maken voor montaan bos, wat de Noren 'de wilgenzone' noemen. Het montane systeem van wilgen en lijsterbessen bereidt in de loop der tijd de grond voor de dennen voor en vormt zo de eerste fase van het bos. Maar herten houden het meest van wilgen en lijsterbessen. Sommige wilgensoorten zijn zo zwaar begraasd dat er in Schotland nog slechts één of twee exemplaren in het wild overblijven. De montane zone van delicate struiken en bessen die doorloopt tot voorbij de grens van het aaneengesloten bos, is het grootste slachtoffer van overbegrazing door herten in de Highlands. Ze is gewoon verdwenen.

Ben Lavers, een reservaat van de National Trust for Scotland dat een paar uur zuidelijker ligt, heeft de beste collectie montane soorten van het VK en is een soort zaadbank voor de zeldzaamste habitat van het land. Het bestaat uit een paar hectare omheind terrein op het zuiden, beschermd door een hoge en veilige hertenomheining met toegangshekken die vanzelf weer sluiten dankzij een veerconstructie. Toen ik er op weg naar Fort William was, vond ik op bijna elke tweede plant keurige cirkels uit de bladeren geknipt, hetgeen de aanwezigheid verraadt van rupsen, strak in hun pluizige pop aan de harige onderkant van het blad. Vlinders fladderden overal boven de weide en het aantal vogels per vierkante meter was verbijsterend. Door de schaarste van dit type habitat is het een toevluchtsoord geworden voor soorten die wanhopig op zoek zijn naar hun traditionele voedsel. Het kreeg bijna het gevoel een dierentuin te bezoeken, een piepklein stukje botanische tuin dat per ongeluk halverwege een uitgestrekte, ontzagwekkende berg lag, beschermd door vestingwerken. Er is nog een lange weg te gaan voordat deze zeer zeldzame soorten in het wild weer veilig zullen zijn.

De wilgenzone is een onmisbare habitat voor bepaalde soorten vogels en insecten. Dit is de plek voor ‘randeffecten’. Naarmate het bos de grens van zijn groeigebied bereikt, geven verschillende soorten het op verschillende hoogten op, waardoor een rijke zone met diverse combinaties van soorten ontstaat. Meer licht en grotere temperatuurverschillen leiden tot verschillende soorten overgangszones. Er hoeft maar één belangrijke soort te worden toegevoegd of weggenomen om het hele levensevenwicht te laten verschuiven. Zonder dennen kunnen wilgen de macht overnemen. En onder de wilgen kunnen haargras en vedermos, die bescherming dicht bij de grond nodig hebben, gedijen. Ze zijn echter ook de eerste die verdwijnen als de begrazing uit de hand loopt. Zeldzame korstmossen zijn hier in overvloed aanwezig en vormen samenwerkingsverbanden met de planten van de wilgenzone, zoals die welke groeien tussen de heide of de wollige bisschopsmuts, *Racomitrium lanuginosum*, een redder in nood voor insecten in de winter. Die kan twaalf maanden lang zonder water overleven door vocht uit de atmosfeer op te nemen. In een diepe sneeuwlaag vormt de wollige bisschopsmuts een kussen met een eigen microklimaat dat tot twintig graden warmer is dan het omringende sneeuwpakket. Als je de wollige muts optilt, ontdek je duizenden insecten die zich daaronder warm houden.

Insectenhabitats zijn natuurlijk goed voor vogels. Abrupte veranderingen in het landschap – de rechte lijnen van een dennenplantage – zijn onnatuurlijk en niet bevorderlijk. Vogels houden van mozaïeken, met verschillende insecten, zaden en bessen die op verschillende tijden beschikbaar zijn. Binnen het gebied van Cairngorms Connect worden de overgangen inmiddels weer wat geleidelijker doordat bos en heide weer in elkaar overvloeien. Dit zijn de marginale habitats die de voorwaarden voor diversiteit creëren. De beflijster, bijvoorbeeld, is een boomgrenssoort die zich tussen habitats verplaatst. Morinelplevieren, sneeuwgorzen en blauwe kiekendieven zijn allemaal heidevogels die af en toe het comfort, of het voedsel, van het bos nodig hebben. Hancock vreest dat deze soorten wel eens de 'uitsterfschuld' zouden kunnen zijn die wij nog gaan moeten betalen – hun habitats zijn zo aangetast, hun aantallen zo sterk afgenomen, dat ze zich niet meer kunnen herstellen.

Een van de hoofddoelstellingen van Cairngorms Connect is ervoor te zorgen dat de bomen zich kunnen herstellen tot aan de natuurlijke boomgrens. Dit kan vervolgens als leidraad dienen voor andere inspanningen, zodat andere projecten voor het herstel van montaan bos weten waar te beginnen. De Montane Woodland Action Group is op sommige plaatsen bezig met het planten van wilgen en jeneverbessen op 600 meter hoogte, maar het is delicaat en kwetsbaar giswerk. En de isotherm, de theoretische groeigrens, is niet statisch. Die wilgen kunnen over een paar jaar midden in een dennenbos staan.

'Niemand weet echt waar de boomgrens in Schotland is, of zou moeten zijn,' aldus Mark.

De gangbare opvatting is dat er slechts één gebied is waar de bomen aan hun natuurlijke grens hebben vastgehouden, waar je een juiste gradatie van krummholz kunt zien – bomen die steeds minder volgroeid zijn als gevolg van hoogte en blootstelling. Het is een plek die de schrijver Jim Crumley 'een heiligdom in het bos' noemt, Creag Fhiaclach.

De volgende morgen ging ik al vroeg op pad naar Creag Fhiaclach ('getande rots' in het Gaelic), die begint waar Glen Feshie overgaat in de vallei van de rivier de Spey. Hier staat de Inshriach Forest-plantage van de Forestry Commission als een indringer tussen Kingussie ('hoofd van het dennenbos') en het goed bewaarde dennenbos Rothiemurchus ('brede vlakte van de sparren') rond het schilderachtige meer van Loch an Eilein.

Ik verlaat het gesloten bladerdak van de plantage met zijn grindwegen, rechte lijnen en angstaanjagende stilte, en kom in het verspreide open bos van een moeraslandschap waarin de vogels plotseling overal om me heen zijn. Ik klauter over de hummocks terwijl mijn laarzen wegzakken in zachte kussens van mos. Een glashelder beekje kabbelt rustig tussen rijke oevers van turf bedekt met gras. Langs de oever groeien heide, varens, bergbraambessen, biezen en riet, en daarboven steken harde zwarte veenkoepels uit waaruit oeroude moerasdennen ontspruiten, knoestig en kronkelig, hun gelaagde takken gebeeldhouwd door de heersende wind.

Ik zoek mijn weg door de dichte ondergroei van heide en brem, het zwiepen van jonge lijsterbes, hazelaar en els en het alomtegenwoordige gekras van dennen. Ik herinner me de woorden van de dendrochronoloog van de moerasdennen, Rob Wilson: 'Bedenk dat de den een onkruid is als hij ook maar even de kans krijgt.'

Een kleine bruine vogel volgt me op een afstand en roept *pie-wit*. Ik vind veren van een uil bij een hol en vervolgens een groot gebarsten wit ei zo groot als een grapefruit onder een dennenboom met een afgeplatte bovenkant. Als ik omhoog kijk, zie ik op de kruin nog net de rommelige stokjes van het nest van een steenarend. Er liggen konijnenkeutels. Kikkervisjes in een poel. Onlangs zijn hier nog herten geweest, een lijsterbes van drie meter hoog is tot halverwege kaal gevreten. Ik heb het gevoel dat dit het boreale bos is zoals het hoort te zijn. Zonder uiteraard de beren, lynxen en wolven die hier ooit ook nog waren. Het is ouder dan Glen Feshie, zonder de opdringerige nieuwigheid van een generatie van pas ontsproten dennen. De herbewilderde vallei voelde als blije verrassing, als uitbundige vrijheid, terwijl de meer gevestigde ritmes hier getuigen van een vast patroon in het leven.

Ik blijf klimmen in de richting waar ik water hoor en kruis eindelijk een pad dat in de zwarte, minerale aarde is getreden. Het bos is hier wat opener: er is ruimte tussen de oude bomen de ondergroei vult die open plekken op. De reusachtig hummocks vormen een ecosysteem op zich. Er staan meer berken dan ik had verwacht: eerbiedwaardige, oude schepsels die met hun rode wortels in de beek hangen, met een huid als van oude hagedissen, geribbeld en gebarsten. De beek is vol en helder, raast luidruchtig tussen de bomen en benevelt de oevers van mos en varens.

De dichte vuisten van varens beginnen zich te ontvouwen, en kleine rode haartjes van vedermos kriebelen de lucht. Allerlei soorten mos rondom: veenmos, Lycopsida, vedermos en *Syntrichia papillosissima*, die hun kleine sporen op fragiele doorschijnende stengels naar buiten duwen. Ze houden het vocht van het bos vast – een hyaliene chemische stof staat de mossen toe duizend keer hun eigen gewicht in water vast te houden. Het mos is de eerste spons, vangt de regen op en geeft die langzaam weer af naar gelang van de absorptiecapaciteit van de bomen en de bodem. Daarbij wordt stikstof gebonden waarmee het bos wordt bemest.

De dominante soort is sphagnum – veenmos. De soort die het grootste deel van steenkool en diamanten vormde. Dit is een van de winnaars van de opwarming van de aarde – veenmos houdt wel van kooldioxide. Te veel van het spul kan echter de ondergroei verstikken en het successiepatroon van het bos veranderen. In Siberië wordt het succes van larikszaailingen nu al belemmerd door welig tierend mos. De ophoping van kooldioxide verzuurt de bodem, precies zoals CO2 de oceaan verzuurt, en dat verstikt andere planten.

In het Carboon, toen de atmosfeer veel minder zuurstof bevatte dan nu, waren mossen en varens zoals de paardenstaart tientallen meters hoog, monsterlijke, Triffid-achtige planten die zich tegoed deden aan kooldioxide. De triomf van de gymnospermen en angiospermen – naald- en bladverliezende houtgewassen die de atmosfeer langzaam van zuurstof voorzagen – bracht de paardenstaarten, de varens en de mossen, terug tot een bescheidener grootte. Met de huidige opwarming kunnen we verwachten dat ze weer groter zullen worden, met ernstige gevolgen voor bosbouw en landbouw omdat de zure lucht het mos versterkt en de velden verstikt.

Het pad loopt meedogenloos steil omhoog naar de open heide die nu boven ons zichtbaar is, over de beek die zich versmalt tot een geul. De noordkant van de geul is nog bebost en kijkt uit op het zuiden. Aan de overkant maken de bomen abrupt plaats. Vijftig meter verder, aan mijn kant van de beek, begint krummholz te verschijnen om vervolgens ook weer snel te verdwijnen. Ik tel de bracteeën, de inkepingen die de jaarlijkse groei markeren, van de laatste dennenboom aan het pad. Die komt maar tot mijn middel, maar is toch zestien jaar oud. Verderop staat een complete miniatuurberk ter grootte van mijn hand die minstens tien jaar oud is. Jeneverbes en wilg groeien nu plat tegen de heuvel. In een holte daarboven zie ik een lijsterbes en meer rechtopstaande wilgen. Hier is het voorzichtige begin – of misschien zijn het de overblijfselen – van Groot-Brittannië's enige boomgrens-overgangszone.

Voor mijn bezoek had ik geen idee dat deze wilgenzone zo zeldzaam of zo belangrijk was. Hier horen de beflijster, de blauwe kiekendief, de sneeuwgors, de fitis en de kleine barmsijs thuis. Hier zouden de koperwiek, de ijsgors en de blauwborst zich kunnen vestigen, als de habitat zou worden hersteld. Er gaat zoveel geschiedenis schuil achter de lichtvaardige en ogenschijnlijk onschuldige term 'habitatverlies', dat het vaak moeilijk is te begrijpen wat er werkelijk bedoeld wordt en daarmee wat we anders zouden moeten doen om de schade te herstellen. De vogels hebben behoefte aan het delicate evenwicht tussen korstmos, mos en insecten, dat op zijn beurt berust op de gelaagde bescherming van enkele wilgensoorten, waarvan sommige op de Britse eilanden zeldzamer zijn dan panda's in China. Ik dacht dat ik goed oplette, maar er is een heel ander niveau van opmerkzaamheid vereist.

Het palet van de heuvel is rood van het mos, roze van het graniet, felgroen van de scheuten van de bosbes, het oranje, rood en wit van het korstmos, en dit alles tegen de grijze deken van zware regenwolken die het geheel bedrukt. Onder mij is het bos oneindig groen, onderbroken door vrachtwagens op de snelweg en het ijzergrijs van de rivier de Spey die tussen de bomen door kronkelt. In de verte liggen de kale, verbrande, bruine hoogvenen waar op korhoenders wordt gejaagd en de geometrische blokken van de plantages die me nu als het impliciete geweld van brutalistische betonarchitectuur voorkomen.

Ik bereik de top van Creag Dhubh (756 meter – 'zwarte rots') terwijl de regen me horizontaal tegen het lijf slaat. Ik ga bergafwaarts bij de Argyll Stone. Iets ten oosten hiervan ligt Carn a'Phris-ghiubhais – 'heuvel in het dennenstruweel', wat erop duidt dat deze dorre heuvel niet altijd zo winderig was. En inderdaad, tussen de koude watermassa's uit het oosten kijk ik naar de tegenoverliggende bergkam van Creag Follais en wat zie ik, verlicht in het veranderlijke grijze licht van de storm? De onmiskenbare contouren van pijnbomen, inmiddels stevig geworteld maar nu al met de wind meebuigend, alsof ze lachen om hun eigen vermetelheid, ver boven hun broeders lager op de berg.

De berghut in Ruigh-aiteachain, een van een netwerk van berghutten die gratis ter beschikking van wandelaars worden gesteld, ligt aan de kop van Glen Feshie bij de spectaculaire samenloop van de rivier Feshie en de Lorgaidh-beek, waar de vallei uiteengaat in zijn iconische gletsjerkommen. Afdalend van Creag Fhiaclach is het een lange wandeling over de lengte van de vallei door een lappendeken van landschappen: heide en moerasgras naast de rivierbedding vol grind, heldere bospoelen vol insecten en het hoge, ritmische landschap van een oude dennenplantage.

Aangezien dit het Glen Feshie van Wildland is, wordt de plantage bewust verwaarloosd om de natuurlijke processen weer op gang te brengen. Hier en daar liggen omgevallen stammen te rotten, er is wat uitgedund en op open plekken gedijen jonge boompjes goed. De structuur van de plantage is echter eentonig: alle bomen zijn even oud, de stammen kaarsrecht en ze concurreren om het licht waar ze opzettelijk dicht op elkaar zijn geplant. Door het uitdunnen van de bomen kon het licht de bosbodem bereiken, zodat de grond tussen de bomen nu een helder groen is van de blauwe bosbes, heide en vedermos. Te veel zonlicht en de heide neemt het over, te weinig en de bosbes kan niet groeien. De wereld van de ondergroei is een precieze afstemming van licht, voedingsstoffen en mycorrhiza's die rechtstreeks verband houdt met de dichtheid van het bladerdak, waardoor de omstandigheden voor wat eronder kan leven nauwkeurig worden bepaald. Daarom zijn de auerhoen en andere vogels teruggekeerd.

Op een heuvel aan de rivier ligt Glenfeshie Lodge, waar gasten veel geld betalen voor een 'wildervaring', een beetje zoals bij een Afrikaanse safari. Verderop, verscholen in een open plek tussen eeuwenoude dennen, ligt een stenen hut, gebouwd en onderhouden voor minder welgestelde toeristen. De hut heeft twee kamers met ruwe planken, verwarmd door Noorse gietijzeren kachels. Buiten is een composttoilet en een emmer naast een koele heldere beek.

De midzomer ceilidh waar Thomas het over had is niet echt een dansfeest te noemen. Er is nauwelijks plaats om op te staan in de kleine kamer, die gloeiend heet is van de razende houtkachel. Ongeveer twintig mensen zijn gekomen om te luisteren naar een Gaelische legende die liederen zingt over hoe het vroeger was.

Margaret Bennett is een zangeres die verschillende boeken heeft geschreven, waaronder *Scottish Customs from the Cradle to the Grave*. Voor ze zal zingen, legt ze haar stok neer, neemt haar dikke bril af en nestelt zich naast me voor de kachel. Margaret wil me vertellen over de magie van bomen. Thomas heeft haar verteld dat ik over het bos schrijf. Haar zwart met zilveren haar is in een eenvoudige knot samengebonden en haar blauwe ogen gaan onderzoekend de ruimte rond terwijl ze spreekt.

Ze vertelt hoe meisjes in het voorjaar hun haar wasten in een extract van berkenknoppen en dan naar de kerk gingen, geurend naar berk, hoe haar moeder een lijsterbes voor hun huis plantte omdat die geluk zou brengen. Die staat er nog steeds. We hebben het over de geneeskrachtige werking van dennenhout, waarvan de naalden van oudsher werden gebruikt voor het uitroken van huizen, bij aandoeningen van de luchtwegen en nu voor industriële toepassingen zoals kamfer, insecticiden, oplosmiddelen en parfum. De inheemse Amerikaanse Cayuga kookten het merg van dennenknoppen om er het antibioticum pinosylvin aan te onttrekken, dezelfde chemische stof die in antibiotische zalven wordt gebruikt om huidaandoeningen en beten te behandelen. Margaret spreekt over het goedwerkende systeem van de clan, waarin niemand een eigendomsbewijs had voor welk land dan ook. Het bos en de heuvels werden onderhouden ten bate van allen. Zij betreurt het dat de koningen landrechten toekenden aan de clanleiders in plaats van aan het collectief, waardoor het mogelijk werd om land te kopen en te verkopen. Dat is de achtergrond van haar liederen: de oude bevolking van de Highlands, verdreven om plaats te maken voor schapen en herten en nog steeds afwezig in de heuvels. Het moderne beeld van de valleien is nauw verbonden met de geschiedenis van uitbuiting, ontginning en militarisme, aangestuurd vanuit het zuiden.

Later, als andere gasten zijn gearriveerd en wij enkele kilo's hertenburgers hebben verorberd, zingt Margaret liedjes over jonge meisjes die wachten op de jongens die op weg zijn met de Royal Navy of de Black Watch, verhalen over kapitein Macleod en zijn spookachtige doedelzakspeler. Er zijn er over de *redshanks*, de Schotse en Ierse huurlingen, en over een knappe veedrijver met 'kalveren als zalm' die Schotse hooglanders over de heuvels naar Crieff brengt met takken van de lijsterbes in hun staart gevlochten, in de hoop dat die geluk brengen. Thomas' broer Sandy begeleidt Margaret op de doedelzak, en de hoofd-ecoloog van het Cairngorms National Park, een lange donkerharige man genaamd Will, speelt mee op zijn banjo. Margaret laat ons met z'n twintigen in het Gaelic meezingen, en aan het eind staan menigeen de tranen in de ogen.

'Je ziet het, we zijn de oude gebruiken nog niet helemaal vergeten,' zegt Margaret, terwijl haar irissen dezelfde kleur lijken te hebben als de midzomernacht die buiten op haar hoogtepunt is.

Die ochtend ben ik alweer vroeg op in de melkachtige dageraad. De maan hangt nog steeds boven de berghelling in het zuiden, terwijl de zon erachter brandt. Het is de zomerzonnewende. Binnen liggen twintig lijven in slaapzakken op de vloer. Tijdens het ontbijt leg ik Will uit waarom ik deze merkwaardige, geïmproviseerde bijeenkomst bezocht. Ik vertel hem over mijn pelgrimstocht de vorige dag naar Creag Fhiaclach en de boomgrens, en hij glimlacht licht en knikt begrijpend.

'Maar dat is niet de boomgrens,' zegt hij, terwijl hij zijn telefoon tevoorschijn haalt.

Eerder die week had Will net een late avond op kantoor achter de rug om de bosbouwstrategie voor het nationale park uit te stippelen, en zoals hij graag doet om te ontspannen, beklom hij de heuvel om daar voor de nacht zijn tent op te slaan op een plek waar hij nog niet eerder was geweest. Hij zette zijn tent op in het donker, en toen hij wakker werd en zijn hoofd naar buiten stak, besefte hij dat hij nog steeds in het bos was. Rondom hem stonden verspreid overal kleine boompjes. Hij bevond zich hoog op de Cairngorm-hoogvlakte. Hij laat me een foto zien van een stevig gewortelde boom met veel stammen die tussen het veengras en de heide groeit, en er is ook een hoogtemeter in beeld. Die geeft 1045 meter aan. Het verbaast hem niet dat ik dennenbomen tegen de helling op zag groeien, nog hoger dan bij Creag Fhiaclach. De natuurlijke boomgrens in Schotland zou best al eens hoger dan de toppen van de hoogste bergen kunnen liggen, zegt hij. En als dat nog niet het geval is, zal het zeker niet lang meer duren. In Zweden, waar de intacte dennenboomgrens al tientallen jaren nauwlettend in de gaten wordt gehouden, is deze sinds de jaren

1960 met tweehonderd meter gestegen.[14] En onlangs, toen de zomerdroogte de voorste rand van de berken in Zweden doodde, nam de meer veerkrachtige grove den het over in de voorhoede van de boomgrens en overvleugelde daarmee de berk.[15]

Cairn gorm is Gaelic voor 'blauwe bergen'. Afgezien van enkele maanden tussen juni en oktober, is de hoogvlakte bedekt met sneeuw. Van een afstand kan dit de ruggen een blauw tintje geven. Maar in oud-Gaelic duidt *gorm* eerder op een groenig-blauw.

De van oorsprong Ierse Canadese botanicus en scheikundige Diana Beresford-Kroeger heeft uitvoerig geschreven over het boreale woud. Zij vertelde me dat de kleur van dennennaalden van doorslaggevend belang is voor hun veerkracht en aanpassingsvermogen. Naalden die blauwgroen zijn, hebben een cuticulair oppervlak dat twee tot drie micron dikker is. De wasachtige laag dempt minder licht, zodat het chlorofyl in de cellen van de naalden blauwachtig lijkt. Deze extra dikte beschermt tegen extreme hitte of extreme koude en ze is bepalend voor het epigenetische vermogen van de den om zich flexibeler op te stellen naar gelang van het klimaat. Bij het verzamelen van specimen, adviseert Diana, moet je altijd de blauwste coniferen van de hoogste hoogten zoeken als toekomstige bron van zaad. Die zullen het sterkst zijn, stelt ze. Een verschil in tint kan een soort 'honderden jaren' kosten. Bomen op grote hoogte hebben de neiging deze eigenschap sneller te ontwikkelen, en daarom zien hoge bergen die met naaldbomen zijn begroeid er vaak blauw uit. Waren de 'beboste hoogten' van Schotland misschien ooit dit soort *cairn gorms*? En zouden ze dat weer kunnen worden?

De restauratie van het verloren gegane grote woud van Caledonia is een prachtig project en noodzakelijk als wij onze eerbied voor en onze verbondenheid met de levende wereld willen herstellen. Wildland en de 'herwilderings'-beweging in ruimere zin slagen erin miljoenen mensen opnieuw te bekoren en beginnen de agenda te verruimen om ook over de herbevolking van de Highlands te praten. Er zal echter meer voor nodig zijn dan bekoring, wil het nieuwe grote bos geen zombiebos worden.

De Forestry Commission van het Verenigd Koninkrijk voorspelt dat de grove den het deze eeuw in Groot-Brittannië goed zal doen met de toegenomen hoeveelheid kooldioxide, warmere temperaturen en een langer groeiseizoen.[16] Als de mens het toelaat, zullen de Schotse dennen de bergen inderdaad weer blauw kleuren. Maar misschien niet voor lang.

Op dit moment vinden we grove dennen in een brede klimaatniche van de boomgrens tot Zuid-Europa. Hoewel Schotland zich momenteel aan de noordelijke grens van dat verspreidingsgebied bevindt, verschuift het territoriale venster voor de grove den naar het noorden. Verder naar het zuiden in Europa zorgen droogte en hittestress er nu al voor dat dennennaalden vroeg bruin worden en afbrokkelen. Onderzoek uit 2008 voorspelde dat 1 tot 4 graden Celsius opwarming de overlevingskansen van grove dennen op breedtegraden lager dan 62°N zou beperken. De Cairngorms liggen op 57°N.[17] Dit grimmige vooruitzicht laat goed zien wat de klimaatcrisis betekent voor bomen en bossen.

Opwarming van de aarde heeft hetzelfde effect als recht naar het zuiden reizen. De huidige snelheid waarmee het klimaat in het VK verandert komt overeen met een zuidwaartse beweging van ongeveer twintig kilometer per jaar. Tegen 2050 zal Londen naar verwachting een klimaat hebben dat vergelijkbaar is met dat van Barcelona.[18] Sommige mensen zullen misschien blij zijn met dat vooruitzicht, maar voor de Schotse den is het een probleem. Twee afzonderlijke modellen – ontworpen door het UK Met Office en de Universiteit van Oregon – voorspellen dat bij de huidige emissies de grove den tegen het eind van de eeuw uit het laagland van Europa, inclusief Schotland, zou kunnen verdwijnen. Het Met Office-model gaat nog verder en voorspelt dat de grove den alleen in het noorden van Fennoscandinavië, Rusland en de Alpen zal overleven.[19] Dit sluit aan bij andere bevindingen die voorspellen dat zelfs bij een gemiddelde opwarming van 1 à 2°C de levensvatbaarheid van de bestaande bossen al minder begint te worden.[20] De veilige ruimte, de klimaatniche van het grote bos van Schotland, is in beweging en laat de bomen daarbij achter.

Tenzij er iets drastisch gebeurt, zal de bewonderenswaardige visie die Cairngorm Connect voor de komende tweehonderd jaar heeft ontwikkeld worden ingehaald door de opwarming van de aarde. Meer dan achtduizend jaar bosgeschiedenis en alle vogels, insecten en zoogdieren die deel uitmaken van het precaire evenwicht van de bossen dat zich rond de grove den heeft ontwikkeld, kunnen binnen de levensduur van één enkele boom worden uitgewist. Terwijl Schotland ooit aan de noordelijke boomgrens lag, waarboven het te koud of te hoog was voor dennen om te groeien, kan het zich in minder dan honderd jaar onder de zuidelijke grens van die zone bevinden.

2.

De rendieren achterna

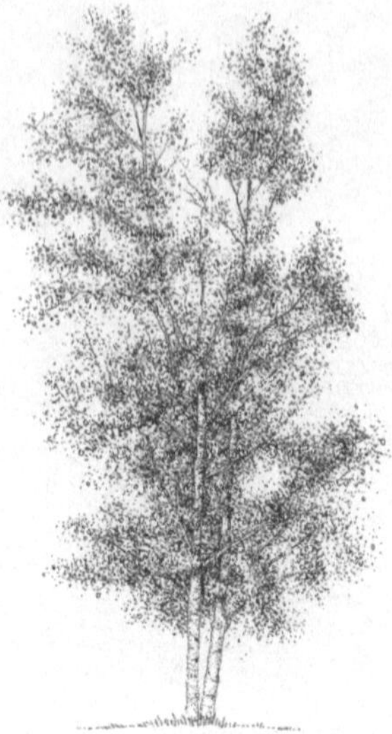

Zachte berk, *Betula pubescens*

Finnmarksvidda, Noorwegen
69° 58' 07" N

Altafjord is een wijde zwarte watervlakte, omringd door grote witte bergkoepels. Die nacht is de eerste sneeuw van de winter gevallen. De ochtendwind drijft de zee de trechtervormige fjord binnen, naar de stad, en stuwt deinende massa's zwart water tegen de golfbreker onder het raam van het pension waar ik logeer. Het schuim op de golven is kortstondig. Elk sprankje licht wordt onmiddellijk teruggezogen en opgeslokt in de duisternis van de Barentszzee.

Alta is de hoofdstad van de Noorse provincie Finnmark, de kroon van de manen van het paard die de grillige kustlijn van Noorwegen en de noordkust van Europa vormen. Ik ben hier veel noordelijker dan in Schotland, maar hier op zeeniveau bewegen de meest noordelijke bomen van Europa zich zowel in de hoogte als de geografische breedte in de richting van de pool. Het probleem is alleen dat er niet veel ruimte is voor uitbreiding. Vanaf Alta is er zestienhonderd kilometer lang niets dan water tot aan het begin van het zee-ijs van de Noordelijke IJszee. De toendra zit gevangen als in een bankschroef. En de mensen en dieren die hier leven proberen de snelle veranderingen te bevatten met een mengeling van verwarring, ontkenning en paniek.

De dageraad op 70 graden noord in de winter is onheilspellend en oneindig. Hij duurt bijna de hele dag. Om acht uur 's morgens verlicht een numineus lila licht de bergen in het zuiden van achteren. Dunne wolken erboven zijn roze gekleurd, het enige teken van de machtige afwezige zon die achter de horizon weggedoken blijft. Het is een licht voor de zonsopgang, een soort gloed, maar de overgang komt nooit, want de zon komt nooit op en de dag staat voortdurend op punt van aanbreken. Het is desoriënterend. Een half uur later hangt de zon nog steeds achter de rand van de wereld en gloeit de maan nog steeds paars, nu iets lager boven de kolkend zwarte zee. De steile fjord erachter ligt in de schaduw, en doet denken aan de met vuur omringde bergen in de volksverhalen over het koninkrijk Thule aan de rand van de bekende wereld.

De poolnacht verstoort de routine van de moderne werkweek niet. Het is maandagmorgen en de inwoners van Alta kruipen uit bed, pakken zich warm in, ontdooien voorruiten en stappen in hun auto's om zich een weg te banen door het halfduister, beneveld met uitlaatgassen die in de koude lucht niet verwaaien.

Op weg van het pension naar het stadhuis zie ik kinderen in klaslokalen en verschillende rijen auto's die voorzichtig op sneeuwbanden over de ijzige weg schuiven, maar weinig voetgangers. Alta is een stad, gebouwd volgens Amerikaanse principes – dat wil zeggen, een stad gebouwd voor een wereld waarin benzine goedkoop is en auto's vanzelfsprekend zijn. Het is een landschap van winkelcentra, benzinestations en wijds opgezette woonwijken met huizen op grote percelen. Normaal gesproken is het in deze tijd van het jaar niet veilig om lang buiten te zijn zonder bont te dragen. Vandaag is het slechts -1 Celsius, maar de gewoonte om te rijden, aangemoedigd door de stadsplanning, is moeilijk te doorbreken.

Langs de hele weg naar het stadscentrum staan rijen jonge grove dennen, waarvan de oranje schors afsteekt tegen de verse sneeuwlaag, en ertussen staan kortere, haveloze bomen met bobbelige stammen, versleten takken en fijne twijgen als knoestige vingers: *Betula pubescens*, zachte berk. Dit zijn de bomen waarvoor ik hier ben, in het kantoor van Hallgeir Strifeldt, directeur ruimtelijke ordening van de gemeente Alta, op een maandagochtend om negen uur, midden in de winter.

De zachte berk is veel korter en rommeliger dan zijn sierlijke neef, de *Betula pendula*, de ruwe berk, en geëvolueerd om veel noordelijker te overleven. Het is een van de weinige bladverliezende loofbomen in het noordpoolgebied en zelfs beter bestand tegen de winterse omstandigheden dan de meeste naaldbomen. Het 'zachte' is een zachte bekleding van trichomale haren die als een soort bontmantel werkt tegen de barre kou. Op een lagere breedtegraad en hoogte vindt men de berk vaak samen met dennen en sparren, maar boven een bepaald punt laat hij de anderen achter zich en gaat nog honderden kilometers alleen verder. Betula pubescens en zijn variant, de dwergberk, *Betula nana*, worden soms ook wel veenberk, witte berk of bergberk genoemd en vormen het leeuwendeel van de Arctische boomgrens van Europa, van IJsland (waar hij de enige boom is die een natuurlijk bos vormt) over het noorden van Noorwegen tot in Finland en de waterrijke gebieden van Karelië, beroemd geworden door Sibelius, over het Russische schiereiland Kola tot aan de Witte Zee, waarna de lariks van Siberië het stokje overneemt.

Hij mag dan onooglijk zijn, zelfs lelijk, met zijn stompe takken en pokdalige schors, maar deze taaie kleine boom is een overlever en een pionier, essentieel voor bijna al het leven in het noordpoolgebied: zowel menselijk, dierlijk als plantaardig. Hij wordt door de mens gebruikt voor gereedschap, huizen, brandstof, voedsel en medicijnen, vormt een thuis voor microben, schimmels en insecten die een centrale rol spelen in de voedselketen en biedt de onmisbare beschutting aan de andere planten die nodig zijn voor een bos. Zonder de pioniersrol van de berk zouden de ecosystemen van het noorden zich anders hebben ontwikkeld. De zachte berk dicteert de voorwaarden voor wat er kan groeien, overleven en bewegen in de gebieden waar hij weet te wortelen. En dat bereik breidt zich snel uit naarmate de Noordpool opwarmt. In de opwarmende ecosystemen van het hoge noorden van Europa is het niet alleen de mens, maar ook de zachte berk die de agenda bepaalt.

Ik heb moeite mijn weg te vinden in deze sombere wereld waar alles slechts een andere tint blauw lijkt, maar uiteindelijk bereik ik het stadhuis, een modern, met hout bekleed gebouw dat oranje licht uitstraalt. Binnenkomen doe je er in stappen, als door een luchtsluis in een onderzeeër, waarbij je door een bad van gloeiend hete lucht moet. De receptioniste is in een goede bui. Net als iedereen in Alta, is ze opgelucht. Eindelijk valt er wat sneeuw en is de temperatuur onder het vriespunt, al is het maar net. Zo hoort de winter te zijn.

'Het wordt hier heel erg donker als er geen sneeuw ligt,' zegt Hallgeir, die in zijn moderne kantoor zit dat is ingericht met kaarten en stijlvolle planken. 'Toen ik jong was, zeiden mijn ouders altijd dat we op 10 oktober klaar moesten zijn voor de winter.' De winters zijn de afgelopen jaren geleidelijk warmer geworden, maar de warmte in november en december 2018 is volgens hem 'extreem'. De hele gemeenschap is in paniek en rendierhoeders plaatsen foto's van een sneeuwloze toendra op Facebook.

Hallgeir is een stadsmens, een milde man met een randloze bril en een gereserveerde houding. Hij is bovendien half-Sami, het inheemse volk van Arctisch Europa dat DNA en een gemeenschappelijk taalkundig erfgoed deelt met de volkeren van het circumpolaire gebied van Finland tot Rusland via de Beringstraat naar Alaska, Labrador en terug naar Groenland. Vroeger migreerden de Sami ongehinderd door het landschap, maar nu zijn de tachtigduizend overgeblevenen burgers van een van de vier verschillende moderne naties: Noorwegen, Zweden, Finland of Rusland. Zij zijn de enige inheemse groep in Europa die door de Verenigde Naties is erkend.

Sinds de rendiergod tienduizend jaar geleden voor het eerst het bloed van het rendier liet vloeien om de rivieren te vormen, de grond met zijn vacht bezaaide om het gras en de bomen te maken, en de ogen van het dier in de nachtelijke hemel wierp als sterren, hebben de Sami geleefd in wat andere Europeanen Lapland, en zij Sapmi (het land van de Sami) noemen. Hun rotskunst toont een consistente manier van leven gedurende duizenden jaren. Op afbeeldingen die volgens koolstofdateringen tot achtduizend jaar geleden werden gemaakt, zijn stokjesfiguren in boten te zien die aan het vissen zijn en dezelfde figuren die jagen op beren en elanden, en rendieren hoeden. In andere afbeeldingen die volgens koolstofdateringen tot tweeduizend jaar geleden werden gemaakt, zijn stokjesfiguren in boten te zien die aan het vissen zijn en dezelfde figuren die jagen op beren en elanden, en rendieren hoeden. Het enige wezenlijke verschil is dat de kunstenaar van achtduizend jaar geleden er beter in is geslaagd de dieren weer te geven.

Rendieren staan centraal in de identiteit van Hallgeir, zoals voor alle Sami. De familie van zijn moeder bestond uit rendierhoeders, maar toen zijn grootmoeder in het kraambed op de hoogvlakte stierf, bracht zijn grootvader zijn jonge moeder naar de stad, naar Alta, en liet haar bij een Noorse familie achter om door hen opgevoed te worden. De grootvader ging terug naar zijn kuddes onder de wijde hemel van de hoogvlakte, naar zijn *laavo* – een traditionele tent die veel weg heeft van een tipi – en trouwde opnieuw. Hallgeir is zowel thuis in de stad als in een laavo. Wanneer ik hem later die week zie op een Sami culturele manifestatie, draagt hij de traditionele Sami-jas van vilt, geborduurd met goud, een zijden sjaal, een broek en laarzen van rendierhuid en een rijk bewerkte zilveren riem. Hij is een vertegenwoordiger van de rationele staat, leverancier van bureaucratie en beton, maar hij heeft ook het gevleugelde bloed van de nomade en verlangt ernaar niet door de mens te worden geregeerd, maar alleen door de behoeften van de kudde.

Rendieren zijn karaktervolle dieren, met hun wijd open bruine ogen, oneindig gevarieerde harige geweien, zachte vacht waarvan al het haar één kant op staat en enorme sneeuwbestendige hoeven met kussentjes die in een onbeholpen vertederende tred klapperen. Hun constante waakzame blik is mysterieus en wijs, achterdochtig en veroordelend tegelijk. Elk rendier heeft een Sami-naam en herders herkennen elk lid van hun kudde individueel, zelfs op de tast. 'Liefde' dekt niet goed wat ze met elkaar hebben. Onderlinge afhankelijkheid is een betere beschrijving. De dieren stellen de Sami in staat te overleven in een meedogenloze wereld van kou en ijs die voor iedereen zonder kleren en schoenen gemaakt van hun huid de dood zou betekenen. De mensen verplaatsen zich omdat de rendieren op zoek zijn naar weidegrond. Hun hele cultuur heeft zich ontwikkeld rond de migratiebehoeften van de kuddes.

De berk is daarbij het hulpje van de herder. Van onderdak tot brandstof tot transport voorziet de berk hier in de essentiële onderdelen om te kunnen overleven. Hij wordt gebruikt voor tentstokken. Hij werd gebruikt voor ski's en sleeën om de mensen in staat te stellen zich in de winter van de weelderige zomerweiden aan de kust naar de toendra op de hoogvlakte te verplaatsen. Maar door de verstoring van het weer verstoort ook deze cyclus. De Sami behoren tot de eerste slachtoffers van de klimaatverandering, iets eerder dan de rest van ons moeten zij de ineenstorting van een hele cultuur onder ogen zien.

De rendieren zijn de enige overgebleven pijler van wat ooit een meer gediversifieerde beschaving was, met inbegrip van bos-Sami die tussen de bomen leefden en visser-Sami die aan de kust woonden. De bos-Sami woonden in plaggenhutten en hadden een hekel aan de verkwisting van de Noren die hun huizen van hout bouwden – hout was alleen voor gereedschap, boten en brandstof. Zij zijn echter al lang verdwenen, meer dan een eeuw geleden door de Noorse regering gedwongen om te kiezen tussen rendierhouderij of assimilatie. Het fokken van dieren voor het vlees werd door de regering wel op prijs gesteld, maar het overleven in de bossen diende geen economisch doel dat ze kon begrijpen. De integratie van de vissende Sami heeft langer geduurd, maar de dramatische achteruitgang van de kabeljauwstand heeft ertoe bijgedragen dat de trek naar de steden is versneld, een proces dat

Hallgeir in goede banen moet leiden. Alta is een bloeiende stad met vijftigduizend inwoners, die groeit naarmate het platteland rondom verder ontvolkt raakt.

De rendierhouderij wordt gewaardeerd door de rest van Noorwegen en is daarom blijven bestaan. De Sami hebben hun vlees altijd verkocht aan de zuiderlingen, en rendiervlees is een dure delicatesse die al lang geleden deel is gaan uitmaken van de bredere Noorse cultuur. De Noorse overheid beschouwt rendieren als een veeteeltproduct, en heeft quota bepaald en subsidies en strenge controles ingesteld op het afmaken van dieren. Voor de officiële instanties zijn ze handelswaar, een nuttig exportproduct van de verder onproductieve uitgestrekte hoogvlakte van het noorden, maar voor de Sami is het belang van het rendier niet alleen economisch en cultureel, maar ook symbolisch, zoals Hallgeirs leren broek getuigt.

'Rendieren zijn leven. Ze zijn alles. Zonder rendieren, sterven we.' En nu wordt de rendierhouderij, een manier van leven die tienduizend jaar lang ongeschonden heeft kunnen voortbestaan, bedreigd. Deze keer is het niet de Noorse regering die het grootste gevaar vormt – hoewel ze een rol speelt – maar het klimaat. De warmere winters zijn op twee manieren dodelijk voor de rendieren: de ene acuut en dodelijk – het ijs. De andere is langzaam maar onontkoombaar – te veel bomen.

Ooit viel de eerste sneeuw van de winter ergens in oktober, eerst op de toendra, de hoogvlakte boven de boomgrens, en vervolgens op de dennen- en berkenbossen van de rivierdalen en de kusten. Kort daarna daalde het kwik in de thermometer tot onder het vriespunt en bleef daar tot april of mei, wanneer de sneeuw begon te smelten en de rivieren stroomden met het heldere turkoois van superzuurstofhoudend ijs. Tot 2005 bedroeg de gemiddelde wintertemperatuur -15 graden Celsius en kon men ervan uitgaan dat de temperatuur tijdens de winter minstens één keer onder de -40°C dook, waardoor zelfs de meest winterharde insectenlarven werden gedood, een proces dat het Noordpoolgebied in de zomer ongerept en vrij van plagen hield. Deze wereld van de winter was donker, koud en droog. Bij die temperaturen was er helemaal geen vocht. De sneeuwmassa had de consistentie van zand en bestond uit verschillende lagen grote sneeuwkristallen, de zogenaamde seayas. Bij -40 of -50 graden Celsius in hartje winter zijn de kwaliteit en de aard van de sneeuwkristallen van doorslaggevend belang voor het overleven van mens en dier.

Seayas zijn cruciaal voor een gezond sneeuwpakket met een evenwichtige dichtheid – *guohtun*. Seayas maken dat de rendieren de sneeuw kunnen wegvegen met hun geweien, hoeven en snuiten om de *Cladonia stellaris* te bereiken, het koolhydraat- en suikerrijke korstmos dat op de grond groeit in symbiose met het gras van de toendra, een energierijk voedsel voor snelle bewegingen in de winter. Het ontbreken van bomen op de toendra betekende dat de felle heersende winden van Finnmark vrij spel hadden op de hoogvlakte en de fijne poedersneeuw tot een dun beschermend tapijt bliezen dat de korstmossen eronder beschermde. Zware sneeuwjacht kan de vegetatie verpletteren.

Maar wanneer de temperatuur weer richting nul klimt, of nog erger, erboven, stort dit delicate winterse ecosysteem in. Zelfs een beetje opwarming van de sneeuw kan een ravage aanrichten. Bij -5 of -6 begint de sneeuwmassa vochtig te worden en verliest hij zijn zandachtige karakter, de seayas smelten en de sneeuw wordt samengedrukt onder de hoeven van de rendieren, waardoor de weiden eronder worden vernield. Als de thermometer helemaal in de positieve richting gaat, zoals de laatste jaren steeds vaker het geval is, is dat een catastrofe. Smeltende sneeuw of regen zal bevriezen wanneer de temperatuur weer onder nul gaat, en een ijskorst over de grond vormen, waardoor de vegetatie wordt afgeschermd van de rondzwervende rendieren. Dat gebeurde in 2013 en opnieuw in 2017. Tienduizenden rendieren stierven, sommige herders verloren meer dan een derde van hun dieren. In de afgelopen 130 jaar is de thermometer in de winter driemaal boven nul gekropen, waarvan tweemaal in het laatste decennium. Volgens de prognoses zal vanaf nu elke winter dagen boven nul kennen, wat betekent dat deze afscherming bijna onvermijdelijk wordt.

De kuddes kunnen tot twintig- of dertigduizend dieren groot zijn en ze zijn verspreid over duizenden vierkante kilometers van de hoogvlakte van Finnmark, een gebied zo groot als Zwitserland. Kunstmatig bijvoederen is ondoenlijk en bovendien veel te duur. Er zal dus onherroepelijk iets moeten veranderen.

Rendieren zijn zeer intelligente dieren. Ze zijn terecht wantrouwig tegenover mensen, windmolenparken, vliegtuigen en voertuigen. Door het steeds verder oprukken van de menselijke invasie in Finnmark wordt hun verspreidingsgebied nog kleiner. Ze hebben de typische achterdochtigheid van prooidieren. Hun ogen, nog groter dan die van hun neefjes de herten, houden alles nauwlettend in de gaten. Zelfs wanneer ze zich met stilstaande kop tegoed doen aan gras of korstmos, behouden ze een gezichtsveld van 300 graden en missen bijna niets. Het dier hoeft zijn kop slechts een beetje te kantelen om 360 graden in het rond te kunnen zien. Het grootste deel van dat groothoekperspectief is scherp, in tegenstelling tot het sterk gefocuste zicht van mensen of andere roofdieren, dat is geëvolueerd om diepte en afstand te peilen. Bij het geringste teken van gevaar zetten de rendieren het gewoon op een lopen.

Ze hebben een uitstekend geheugen voor het terrein en een perfect innerlijk kompas dat hen vertelt waar ze in de zomer en in de winter naartoe moeten trekken. Ze weten niet altijd hoe ze door de ravijnen en de rivieren moeten navigeren, maar hebben een instinct dat hen terugbrengt naar weiden waar ze al generaties komen. Ze hebben bovendien een innerlijke thermometer die hen vertelt wanneer het tijd is om verder te trekken. Als het niet koud genoeg is om de herfstweiden te verlaten en naar de winterweiden te trekken, zal de kudde niet gaan, maar het risico lopen één gebied of een bereik buiten haar normale territorium te overbegrazen. En als er te veel vocht is, zodat de bodem dichtvriest, of als het voedselaanbod slecht is, kan een vrouwtjesrendier zelfs bewust haar ongeboren jong aborteren, een eigenschap die zij deelt met enkele andere zoogdieren zoals muizen, apen en orka's.

Warmere winters betekenen dat de rendierkuddes meer ruimte

nodig hebben om zich te voeden. De concurrentiestrijd om de grazige toendra van de hoogvlakte neemt toe tussen de rendieren onderling, maar ook met de windmolenparken, hoogspanningsmasten, wegen en mijnen. De meest geduchte uitdager ziet er echter veel onschuldiger uit, ook al zal hij uiteindelijk de meest effectieve zijn: de nederige zachte berk.

Het kantoor naast dat van Hallgeir is van Tor Havard Sund, manager van de Finnmark Forest Service. Tor is een grote man in een geruit hemd met een open gezicht en een warme glimlach. Dertig jaar geleden begon hij als leraar aan een bosbouwschool, waarna hij zijn liefde voor bomen volgde en boomspecialist en boswachter werd. Bij het begin van ons gesprek raadplegen we meteen de enorme kaart die een muur van zijn kantoor vormt, maar hij raakt al snel gefrustreerd.

'Wanneer werd deze kaart gedrukt?' We vinden de datum in kleine lettertjes aan de rand: 1994.

'Die is voltrekt nutteloos,' zegt hij. 'We hebben nieuwe kaarten nodig. De boomgrens gaat alle kanten op.'

Verscheidene onderling samenhangende factoren zijn van invloed op het verspreidingsgebied van boomsoorten: de beschikbaarheid van zonlicht, water en voedingsstoffen zijn een eerste vereiste, maar ze vormen in wisselwerking met andere variabelen zoals wind en temperatuur een delicaat evenwicht. Kleine gradaties in hoogte of breedtegraad kunnen grote verschillen in de vegetatie betekenen, en dat geheel is natuurlijk ook nog in beweging. De tropen en de polen, met hun veel fijnmaziger weerpatronen en ecosystemen, zijn veel gevoeliger voor de opwarming van de aarde dan de gematigde zones die gewend zijn aan een wisselvallig klimaat. De zachte berk heeft de huidige opwarmingstendens veel eerder aangevoeld dan de meeste wetenschappers. De bomen waren als de kanarie in de mijn, maar weinig mensen begrepen het signaal dat ze afgaven.

De belangrijkste verandering is dat de winters warmer en korter zijn geworden. De Sami zeggen al minstens vijftien jaar dat de winters 'raar' worden. De hoeveelheid licht is niet veranderd en de grond is dezelfde, maar meer regen en meer warmte hebben een groot verschil gemaakt. De zachte berk houdt van het warmere weer. Vroeger groeide hij alleen in de depressies en geulen van de hoogvlakte, weg van de ijzige wind, maar ontketend als hij is door de warmte, is hij daaruit geklommen, naar de open lucht, met een snelheid van veertig meter per jaar. Een enorme hoeveelheid gebied verandert razendsnel van toendra in bosgebied.

Op het eerste gezicht lijkt een groter aantal bomen een goede zaak. Behalve dan dat de vergroening van de toendra nauw verband houdt met opwarming, aangezien de berk de bodem verbetert en deze verder opwarmt door microbiële activiteit, waardoor de permafrost smelt en methaan vrijkomt – een broeikasgas dat 85 keer krachtiger is dan kooldioxide in zijn opwarmende werking, en gedurende een kortere tijdspanne.

De zachte berk is de rockster onder de bomen. Hij leidt een snel leven en sterft jong. Hij verbruikt een enorme hoeveelheid energie om in marginale omgevingen te overleven, maar kan dat niet veel langer dan zestig jaar volhouden. Trager groeiende naaldbomen zoals de den zullen er langer over doen om zich te vestigen, maar ze hebben de berk nodig als wegbereider. De berk is een pionier onder de bomen. In het voorjaar voelt hij aan wanneer de nachten korter worden en de temperatuur hoger, en als hij merkt dat het juiste moment is aangebroken, bloeit hij met twee sets katjes. Het mannelijke is geel en bruin, als een harige rups, en hangt in groepjes van vier aan de uiteinden van de scheuten. Het vrouwtje is kort, groen en staat recht overeind. De berk is eenhuizig, zoals de den, hetgeen betekent dat hij zichzelf kan bevruchten en geen andere bomen nodig heeft voor de bestuiving, alleen de wind. De spectaculaire wind van het Finnmark-plateau is ideaal voor de bestuiving en de verspreiding van de bevruchte zaden van de berk wanneer die in de herfst ontstaan.

Na de bestuiving breken de donzige, met fijn haar bedekte knoppen open om meer dan een miljoen kleine gevleugelde zaden als harde kevers op de wind los te laten. Een goed jaar voor de verspreiding van het zaad wordt een mastjaar genoemd. Tegenwoordig is elk jaar een mastjaar. De kleine zaaddoosjes sluimeren onder de sneeuw tot het voorjaarslicht en de warmte het kiemen op gang brengen en het zaad een wortelpunt uitsteekt, op zoek naar waar de bodem meegeeft. Meer dan ooit slagen er ook daadwerkelijk in wortel te schieten tussen de matten mos en korstmos van de toendra. Voorheen hadden de zaden, zelfs als ze met succes ontkiemden – en dat was zeker niet vanzelfsprekend – slechts een korte tijdspanne (van juni tot oktober) om in knop en blad te komen en de nodige voorraden aan te leggen om de extreem lage temperaturen van de poolwinter te overleven. Vooral berken zijn hier goed in: ze maken in recordtijd een taaie houtachtige schors aan en besteden veel energie aan de productie van oliën en eiwitten om de kou te weerstaan. Desondanks doodde de vorst gewoonlijk de meeste jonge boompjes die zich met moeite op de toendra hadden gevestigd en handhaafde zo de boomgrens op een bepaalde hoogte. Vroeger liep het groeiseizoen van mei tot oktober, nu van april tot november, en het is zowel in de zomer als in de winter een stuk natter. Dat zijn ideale omstandigheden voor de berk.

De rendierhoeders grappen dat dit ook ideale omstandigheden zijn voor de parasieten van de berk. De larven van de berkenetende herfstmot, *materjokt* in het Noors, sterven bij -36 graden Celsius. In de afgelopen warmere winters, waarin het niet zo koud is geweest, hebben ze het overleefd en een ravage aangericht in duizenden hectaren berkenbos, maar zelfs deze insectenplaag heeft de aanval van de berk op de toendra niet substantieel weten af te remmen.

'De natuur is ingewikkeld,' zegt Tor. Hij heeft tijdens zijn leven al grote veranderingen meegemaakt en gelooft dat de natuur een nieuw evenwicht aan het vinden is, de verschillende permutaties van de natuurlijke selectie aan het uitproberen is en verschillende opties onderzoekt om een nieuwe balans te vinden.

'Vroeg of laat zal de hele hoogvlakte bedekt zijn met bomen.' Er waren hier natuurlijk al eerder bomen. Voor de laatste ijstijd reikte het bos tot aan de kust. De bomen zijn nog maar tot halverwege teruggekeerd, maar terwijl de reis destijds millennia duurde, hebben ze de afstand nu in slechte enkele tientallen jaren afgelegd. Die snelheid is een probleem. De meeste soorten kunnen zich niet zo snel aanpassen. Er heeft altijd een relatie bestaan tussen de toendra en het bos, en de Sami hebben steeds op de overgang tussen die twee geleefd. Maar het woord 'bos' betekende iets anders voordat de opwarming vijftig jaar geleden zijn intrede deed. Voorheen was het een langzaam bewegend en ontwikkelend landschap met een voorhoede van berken die steeds noordelijker kropen, waarbij de berken de jonge, kwetsbare dennen beschermden. De oeroude dennen creëerden een gevarieerd bos met honderden verschillende soorten planten die de rendieren konden eten. Van dit oerbos is in Noorwegen bijna niets meer over, hoewel er over de grens in Finland nog wel delen van resten.

Het duurt honderdzestig jaar om een oerbos van dennen en berken te vormen, een bos dat geschikt is voor rendieren om in te grazen. Jonge dennen werpen te veel naalden af en verstikken het op de grond groeiende korstmos. Na dertig jaar creëren dichte jonge en kleine boompjes een vochtig microklimaat waarin de korstmossen afnemen en mossen in het bladerdak gedijen. De korstmossen ontwaken in natuurlijke bossen na zo'n honderd jaar, wanneer het bos is uitgedund. Het korstmos dat in deze oude dennenbossen groeit is net koraal. Het bloeit met grote sponsachtige bladeren en hangt aan de dode takken van oude bomen. Naast het versterkte vermogen om koolstof te absorberen en op te slaan, is dit korstmos het belangrijkste verschil tussen jonge en oude bossen en de reden waarom oude bossen van cruciaal belang zijn als alternatief voor de toendra om in de winterbegrazing van de rendieren te voorzien.

Is dit ook waarom een oud bos goed aanvoelt voor de menselijke ziel? Wanneer we wandelen tussen een rijke intergenerationele gemeenschap van bomen, vergezeld van een overvloed aan andere soorten, is er die overvloed en die rijkdom, maar we voelen ook voldoening bij het zien van een natuur die een natuurlijk evenwicht heeft bereikt. Een rendierhoeder die campagne voert om te voorkomen dat de oerbossen van Finland worden gekapt, zei eens tegen Greenpeace: 'Je gaat niet naar een jong bos om je herboren te voelen, je verlangt naar een oud bos.'[1]

In Noorwegen zorgt de agressieve groei van bomen nu voor enorme problemen. De berk raast sneller over de toendra dan de dennen kunnen bijhouden. Dit is slecht nieuws voor de rendieren en de mensen die ervan afhankelijk zijn. Een beetje berkenbos ontwikkelt geen bladerdak, maar is eerder een soort struikgewas. Zonder bladerdak houdt het meer sneeuw vast, buigen en barsten de takken door het gewicht en vormt hun massa een windscherm voor ophopingen die te diep zijn voor de rendieren om erdoorheen te lopen of in te graven. Hun wortels warmen de grond op, waardoor rondom het ijs smelt. Na verloop van tijd zal een hectare berk drie tot vier ton bladafval op de bodem deponeren, waardoor de organische samenstelling van de bodem verder wordt verbeterd en de groei van andere planten wordt gestimuleerd. Rendieren knabbelen wel aan de twijgen van jonge berken, 'maar zelfs als je het aantal rendieren in de provincie Finnmark zou verdubbelen, zou je de berk niet kunnen tegenhouden.'

Tor glimlacht spijtig. Hij is een wetenschapper, voor emoties is weinig ruimte in zijn kantoor. Hij accepteert de oprukkende boomgrens als iets onvermijdelijks. Toch ziet hij ook een voordeel. Tor geeft toch vooral om dennen. De berk, essentieel voor de Sami, is lang niet zo waardevol in een moderne economie. De bosbouw in Finnmark is gebaseerd op de grove den en komt nog maar net weer tot leven na een reeks catastrofes. De levenscyclus van dennen is lang. Tien generaties berken kunnen leven en sterven binnen de levensduur van één enkele den. Net als hun neven in Schotland hebben sommige van de vandaag nog levende dennen grote delen van de menselijke geschiedenis meegemaakt, van de tochten van de Vikingen naar Groenland in de middeleeuwen tot nu. En voor hen was de twintigste eeuw de meest traumatische tijd.

In de jaren 1930 stond de grootste zagerij van Europa in Kirkenes, een Noorse haven aan de Barentszzee, niet ver van Moermansk, over de Russische grens. Kirkenes verbruikte 130.000 ton dennenhout per jaar. Toen de nazi's in de Tweede Wereldoorlog binnenvielen, brandden ze die houtzagerij echter plat. In plaats daarvan plunderden ze de bossen van Noorwegen voor scheepsbouw en export op een ongekende schaal. En toen ze zich terugtrokken, verwoestten ze alle houten stadjes en dorpen van Finnmark. Tors moeder herinnerde zich dat ze vanaf de heuvel toekeek hoe haar stad Vardsø afbrandde. De inwoners van Finnmark beschrijven die vernietiging nog steeds als een soort holocaust. Na de oorlog werd wat overbleef van het oerbos gekapt om nieuwe huizen voor hen te bouwen.

De dennen van Finnmark zijn dan ook jong, legt Tor uit, meestal niet ouder dan zestig jaar. Ze zijn pas geschikt om te worden geoogst wanneer ze honderdtwintig jaar oud zijn. Daarna groeien ze langzamer. Ze kunnen drie- of vierhonderd jaar oud worden, maar er is, zoals Tor het zegt, niet veel 'toegevoegde waarde' na honderdtwintig jaar. De bossen van Finnmark zullen nooit oud worden. Het rendier kan misschien overleven in een veranderd landschap, maar alleen als het bos voldoende tijd krijgt om te rijpen en zich te ontwikkelen, en het is nog niet duidelijk of dat ook het geval zal zijn. In elk geval is het zo lang geleden dat de rendieren in een oud bos hebben gegraasd dat het lijkt alsof zelfs de Sami niet weten wat ze zijn kwijtgeraakt.

'De Sami in Noorwegen hebben nooit oude dennenbossen gekend zoals die in Finland, ze zijn opgegroeid met bosbouw,' zegt Tor.

Tor wordt geacht zijn bossen te beheren in overleg met de Sami-rendierhoeders, en elk jaar smeken meer en meer herders hem de pionierende berk te kappen om de kostbare toendrahabitat te beschermen die nodig is voor de rendieren. De hoeders die zichzelf van oudsher beschouwden als een integraal onderdeel van de natuurlijke wereld en niet als losstaand ervan, vechten een hopeloze strijd tegen de natuur. Tor is hard.

'De Sami zullen een andere levensstijl moeten ontwikkelen.'

In het voorjaar en de zomer brengen de Sami hun rendierkudden naar de kust, naar de majestueuze grillige heuvels die de fjorden doorklieven, of naar de eilanden voor de kust die als ruwgehouwen juwelen de Barentszzee omzomen. Vroeger zag je in het voorjaar vaak kuddes door een fjord zwemmen om het sappige gras van een ongerept eiland te bereiken, de herders en hun honden volgend in kajaks of roeiboten. Tegenwoordig maken de meeste kuddes de overtocht met veerboten die anders voor auto's worden gebruikt.

In de zomer trekken veel Sami rond met de kuddes en wonen in hun laavo, traditionele tenten van geweven wol, gespannen over een in elkaar grijpende piramide van berkenstokken. Kinderen die voor de vakantie van school komen, blijven vaak nog wekenlang in het zomerverblijf van hun familie en gaan zelden naar huis. Pas onlangs begonnen hoedersfamilies zich overwegend op één plaats te vestigen, verplicht door de regering om langs een weg te wonen en hun kinderen naar overheidsscholen te sturen – een poging om de nomaden te kortwieken en ze daar te houden waar ze gezien konden worden, en hun dieren belast. Vroeger was het hoeden een familieaangelegenheid, nu is het vooral een mannenactiviteit omdat de vrouwen voor de schoolgaande kinderen zorgen.

In de herfst en de winter keren de kuddes echter terug naar de hoogvlakte, naar hun 'winterplek' – een gebied waar een familiegroep (een *siida* genoemd) al sinds mensenheugenis komt. Juist tijdens de winter vindt het sociale leven van de Sami plaats, wanneer de kuddes zich verzamelen op de hoogvlakte, meestal op een steenworp afstand (een dag stevig doorrijden met een sneeuwscooter) van het middelpunt van het culturele leven van de Sami, de plaats Kautokeino. De naam in het Sami – Guovdageainnu – betekent 'het midden', en het is letterlijk het midden van het Finnmark-hoogvlakte, of – zoals sommigen grappen, aangezien de hoogvlakte wordt gekenmerkt door zijn leegte, tot de laatste decennia verstoken van bomen en elke permanente menselijke nederzetting – *the middle of nowhere*, het midden van nergens.

In Kautokeino zijn het Sami University College, het Sami Cultural Centre, het Beaivvas Sami Theater en het International Centre for Reindeer Husbandry gevestigd. Voor het middelpunt van Europa's oudste ononderbroken voortbestaande beschaving – een manier van leven eigenlijk die al meer dan tienduizend jaar ongeveer dezelfde is – is het verrassend klein. Er zijn slechts 1500 permanente inwoners. Op foto's uit de jaren 1950 zien we de gebouwen van Kautokeino omgeven door het ononderbroken wit van besneeuwde toendra, zonder een boom in zicht. Nu ligt de plaats midden in een berkenbos.

Vanuit Alta neem ik de weg naar Kautokeino, 250 kilometer pal naar het zuiden. Hij begint tussen de gemengde dennen- en berkenbossen die grenzen aan de brede kiezelbochten van de rivier de Alta, naar men zegt 's werelds beste rivier voor zalm. Dan klimt hij snel door een smalle kloof onder steile, honderden meters hoge kliffen naar de hoogvlakte erboven. Een heldere beek klatert door de rotsspleten naast de weg.

De Sami vereerden van oudsher rotsen, bomen, rivieren, bergen en andere heilige plaatsen, en offerden vis, albino rendieren en andere dieren om een goede jacht, visvangst of gewoon geluk te verzekeren. Zij spraken met hun omgeving en de dieren en planten vormden hun gemeenschap. Eenheid staat centraal in de kosmologie van de Sami. Ze kennen helemaal geen concept van 'mens' of 'natuur', alleen een circulair systeem dat op de magische trommel van de Sami-sjamaan is afgebeeld: in het midden een ruitvormige zon met vier stralen, de heersende goden van de donder, de wind en de maan, de 'hond der goden' – de beer – en op het laagste niveau de Sami, zijn thuis, zijn rendieren en de vogels en het wild van het woud. De goddelijke krachten die zich via de goden manifesteerden eisten respect, en wanneer Sami heilige plaatsen passeerden, kleedden zij zich in hun beste goed, brachten een lied ten gehore of ontblootten hun hoofd als teken van eerbied. Er zijn nog mensen in leven die zich herinneren dat ze van hun ouders te horen kregen dat ze goedemorgen moesten zeggen tegen een bepaalde boom of rots.

De kloof is in spiritueel opzicht belangrijk. Hij galmt als een kathedraal – of een bos – en moest toch zeker wel een heilige plaats zijn. Het is een herinnering aan het feit dat namen, verhalen en geesten ooit overal te vinden waren waar mensen leefden. Voor de meesten van ons zijn die stemmen verre echo's, verloren in een mysterieus verleden, maar voor de Sami zijn ze nog maar net buiten gehoorsafstand. Het land is niet stilgevallen. Wij zijn gewoon gestopt met luisteren.

Aan het begin van de kloof kabbelt het water over kiezelstenen en wordt dan stil en steeds breder naarmate de vallei wijder wordt, als een deur naar een bovenwereld die openzwaait. De sneeuw is hier dikker, dieper dan aan de kust, maar de rivier is nog niet bevroren. Dan, na ongeveer een kwartier slingeren langs de oever van de rivier, doorsnijdt een vage rand ijs schuin de trage watervlakte, alsof er een plaat glas in het water ligt. Water glijdt erover en eronderdoor. Dit is het langverwachte, lang uitgestelde, begin van de vorst. Vanaf hier is het oppervlak van de rivier ondoorzichtig en hard. Wervelingen van wit en scherven van blauw flitsen in de scherpe ochtendlucht. In het zuiden zie ik de roze en oranje oven van de dageraad. Zonder de bergen om zich achter te verschuilen is de zon dichterbij, hoewel nog steeds schuchter, en blijft net uit het zicht. Rode en gele flitsen doorkruisen de hemel als lichtspoorkogels, en de gespikkelde hellingen, sneeuw en struikgewas, gonzen met een warme roze gloed.

Sinds Alta, honderd kilometer achter ons, hebben overal langs de kant van de weg struikachtige berken de auto gezelschap gehouden, en dat zal tot Kautokeino zo blijven. Slechts één keer, wanneer een geprononceerde berg boven het niveau van de open riviervallei uitsteekt, is er een glimp te zien van een onbeboste toendra: gladde, ongeschonden sneeuw, doorsneden door een rij gebogen en gedraaide figuurtjes, een bataljon berken dat grimmig omhoog marcheert. De bomen zijn hier niet zo hoog als aan de kust, zelden hoger dan twee tot drie meter. Hun zilveren schors is ook ernstiger misvormd: niet de gladde papierachtige laag van rechte krachtige stammen, maar een knoestige huid vol blaren om de bomen tegen de kou te beschermen. De witte kleur is afkomstig van de peridermis, een poedervormige oppervlaktelaag die het zonlicht weerkaatst en de boom beschermt tegen zonnebrand en tegen de lage winterzon die het onder druk staande sap in de stam zou kunnen bevriezen en de boom zou kunnen doen barsten. Ze wordt bovendien door de Sami als medicijn gebruikt. Dit is krummholz: onvolgroeide, traaggroeiende bomen die overleven aan de rand van hun natuurlijke verspreidingsgebied. Sommige mensen vragen zich af of ze de naam boom überhaupt verdienen. Maar is een bonsai van honderd jaar oud, een halve meter hoog, geen boom? Verdienen ze misschien juist meer respect voor hun ongelooflijke overlevingsprestatie?

Een eindje van Kautokeino bereikt de weg een bergkam, en beneden ontvouwt zich het plateau in een wijds vergezicht van zwart – de bomen – en oranje – de lucht weerspiegeld in de sneeuw. Een slingerende rivier baant zich een weg door het midden van het tafereel en stroomt hier en daar weer, niet bevroren, met een oppervlak dat glinstert als vloeibaar goud. De griezelige bijna-dageraad is overgegaan in het moment vlak na zonsondergang zonder dat de zon ook maar even te zien is geweest. De halve hemel staat in brand. Het is één uur 's middags. We staan aan het begin van een twintig uur durende nacht. Vanaf dit uitkijkpunt is de bomenplaag angstaanjagend duidelijk. Zo ver het oog reikt is de toendra van de hoogvlakte bezaaid met zwarte strepen, als de gespikkelde borst van een sneeuwuil. Het patroon is geschilderd door de heersende wind, die de harde zaaddozen op hun kleine vleugels in vlagen en stromen over de glooiende heuvels meevoert. Uit de wind, waar de zaden zijn neergekomen in de plooien en de holten, is de berk groter en dikker.

Het is een prachtig tafereel, maar het feit dat de bomen er niet zouden moeten staan en de rivier op dit punt midden in de winter keihard zou moeten zijn met metersdik ijs dat het gewicht van een kudde rendieren of een vrachtwagen met oplegger zou kunnen dragen, maakt het moeilijk de schoonheid ervan te waarderen. Misschien was het anders geweest als we niet had geweten hoe het er vroeger heeft uitgezien, als we konden doen alsof het een vreemd jaar was en geen deel van een versnellend patroon. In feite ondergaat dit deel van een verder ongerept gebied een enorme omwenteling. Op deze winterdag, op deze plek in de poolcirkel, bij -1 graad (14 graden boven het gemiddelde voor deze tijd van het jaar), kan men zich moeilijk aan het gevoel onttrekken dat, als er een omslagpunt is in het klimaatevenwicht van de aarde, we dat al ver achter ons hebben gelaten.

In een geel, laag huis aan de rand van Kautokeino houdt Berit Utsi haar tweejarig zoontje tegen haar borst en kijkt in de toenemende duisternis naar het meer dat bedekt is met een flinterdunne laag ijs en omringd is door berkenbomen. Ze is de secretaresse van de plaatselijke vereniging van rendierhouders en zij heeft ermee ingestemd om met mij te praten over de problemen die worden veroorzaakt door de oprukkende bomen. Zij heeft een kalme gelaatsuitdrukking, maar er is een rusteloosheid die nu en dan achter haar ogen opvlamt. Ze weet haar ongerustheid niet geheel te verbergen.

'In onze cultuur zijn we niet gewend om dramatisch te doen,' zegt ze. Dat is een understatement. De Noren, die bekend staan om hun terughoudendheid, zijn uitbundig vergeleken met de Sami, bij wie emoties hooguit waarneembaar zijn als een huivering of een stille glimlach, een vage lijn in een verder bevroren gelaatsuitdrukking.

'Iedereen hield zich rustig, maar stilletjes waren we allemaal erg bezorgd.' Zij heeft het over de ongelooflijk warme winter, die zojuist is gezegend met zijn eerste sneeuw. Maar Berits zorgen zijn nog niet voorbij. Haar man is nog steeds daarbuiten ergens, en ze weet niet precies waar. Hij verplaatst zich veel, en het gsm-signaal is vaak slecht. Zelfs in een goed jaar is dit een zeer stresserende periode voor rendierhoeders: de kuddes van de herfst naar de winterweiden brengen, de kudde over honderden vierkante kilometers bijeenhouden.

De kleurverandering van de toendra heeft ernstige gevolgen.

Rendieren zijn de enige zoogdieren die ultraviolet licht kunnen zien – onzichtbaar voor mensen. In het lage licht van de poolnacht, wanneer de zon niet opkomt, is dit vermogen cruciaal om te overleven. Korstmossen absorberen UV en lijken zo zwart tegen de sneeuw. Er zijn bovendien steeds meer aanwijzingen dat korstmossen in verschillende kleuren fluoresceren en dus door de sneeuw heen zichtbaar kunnen zijn voor rendieren.[2] Hun oog heeft een speciale strook, *tapetum lucidum* genaamd, die gebruikelijk is bij nachtdieren en insecten, een 'helder tapijt' dat licht absorbeert en terugkaatst naar het netvlies om hun zicht bij weinig licht te verbeteren. Alleen bij rendieren is het tapetum in de zomer goudkleurig en in de winter diepblauw om de UV te absorberen. In een ongebroken sneeuwlaag zijn de rendieren kalm en blijven ze meestal op één plaats staan, gravend in de sneeuw om bij hun voedsel te komen. Maar een gespikkeld zwart-wit is verleidelijk en verwarrend, omdat dan de indruk bestaat dat er gemakkelijker toegankelijk voedsel is. Ze graven niet, maar knabbelen aan het gras en het korstmos dat aan de voet van de bomen ligt. Ze leggen veel grotere afstanden af en bezorgen de hoeder veel hoofdbrekens, omdat hij ze in het oog moet houden en ze bij elkaar moet houden om te voorkomen dat ze afdwalen naar het territorium van een naburige siida of, erger nog, zich vermengen met een andere siida. Het scheiden van tienduizend rendieren kan twee weken duren.

Afgezien van vorige week, toen hij voor een paar dagen terugkwam omdat zij geopereerd was, is Berits man al twee maanden achter elkaar op de hoogvlakte met de kuddes. Het volledige inkomen en al het spaargeld van de familie wordt in de kudde geïnvesteerd. Een dier is in het slachthuis meer dan twaalfhonderd euro waard en elk deel van het karkas – huid, gewei, hoeven en pezen – wordt door de Sami gebruikt voor kleding, gereedschap en ambachtelijke producten. Die grote waarde nodigt uit tot het nemen van risico's.

'Er zijn de laatste tijd veel ongelukken gebeurd,' zegt Berit. Een 'puntcontrole', een cirkel rijden rondom de kudde, is de dagelijkse routine van een hoeder. Onder koude omstandigheden zijn de sporen van een verdwaald dier gemakkelijk zichtbaar op de sneeuw, en een sneeuwscooter kan in een rondje van dertig kilometer over open toendra, bevroren meren en rivieren zoeven. In een niet-bevroren landschap vol struiken is dat veel lastiger. Zonder voldoende sneeuw voor de sneeuwscooter, en zonder ijs, moet een herder op een quad om de meren, rivieren en bomen heen rijden, soms wel zestig of zeventig kilometer verder dan voorheen. Dat kost een hele dag en veel brandstof, en plet veel korstmos dat honderden jaren nodig heeft om zich te herstellen. En de volgende dag moet het gewoon opnieuw.

'Mensen rijden met hun sneeuwmobiel op stenen, raken bomen en komen in het ziekenhuis terecht... of misschien is het ijs wel sterk genoeg om een rendier te dragen, maar zakt een quad er doorheen. Soms neem je een risico – als het te ver is om helemaal om te rijden. Vorig jaar zijn twee mensen door het ijs gezakt en niet meer bovengekomen,' aldus Berit.

Als tiener probeerde Berit in de stad te werken, maar het voelde niet goed. Ze miste haar rendieren. Ze was met hen opgegroeid en bracht elke zomer met haar familie en de dieren door in de Lyngen Alpen, in de buurt van Tromsø. Ze herinnert zich dat er op de toendra minder bomen groeiden toen ze nog een kind was. Die verandering voelt als een verlies, maar zoals de meeste Sami die ik leer kennen, is ze pragmatisch: 'We passen ons aan, dat hebben we altijd al gedaan.' Maar het veranderende weer en het oprukken van de bomen, samen met andere manieren waarop de weidegronden onder druk staan – wegen, mijnen, windturbines – betekenen dat het rendierhoeden steeds moeilijker wordt. En tot overmaat van ramp is de regering zich bewust van de krimpende begrazing en eist zij elk jaar steeds grotere ruimingen van de dieren. Haar gezin heeft een andere inkomstenbron nodig.

Berit zou graag zien dat haar kinderen de kans krijgen rendierhoeder te worden als ze dat willen – het is een sterke traditie – maar als de kinderen niet het hele jaar door met de kuddes leven zoals haar ouders deden, zullen ze onherroepelijk minder kennis vergaren. En het is niet alleen de typische manier van doen van het rendier die ze moeten leren kennen. De nachten in het wild waren ook het moment waarop verhalen werden verteld en werktuigen werden gemaakt.

De *soahki*, zoals de berk in de Sami-taal wordt genoemd, is bijna even essentieel voor het traditionele Sami-leven op de toendra als het rendier. Hij was van cruciaal belang voor onderdak: voor het maken van de palen van de laavo, en voor isolatie – geurige berkentwijgen werden op de grond gelegd als vloer. Het hout was essentieel voor het vervoer, werd gebruikt voor het maken van sleeën, ski's en sneeuwschoenen, en als brandstof. En in de herfst beperkt de berk, zoals alle bomen, het vochtgehalte in zijn xyleem – het binnenste gedeelte van de stam – klaar voor de winterslaap. Dat betekent dat berken die in de winter worden geoogst, goed branden, zelfs als hun hout niet eerst de tijd heeft gehad om te drogen. Het looizuur en de oliën worden gebruikt voor de behandeling van kleding en huiden en voor het maken van geolied papier. De schors werd gebruikt voor de bekleding van kano's en gefermenteerd in zeewater. Het looizuur werd ook gebruikt voor het drogen van de wollen, hennep- of linnen zeilen van traditionele boten. In het voorjaar kan het sap worden afgetapt als een mineraalhoudende drank of om te gisten als basis voor een soort mede.

'En in de herfst, paddenstoelen!' Er zijn meer dan zeventig soorten schimmels te vinden in de habitat van berkenwortels.[3] Het lot van de Sami is nauw verbonden met dat van de berk.

De berk is een voorbode van de lente en heeft altijd al een rol gespeeld als vruchtbaarheidssymbool voor de Sami – en ook elders. In de Schotse folklore zal een onvruchtbare koe die met een berkenstok wordt gehoed, vruchtbaar worden, en verder naar het zuiden in Engeland werd van oudsher een meiboom van berk gemaakt. Een *besom birch wedding*, waarbij een bruidspaar over een bundel twijgen springt om te trouwen, was tot voor kort een gebruikelijk alternatief voor het Engelse kerkelijk huwelijk. Dit werd ook in verband gebracht met zuivering en reiniging, vandaar dat het *beating of the bounds*, het slaan van de grenzen, van een parochie altijd werd gedaan met berkentwijgen.

'De berk is onze vriend!' zegt Berit, alsof ze zich schuldig voelt omdat ze de boom belasterd heeft waar ze eigenlijk zo sterk op vertrouwt.

Maar daarbuiten, op de toendra, maken de bomen het leven van haar man moeilijk en gevaarlijk. Hier, in de keuken, is overal berkenhout te vinden. Berits moderne keuken staat nog vol met het traditionele handwerk van de nomaden, gemaakt tijdens haar zomertochten naar de bergen. Haar houten lepels en pollepels zijn allemaal gesneden uit berkenhout – 'veel sterker dan grenenhout'. De bekers en kommen op een plank zijn ook uit berkenhout gesneden, terwijl de handvatten van handgemaakte messen van gewei en been zijn. Een koffiezak van bewerkt rendiervel hangt naast de ketel, en daarnaast ligt een muts van vossenbont en rendiervel. Haar zoon draagt laarsjes gemaakt van rendierhuid, geïsoleerd met holle stengels toendragras. En in een klein potje op het werkblad zitten snippers berkenschors voor infusies en medicinale brouwsels.

'Maar nu zijn de bomen te veel geworden,' zegt Berit fronsend. Ze volgt een opleiding tot lerares.

Net als in Schotland is het evenwicht tussen grazende dieren en bomen verstoord en zijn de mensen in de war. Maar, opnieuw net als in Schotland, is de teerling hier inmiddels geworpen. De uitstoot die nu al in de atmosfeer zit, zal de toekomstige vorm van het bos bepalen. Wij staan nu voor dezelfde taak als Berit: proberen te aanvaarden wat er gebeurt en ons aanpassen.

Kautokeino lijkt een stad in winterslaap. Dat, of het is helemaal geen stad, maar een kunstmatige constructie, een soort filmset. In het Arctic Motel is een klop op de deur in de duisternis tevergeefs. In de jeugdherberg gluurt een eenzame oudere vrouw uit het enige verlichte raam van een betonnen gebouw uit de jaren 1970 en wuift me weg te gaan. De deur van het ambachtencentrum staat open, maar er is niemand. Boven lezen drie oudere mensen in grote jassen de krant. Ze wijzen terug naar beneden, naar de werkplaats. In de werkplaats is een man met gehoorbeschermers op zijn hoofd in concentratie verzonken aan een draaibank. Zelfs wanneer hij me duidelijk kan zien, lijkt hij niet van plan zijn werk te onderbreken. Winkels schijnen open te zijn wanneer dat zo uitkomt, en net als in Alta zijn er geen voetgangers op straat, alleen lege auto's voor de huizen, hun motoren draaiend om ze warm te houden, of op de wegen mysterieuze, langzaam rijdende auto's met knipperende remlichten in het donker.

De volgende dag is het vijftig jaar geleden dat de Noorse Samivereniging werd opgericht, een politieke groepering die op de rechten van de Sami aandringt. Misschien gaat iedereen volledig op in de voorbereiding op deze belangrijke gebeurtenis?

'Wat? Nee!' De twee vrouwen die koffie drinken in hun keuken lachen en sputteren. 'Daar geeft niemand wat om!'

Marija draagt een zwart horloge dat past bij haar zwarte nagels en zwart-witte chiffon blouse. Haar halsketting en oorbellen zijn van goud, en haar gedeeltelijk kortgeschoren haar is rood geverfd. Sara-Irene draagt ook een zwart-wit hemd, en haar haar is ook kortgeschoren aan de zijkanten, hoewel haar pony blond geverfd is. Ze heeft drie paarlen oorbellen in één oor. Aan haar middelvinger draagt Sara-Irene een ring die haar man voor haar heeft gemaakt: het is het 'oormerk' van haar rendierkudde. Bij de dieren van elke kudde worden de oren in een bepaald patroon ingeknipt om aan te geven wie de eigenaar is. In de kraal, tijdens het tellen, herkent een ervaren hoedster haar dieren in een oogwenk door gewoon aan de oren te voelen. Sara-Irene is enorm trots op haar rendieren. Ze wil niet zeggen hoeveel ze er heeft: 'Het is niet beleefd om dat te vragen.'

'Ze heeft er zat,' zegt Marija lachend.

'Maar niet zoveel als Marija,' antwoordt Sara-Irene, en ze slaan beide aan het giechelen.

Ze doen niet aan politiek en delen de traditionele minachting van de inheemse bevolking voor de regering: 'De regering geeft niets om de Sami.' Het heeft geen zin om te proberen dingen te beïnvloeden door naar de vergadering te gaan. Maar Marija is het hoofd van de uitkeringsinstantie in Kautokeino, dus eigenlijk werkt ze toch voor de staat?

'Ja! Stel je voor! De vijand!' En ze lacht zich weer een hoestbui. Haar betovergrootvader werd in 1852 door de Noren onthoofd omdat hij tegen de regering in opstand was gekomen. Ze heeft zijn oormerk geërfd. Het is een nobel, beroemd oormerk.

Als ik over klimaatverandering begin, slaat de stemming om. 'De regering wil gewoon ons en onze kuddes controleren. Het is niet meer dan een excuus... om ons te dwingen onze dieren af te maken. Klimaatverandering is onzin. Toen mijn moeder jonger was, was het weer precies hetzelfde als nu, negentig jaar geleden. Dus ik maak me geen zorgen. We hebben dit eerder gezien.'

Voor de bomen heeft ze geen verklaring. Wanneer ik volhoud, vloekt ze zachtjes op de Noorse regering en maakt Sara-Irene aan het lachen met een grap die ik niet begrijp, voordat ze naar buiten gaat om een sigaret te roken. Als ze weer binnenkomt, is het gesprek al een heel stuk gevorderd.

Rendierhoeders staan niet los van de kudde, maar maken er deel van uit. Ze kunnen dagen of weken op voorhand aanvoelen wanneer de kudde zich zal verplaatsen. Ze kunnen niet eten tenzij hun kudde heeft gegeten. Bedreigingen voor het welzijn van de kudde, zoals de klimaatverandering, moeten net zo aanvoelen als je eigen kinderen dood of uitgehongerd zien. Ontkenning is natuurlijk het eerste stadium van rouw.

Sara-Irene en Marija werken beide in de stad. Sara-Irene runt een nagelsalon. Zij heeft Marija's nagels zwart gelakt. Er zijn echter perioden van het jaar waarin ze de aanwezigheid van de rendieren niet zullen missen: de tijd van het kalven in de zomer en van het oormerken van de jonge kalveren in de late winter, wanneer de hele familie nodig is om dag en nacht duizenden rendieren bijeen te drijven.

'Soms,' zegt Sara-Irene, 'voelen we ons schizofreen!' Beide vrouwen lachen wild. Ze zijn misschien goed in hun werk en er zelfs trots op, maar hun ziel ligt niet in de stad. Die is daarbuiten, in de heuvels, en rent vrij rond met de rendieren.

De volgende morgen is de stad weer half in slaap, verdoofd door het donker en de kou. Het is nu -8, nog steeds niet koud genoeg, klaagt de vrouw in het pension. De lucht is bewolkt, en zonder de heldere hemelkoepel is het licht een soort troebele soep. De rivier onder de brug is nog gedeeltelijk vloeibaar en beweegt zich langzaam langs de donkere kerk op zijn landtong. Licht brandt in de huizen en er zijn nog nauwelijks auto's en geen voetgangers.

Maar bij het benzinestation is dat wel anders. Daar is het voorterrein fel verlicht door koplampen. Rijen enorme pick-ups, vaak door dezelfde 'Arctic Truck Co.' uitgerust met enorme winterbanden, staan er met draaiende motoren en vullen de koude lucht met dieseldampen. Achter elk ervan hangt een aanhangwagen met daarop een sneeuwscooter, een quad of beide. Ik drink een kop koffie op een stalen kruk, zoals in een Amerikaanse diner, en kijk toe hoe mannen, van top tot teen gehuld in sneeuwpakken en bontmutsen, zich uit hun wagens laten zakken en jerrycans vullen met brandstof. Ze bewegen snel, doelgericht en energiek. Ze komen met lange passen de winkel binnen, knallen hun geld op de toonbank, begroeten het personeel luidkeels, vullen hun armen met snacks en suikerhoudende drankjes en roepen weer ter afscheid. Dan springen ze in hun enorme vervuilende machines, zetten ze in de versnelling en brullen weg in de duisternis die voor ochtend doorgaat. Het zijn de rendierhoeders, op weg om hun puntencontrole te doen. Sommigen zijn wellicht vanavond terug, anderen blijven misschien weken weg en een enkeling zal nooit meer terugkeren.

Overal in Kautokeino zijn afbeeldingen van rendieren te vinden – op de muren van winkels, in de logo's van overheidsinstanties en culturele organisaties van de Sami. Je vindt ze in ambachtswinkel, op ansichtkaarten, afgebeeld in de lichtjes buiten de supermarkt. Maar er zijn geen echte rendieren. In drie dagen tijd heb ik er nog niet een gezien.

Als Kautokeino zielloos en vreemd aanvoelt, komt dat omdat

de stad niet het middelpunt van het leven op de hoogvlakte is. De historische functie van Kautokeino is altijd die van een soort tankstation geweest, een stopplaats met essentiële diensten. Afgezien van de fast-foodbalie van de benzinepomp zijn er geen restaurants, geen winkels behalve de supermarkt en slechts één ambachtelijke boetiek voor het stroompje toeristen dat hier komt, meestal in de zomer. De identiteit van de mensen, hun rijkdom, hun echtgenoten, het welzijn en de toekomst van hun familie en hun cultuur, is afhankelijk van het lot van de kuddes daarbuiten, op de toendra.

Kautokeino lijkt misschien een slaperig stadje in de binnenlanden, maar bij nader onderzoek blijkt het in de greep te zijn van een soort collectieve neurose. Iedereen is zich bewust van de strijd op leven en dood tussen mens en natuur die zich afspeelt in de heuvels en toendra rondom, maar bijna niemand is bereid de waarheid te erkennen: dit kan zo niet doorgaan in zijn huidige vorm. Het is een microkosmos van de strijd die zich wereldwijd afspeelt. Op een niveau is er het prozaïsche patina van het dagelijkse leven in een koolwaterstofmaatschappij: naar het werk gaan, naar school, naar de supermarkt, benzine tanken, sinaasappels en mango's van ver weg, en toch, vlak daaronder, op een ander niveau, zijn er de geesten van de toendra en het bos die hun waarschuwingen uitschreeuwen.

Het Samische Dodenrijk, *Jabmiidaibmu*, bevond zich onder de grond en werd bestuurd door Jabmiidahkka, de moeder van de doden. Een rivier van bloed scheidde het land van stervelingen van het mythische land van de rendieren, maar was altijd aanwezig. Net als in de oude Keltische cultuur of bij hedendaagse inheemse volkeren wereldwijd, was het de rol van de *noadi* – sjamaan – om een dialoog aan te gaan met de voorouders en de geesten, en hen om hun advies te vragen. Maar noadi zijn er allang niet meer.

In het enige hotel in de stad houdt de jeugdafdeling van de Noorse Sami-vereniging een voorbereidend evenement voor haar jaarlijkse algemene vergadering. Jonge activisten in prachtige traditionele kostuums en bijpassende sportschoenen zitten met gekruiste benen op rendierhuiden, achter een namaak-politieafzetting met de tekst 'gedekoloniseerde zone', met hun iPhones in de aanslag. De titel van de bijeenkomst is 'De toekomst is inheems'. Het is een verleidelijk en romantisch idee, maar de meesten van deze serieuze kinderen die hier in het rond zitten, komen niet uit Kautokeino en zijn geen rendierhoeders. Ze hebben al evenmin het verlangen om in laavo te leven en de helft van het jaar rendieren te voet door de sneeuw te volgen.

Iedereen kent wel iemand die zijn rendieren heeft opgegeven. Marija en Sara-Irene zweren dat ze dat nooit zullen doen en hebben medelijden met wie dat wel heeft gedaan. Wie wil er nou deze heilige en oude manier van leven, dit geboorterecht, vrijwillig opgeven? De volhouders zijn ofwel van de hoedersaristocratie zoals Marija, die zoveel dieren heeft dat ze de tegenslagen voorlopig kan doorstaan en tweede huizen in Tromsø en derde huizen in Oslo kan kopen, of het zijn echte toegewijden: misschien verslaafd, of gek. Ik weet niet goed tot welke categorie Issat behoort, maar zijn ervaring geeft perfect de cognitieve dissonantie weer die ons door de opwarming wordt opgedrongen. Rationeel weten we wat er gebeurt en wat er waarschijnlijk staat te gebeuren, maar praktisch en emotioneel lijken we er alles aan te willen doen om de feiten niet te hoeven accepteren.

Ik ontmoet Issat om negen uur 's avonds in zijn onopvallende kantoor aan de achterkant van een gebouw van de gemeente in Kautokeino, na een lange dag. Zijn organisatie, Protect Sapmi, is een ngo die juridisch advies verstrekt aan Sami-gemeenschappen die de overname van hun land door multinationals en parastatale overheidsorganisaties aanvechten, en heeft daar de handen vol aan. De opwarming van het Noordpoolgebied heeft geleid tot massale belangstelling voor de 'ontsluiting' van het noorden, niet alleen in Noorwegen maar in de hele wereld van het poolgebied: Rusland, Groenland, Alaska, Canada. Noorwegen is zelfvoorzienend op het gebied van hernieuwbare energie, maar er is een enorme vraag uit Duitsland, het VK en Nederland, en windmolenparken binnen de poolcirkel koloniseren in hoog tempo de weinige overgebleven boomloze bergketens van Finnmark. De Sami-bevolking zou volgens een recente wet 96 procent van het land van Finnmark in handen moeten hebben en de Noorse regering zou de VN-beginselen van 'vrije, voorafgaande en geïnformeerde toestemming' moeten volgen voor de vervreemding van inheems land, maar doet dat niet. De enige organisatie die zich wel aan het internationale recht houdt is, vreemd genoeg, de NAVO, die grote stukken land van de Sami heeft gepacht voor militaire manoeuvres.

Aan het eind van ons gesprek, rond elf uur 's avonds, als ik wel aan mijn bed toe ben, kondigt Issat aan dat hij nu aan zijn 'tweede baan' zal beginnen: rendierhoeden. Hij nodigt me uit om mee te gaan. Zijn huis staat hoger op de heuvel, een rijtjeshuis in een kleine woonwijk die lijkt op talloze andere in Europa. Terwijl ik buiten wacht, gaat Issat naar binnen om zijn vrouw en zijn vier slapende kinderen te kussen en dan zijn rendierhoederskleren aan te trekken: twee paar dikke wollen sokken, een thermische jas, een donsbroek, een fleece, een knielange bovenjas, een sneeuwscooterjas met het logo Sinsalo, dikke rubberen sneeuwlaarzen, wanten en een gehavende oude rendierhuidenmuts gevoerd met vossenbont. Hij komt tien minuten later tevoorschijn. Zonder zijn bril en pak en keurig gekapte haar is hij getransformeerd. Hij is niet langer de rustige, bedeesde jurist, maar een man van actie geworden.

Buiten is het maar -5, maar we moeten erop voorbereid zijn de hele nacht buiten te blijven als een dier zoek is of we een ongeluk krijgen. Onlangs zat een herder twaalf uur vast onder een sneeuwscooter voordat zijn vrienden hem kwamen zoeken. Issat fluit naar zijn hond, die achterop zijn quad naast me springt – zij weet waar we naartoe gaan.

Door de donkere straten met rijtjeshuizen aan de rand van Kautokeino rijden we met de quad de stad uit, langs de schamele berken die zich de heuvel op worstelen tot de groepjes steeds lager worden. We snellen voorbij het '60km/u' bord, doorzeefd met kogelgaten, en op naar het plateau. Op de top zijn de bomen slechts manshoog. Issat remt af en stuurt de quad naar de zijkant van de weg. Hij gaat rechtop staan op en tuurt in de lichtbundels van zijn koplampen die de rand van het asfalt volgen. Die lijn is gemarkeerd met rode palen. Als de sneeuw weer zoals gewoonlijk komt, zullen die de rand van de weg markeren. Hij is op zoek naar sporen.

Waar het sneeuwdek verstoord is, beweegt hij bijzonder langzaam. Sporen in de sneeuw betekenen dat zijn rendieren de weg zijn overgestoken en zijn afgedwaald. De bomen zorgen ervoor dat de rendieren meer gaan zwerven, wat leidt tot meer conflicten over territorium en graasgebieden en meer geschillen met buren. Issat moet elke nacht patrouilleren om zeker te zijn dat zijn rendieren aan de goede kant van de weg staan. De veranderingen dreigen de Sami-gemeenschap te verscheuren. Ze leggen daarnaast een enorme druk op de hoeders en hun gezinnen.

'Vindt je vrouw het niet erg dat je elke avond weg bent?' vraag ik.

'Ze is het gewend,' zegt hij.

Issat concentreert zich op de sneeuw, op de rendieren die op verboden terrein zijn gekomen. De vraag die hij probeert te beantwoorden is 'wanneer?' Hij wijst en roept en praat snel en vloeiend, in het Engels, helemaal niet zoals de gereserveerde man in het beige kantoor die een uur geleden nog grafieken raadpleegde en met moeite de juiste woorden kon vinden. Op het plateau onder de sikkel van de maan, gezeten op zijn krachtige machine, is hij uitgelaten – een ander mens, zijn blauwe ogen dansend in het licht van de koplampen.

Hij knielt om de sneeuwkorst te onderzoeken op sporen en de richting waarin ze wijzen. De Sami kennen zeventien verschillende termen voor sneeuwkorst, en zeven graden van hardheid. Overleven hangt af van precisie. De sporen zijn oud.

Terug op de quad snellen we verder over open terrein – *oppas* – een gebied dat nog niet door rendieren is betreden, de sneeuw afkijkend als een kerkuil, op zoek naar sporen. Issat ziet er een, en vervolgens vele, die de verkeerde kant op gaan. Hij zwenkt op hoge snelheid en volgt de sporen. De quad komt even los van de grond en landt dan met een krakend geluid op een bevroren meer. In het licht van de koplampen lopen de sporen rechtdoor. Issat houdt zijn adem in terwijl het ijs kraakt onder de hoge druk en af en toe een geluid laat horen als van een geweerschot. De afgelopen maand is hij twee keer door het ijs gezakt. De laatste keer was hij tot aan zijn borst weggezakt in een ondiepe poel en doorweekt geraakt, en moest de quad er met een lier worden uitgetrokken, waarna het ding enkele dagen lang heeft staan drogen in de garage.

'Dit is de gevaarlijkste baan in Noorwegen!' grijnst hij. En het is waar: hoeden is gevaarlijker dan werken op een booreiland of in het leger.

De sterren zijn te zien en vormen een prachtig schouwspel. Issat wijst en schreeuwt de Sami-namen voor de sterren, maar ik versta geen woord. De wind buldert in onze oren, de quad vliegt over de toendra, stuitert over rotsen en keien en dan door een berkenbos, waar de twijgen in onze gezichten slaan.

Na anderhalf uur, om bijna twee uur 's nachts, laat Issat de quad uitglijden tot hij stilstaat.

'Hier zouden ze moeten zijn.'

'Heb je gps?' vraag ik.

De kudde telt tien rendieren met een gps-label, maar de batterij van Issats telefoon is leeg. Hoe dan ook, hij doet hij het liever op deze manier. Zijn instincten laten hem zelden in de steek.

Hij zet de motor en het lichten uit, en luistert of hij de bellen hoort die sommige rendieren dragen. De stilte is immens. Niets. De sterren stralen zo intens dat het lijkt alsof we ze kunnen aanraken. De takken van de bomen werpen schaduwen op de sneeuw.

'Ach,' zegt hij, terwijl hij de sleutel omdraait en de quad keert richting huis.

Het is moeilijk voorstelbaar, al die moeite doen om op het laatst toch op te geven. Issat zegt dat zijn broer morgen verder kan zoeken. Ik ben geschokt, maar ik besef dat ik het doel van deze tocht verkeerd begrepen heb. Door de nacht scheuren, alleen in de stille uitgestrektheid, wilde dieren opsporen in een spel van leven en dood – het lijkt wel een computerspel met hoge inzet dat zich voordoet als een manier van leven. Het gaat daarbij niet altijd om het daadwerkelijk vinden van de rendieren. Dit zijn de daden van een man die zijn erfgoed voor zijn ogen ziet verdwijnen. Issat weet dat rendieren hoeden op deze manier niet langer een haalbare kaart is. Hij maakt de hele dag ruzie met de regering en de mijnbouwbedrijven over schadevergoeding, maar 's nachts droomt hij van het tegendeel. Terwijl de quad de heuvel afjakkert in de richting van het neonverlichte, slapende stadje in de vallei beneden, worden de bomen langs de weg geleidelijk weer hoger en het gehuil van de honden van Kautokeino vult de nachtlucht. De laatste dagen is in de buurt een wolf gesignaleerd – nog een gevolg van het uitdijende bos. Issat stopt de quad voor zijn huis dat gehuld is in duisternis, en ik klim eraf, stijf van de kou. Terwijl hij zijn bovenkleren uittrekt en naar binnen gaat om te gaan slapen, gaat bij de buren, in het huis van zijn zus een licht aan. Haar dochter, zijn nichtje Māret, is net wakker geworden.

Het is de dag van de grote bijeenkomst, de vijftigste verjaardag van de Noorse Sami Associatie. Māret is een chef-kok en zij kookt voor de tweehonderd afgevaardigden. Ze moet al vroeg beginnen.

Ze loopt door de stad naar een groot blauw en zwart rechthoekig gebouw naast de supermarkt, de sporthal waar de bijeenkomst zal worden gehouden. Aan de ene kant is er een professionele keuken van roestvrij staal. Māret trek haar witte kokshemd aan, maar combineert het met een *gotki*, de traditionele veelkleurige vierhoekige muts van de Sami. Māret is een beroemdheid onder haar volk. Zij is een van de weinige Sami-koks die proberen de keuken en de traditionele gebruiken rond voedsel en het medicinale gebruik van planten in stand te houden.

'Ik wil mensen met hun maag laten denken!' zegt ze als ik later bij haar kom zitten na even kort te hebben geslapen om bij te komen van de manische nacht. Over haar ronde gezicht glijdt even een wrange glimlach en haar ogen glinsteren onder haar zware oogleden. Ze ziet er moe uit.

'Ik ben erg moe, en erg boos, maar ik heb het nog niet opgegeven. Ik kan protesteren met mijn eten. Alles komt uit de natuur.'

Ze bereidt rendier. Het zijn haar eigen rendieren, geslacht volgens biodynamische principes, bij een wassende maan. Ze kan zeker zijn van de smaak. Je proeft de veranderingen in het vlees, zegt ze: het nattere klimaat, de oprukkende bomen en de afname van korstmossen in het dieet van het rendier. Winterdieren van de hoogvlakte werden vroeger het meest gewaardeerd, met het magerste vlees, de beste combinatie van spiermassa en vet. Maar nu smaakt het meeste rendiervlees naar de kust – te veel gras.

Na de rendiersoep volgen er pannenkoeken van berkenmeel en bloedworst van rendierbloed. Het binnenste gedeelte van de berkenschors, het rode cambiumweefsel, wordt gedroogd en vermalen tot meel, dat soms puur wordt gebruikt en soms wordt gemengd met spelt of tarwe of ander meel. Het heeft een houtachtige, aromatische smaak. Er wordt ook brood gemaakt van gedroogd rendierbloed, rendierhersenen en meel van gemalen pijnboomschors. Dit is een belangrijke bron van vitamine C en andere mineralen die ervoor zorgden dat de Sami nooit last hadden van scheurbuik, ondanks het tekort aan groenten tijdens de lange winters. Dit is een van de redenen waarom de den, door de Sami *bèahci* genoemd, heilig is – hij is nodig om te overleven.

'Deze inheemse kennis is grotendeels verloren gegaan. Toch is ze essentieel voor ons overleven in deze vervuilde wereld,' zegt Māret.

Het was moeilijk om aan het bloed te komen. Ze mag het niet vers opdienen, en de directeur van het plaatselijke slachthuis lijdt, ook al is hij haar neef, volgens haar aan 'assimilatiedenken'. Ze bedoelt dat hij een gevangene is van de voorschriften van de Noorse regering.

De rest van het menu bestaat uit kabeljauw, gevangen in Alta, gehaktballen gemaakt van eland en gefrituurd zeewier, een oude Sami-delicatesse.

De familie van Mārets man komt van de kust, waar ze nu woont, maar zij is opgegroeid in Kautokeino. 'Toen mijn vader me leerde rijden op een sneeuwscooter, zei hij dat ik moest mikken op die ene berkenboom op de toendra als oriëntatiepunt. Haha! Nu zou ik die plaats niet meer herkennen.' Maar ze gebruikt geen sneeuwscooter meer. Zij leert haar kinderen te voet hoeden, met honden, op de oude manier. Ze wil niet meer benzine gebruiken dan strikt noodzakelijk.

'Als mens mag je het voedsel of de habitat van andere dieren niet vernietigen. Je neemt slechts wat je nodig hebt, want je bent niet alleen.' Dit is het Samische concept van toereikendheid, *birgejupmi* genaamd: je neemt alleen wat nodig is uit de natuur, nooit meer dan dat. Het is precies het tegenovergestelde van het moderne idee van duurzaamheid, dat gebaseerd is op het maximale overschot dat kan worden onttrokken zonder de capaciteit van de natuur om de hulpbron in stand te houden, te vernietigen. Het is een belangrijk onderscheid. De natuur begrijpen en er goed gebruik van maken was niet alleen essentieel voor het leven in het noordpoolgebied, maar ook een waarde op zich. Maar birgejupmi gaat volgens Māret verloren door 'dit gelddenken'.

Ze gaat er prat op de oude kennis te leren en te bewaren. Kunnen zien of een berkenboom ziek is en dan weten dat een zieke berkenboom antilichamen zal produceren die ook voor zieke mensen heilzaam zijn. De lucht en de planten kunnen lezen om te zien wanneer het gaat sneeuwen, wanneer het droog wordt en hoelang de sneeuw zal blijven liggen.

'Ik lees de natuur en dan check ik mijn apps op mijn telefoon en zie: Ik heb gelijk!'

Bliksem in de herfst betekent dat de vroege zomer volgend jaar warm zou moeten zijn. En de kleur van de berkenbladeren in de herfst en de tijd die ze nodig hebben om te vallen, geven aan hoelang de sneeuw in het voorjaar zal blijven liggen. Dit jaar waren de kleuren slecht: groen en bruin zonder rood en geel, niet het klassieke, mooie scala van geel en rood. Māret vreest dat het een natte en lange winter wordt in plaats van een koude, droge, korte winter.

Haar eigen voorspellingen zijn gebaseerd op het evolutionaire geheugen van de bomen zelf. De berkenbladeren worden in de herfst zo spectaculair rood omdat de boom zich op de winter voorbereidt door al het chlorofyl uit zijn bladeren te trekken en op te slaan voor het voorjaar, door overtollig vocht uit zijn stam te weren en door de haarvaten in het floëem, de binnenste schors die als een stelsel van bloedvaten fungeert, af te sluiten. Het resterende caroteen veroorzaakt de rode kleur. Maar als een boom te nat is of de omstandigheden te warm, waagt hij een gokje door de bladeren langer aan de takken te laten zitten, waardoor een deel van het chlorofyl actief blijft en de bladeren zoveel mogelijk energie kunnen verzamelen. Het is alsof de boom weet dat de winter lang zal duren.

'Ik ben niet boos op de bomen,' zegt Māret droevig, ook al zuigt de berk al het licht en alle voedingsstoffen op, zodat het korstmos dat de rendieren nodig hebben, niet kan overleven. 'Ik kan me altijd aanpassen aan de natuur. De natuur verandert voortdurend – we moesten altijd al voorbereid zijn. Ik ben hoopvol voor de natuur, maar niet voor de mens.'

Mārets helpers spreiden rendierhuiden uit op banken en dekken de tafels. Zij gaat verder met het snijden van vlees als de eerste afgevaardigden in de zaal beginnen aan te komen, gekleed in hun fijn geborduurde traditionele vilten jasjes en rendierleren broeken en schoenen. Hallgeir komt hallo zeggen en tapt water uit een grote koelbox in zijn eigen persoonlijke handgesneden berkenhouten beker. Ik zie dat de meeste afgevaardigden hun eigen beker aan een touwtje aan hun riem dragen.

'Een grote bijeenkomst! Een zeer grote bijeenkomst!' zegt hij met een stiekeme knipoog, alsof hij een dubbelagent is, wat hij in zekere zin ook is.

Vertegenwoordigers van de Sami uit het hele noorden van Noorwegen zijn bijeengekomen om te praten over de nieuwe rendierwet, de voorgestelde ontwikkelingen op het gebied van mijnbouw, windmolenparken in Finnmark en Tromsø en een fonds voor aanpassing aan de klimaatverandering om de Sami te helpen bij de overgang naar nieuwe middelen van bestaan.

Volgens Māret reikt het probleem echter al veel verder dan Noorwegen alleen. 'Iemand moet de rekening betalen voor dit leven, deze levensstijl – en het ziet ernaar uit dat het de dieren en onze inheemse manier van leven zijn. Dat is de prijs.'

De Sami-identiteit, hun eenheid met de natuur, sterft met de habitat die haar in stand houdt. Zij ondervinden nu het leeuwendeel van de gevolgen van de klimaatverandering, maar op lange termijn zullen het de mensen in warmere oorden of in kuststeden zijn die meer te lijden hebben van overstromingen en hittegolven. Het Noordpoolgebied zal naar verwachting steeds meer onder druk komen te staan van vluchtelingen, aangezien mensen verder zuidelijk op de vlucht zullen slaan vanwege misoogsten en extreme temperaturen.[4] De Sami zullen zich waarschijnlijk wel kunnen aanpassen waar ze zijn.

Māret is echter niet zelfgenoegzaam en maakt zich zorgen om alle anderen. Ze wil dat de mensen de gebeurtenissen in Noorwegen zien als een waarschuwing: 'Je staat niet bovenaan de keten. De natuur staat bovenaan. En als je haar tegenwerkt, zal ze je aanvallen. Dat is wat er nu gebeurt.'

3.

De Slapende Beer

Aziatische lariks, *Larix gmelinii*

Krasnojarsk, Rusland
56° 01' 00" N

Van alle bossen in de wereld is de Russische taiga het grootste. Hij beslaat meer dan de helft van de Russische landmassa en strekt zich uit over bijna acht miljoen vierkante kilometer, twee continenten en tien tijdzones. Het is een groen tapijt van bomen bovenop de permafrost en vormt meer dan de helft van de planetaire motor van de boreale zone, die de patronen van wind, neerslag, klimaat en oceaancirculatie op het noordelijk halfrond regelt. Het boreale gebied bestaat grotendeels uit de Russische taiga, en de taiga bestaat voornamelijk uit lariks.

Vanaf de Witte Zee, onder de kin van de paardenkop van Fennoscandinavië, waar Noorwegen en Rusland elkaar ontmoeten, tot aan de internationale datumgrens in de Beringstraat, bestaan de boomgrens en het noordelijke deel van de taiga uit eindeloze wouden van één geslacht, de Larix. Meer dan een derde van de taiga (37 procent) bestaat uit lariksen, die als soort de hoeksteen vormen. Net als de den in Schotland heeft de lariks beter dan welke andere boom ook met zijn omgeving leren omgaan en domineert hij daarom het ecosysteem, waarbij hij de levenscycli en de evolutionaire paden van andere planten en dieren vormgeeft. Zijn bladafval vormt de basis van de bodem, zijn cycli van zaadproductie regelen de populaties van vogels en knaagdieren, zijn vraag naar licht bepaalt waaruit de ondergroei kan bestaan, en zijn weerstand tegen vuur en zijn bereidheid tot het koloniseren van verbrande grond betekenen dat hij de architectuur van het taigabos in Siberië zoals wij het kennen, heeft bepaald.

Om over de toekomst van het boreale bos na te denken, moet je kijken naar wat er op de taiga gebeurt. De veranderingen hier hangen af van hoe de lariks reageert op de ongelooflijke opwarming die in heel Siberië plaatsvindt. Niemand weet meer over lariks dan de wetenschappers van Ruslands topinstituut voor bosonderzoek, het V.N. Soekatsjev Instituut voor het Bos van de Siberische Afdeling van de Russische Academie van Wetenschappen, gevestigd in de stad Krasnojarsk. Het district Krasnojarsk is ook de thuishaven van Ary Mas, het fabelachtige bos hoog op de wereld, de meest noordelijke bomen op aarde.

Krasnojarsk ligt vier tijdzones ten oosten van Moskou en iets ten noorden van het punt waar de grenzen van Kazachstan, Mongolië en Rusland samenkomen. Er is ook een van 's werelds grootste aluminiumsmelterijen gevestigd. Op mijn eerste ochtend in de stad word ik wakker in een backpackershostel. Het zwakke februarizonlicht heeft moeite om door de nevel te dringen die boven de skyline hangt. De kamer is bloedheet door een enorme radiator die over de hele lengte van een muur loopt. Het is maar -10, zei de receptioniste me toen ik incheckte na mijn lange vlucht uit Moskou, de avond tevoren. De verwarming werd ontworpen voor kouder tijden. Ik open het dubbele raam en besef onmiddellijk mijn vergissing: ijzige lucht stroomt binnen, maar is niet verfrissend. Ze heeft een nare bijtende smaak.

De reden waarom het koudste deel van het jaar in Siberië, en het Noordpoolgebied in het algemeen, februari is en niet het midden van de winter, wanneer de dagen het kortst zijn, is dat de met sneeuw bedekte grond warmte blijft uitstralen naar de atmosfeer, waardoor de aarde afkoelt. Sneeuw weerkaatst de kortegolfstraling en isoleert de grond eronder tegen zowel het opwarmende effect van de zonnestralen als tegen het afkoelende effect van de koude lucht, waardoor de temperatuur onder de sneeuw constant blijft. Maar terwijl sneeuw kortgolvige straling – het rood en geel in het lichtspectrum – weerkaatst, absorbeert het langgolvige straling – het blauw en groen – die het 's nachts weer de ruimte instraalt. 's Nachts is de koudste lucht die welke zich het dichtst bij het oppervlak van het sneeuwpak bevindt. Dat is de reden waarom je het warmer hebt als je onder een boom slaapt, want de boom kaatst de langgolvige straling terug naar de oppervlakte in plaats van deze naar boven te laten ontsnappen. Dit afkoelende effect van het sneeuwpakket creëert een energietekort, dat bij rustig weer kan resulteren in een temperatuurinversie waarbij de lucht aan de grond kouder is dan de atmosfeer erboven. In stabiele hogedruksituaties die dagen- of wekenlang aanhouden en waarbij de sneeuw warmte van de aarde blijft wegstralen, kunnen temperatuurinversies van enkele honderden meters ontstaan waarin het normale proces van het opstijgen van warme lucht wordt onderbroken. In de heldere lucht van de toendra kan waterdamp vast komen te zitten en bevriezen als mist. In steden wordt in plaats daarvan de luchtverontreiniging die normaal zou opstijgen op dat lagere niveau vastgehouden, en Krasnojarsk, dat ooit door Anton Tsjechov werd uitgeroepen tot 'de beste en mooiste van alle Siberische steden', staat nu bekend om een wazige smog die het leven van veel van zijn inwoners bekort.[1]

Tsjechov was gebiologeerd door de pracht van de rivier de Jenisej, en het is de rivier die de stad toen en nu nog steeds bepaalt. De op twee na grootste stad van Siberië werd gesticht als onderdeel van de Russische expansie naar het oosten in 1628 toen Kozakken een fort bouwden aan de samenloop van de rivieren de Jenisej en de Katsja om aanvallen van de inheemse bevolking af te slaan. Net als de West-Europese naties in de zeventiende en achttiende eeuw expedities en veroordeelden verbanden naar nieuwe overzeese gebieden, deed Rusland hetzelfde op het land, waarbij het de inheemse bevolking van Siberië uitbuitte, volgens

Tsjechov met 'de gebruikelijke methode, door hen verslaafd te maken aan drank.' Serieuze kolonisatie van Siberië moest echter wachten op een weg en de beroemde brug van Krasnojarsk over de enorme rivier de Jenisej, die in 1741 gereed kwam en nu het Russische tienroebelbiljet siert. De ontwikkeling kwam weer in een stroomversnelling na de ontdekking van goud en de aanleg van de Trans-Siberische spoorweg in 1895. Krasnojarsk was ook het verbanningsoord voor acht decembristen na het mislukken van hun opstand tegen tsaar Nicolaas I in 1825 en vormde, in die traditie, een knooppunt van het systeem van werkkampen, de Goelag, tijdens het stalinistische tijdperk. Tot op de dag van vandaag is er nog steeds een strafkolonie. Tijdens de Tweede Wereldoorlog werden talrijke fabrieken van de westelijke Sovjet-Unie overgebracht naar Krasnojarsk, buiten het bereik van de binnenvallende Duitse legers en dicht bij de slavenarbeiders van de Goelag.

Als toegangspoort tot Siberië werd Krasnojarsk onder de Sovjets een wetenschappelijk en educatief centrum met instituten voor metallurgie, lucht- en ruimtevaart, geneeskunde, landbouw en technologie. De grootste en meest voor de hand liggende natuurlijke hulpbron was de taiga, en het eerste academische instituut dat er werd gesticht was dan ook het Siberisch Instituut voor het Bos in 1930. Na de oorlog groeide deze uit tot de Technologische Staatsuniversiteit van Siberië, een van de zes universiteiten in de stad, en het Soekatsjev-Instituut, dat in 1944 in Moskou werd opgericht en in 1959 naar Krasnojarsk werd overgeplaatst, werd het belangrijkste centrum voor bosbouwonderzoek in Rusland.

Het instituut is genoemd naar zijn stichter, Vladimir Soekatsjev, een lariksspecialist en een weinig bekende pionier op het gebied van mondiale ecologie en milieubescherming. Soekatsjev schreef een baanbrekend werk over ecologie, *Moerassen: Hun ontstaan, ontwikkeling en eigenschappen* (1926), dat ijverige Leninisten, die uit waren op een maximale landbouwproductie, ervan overtuigde er niet te veel droog te leggen. 'Biogeocoenose' was zijn ruimere definitie van Karl Mobius' concept van een ecosysteem dat zowel de atmosfeer als rotsen, bodem, planten en dieren omvat, die allen in een zich voortdurend ontwikkelende wisselwerking verwikkeld zijn. Hij inspireerde een studentenbeweging van een miljoen natuurbeschermers in de USSR in de jaren 1950 en was de eerste die ontdekte dat lariksen bijwortels kunnen vormen (uit niet-wortelweefsel) om vocht te onttrekken aan permafrost. Dit inzicht is misschien wel zijn belangrijkste bijdrage tot het begrip van de vroegere evolutie van de taiga en daardoor van haar toekomst. Het was Soekatsjev die als eerste begreep dat de relatie van de lariks met het ijs de basis vormde van het Siberische landschap zoals wij dat kennen.

Telkens wanneer een ijstijd een golf van gletsjers uit het noorden deed afzakken, werd de vegetatie weggevaagd en werden de soorten in hoeken gedwongen waar de gletsjers niet konden komen. Na elke dooi kwamen de planten, bomen, dieren en later ook de mensen tevoorschijn uit hun schuilplaatsen – refugia zoals wetenschappers ze noemen – en begonnen het proces van kolonisatie opnieuw. Het strategische antwoord van de lariks op dit lange spel van natuurlijke selectie is haar bereidheid tot hybridisatie, die blijk geeft van een extreem groot ecologisch aanpassingsvermogen aan uiteenlopende groeiomstandigheden van de Oostzee tot de Stille Oceaan en van de boomgrens in het hoge noorden tot aan de zuidgrens van de taiga op de 45e breedtegraad in Mongolië.

De enorme verscheidenheid aan aanpassingen in de grootte van de kegels, het aantal zaden, de kleur van de naalden en de hoeveelheid rode en roze kleur op de helmknoppen van de bloemen van de bomen hebben in de Russische bosbouw gedurende het grootste deel van de twintigste eeuw tot langlopende ruzies en obsessief onderzoek geleid. Sovjetonderzoekers van het Soekatsjev-Instituut wogen zaden, telden naalden, distilleerden de oliën van meerdere soorten en ondersoorten en testten vermeerderingsmethoden. Eén bevinding, namelijk dat grondwater op niet meer dan 1,5 meter diepte een noodzakelijke voorwaarde was voor de succesvolle vestiging van zaailingen, zou belangrijk blijken voor de toekomst. Eén arme onderzoeker, Abaimov, heeft het grootste deel van de jaren 1980 besteed aan het meten van dertigduizend larikskegels, op zoek naar een meetmethode om soorten uit elkaar te houden, maar hij kwam tot de conclusie dat het een nutteloze exercitie was. De hoek van de zaadschubben in elke kegel, zoals ontdekt door Soekatsjev in 1924, blijft een van de enige consequente verschillen tussen de soorten, die voor het overige zeer moeilijk uit elkaar te houden zijn.

Alle lariksen hebben een edele uitstraling. Hun fijne naalden, heldergroen in het voorjaar, glanzend oranje in de herfst, contrasteren met een grijze, enigszins geschubde schors zoals die van de grove den. In hun massale gelederen kunnen ze over een heuvel flitsen. Lariks is de enige loofverliezende naaldboom. Een kurkentrekkervormige top garandeert maximale lichtinval, waarbij elke tak zich naar beneden welft in elegante bochten die lijken te druipen van de naalden. In het voorjaar vormt hij kleine paarsachtige kegels die op snoepjes lijken en in de loop van het jaar langzaam oranje worden.

Men is het er nu algemeen over eens dat de taiga bestaat uit vier afzonderlijke zones met larikssoorten (taxa), die als verticale strepen over Siberië zijn getrokken.[2] Van de Witte Zee in het westen tot de Oeral ten oosten van Moskou is de ondersoort *Larix sukaczewii*, ontdekt en benoemd door Soekatsjev, dominant. Vanaf de Oeral neemt de veelzijdige, maar permafrost-schuwende *Larix sibirica* (Siberische lariks) het stokje over tot aan de ontmoeting met de *Larix gmelinii* (Aziatische lariks) aan de Jenisej, waar de twee soorten elkaar hebben gevonden in een smalle strook van honderddertig kilometer breed van een hybride die *Larix czekanowskii* wordt genoemd, ter ere van de Poolse botanicus die hem heeft ontdekt. In het uitgestrekte midden van Siberië, het hoge noorden vanaf het schiereiland Tajmyr tot aan de rivier de Lena, is L. gmelinii dominant, de onbetwiste koning van de koude. Een verwante ondersoort, *Larix gmelinii var. japonica*, soms *Larix cajanderi* (de Aziatische lariks) genoemd, vormt de oostelijke band van het woud van de Lena naar het oosten tot de Tsjoektsjenzee en de Beringstraat, Kamtsjatka en de Zee van

Sachalin, de geboorteplaats van de grote Pacifische walvissen.

Soekatsjev veronderstelde dat het moment dat deze verschillende soorten met elkaar in contact kwamen en hybridiseerden relatief recent moest zijn en dat ze allen waren ontstaan in verschillende refugia aan het begin van het Pleistoceen. Hij toonde aan dat de dominantie van de Aziatische lariks hand in hand ging met de permafrost. Naarmate men verder het binnenland van Siberië ingaat, vormen deze soorten een steeds groter percentage van het bos, totdat in het uiterste noorden duizenden kilometers lang uitsluitend nog zuivere lariksbossen door het landschap lijken op te rukken. Overal waar ijs lag, maakten de Siberische lariks en andere ondersoorten plaats voor de jongste, taaiste, nieuwkomer op het terrein, de Aziaat. Maar nu de permafrost aan het smelten is, verschuift het machtsevenwicht in Siberië. Het lot van de taiga en de permafrost zijn altijd met elkaar verbonden geweest, maar tot voor kort keken de boswachters van het Soekatsjev-Instituut alleen maar omhoog naar de bomen, niet naar beneden, naar de grond onder hun voeten.

In het Sovjettijdperk was het gebruikelijk om wetenschappelijke instellingen te clusteren in een eigen wijk, een beetje zoals een modern bedrijvenpark, hetzij om innovatief denken te bevorderen door wetenschappers bij elkaar te plaatsen, hetzij om hen beter te controleren. De academische wijk van Krasnojarsk, Akademgorodok, ligt ongeveer acht kilometer buiten de stad. Een taxi, zegt de receptioniste van mijn hotel, is de enige manier om er te komen. Ze heeft liever niet dat ik de stadsbus neem.

Terwijl ik naar de taxistandplaats loop, word ik onafgebroken aan het industriële doel van de stad herinnerd doordat mijn neusgaten worden bekleed met een zwarte laag. Ik doorkruis grote parken, beplant met boreale soorten en met geplaveide paden die een lus vormen langs een steile helling boven de rivier de Jenisej. Zelfs hier, drieduizend kilometer ten zuiden van de Arctische kust waar hij uitmondt in de zee, is de Jenisej enorm, al bijna tweeduizend kilometer verwijderd van zijn oorsprong in het Baikalmeer. De rivier vormt het hart van de stad en de mist wervelt in achtvormige figuren op het zwarte water in zijn omlijsting van ijskorsten. De rivier is vloeibaar vanwege de waterkrachtcentrale dertig kilometer stroomopwaarts, die voorkomt dat het water bevriest en die het grootste deel van de energie voor de regio levert. Ver weg op een bevroren plaat boren figuren met capuchons gaten in het ijs en laten lijnen zakken, op zoek naar vissen die genetisch zijn aangepast aan overwintering onder ijs.

Aan de andere kant van het park loop ik door een regelmatig patroon van straten, bezaaid met negentiende-eeuwse houten herenhuizen met gebeeldhouwde filigrein gevels. In een ander park is een kinderspeelplaats gemaakt van ijs en uit een omroepinstallatie op een paal klinkt muzak. Het pad is afgezoomd met berken, lariksen, dennen en sparren waaronder stapels versnipperd zaad liggen, vogels plunderen de dennenappels voor hun wintervoorraad. Het centrale plein met het theater, het stadhuis en het ballet wordt aan één kant gedomineerd door een enorm kruispunt met acht rijstroken en een betonnen systeem van voetgangersbruggen waar daklozen zonder handschoenen papieren bekertjes omhoog houden en vragen om wat kleingeld. Het is in elk geval maar -18 volgens de digitale display aan de voorkant van het theater.

'Akademgorodok!' De taxichauffeur knikt, en we haasten ons vooruit over een brede snelweg, het bos in. Krasnojarsk ligt midden op de taiga. Aan alle kanten hebben we uitzicht op de scherp met bomen afgetekende heuvels in de verte. De academische stad wordt aan de ene kant begrensd door een steile val naar de rivier over de hoge zandstenen kliffen waaraan de stad haar naam dankt: *krasnyi* - 'rood' en *yar* - 'klif', en aan de andere kant door een ondoordringbare muur van bos. De lucht klaart op en reusachtige grove dennen lichten oranje op in het ochtendlicht, terwijl de zilveren strepen van de berken ertussen als lichtflitsen flikkeren. De lariks begint verder naar het noorden, maar voordat ik de bomen zelf bezoek, moet ik met de wetenschappers praten, om te leren hoe ik naar het landschap moet kijken.

De veranderingen in Siberië zijn complex. Het is niet simpelweg een kwestie van ontbossing, zoals in Schotland, of bebossing, zoals in Noorwegen, maar een traag verlopende transformatie van de structuur en de samenstelling van het bos. Op sommige plaatsen verschuift de boomgrens helemaal niet, op andere trekt hij zich juist terug, terwijl in het zuiden het bos opbrandt en niet meer aangroeit, en in het midden maakt de lariks plaats voor andere soorten die minder efficiënt zijn in het opnemen van koolstof en het produceren van zuurstof. En ondertussen ontdooit de permafrost, een fenomeen dat al het andere overschaduwt.

We passeren wat ooit een controlepost was en komen in een raster van grote hoekige betonnen gebouwen die in de sneeuw zijn weggedoken en me het gevoel geven in een industriegebied te zijn. In het midden staat een kolencentrale die geelbruine rook uitblaast. De woonwijken lijkt men er achteraf nog even bij te hebben verzonnen: flatgebouwen met identieke bevroren kinderspeelplaatsen – ijskoude schommels die stijf in de windstille ochtendlucht hangen – markeren elke derde of vierde straat, maar er is geen levende ziel te zien.

De taxi zet me af voor een onopvallend betonnen blok dat niet te onderscheiden is van alle andere, gebouwd in de jaren 1950.

'Soekatsjev? vraag ik.

'Soekatsjev.' Hij knikt en stopt het rolletje roebels dat ik hem aanbied zonder omkijken in zijn zak.

Op de trappen in de felle zon, met een muts, handschoenen en een redelijk dunne jas aan, wacht Nadezjda Tsjebakova op mij. Zij heeft kort grijs haar en de snelle, maar even snel weer vervagende glimlach van een menslievende wetenschapper die worstelt om de kennis die ze vergaard heeft te verzoenen met de waanzin van de wereld om haar heen. Ze lacht veel, maar dat betekent niet dat ze de dingen leuk vindt. De genereuze onderzoekssubsidies en het hoge aanzien van het Sovjettijdperk zijn voorbij, maar de Russische cultuur van geheimhouding en achterdocht is nog springlevend. Ik mag het instituut niet binnen zonder allerlei brieven en goedkeuringen die drie maanden van tevoren moeten worden afgegeven, dus Nadezjda wuift het hele idee weg en stelt voor dat we in plaats daarvan een eindje gaan wandelen.

Beneden ons snijdt de zwarte stroom van de rivier een lijn tussen de met verblindende sneeuw bedekte rotsen. Boven ons blijft een halve maan hangen in de inmiddels korenbloemblauwe ochtendhemel. Aan de andere kant van de vallei stoten schoorstenen linten zwarte rook uit, en rode en zwarte torenflats werpen schaduwen over het water. Aan deze kant schittert de gouden koepel van een gloednieuwe orthodoxe kerk tussen de bomen, als bewijs van de vroomheid van een oligarch. Vanaf het instituut naar de rivier loopt een bos binnen een omheining, het onderzoeksarboretum, een verzameling van vierhonderd soorten waar de oligarch blijkbaar graag datsja's wil bouwen. Alle boreale soorten en meer zijn er te vinden, een hele menigte glinsterende bomen, in hun zware jassen van sneeuw, naalden omhuld door ijs.

'Ik vind het hier geweldig,' zegt Nadezjda, terwijl ze het uitzicht op de rivier in zich opneemt en de rand van haar bril de ochtendzon vangt. 'De natuur, de dieren, het bos, dat is mijn ding.' Maar toen ze hier 47 jaar geleden aankwam, was dat wel anders. Ze was gedeprimeerd en miste haar familie. Haar ouders hadden veel opgeofferd voor haar carrière, maar die hield haar vervolgens bij hen vandaan. Ze waren boeren die tijdens de harde stalinistische tijden van de jaren 1930 de Wolga hadden verlaten en werk hadden gevonden in een automobielfabriek in de buurt van Moskou. Later werd Nadezjda's moeder kokkin op een kleuterschool. Ze moedigden haar aan om gaan studeren en uiteindelijk studeerde ze Engels aan de beste universiteit van Moskou. Haar moeder stuurde haar hele salaris naar Nadezjda om haar te steunen, maar die slaagde niet voor haar eerste jaar en maakte vervolgens de allesbepalende overstap naar aardrijkskunde.

In de jaren 1960 was de Academie van Wetenschappen in Moskou en Leningrad, vooruitlopend op het Westen, het centrum van geavanceerd onderzoek naar wat de wereldberoemde klimatoloog Mikhail Budyko 'het probleem van de klimaataanpassing door de mens' zou gaan noemen. In 1961 had Budyko zijn paper 'De theorie van het evenwicht tussen warmte en water op het aardoppervlak' gepresenteerd tijdens het derde congres van het Geografische Genootschap van de USSR, waarin hij stelde dat antropogene klimaatverandering nu onvermijdelijk was en dat het menselijk energieverbruik moest worden aangepakt. In 1962 publiceerde hij het baanbrekende artikel 'Klimaatverandering en de manier waarop deze plaatsvindt' in het *Bulletin van de Academie van Wetenschappen* van de USSR. Daarin legde hij uit hoe de vernietiging van de ijsbedekking zou leiden tot 'een belangrijke verandering in het regime van de atmosferische circulatie'. Nadezjda was net begonnen aan de Academie van Wetenschappen toen Budyko in 1969 zijn artikel 'Het effect van zonnestraling op het klimaat van de Aarde' publiceerde, waarin hij uitlegde hoe het polaire zee-ijs/albedo-terugkoppelingsmechanisme de klimaatverandering zou voortstuwen. Zij begon aan haar postdoctorale onderzoek toen zijn baanbrekende boek *Klimaat en leven* uitkwam. Nadat het twee jaar later, in 1974, in het Engels was vertaald, zou het de basis leggen voor het nieuwe vak van de klimatologie. Inmiddels was Nadezjda volstrekt gefascineerd geraakt.

Toen ze op het Soekatsjev-Instituut aankwam om haar postdoctorale werk voort te zetten met onderzoek naar de invloed van het klimaat op de boreale vegetatie in de bergachtige bossen ten zuiden van Krasnojarsk, was ze verbaasd te ontdekken dat zij de enige was die aan klimaatmodellering deed op een faculteit vol bosbouwers. Gewend als ze waren aan hun jaarlijkse zomerritueel van veldstudies in het bos, hadden ze een hekel aan modellen. Bijna een halve eeuw later is ze nog altijd de enige.

Na het vertrek van Soekatsjev werd het instituut geleid door dendro-klimatologen die vooral druk waren het vroegere klimaat van Siberië te reconstrueren, en niemand leek geïnteresseerd in vooruitkijken. Internationale wetenschappers werden zich echter bewust van Nadezjda's werk en in 1989 werd zij uitgenodigd om in Wenen te komen werken aan het Internationaal Instituut voor Toegepaste Systeemanalyse met topklimaatwetenschappers van over de hele wereld. In Wenen werkte Nadezjda aan grote modellen voor de wereldwijde vegetatie. Ze keerde terug naar

Krasnojarsk met een hernieuwd gevoel van urgentie en verwondering over wat er mogelijk was, en begon met het bouwen van toekomstmodellen voor de bossen van Siberië aan de hand van de nieuw ontwikkelde scenario's van het Intergovernmental Panel on Climate Change. Haar bevindingen waren alarmerend. De noordelijke boomgrens zou iets naar de pool verschuiven, maar de echte verandering betrof de zuidelijke grens van de taiga. Door toenemende droogte en frequentere branden zou de steppe van Centraal-Azië zich uitbreiden en de uitgebrande taiga opslokken, zodat deze niet meer kon regenereren: het grootste bos ter wereld zou van onderaf afsterven.

'En dat,' zegt Nadezjda, 'is wat we nu zien gebeuren.'

In een warm café waar schuimende warme chocolade en taigathee – een mengsel van munt, wilgenkruid en wilde frambozen – wordt geserveerd, ontmoet ik Elena Kukofskaja, Nadezjda's collega en een van de meest vooraanstaande deskundigen op het gebied van bosbranden in Siberië. Terwijl studenten om ons heen op laptops tikken, legt zij uit dat brand een natuurlijk onderdeel van de boscyclus is, en zelfs de reden dat de taiga zijn huidige vorm heeft aangenomen. Lariksbossen zijn betrekkelijk open met grote ruimten tussen de bomen en een dichte bladstrooisellaag die de grond vochtig houdt en voorkomt dat er onder de bomen een dichte ondergroei ontstaat die extreme branden kan aanwakkeren. De lariks met zijn bladverliezende naalden en dikke schors is brandbestendig en heeft een lange levensduur, op voorwaarde dat de branden niet te hevig zijn. Tijdens ons huidige Holoceen (de periode na de laatste ijstijd) richtte het vuur maar weinig schade aan in de zuivere lariksbossen en schroeide takken en stammen zonder de volwassen bomen te doden, maar het bladafval en de bovenste bodemlaag werden verteerd zodat de minerale bodem eronder tevoorschijn kwam – de bodem die de larikszaden nodig hebben om te ontkiemen. De bossen van Noord-Amerika zijn ondertussen over het algemeen veel jonger, minder dan 200 jaar oud, aangezien branden hele opstanden van sparren, espen en dennen vernietigen, hetgeen betekent dat cohorten zaailingen zich op hetzelfde ogenblik vestigen, wat leidt tot wat bosbouwers 'opstanden van gelijke leeftijd' noemen. Maar de dynamiek van de branden is aan het veranderen. Na recente branden die Elena heeft bestudeerd, zijn de bomen helemaal niet meer teruggekomen.

In de hoge taiga aan de boomgrens, in Ary Mas bijvoorbeeld in het noorden van het district, was vuur altijd een zeldzaamheid en meestal het gevolg van blikseminslag. Daar is de interval tussen de branden lang, tot soms wel 300 jaar, maar de frequentie en intensiteit nemen toe naarmate je zuidelijker gaat. In de lagere breedtegraden bedroeg de brandinterval vroeger 5 tot 30 jaar, afhankelijk van de regenval. Op sommige plaatsen zijn branden inmiddels een jaarlijks terugkerend fenomeen. Naarmate de temperaturen zijn gestegen en de bodem droger is geworden, werden de branden heter, langduriger en frequenter, waardoor meer van de bodem wordt aangetast en het voor de lariks moeilijker wordt om zich nog te herstellen.

'Mensen hebben geprobeerd nieuwe bomen aan te planten, maar die worden een jaar later ook verbrand,' zegt ze.

Herhaaldelijk afbranden maakt het terrein bijna onmogelijk voor bomen om in te wortelen. In de plaats daarvan zijn planten gekomen die van zeer marginale bodems houden. Dit betekent dat struiken zoals wilgen de lariks verdringen en dichte houtclusters vormen die de volgende keer heter zullen branden. Na verloop van tijd zetten de brandcycli de deur open voor grassen uit de steppe die bomen verhinderen te ontkiemen en al het andere verstikken.

Verder naar het noorden zorgen hetere branden en drogere zomers ervoor dat op de middelste taiga, ten noorden van Krasnojarsk, de grove den de plaats inneemt van de lariks op plaatsen waar brand heeft gewoed. Dit heeft grote gevolgen voor de structuur van het bos en voor de wijze waarop andere wetenschappers de 'ecosysteemdiensten' ervan kwantificeren en modelleren. Aangezien verschillende soorten een verschillende waterhuishouding hebben, is hun bijdrage aan de atmosfeer en het klimaat gevarieerd en uniek. Van de kooldioxide die de taiga vastlegt, neemt de lariks

55 procent voor zijn rekening, hoewel deze hooguit 40 procent van de bomen uitmaakt. Deze ene soort is de grootste bosvormige bron van zuurstof op aarde. Omdat lariks bladverliezend is, transpireert hij veel meer water dan altijdgroene bomen, neemt 20 procent meer koolstofdioxide op dan dennen, en de bodem onder lariks, bedekt als hij is met half vergane lariksnaalden, stoot een kwart minder koolstofdioxide uit dan die onder dennen. Bovendien is een bos dat opwarmt minder efficiënt in het afvangen en vastleggen van koolstof, omdat bomen te weinig water hebben om te fotosynthetiseren, stoppen met groeien of eerder hun bladeren verliezen.[3] En toch zijn veel mondiale modellen gebaseerd op vaste aannames over de hoeveelheid koolstof die bossen kunnen opslaan en negeren ze hoezeer die bossen aan het veranderen zijn. Volgens één studie zullen de bossen wereldwijd tegen 2040 de helft minder kooldioxide absorberen dan nu het geval is als de huidige opwarmingstendensen aanhouden.[4]

Veel zorgwekkender, zegt Elena, is de vraag of er überhaupt nog bos over zal zijn. Wat haar nu zorgen baart, is de enorme hoeveelheid bos die inmiddels verbrandt. Het bos is droger. Door houtkap zonder vergunning om China's explosieve groei in de bouw te voeden, is er veel brandbaar afval. Bovendien betekent een warmere, vochtigere atmosfeer een verdubbeling van het aantal onweersbuien en een verdubbeling van het aantal ontbrandingen als gevolg van blikseminslagen. Elena's interesse is niet langer louter academisch. Ze is net bevallen van haar tweede kind. In 2019 bedekte zwarte rook wekenlang de stad Krasnojarsk, en konden de mensen geen adem halen.

'Elk jaar, elk brandseizoen nu, wachten we af, zetten we ons schrap.'

In 2019 verbrandde meer dan vijftien miljoen hectare, een gebied groter dan Oostenrijk. Vóór 2018 bedroeg de gemiddelde omvang van de uitstoot door natuurbranden 2 megaton kooldioxide per jaar. In 2019 was dat 5 megaton. Later in 2020, nadat ik haar had bezocht, zouden de branden in Siberië alle records breken, met een uitstoot van 16 megaton alleen al in de maand juni. Bosbranden op deze schaal waren niet voorspeld tot 2060.

Tijdens onze lunch in het Huis van de Wetenschappers, glimlacht Nadezjda wanneer ik haar vertel wat Elena zei. Deze veranderingen had ze een decennium geleden al voorspeld met haar modellen. Ze geeft me een kaart. Het is een uitdraai van haar laatst gepubliceerde onderzoek in het Amerikaanse tijdschrift *Environmental Research Letters.*[5] Wat haar nu interesseert is wat de veranderingen in het ecosysteem betekenen voor de mens. Het artikel, dat later in de *New York Times* verscheen, heeft een technisch klinkende titel ('Een bepaling van het landschapsvormende potentieel voor de leefbaarheid en "aantrekkelijkheid" van heel Russisch-Azië in een warmere eenentwintigste eeuw'), maar dramatische implicaties.[6]

Nadezjda's eerdere werk toonde aan dat zelfs bij gematigde opwarmingsscenario's Siberië een veel hogere regionale opwarming zou blijven ondervinden en dat het bos naar het noorden zal opschuiven als het niet voor die tijd al verbrandt. Aangezien er echter in het noorden niet veel land is om te koloniseren, betekent dit uiteindelijk dat 50 procent of meer van het bos tegen het einde van de eeuw in steppe zal zijn veranderd.

In de jaren 1930 ontwikkelde de USSR een systeem om de leefomstandigheden van de mens te classificeren op basis van de ernst van het klimaat en het comfort. Het systeem werd gebruikt om de barre levensomstandigheden te compenseren met salarisbonussen en vormde de basis voor opeenvolgende bureaucratische pogingen om migratie naar het oosten van Rusland aan te moedigen, gesubsidieerd door de staat. Het kent zeven categorieën, en de twee beste zones, 'gunstig' en 'meest gunstig', zijn momenteel niet te vinden in Siberië, maar uit Nadezjda's model blijkt dat dit binnenkort zal veranderen.

De lijnen op de kaart geven aan dat bij de hoogste voorspellingen – een opwarming tot 9 graden Celsius voor het noordoosten van Siberië – de zuidelijke grens van het bos duizend kilometer naar het noorden zal opschuiven, waardoor tegen het einde van de eeuw tot 85 procent van Siberië, drie miljoen vierkante kilometer, geschikt zal zijn voor landbouw. Er zijn nu al veranderingen op til: Het Russische agrarische megabedrijf RusAgro breidt zijn uitgestrekte tarwevelden in de buurt van Vladivostok uit en immigranten uit China worden aangemoedigd om landerijen aan de overkant van de rivier de Amoer te exploiteren. Ondertussen vertoonden de Noord-Amerikaanse rendementen in 2019 en 2020 de eerste tekenen van een achteruitgang.[7]

Volgens Nadezjda's laatste model zal tot de helft van Siberië 'gunstig' of beter worden voor menselijke bewoning, maar Nadezjda en haar co-auteurs wagen zich niet aan de onvermijdelijke politieke conclusie. Gedurende het grootste deel van de menselijke geschiedenis heeft de mensheid over de hele planeet een zeer smalle strook land bewoond, binnen een bepaald temperatuurbereik. Hier en daar raakt die strook nu echter al de bovengrens van dat bereik, en tegen 2070 zullen meer dan drie miljard mensen buiten die strook leven – de meesten van hen in Zuidoost-Azië, slechts een grens of twee verwijderd van het uitgestrekte, onlangs vruchtbare geworden oosten van Rusland.[8] Binnen enkele decennia zullen delen van het Midden-Oosten en Zuidoost-Azië te heet worden voor mensen om veilig buiten te werken of te slapen zonder airconditioning. Siberië is het voor de hand liggende toevluchtsoord voor de grote bevolkingsgroepen verder naar het zuiden die reeds onder druk staan door hittestress, overstromingen, droogte en hongersnood: de door het klimaat geteisterde gebieden in Oost-China, Bangladesh, Pakistan, Nepal, Oezbekistan, Kazachstan en het Midden-Oosten.

De niches voor bomen en die voor menselijke bewoning zijn zeer vergelijkbaar. Dezelfde dynamiek van uitbreiding van woestijn en steppe ten koste van bossen is ook al zichtbaar in Zuid- en Midden-Amerika en in de Sahel in Afrika. Als we de migratie van mensen op dezelfde manier modelleren als die van bomen, zonder rekening te houden met politieke grenzen, is een massale verschuiving naar het noorden te verwachten.

Dit verband tussen de niches voor menselijke bewoning en bomen is iets waar ik meer over wilde weten. De menselijke samenleving is pas recentelijk – in de tweede helft van de twintigste eeuw – losgekoppeld van haar omgeving, met aanvoerketens naar afgelegen en onherbergzame oorden die mogelijk zijn gemaakt door fossiele brandstoffen. Maar daarvoor heeft de mens, afgezien van de Inuit met hun energiebron uit de speklaag van walvissen en zeehonden, het nooit lang zonder hout kunnen stellen. Door het definiëren van ecosystemen en habitats heeft de boomgrens de mogelijkheden voor het menselijk bestaan bepaald en, bij uitbreiding, de voorwaarden voor de menselijke cultuur. Onze plaats is altijd aan de rand van het bos geweest, in een relatie ermee.

Een van de redenen waarom ik zo graag de lariks-boomgrens bij Ary Mas in het noordelijke deel van het district wil bezoeken is om deze relatie in actie te zien bij de Nganasanen, een unieke inheemse groep die al duizenden jaren boven de Siberische boomgrens leeft en overwintert in het meest noordelijke bos ter wereld, terwijl ze de korte zomermaanden doorbrengen met het jagen op rendieren op de toendra dichter bij de Noordpool. Ik vraag Nadezjha of er antropologen zijn onder haar collega's in het instituut, maar het antwoord is nee, zij bestuderen alleen bomen. Ze stelt me voor aan een van hen, een larikspecialist genaamd Aleksandr Bondarev die Ary Mas al tientallen jaren bezoekt, en we maken een afspraak voor een telefonisch gesprek.

Nadezjda heeft nauwelijks contact met haar collega's. Zoals op alle campussen zijn de meeste onderzoekers druk bezig met hun eigen werk en zich niet bewust van anderen op dezelfde gang. Nadezjda werkt dag en nacht in haar laboratorium en is ook wanneer ze terugkeert naar huis, naar het appartement op de campus waar zij het grootste deel van haar leven heeft gewoond, alleen met haar vele katten. Haar missie is dringend, misschien deels omdat de rest van de maatschappij zo zelfgenoegzaam is.

'Er is geen jong talent voor het modelleren van vegetatieve veranderingen. Ze zijn er niet in geïnteresseerd. Misschien ben ik een slechte docent. Ik ben ongeduldig,' zegt ze nuchter. 'Dit onderzoek houdt na mij op.'

Modelleren moet eenzaam werk zijn, turen in de kristallen

bol van gesofisticeerde klimaatmodellen om een glimp van de apocalyps op te vangen. En de emotionele tol moet aanzienlijk zijn, hoewel Nadezjda, als goede stoïcijnse Russin of voldoende afstandelijke wetenschapper, geen emotie toelaat, ook al betekent haar naam 'hoop'.

'Ik heb geen gevoelens over de toekomst. Ik kan de dingen niet veranderen. Ik waarschuw de mensen alleen. Het is niet mijn verantwoordelijkheid om het op te lossen,' zegt ze zonder te glimlachen.

Wanneer we het hebben over andere onderzoekers van wie het werk relevant zou kunnen zijn voor mijn project – voor de toekomst – lijkt het toepasselijk dat de persoon die zij voorstelt uit te nodigen voor de lunch, een vage kennis van vijftig jaar geleden, op zijn eigen manier ook dezelfde vraag stelt: waar moeten alle mensen toch heen?

Professor dr. Alexander Tikhomirov is een rustige, voorzichtige man. We ontmoeten hem in het personeelsrestaurant van de sociëteit, waar hij langzaam eet en de borsjt van zijn gladgeschoren kin dept. Hij heeft volledig wit haar, borstelige wenkbrauwen en kleine grijze ogen die glinsteren met een wrange humor. Gekleed in een trui, hemd en broek, houdt hij zijn zwarte militaire laarzen stevig op de grond terwijl we praten.

Net als Nadezjda begon Alex zijn carrière in Krasnojarsk, zo'n vijftig jaar geleden. Hij begon in het Bosinstituut onderzoek te doen naar de wijze waarop bomen genezen na verwonding door insecten, wind of overbegrazing door dieren en was geïnteresseerd in de wijze waarop cellen zich herstructureerden. Daarna schakelde hij over op gekweekte planten en werd hij aangeworven in het Instituut voor Biofysica om te werken aan een uiterst geheim project genaamd 'Bios-3' op het Departement voor Levensondersteunende Systemen, dat hij nu leidt binnen de Siberische Lucht- en Ruimtevaartuniversiteit. Bios-3 had betrekking op het overleven van mensen in de ruimte gedurende langere perioden – hetzij in ruimtestations, hetzij voor een geplande missie naar

Mars. Dat is wat men noemt een gesloten-ecosysteemexperiment. Eigenlijk een beetje spelen met klimaatverandering in het klein.

In 1972-1973 brachten drie kosmonauten 180 dagen door in een volledig afgeschermde ruimte in Bios-3. Zij aten tarwe en groenten uit een algenkwekerij met xenonlampen die het zonlicht benaderden, en waren elk afhankelijk van 85 vierkante meter blootgestelde chlorella-algen om hun zuurstof te produceren. De totale faciliteit was 315 kubieke meter groot en omvatte drie hutten, een kombuis, een toilet en een controleruimte. Menselijk afval werd gedroogd en opgeslagen, maar vlees en water werden ingevoerd. Het Bios-experiment behaalde ongeveer 85 procent rendement. Een later soortgelijk experiment in Arizona, in de Verenigde Staten, uitgevoerd door een particuliere onderneming met de naam Biospace Ventures, beweerde 100 procent efficiëntie te hebben bereikt zonder dat extra water en zuurstof nodig waren. Het experiment in Arizona mislukte echter toen na een ruzie een manager genaamd Steve Bannon (de latere stafchef van president Donald Trump) inbrak in de verzegelde kamer, waardoor de astronauten binnen in gevaar kwamen. Veel van de onderzoeksgegevens zijn verloren gegaan. De faciliteit werd overgenomen door Columbia University en daarna door de University of Arizona. Ze wordt nog altijd gebruikt voor onderzoek naar habitatmodellering. Bij andere projecten groeit een halve hectare regenwoud in een glazen piramide bij extreem hoge temperaturen, wat suggereert dat sommige bossen, met voldoende water, een broeikasaarde zouden kunnen overleven als de kooldioxide-fractie constant blijft, al is dat laatste maar zeer de vraag.[9]

Een ander gezamenlijk experiment van Bios-3, de faciliteit in Arizona en het Europees Ruimte-Agentschap levert cruciale informatie op over wat er met planten en mensen gebeurt in een kooldioxiderijke omgeving. Dit onderzoek heeft aangetoond hoe oceanen en koraalriffen door de verzuring zullen worden verwoest en, wat belangrijk is, dat sommige ecosystemen een verzadigingspunt voor koolstofdioxide hebben. Planten kunnen blijkbaar niet omgaan met een steeds hoger kooldioxidegehalte. Fotosynthese is afhankelijk van een evenwicht om te kunnen werken. Als planten niet genoeg water en licht krijgen om gebruik te maken van de beschikbare kooldioxide, kan die hen overweldigen. Sommige soorten zijn natuurlijk beter aangepast dan andere: de prehistorische varens en ginkgo's die zich het carboontijdperk herinneren, vinden in hun genen misschien verre aanwijzingen die zullen helpen. Wat de mens betreft, ontdekte het team van Alex dat een atmosfeer met meer dan 1 procent kooldioxide (10.000 ppm) duidelijk schadelijk was voor het menselijk functioneren – de kosmonauten raakten verward en hadden een slechte coördinatie.

Alex zal geen mensen meer in een gecontroleerde omgeving plaatsen tot ze verschillende problemen met Bios-3 hebben opgelost. Ten eerste is het erg moeilijk om het atmosferisch evenwicht te bewaren zonder menselijk afval op te slaan of uit te stoten. Methaan, ammoniak en andere afbraakproducten zijn in hoge concentraties zeer slecht voor planten – ze verouderen sneller.

'En dat geldt ook voor de mens zelf!' zegt Alex met zijn kenmerkende droge grinnik.

Momenteel is hij volledig geobsedeerd door methaan. Zijn team gebruikt de afgesloten kamers om aan kunstmatige opwarming te doen.

'We willen weten wat de kritieke temperatuur is waarbij methaan de opwarming van de aarde versnelt. Dat is een belangrijke vraag!'

Hij raakt opgewonden als hij over de details van het experiment praat: hoe zijn collega's blokken toendra vervoeren en invriezen, ze dan geleidelijk in het herbarium opwarmen en het gas opvangen, maar als ik hem vraag wat de betekenis daarvan is, is hij stil.

'Ik heb kleinkinderen,' zegt hij, plotseling somber. 'Ik wil dat ze gelukkig zijn, maar...' Hij kijkt omhoog naar het gele plafond en dan naar de berijpte campus die schittert in het licht van de vroege middag. 'Ik zie drie fasen. Eén, misschien brengt opwarming voordelen. Die fase is voorbij. Twee, flora en fauna zullen verschuiven. Daar zitten we nu in. Drie, de mens zal zich moeten aanpassen aan nieuwe omstandigheden – bodem, landbouw, strijd om land, water, hulpbronnen. En als je daarbij bedenkt dat we over kernwapens beschikken... roept dat angstaanjagende beelden op.'

Buiten het raam is een bende pestvogels luidruchtig een lijsterbes aan het plunderen.

'Het is dringend dat we proberen Mars te bereiken. Als we een wereldwijde inspanning zouden doen, zouden we er binnen twintig jaar kunnen zijn. Daar een station installeren. Het hangt ervan af hoe het op Aarde zal gaan.'

Na de lunch brengt Nadezjda me naar de bushalte. Door ons gesprek tijdens de lunch lijkt ze zich vrijer te voelen. Het is alsof ze, aangemoedigd door Alex, nu haar mening kan geven.

'Ik ben ervan overtuigd dat er al een kettingreactie op gang is gekomen. De permafrost is al aan het smelten. Ik zie niet goed hoe we dat kunnen tegenhouden.' Ze trekt haar dunne jas dichter om zich heen. Ze heeft haar oude dikke winterjas niet vervangen. De winters zijn niet koud genoeg meer om zo'n jas te rechtvaardigen en Nadezjda is een zuinig mens. Ze wenst me succes in Ary Mas en raadt me aan informatie over de Nganasanen te zoeken in het Regionaal Museum van Krasnojarsk en ook om naar het ballet in de stad te gaan, 'gewoon daarom'.

Bij de bushalte wil ze niet te lang blijven wachten. 'Ik heb veel werk te doen, dat begrijp je wel.'

Door de ramen van de bus op de terugrit naar het stadscentrum flikkert het lage middaglicht voor mijn ogen door het spookachtig berijpte berkenbos, dat de zwart-witte strepen van een Siberische tijger aanneemt voordat de reclameborden en het vervallen beton van de buitenwijken van de stad het overnemen. Op het eindpunt volg ik Nadezjda's raad op en ga op zoek naar het Regionaal Museum van Krasnojarsk. Het blijkt om verschillende redenen de meest geschikte plaats te zijn om informatie over de Nganasanen te zoeken. De taal en cultuur van de Nganasanen zijn bijna uitgestorven en wat ervan over is, bevindt zich letterlijk volledig hier in het museum. Het gebouw kijkt ook uit op de beroemde brug die Siberië opende voor de invallen van de Kozakken, de eigenlijke oorzaak van de ondergang van de inheemse bevolking.

Het museum is warm en nogal goed voorzien van personeel, en ik ben blij binnen te zijn terwijl de duisternis over de bevroren, vervuilde stad sluipt. De versierde betonnen Egyptische gevel die de enorme hardhouten deuren van de ingang omlijst, heeft weinig te maken met de inheemse schatten binnen, verzameld onder de bedreigde oorspronkelijke bewoners van Siberië. In een merkwaardige hiërarchie is de grote houten boot die de hele benedenverdieping tegenover de ingang in beslag neemt een koch, een vaartuig met een versterkte romp dat door de tsaristische kolonisten werd gebouwd om de met ijs bedekte Arctische kust te verkennen. Het communistische tijdperk wordt vertegenwoordigd door een tentoonstelling op de eerste verdieping, met beelden van lachende collectieve arbeiders en een geschiedenis van de ruimte-exploratie, compleet met een satelliet die aan het plafond hangt als eerbetoon aan Krasnojarsks geschiedenis als lanceerplaats voor raketten. De prehistorie en de inheemse culturen zijn beperkt tot de raamloze kelder.

In de schemerig verlichte kamer wordt aan de hand van een reeks pentekeningen uitgelegd dat de oudste bewijzen van menselijke bewoning in Siberië dateren van 70.000 jaar geleden. De laatste ijstijd, die in Siberië de Sartansk-ijstijd werd genoemd, bedekte een groot deel van het land gedurende 20.000 jaar tussen 50- en 20.000 jaar geleden. Sindsdien heeft het terugtrekkende ijs nieuwe gebieden blootgelegd waar mossen, korstmossen, grassen, struiken en bomen zich snel hebben gevestigd. Dieren volgden de begrazing en mensen volgden de dieren. De meeste Siberische volkeren delen een achtergrond met de neolithische volkeren van vóór de Samojeden, bekend als de Joekagieren, die uit hun glaciale toevluchtsoord in de bergen van Noord-Oost-China tevoorschijn kwamen, achter de steeds verder migrerende rendieren aan. Zij verspreidden zich over het gehele Aziatische continent, van de Stille Oceaan tot de Oeral, en staken zeer waarschijnlijk de Beringlandbrug over naar Alaska. In één richting heeft linguïstische analyse verbanden gevonden tussen Joekagiers en de

Fins-Oegrische talen van de Baltische staten en Hongarije. En in de andere is 'berk' een van de 36 woorden die de bedreigde Ket-taal van Siberië gemeen heeft met de Athabaskan Na-Dene-groep van Noord-Canada.

De inheemse kunstvoorwerpen in het museum vertonen opmerkelijk veel gelijkenis tussen de groepen: cilindrische nomadententen, rendierhuiden die tot kleding zijn genaaid, versierd met kralen, metalen ornamenten en kleurstoffen en jachtuitrustingen, kano's en sneeuwschoenen gemaakt van lariks en berk. De Selkup, Ket, Evenks, Nenets, Enets, Dolgans, Khakas en Nganasanen bewoonden een grote verscheidenheid van gebieden en omgevingen, maar ze deelden een zeer gelijkaardig animistisch geloof. *Saitan*, een Dolgan-woord, betekende een geest die een voorwerp bewoonde. Geesten waren een centraal organiserend principe voor de mensen van de taiga. Het gezag dat in elke cultuur verantwoordelijk was voor het bemiddelen tussen de geestenwereld en de 'bovenwereld' van de mensen, was de sjamaan. De taigavolkeren geloofden dat bomen antennes waren, cruciaal voor de communicatie tussen de bovenwereld en de onderwereld.

In de afgesloten vitrines liggen de trieste, in beslag genomen heilige voorwerpen van de sjamanen: ronde met huid beklede trommels versierd met afbeeldingen van rendieren, vogels, mensen, de zon, de maan en de sterren. De trommel was een boot om in te varen, een rendier om op te rijden, een voertuig voor de sjamaan om ver te reizen, om te zien wat er elders gebeurde en verslag uit te brengen. Zijn gebruiksvoorwerpen waren meestal gemaakt van lariks – de reinste boom, vrij van geesten. De trom symboliseerde het cirkelvormige karakter van het universum. Samen met unieke liederen en gedichten, een vreemde muziek geïnspireerd op de geluiden van de natuur, van vogels, wind, water en bomen, met strikte regels van metrum en rijm, werden de trommels gebruikt om geesten op te roepen om te helpen bij de beproevingen van de bovenwereld.

Een Koreaanse professor in de rechten is de enige andere bezoeker in de kelder. Hij legt uit dat het Koreaanse rechtssysteem wortels heeft in het animisme en het boeddhisme, beide religies van het bos. Korea is ook een boreale natie, zegt hij.

De sjamanen van Siberië werden systematisch vervolgd door de seculiere Sovjetstaat, vermoord, gevangen gezet en, volgens één verhaal, uit helikopters gegooid en verteld dat ze moesten vliegen. De geloofssystemen die vandaag de dag nog over zijn, zijn voor het grootste deel flarden van verhalen die door enkelen bewaard zijn, en die spoedig niet langer zullen worden herinnerd. Toen zij de rivier de Ob en vervolgens de Jenisej overstaken naar het hart van Siberië, ontwrichtten de verkennende Russen een rijk web van woudculturen dat razendsnel in verval is geraakt. Veel groepen zijn geassimileerd, andere zijn bijna uitgestorven. Er zijn bijna geen Enets meer. Het tijdperk van de extinctie heeft niet alleen betrekking op dieren en planten, maar ook op etniciteiten, talen en culturen – vele zijn reeds verdwenen.

De Nganasanen ontkwamen het langst aan Sovjetoverheersing. Zij trokken zich terug in hun bevroren schuilplaats in het woud van Ary Mas op het schiereiland Tajmyr, waar zij de boomheer aanbaden die in de lariks woonde. Als de felste van de wilde stammen, met de machtigste sjamanen, waren ze tot in de jaren 1930 eigenlijk onbekend bij de Sovjetautoriteiten. De regering noemde ze Samojeden. De Nganasanen verwijzen naar zichzelf als *nanuo nanasa* – 'echte mens', een naam die de erkenning van een onderscheid suggereert.

Afgezien van incidentele pogingen om de 'Pyasina-Samojeden' te dwingen tribuut te betalen in de vorm van pelzen en een handvol korte beschrijvingen in negentiende-eeuwse werken, komen de Nganasanen niet voor in de geschriften van Rusland of de USSR, tot 1936, toen A.A. Popov, een jonge etnoloog, van het Instituut voor Etnografie van de Academie van Wetenschappen van de USSR de opdracht kreeg hen te bestuderen. Popov leefde twee jaar lang met de nomaden van Tajmyr, de meest noordelijke inheemse volkeren ter wereld, reisde meer dan 9600 kilometer over de toendra ten noorden van Ary Mas tot aan de 75ste breedtegraad, leerde hun taal en gebruiken, nam achthonderd foto's en verzamelde vijfhonderd voorwerpen.

De mensen die Popov ontmoette, leidden een volledig zelfvoorzienend nomadisch leven, jagend op rendieren ver boven de poolcirkel, net zoals hun voorouders dat duizenden jaren lang hadden gedaan. Hij ontmoette vrouwen die rendierzenuwen tegen hun wang rolden om garen te maken, parka's en broeken naaiden van rendierhuid en de zolen van laarzen maakten van de huid van het voorhoofd van rendieren. Zij gebruikten de dikke wintervacht van de dieren voor winterkleding en de dunne voor zomerkleding. En hij ontmoette onvermoeibare, sterke mannen die jaagden met bogen en pijlen gemaakt van de gestripte wortels van lariks, omwikkeld en verstevigd met berkenbast en waterdicht gemaakt met vislijm.

Hij ging twee seizoenen lang met hen mee op jacht, was meerdere dagen onderweg met alleen thee, een ketel, huiden en een slee, en was getuige van de massale rendierjacht, collectieve slachtingen van honderden dieren op dezelfde plaats elk jaar weer, op de trekroutes van de rendieren. Hij beschrijft hoe jagers kilometerslange lanen uitzetten met witte vleugels van sneeuwhoenders aan palen om de herten in een trechter te drijven, een smalle kloof of een klif, die naar een meer leidt waar jagers in kano's de dieren met korte speren in hun achterwerk staken om de huiden niet te bederven. Ze bonden meerdere karkassen aan elkaar en sleepten ze naar de oever. Vervolgens maakten 'deze mensen die geen vermoeidheid kennen' het gedode dier schoon, smolten het vet, verwijderden de ingewanden en de huiden alvorens hun jachtuitrusting te herstellen en twee of drie uur te slapen en het proces vervolgens te herhalen. Massale slachting, zei Popov, was veel gemakkelijker dan de jacht op individuele rendieren te voet, wanneer men het dode dier alleen terug moest dragen.

Het vet en vlees werden gedroogd en gerookt, de hersenen en andere ingewanden rauw gegeten. Vóór de winter aten de mensen tot ze misselijk werden om een voorraad aan te leggen voor de lange koude, minstens 263 dagen onder het vriespunt. In de lente waren ze vaak uitgehongerd tot de trekvogels terugkeerden. Dan gebruikten de Nganasanen lokvogels, netten en pijl en boog om eenden en ganzen te doden, tot wel duizend in één keer, waarbij de huiden, veren en het vlees onmiddellijk helemaal werden verwerkt zonder pauze te nemen om te slapen, en het gesmolten vet werd opgeslagen in rendiermagen. Brandhout van de lariks werd bewaard om te roken en te drogen. Voedsel werd zo mogelijk rauw gegeten, en in hun met bont gevoerde tenten maakten ze vanaf maart geen vuur meer om brandstof te besparen, maar kropen ze dicht tegen hun honden aan om warm te blijven.

Popovs bezoek was echter de laatste glimp van deze eeuwenoude manier van leven. In 1938 schreef hij trots over de impact die zijn veldwerk had gehad:

> Vóór de grote socialistische Oktoberrevolutie waren de Nganasanen een van de sterks verwaarloosde kleine volkeren van het Siberische noorden en waren zij gedoemd geweest om uit te sterven. Verloren op de uitgestrekte toendra, leefden ze geïsoleerd van de buitenwereld. Elementen van de beschaving drongen praktisch niet door in hun manier van leven. [Nu]... gaan Nganasan-kinderen naar de scholen die in afgelegen nederzettingen zijn geopend. De eerste spoorweg is op de toendra verschenen, en aken en stoomboten varen op de rivieren. De landbouw ontwikkelt zich, en boven de poolcirkel groeien nu groenten.[10]

Popov heeft zijn werk te goed gedaan. Het was niet de 'verwaarlozing' die hen met uitsterven bedreigde, maar juist de aandacht van de staat. De kolonisatie, of die nu socialistisch of kapitalistisch is, is zo doeltreffend, zo bruut in het vervreemden van mensen van de natuur, dat een cultuur die zich in de loop van millennia in relatie tot de boomgrens heeft ontwikkeld, binnen één mensenleven bijna spoorloos is verdampt.

Volgens de volkstelling van 2012 waren er minder dan vijfhonderd Nganasan over. Velen van hen spreken hun taal niet meer en houden niet langer vast aan hun oude cultuur, en allen zijn uit hun voorouderlijke streken verdreven om in verafgelegen steden te gaan wonen. Er zijn nog maar een paar grote families over langs de rivier Khatanga op het schiereiland Tajmyr, meer dan honderd kilometer ten zuiden van Ary Mas, ver ten zuiden van hun historische grondgebied. Tegen een flinke prijs heeft een reisorganisatie geregeld dat ik kan beschikken over een speciale Arctische terreinwagen en een tolk, zodat ik kan proberen hen te interviewen en het cryolithische lariksbos te bezoeken dat zij meer dan achtduizend jaar lang als hun thuis hebben beschouwd. En zo heb ik de volgende morgen om vier uur 's ochtends op het vliegveld een afspraak met de voor mij ingehuurde tolk, Dmitry, voor de volgende etappe van mijn reis naar het hoge noorden.

Toch kan ik Nadezjda's aandringen om het Krasnojarsk ballet te gaan zien, niet negeren. Het museum ligt aan de overkant van het centrale plein van het Staatstheater. Hoog op de noordelijke oever van de rivier kijkt het uit over de rode lichtjes die aan de brug hangen en in zwarte water weerspiegelen. Met een glimlach en gebarentaal door een dik raam weet een vrouw met een muts van vossenbont en een bril duidelijk te maken dat er nog kaartjes beschikbaar zijn. Ik neem plaats tussen de in bont geklede en gelaarsde middenklasse van de stad, op lichtblauwe velours zetels in het modernistische betonnen theater met zijn koepel, voor een volledig georkestreerde versie van Het Zwanenmeer, waarin zowel de witte als de zwarte zwaan door mannen wordt gedanst. Ik ben geen balletkenner, maar na afloop ben ik net zo ontroerd als de rest van het publiek en veer overeind om uitbundig te klappen, niet zozeer uit waardering voor de voorstelling, hoewel die een zeldzaam genoegen is, maar uit verwondering over de prestatie om een dergelijke cultuur in stand te houden in zo'n godvergeten oord.

Oetsjoektai – het Dromende Meer - Rusland
73° 08' 81" N

Siberië is zo uitgestrekt dat de afstand van Moskou naar Krasnojarsk – drieduizend kilometer en vijf uur vliegen door vier tijdzones – vergelijkbaar is met de afstand van het zuiden van het district Krasnojarsk aan de grens met Mongolië naar de Arctische havenstad Khatanga in het noorden. Dmitry – ik mag Dima zeggen – en ik vliegen gedurende wat een eeuwigheid lijkt over de lichtloze uitgestrektheid van noordelijk centraal Siberië. Alle stoelen voorin zijn volgestouwd met vracht, en iedereen slaapt tot, tegen het einde van de vlucht, de taiga onder ons in zicht komt: wervelende patronen van een bevroren rivierenstelsel dat zo sterk slingert dat de lussen kort langs elkaar lopen, kleine boompjes hier en daar op de rivieroever. Op de landingsbaan knijpen we met onze ogen in het zwakke licht van een wazige ochtendschemering om een luchtvaartkerkhof van propellervliegtuigen, straaljagers en een Mi-26 helikopter, ingekapseld in sneeuw en ijs, te zien staan.

Onder een lariksboom vol ijs ontmoeten we onze fixer Alexei, zijn grijnzende gezicht omlijst door een muts van vossenbont met oorflappen, gezeten op een sneeuwscooter die een stalen kooi voor onze bagage sleept. De kou is, letterlijk, verblindend. Bij -44 doet het kleinste zuchtje wind je ogen tranen. Die tranen bevriezen op de huid en als je te traag knippert, plakken je oogleden aan elkaar. De ijzige lucht schuurt je keel als schuurpapier. De kou dringt als naalden door je kleren en je kunt niet langer dan zestig seconden zonder handschoenen zitten voordat je huid begint te jeuken alsof hij in brand staat. Het is normaal om twee mutsen, twee jassen, twee broeken en twee paar sokken en dubbele handschoenen te dragen, hetzij van bont, hetzij gevuld met dons.

Op hoge snelheid, door plakkerige, waterige ogen, werp ik een blik op Khatanga, een middelgrote stad met grote vierkante gebouwen. Er staan rijen lichtgroene prefab-blokken en één flatgebouw van rode baksteen, allemaal met elkaar verbonden door enorme pijpen van glimmend aluminiumfolie met daarover bruggen en voetpaden: het gemeentelijke warmwatersysteem. De skyline wordt aan de ene kant getekend door boortorens die stil boven de haven aan de rivier hangen, en aan de andere kant door een elektriciteitscentrale met zijn twee dunne schoorstenen met knipperende rode lichten als brandende sigaretten die grijze rook in een gele, nicotinekleurige lucht verspreiden. Alles is bedekt met een fijne grijze sneeuw, als as. We blijven hier echter niet stilstaan.

Alexej levert ons rechtstreeks af bij onze chauffeurs Kolja en Kolja en hun trots, een reusachtige witte terreinwagen, een zogenaamde 'Trekol', met enorme banden, even hoog als ik zelf ben. De motor draait, een groot stalen vat vol diesel ligt op een aanhangwagen erachter, en een groot bolvormig reservewiel wordt op het dak gebonden. De ene Kolja heeft zandkleurig haar en de andere zwart. Beiden roken ze sigaretten met een wrange glimlach op hun gezicht. Blonde Kolja gebaart met een sigaret in zijn vette, gehandschoende hand dat we de garage binnen moeten gaan.

De deur is een gehavende staalplaat die wit gestraald is, iets wat duidelijk het gevolg lijkt te zijn van de meedogenloze poolwinter met zijn peilloze duister en zijn eindeloze stormen. Drie grote, keihard bevroren vissen, elk ongeveer zo lang als mijn arm, zijn nonchalant bij de deur neergegooid, te midden van machines en een paar bevroren rendierharten die op een laagje sneeuw liggen. Aan één kant gloeit een ijzeren kachel, maar het effect ervan is beperkt. Vette banken, dekzeilen, banden en gereedschap liggen overal opgestapeld in de duisternis. Er is één vieze lamp en geen ramen.

Kolja en Kolja komen met veel tamtam binnen, schudden ons de hand en lachen om dingen die ik niet begrijp. Dima vertaalt echt alleen het hoogstnoodzakelijke. Alexej en Dima hebben een lang gesprek en dan schudt Alexej mijn hand en neemt afscheid. Al snel klauteren we achterin de Trekol met Kolja en Kolja in de twee beklede voorstoelen, en Russische popmuziek uit de luidsprekers. De geïmproviseerde versnellingspook die eigenlijk een moersleutel is, wordt in de eerste versnelling gezet en de enorme truck begint met een ruk te bewegen.

Trekols werden speciaal voor Siberië ontworpen met hun monsterlijke opblaasbare wielen om de moerassen van de zomer en de sneeuw en het ijs van de winter aan te kunnen. Ze beschikken over bijzonder krachtige versnellingen en kruipen als een tank door het landschap, waarbij ze zelden harder rijden dan dertig kilometer per uur. We passeren een verlaten kamp van geologen aan de rand van de stad en een kolenmijn waar de Trekol al stuiterend de weg verlaat, jankend, krakend en slingerend over het bevroren oppervlak van de Khatangarivier, in oostelijke richting naar de Laptevzee, een deel van de Noordelijke IJszee.

Onze eerste stop, legt Dima uit, is Novoribyne, langs de Khatanga, een van de twee meest noordelijke nederzettingen in Rusland, waar een grote familie van Nganasanen woont. Daarna gaan we noordwaarts naar het bos van Ary Mas en bezoeken daar de Dolgan-nomaden, die nog steeds rendieren hoeden boven de boomgrens en zo hun eigen relatie met het bos onderhouden.

'Hoe ver is het naar Novoribyne?' vraag ik.

'Zo'n honderdzestig kilometer.'

De volgende acht uur zitten Dima en ik tegenover elkaar op parallelle banken achterin, met onze tassen en een jerrycan wodka tussen ons in, en houden we ons vast alsof ons leven ervan afhangt omdat we heen en weer worden geslingerd als aan boord van een schip in een storm.

Ik probeer me te concentreren op het golvende uitzicht, maar de zon, die nog maar net terug is na de donkere poolwinter, gaat al achter ons onder met een enkele gele streep over de horizon, iets voor drie uur 's middags, wanneer we de stad verlaten. In de schemering zie ik door de berijpte voorruit een brede vlakke witte rivier met lage heuvels aan weerszijden. We volgen de boomgrens. Langs de zuidelijke oever staat een lint van lariksen, maar aan de noordelijk staat er niet een. Aan die kant van de rivier ligt het schiereiland Tajmyr, een duizend kilometer lange landtong, de noordelijke punt van Siberië die de Karazee scheidt van de Laptev, bijna precies halverwege tussen Noorwegen en Alaska. Duizenden kilometers zuidelijker ligt het Baikalmeer, en nog verder zuidwaarts op dezelfde lengtegraad liggen de steden Ulaanbaatar, Hongkong en Jakarta. Dichter bij de Noordpool dan Tajmyr kun je op een continentale landmassa niet komen, alleen de eilanden van de Noordelijke IJszee zijn dichterbij. Zonder het vreemde kluitje bomen bij Ary Mas – de naam betekent 'boomeiland' in de taal van de Dolgan – zou deze zuidelijke oever van de Khatanga de noordelijkste boomgrens ter wereld zijn.

Het bos, de toendra, de rivier, de lucht zijn niet meer dan verschillende tinten grijs in de vallende nacht. Op een gegeven moment zet blonde Kolja de schijnwerper op een stalen paal die uit het dak steekt aan en ik zie de weg voor me: de rivier lijkt midden in een storm te zijn bevroren, grote plooien ijs en sneeuw lijken op golven. De Trekol, onophoudelijk jankend, op en neer en stotend over die golven, zorgt ervoor dat we zeker niet in slaap zullen vallen.

Rond elf uur 's avonds verschijnen er lichten uit de duisternis, alsof de rivier is ontdooid en we een haven vanaf het water zien. De opluchting is navenant. De Trekol verlaat de rivier en beklimt een steile besneeuwde oever, doorkliefd met de sporen van andere voertuigen. Lampen op palen onthullen een verzameling gebouwen met schuine daken die kreunen onder meters sneeuw en bedekt zijn met ijs. Als de buitenlucht gevaarlijk is, zijn huizen niet alleen woningen, maar toevluchtsoorden, vrijplaatsen, ruimtestations, essentieel om te overleven. Ze liggen diep onder de sneeuw, maar lokken met de belofte van warmte. Het lijkt ongelooflijk, maar Novoribyne is een dorp met enkele honderden inwoners, een kerk, een winkel en een school met meer dan honderd kinderen.

Op het kruispunt waar op de helling een rij huizen staat in iets wat op een straat lijkt, stopt de Trekol. Kolja en Kolja barsten uit een vloed van wat ik denk dat scheldwoorden zijn, en springen uit de truck. Ze hebben maar een korte tijd om de motor te herstarten voordat de brandstofleidingen bevriezen. Als dat gebeurt, moeten ze een vuur onder de motor aanleggen – een gebruikelijke, maar riskante Siberische tactiek. Dima en ik trekken onze sneeuwpakken, handschoenen en mutsen aan en laten ons op straat zakken. Zwarte Kolja gebaart wild naar het dichtstbijzijnde huis en schreeuwt instructies naar Dima die verloren gaan in de wind. We lopen langs wat garages lijken te zijn, bedolven onder de sneeuw en waartussen kabels zijn gespannen die bedekt zijn met ijs, naar een trap die uit de sneeuw is gehakt en leidt naar een houten huis en een deuropening in een poel van geel licht dat flikkert in de sneeuwstorm.

Een dunne overdekte veranda, de muren bedekt met ijs, herbergt een enorme voorraad bevroren rendierkarkassen. We kloppen aan en staan al gauw in de keuken van een vriendelijke man, Konstantin genaamd, in een wit hemd en een joggingbroek. Hij rent door het huis met kinderen, sigaretten en een grote bevroren vis die hij op de tafel met het vinyl tafelkleed legt en in lange ijzige repen begint te snijden - *kyspyt*, een plaatselijke delicatesse. Die eten we met thee, mosterd, zout en een klein schaaltje chilipoeder. Heerlijk!

Een uur later keren de Kolja's terug, triomfantelijk. De Trekol staat buiten gehoorzaam te spinnen. Anna, Konstantins vrouw, staat nu aan het fornuis, in spijkerbroek en gebloemde pantoffels, en praat non-stop met het bezoek terwijl ze vis bakt in een pan die ze met een tang op het elektrische fornuis manoeuvreert. Al snel verschijnt er een volgende maaltijd: gebakken trekzalm met brood en nog meer thee. Het is al na middernacht en we weten nog steeds niet waar we de nacht gaan doorbrengen. Dima en ik zijn al sinds vier uur vanochtend wakker. Konstantins zoontje blijft maar heen en weer lopen, zonder naar bed te willen.

Na de maaltijd gaan alle rokers, ook Anna en Konstantin, op de grond zitten bij de keramische kachel in de grote zitkamer. Bovenop de kachel liggen twee zalmen te ontdooien in een schaal. Er gaat een half uur voorbij waarin ze naar hun telefoons en hun gps kijken en praten. Uiteindelijk legt Dima uit: de Nganasanenfamilie heeft een begrafenis, een familieaangelegenheid. Er is besloten door te gaan naar de volgende stad, Syndassko, waar de Dolgans zijn, en de Nganasanen en het bos te bezoeken op onze terugreis naar Khatanga.

'Morgen?' vraag ik, zwak van vermoeidheid.

'Nee. Nu,' zegt Dima. Ik begrijp kennelijk niet hoe men hier in Siberië zaken aanpakt.

'Syndassko!' zegt de blonde Kolja, terwijl hij opstaat, zich uitrekt en omhoog kijkt als om het dak aan te duiden.

'Hoe ver is het naar Syndassko?'

'Honderdveertig.' De moed zakt me in de schoenen. De Kolja's lijken ondertussen te genieten van de ontberingen, alsof er een elementaire waarheid over de wereld wordt gedemonstreerd aan de verwende westerling. Het verschil tussen dag en nacht betekent zo ver noordelijk niets.

Konstantin en Anna vertellen Kolja en Kolja over de gevaren van het zee-ijs. Blijf dicht bij de oever, ga niet te ver buitengaats. Er zijn plooien en richels die te hoog zijn om overheen te rijden en je zou vast kunnen komen te zitten. De zee is afgelopen winter niet goed bevroren en er zijn scheuren ontstaan door opwellingen van zilt smeltwater, waardoor plooien en richels over elkaar zijn geschoven. De scheuren zijn een nieuw fenomeen.

'Oké!' roept de blonde Kolja, en de Trekol duikt met een ruk weer het donker in, terug de helling af, opnieuw de bevroren rivier op.

Ergens gedurende de nacht, na een paar uur voortjammeren in een sneeuwstorm, stopt de Trekol. We stappen uit om te plassen. De maan is verdwenen in de duisternis, de kustlijn is nergens te zien, en er is niet meer dan mist en de sneeuw op paar meter voor de terreinwagen. Bij Syndassko stroomt de Khatanga op weg naar de Laptevzee in een enorme baai, de Golf van Khatanga, vijftig kilometer breed. Daar ergens bevinden wij ons nu. We hadden evengoed ergens in de ruimte kunnen zijn.

Daar waar de zee onder de stuivende sneeuw tevoorschijn komt, is ze als zwart glas, met een ondoorzichtig en gebarsten glazuur dat soms in plooien is geplet die op tektonische platen lijken. De Kolja's kijken lang op hun gps. Ik maak me zorgen. Onze terreinwagen van twee ton draait stationair op misschien een meter of twee bevroren zee, kilometers ver uit de kust. Een van de Kolja's springt lachend op en neer alsof hij het ijs test. Tot voor kort werd het als vanzelfsprekend beschouwd dat je de helft van het jaar altijd op zee kon rijden. Maar tijdens een expeditie naar de Noordpool deze winter begonnen wetenschappers reddingsvesten te dragen nadat verscheidene van hen door het broze ijs waren gezakt. Zelfs de meest rotsvaste zekerheden zijn plotseling als sneeuw voor de zon aan het verdwijnen.

'Zijn we verdwaald?' vraag ik.

'We zijn op de Noordpool!' grapt Dima. Die is inderdaad niet zo heel ver meer. Drie dagen rijden, zelfs met deze snelheid, en we zouden er zijn – als het ijs tenminste zou houden.

De hemel kleurt wat lichter als we eindelijk het havenplaatsje Syndassko binnenrijden. Bij daglicht wordt de omvang van de Golf van Khatanga duidelijk. Aan de horizon zijn nog net witte heuvels te zien – de rand van Tajmyr aan de verre oever van de uitgestrekte, bevroren zee. Langs de hele zuidelijke oever van riviermonding liggen huizenhoge stapels boomstammen. Er liggen complete bomen opgestapeld, alsof een reusachtige bulldozer een bos heeft gerooid en het hier heeft gedumpt. Het zijn allemaal lariksen uit het bos ver stroomopwaarts, die elke zomer door de vloed stroomafwaarts worden meegenomen wanneer het ijs smelt – historisch gezien rond 20 juli, maar tegenwoordig is dat steeds vroeger. In Novoribyne, nu honderdzestig kilometer zuidelijker, hebben wij het bos in de loop van de nacht achter ons gelaten, maar het bos ver landinwaarts blijft de menselijke geografie vele kilometers stroomafwaarts beïnvloeden: het drijfhout dat gevangen ligt in de kronkel van de baai waar de rivier haar bocht naar zee maakt, is de reden dat hier de plaats Syndassko werd gevestigd. Het is een van de weinige nederzettingen boven de boomgrens die geen militair- of mijnstation is.

Achter een berm van kiezelstenen doemt een verzameling huizen op uit de nacht, half bedolven onder de sneeuw en aangevroren met ijs. We rijden door een soort hoofdstraat die aanvoelt alsof hij thuishoort in een stadje in het Wilde Westen, een brede laan met aan weerszijden huizen van houtskeletbouw, met kabels zwaar van sneeuw die ze met elkaar verbinden. Maar het is moeilijk om gebouwen, auto's en olietanks van elkaar te onderscheiden, want het zijn stuk voor stuk niet meer dan bulten in de sneeuw. We stoppen voor een van de huizen en zitten al gauw aan een kleine ontbijttafel met een man die Sergei heet. Hij gooit een blok ijs in een ketel, snijdt reepjes van een bevroren vis en steekt sigaret na sigaret op terwijl hij de Kolja's om informatie uit Khatanga vraagt. We zijn uit de kou gekomen, en moeten worden gevoed. Hij geeft ons wat we nodig hebben en wil in ruil daarvoor nieuws van Khatanga.

Sergei grinnikt vaak, heeft een rond, stralend gezicht en een flinke buik waarover hij wrijft terwijl hij praat. Iedereen is een tikkeltje beroerd vandaag, legt hij uit. De helikopter komt op donderdag en brengt voorraden, waaronder wodka. De prijs voor een liter is 25 kilo bevroren vis, en er is vis genoeg. Sergei vraagt naar de scheuren in het zee-ijs, of we die hebben gezien? Dat is een nieuw gevaar. Het weer vandaag de dag is zo warm! Inmiddels is het nog maar -27 's nachts. De mannen knikken stilletjes, hun ogen gericht op hun thee. -30 was tot voor kort nog ongehoord warm voor februari.

Toch is dat koud genoeg om een toiletbezoek buiten maar liever kort te houden. In het voorportaal van Sergeis huis bevindt zich een afdak vol grote blokken ijs van een halve meter in het vierkant, en aan de andere kant een kist met wat lijkt op grote plakken steenkool. Geen van de huizen zo ver noordelijk heeft stromend water, omdat de leidingen zouden barsten. Elk huis is in plaats daarvan omringd met een soort spatpatroon van gele sneeuw en bruine menselijke uitwerpselen. Men doet geen poging om dat tot één plaats te beperken. Het zal daar blijven liggen, bevroren, tot de zomer.

Als Sergei hoort dat ik geïnteresseerd ben in bomen, laat hij me bij terugkomst trots de 'versteende bomen' in zijn brandstofmand zien, de overblijfselen van een bos, zoals Ary Mas, dat ooit veel noordelijker lag. De jonge zwarte steenkool komt uit een spleet in de berg ongeveer vijf kilometer ten zuiden van de stad. Syndassko is de meest noordelijke nederzetting in Rusland. Het was oorspronkelijk de plaats van een zomervisserskamp van de Dolgan-nomaden. In de winter trokken zij naar het zuiden, terug naar de boomgrens bij de Popigajrivier. Daarna was het tot de jaren 1950 een handelspost waar nomaden bont en rendieren brachten om te handelen met de 'Russen'. Er was één winkel die per boot werd bevoorraad en geen permanente huizen totdat Syndassko zich na de Tweede Wereldoorlog bij de Goelag-archipel aansloot. Het waren de gevangenen die de steenkool ontdekten en de Dolgan-bevolking lieten zien wat ze ermee konden doen, waardoor deze plek het hele jaar door bewoonbaar werd. Fossiele brandstoffen – prehistorische bomen – waren nog steeds de voornaamste bepalende factor voor waar en hoe de mens kon leven, zelfs – vooral – op dit meest noordelijke punt. Met de Goelag kwamen de Sovjetoverheid en de sovkhoz, het staatsbedrijf voor het hoeden van rendieren dat Syndassko's overgang van tijdelijk tentenkamp naar permanente nederzetting met school, burgemeester en dieselgenerator voltooide.

De communistische regering herstructureerde de levenswijze van de herders met quota's en vaste grondgebieden, maar dankzij de steun van de staat kon deze levenswijze blijven bestaan als die van de meerderheid voor hele gemeenschappen, tot de ineenstorting van de USSR in de jaren 1990 het hoeden economisch onrendabel maakte. Terwijl er hier vroeger meer mensen aan rendierhoeden deden dan in het kapitalistische Noorwegen, zijn er nu nog maar heel weinig mensen bij betrokken. Het is alsof een vloed van bureaucratie de Dolgans had meegesleept en hen deed aanspoelen aan de noordelijke grens van hun oude grondgebied, waarna ze zich had teruggetrokken en hen achterliet. Tegenwoordig is vissen lucratiever, veel gemakkelijker werk en, per calorie voedingswaarde, veel productiever. Je hakt een aantal gaten in het ijs, rijgt het net erdoor aan palen die in de rivierbedding zijn geslagen, gaat weg en wacht af. Rendieren hoeden is vergeleken daarmee een geweldige hoeveelheid werk. Toch staat het nog steeds in hoger aanzien. Als het ijs verdwijnt en je niet meer kunt vissen, wil iedereen Misha's vriend zijn. 'Ze willen allemaal vlees!' lacht Sergei.

Misha en zijn schoonvader Alexej zijn de enige twee die nog rendieren hoeden in Syndassko. Wij hebben afgesproken hen te bezoeken en te vergezellen naar hun winterkamp op de toendra.

'Kunnen we eerst slapen?' vraag ik Dima. Ik ben al 47 uur wakker.

'We zijn te gast. We moeten doen wat ons gezegd wordt.' Er ronken drie sneeuwscooters langs het raam die stoppen in een wolk van sneeuw. Tijd om te gaan.

Dima laat me zien hoe ik de hoge laarzen van rendierhuid die tot op mijn dijen reiken moet aantrekken. Die bieden de beste bescherming tegen de Siberische kou. Zo licht als katoen bijna, met het holle bont van het rendier, zijn ze ongelooflijk warm, als pantoffels, en ze laten ze geen sporen achter als je over de sneeuw loopt. Misha draagt alleen een polyester ski-jack. Zijn vrouw Anna en hun dochter Tanja zijn van top tot teen gekleed in rendierbont, met vossenbontmutsen en -wanten. Alexej, Anna's vader, rijdt op de derde sneeuwscooter met een groene canvas poncho over zijn rendiervacht om de sneeuw tegen te houden. Misha noch Alexej hebben een bril of gezichtsbedekking. Ze kijken met toegeknepen ogen naar de toendra als naar een onbetrouwbare oude bekende.

Als Dima en ik, uitgedost met bivakmutsen, brillen en dubbele handschoenen, in de houten slee zitten die klaar is om achter de machine van Misja te worden getrokken, komt Sergej naar ons toe, wrijft onze mutsen tussen zijn vingers en knijpt in mijn vingers door de handschoenen. Dan lacht hij.

'Het maakt toch niet uit,' zegt hij, 'het is nog niet eens -30.'

Twee uur lang slaat de sneeuw van de rupsband van de sneeuwscooter in onze gezichten. De slee stuitert over het korstige oppervlak van de toendra en een lage rode zon smeult aan de horizon. We vliegen. De toendra-oceaan strekt zich uit zover het oog reikt, tot aan een wazige gele horizon, waarboven wolkenveren zichtbaar zijn tegen een roze-turquoise hemel. Het gevoel van ruimte is duizelingwekkend, alsof we verdwaald zijn in een andere dimensie, een witte wereld onder of boven de echte.

Het kamp is een *baloch*, een tent van lariks op ski's, gemaakt om achter een rendierteam te worden voortgetrokken. Het ding ligt half onder een sneeuwjacht met daaromheen de houten frames van enkele oudere tenten. De baloch is het zomerverblijf van de familie, maar hij is duidelijk al enkele seizoenen niet verplaatst.

'Hij is erg zwaar,' zegt Anna, die zich verontschuldigt voor het gebrek aan nomadisme van de familie. Er zijn acht rendieren nodig om hem voort te trekken. 'We laten hem nu gewoon hier staan.'

Alexej en Misha hebben hem voorzien van triplex in plaats van het traditionele larikshouten frame met canvas en huiden – dat is warmer en stabieler, maar moeilijker te verplaatsen. Maar dat maakt niet zoveel meer uit, aangezien het kamp nu eerder de rol van een weekendhuisje op het platteland vervult. Anna kan zich niet herinneren wanneer de familie voor het laatst met de seizoenen mee migreerde. Toen ze nog een meisje was, woonden haar vader en moeder hier in de zomer, en ging zij naar school in Syndassko en later, toen ze ouder was, naar een kostschool in Khatanga, en keerde voor de vakanties terug per boot of helikopter. De familie bleef ondertussen op de toendra. In de winter trokken ze met een groot aantal andere families naar de boomgrens bij de Papigai-rivier, maar één voor één gaven de anderen het op en gingen vissen.

Aan de ingang van de baloch is een veranda met bevroren rendierhuiden, larikshoutblokken voor brandhout en bevroren vis die op het dak werd gegooid. Binnen steekt Anna een gietijzeren kachel aan met repen lariks. De ruimte is ongeveer vier bij drie meter, genoeg voor ons zessen om naast elkaar te slapen, net. Anna legt huiden op de vloer, doet een blok ijs in de ketel om te koken, haalt de radio en een auto-accu van een plank en begint het bestek en wat andere zaken te sorteren in een doos bij het vuur. Binnen enkele minuten is de baloch behaaglijk warm. Het ijs aan de binnenkant van de dubbele perspex ramen begint te smelten en langs het triplex interieur te druipen. Ik trek mijn buitenste jas uit, ga achterover liggen op de rendierhuiden en val uiteindelijk halsoverkop in een diepe slaap.

Ik word wakker en zie Alexei zijn bovenjas uittrekken en bij het vuur gaan zitten voor thee en rendierstoofpot. Er ligt sneeuw op zijn lange laarzen en er staan zweetdruppels op zijn kale hoofd. Terwijl Misha op zoek was naar hun rendieren, is hij buiten aan het werk geweest, hout hakken dat hij vorige zomer hierheen heeft gesjouwd en dat de hele winter bevroren heeft gelegen. Hij wijst beschuldigend met zijn lepel naar mij.

'Dus jij beweert dat het bos naar het noorden opschuift? Heel goed! Dan hebben we genoeg brandhout.' Hij glimlacht niet. Toen hij nog jong was, was het zoeken naar hout een steeds terugkerende last. Het was zwaar werk en de reis kostte meerdere dagen. De Dolgans zochten niet alleen brandhout. Ze gebruikten de lariks ook voor tentstokken, voor sleeën, voor balochs, voor boten, roeispanen en gereedschap. Bijna alles was van hout gemaakt, behalve het kinderspeelgoed, want dat zou de geesten hebben beledigd. Speelgoed werd meestal gemaakt van eendensnavels of been. Hout was speciaal. Nu is natuurlijk al het speelgoed van plastic, gemaakt in China.

'De bomen waren ver weg!' herinnert Alexei zich, die vroeger, toen hij jonger was, met de rendieren naar de Papigai trok om er te overwinteren. Het was een zwaar leven, maar Alexei kijkt er verwarrend genoeg vol heimwee op terug. Als de opwarming van de aarde het leven makkelijker maakt, is hij er helemaal voor. Toch wil hij niet dat er een einde komt aan het hoeden van rendieren als een manier van leven. Hij houdt van de arbeidsbesparende voordelen van steenkool, benzine, helikopters en sneeuwscooters, maar wijst tegelijkertijd scholen, wodka, markten en smartphones af. Hij is in sommige opzichten het archetype van een knorrige grootvader, een cynische allemansvriend die de opwarming van de aarde aanvaardt, ontkent en dan weer toejuicht, allemaal tegelijk. Is deze verwarring misschien een meer algemeen symptoom van het razendsnelle tempo van de veranderingen in ons koolwaterstoftijdperk? We hebben nauwelijks afscheid genomen van één manier van leven of we moeten er alweer aan wennen om de volgende achter ons te laten.

Hoewel bijna niemand meer rondtrekt met de kudden, is het hoeden nog steeds de spil van de taal en de cultuur. De Dolgans zijn, zoals zoveel culturen die een verandering ondergaan, op de grens van werelden, doortrokken van een cultuur die is losgeraakt van zijn oorsprong. Het is alsof ze zich vasthouden aan de takken van een boom die net boven de wortel is omgehakt. Zonder hoeden is er geen reden om naar de toendra te gaan, of naar het zuiden naar het bos. Er is geen reden om aandacht te besteden aan de subtiele verschillen in de typen sneeuw, om de namen te kennen voor kleine veranderingen in het weer, de vegetatie, de bewegingen van soorten, de tekens en signalen, de taal en de dialoog met de geesten en de natuurlijke wereld. Daarom zal hij nooit gaan vissen, zegt Alexej. Toch neemt hij het zijn schoonzoon niet kwalijk dat hij vist – hij knijpt zijn ogen ver dicht en de diepe lijnen rond zijn ogen plooien zich tot een halve glimlach – zolang Misja ook rendieren hoedt. Alexej was de jongste van veertien kinderen, nu is hij 72 en de enige die nog leeft. Zijn eigen kinderen zijn allemaal verhuisd, behalve Anna. Zij en Misja zijn de laatste erfgenamen van de Dolgan-traditie van rendierhoeders in Syndassko, en Alexej heeft moeite om zijn verwachtingen voor hen te verbergen.

Een tijd lang liet Anna zich verleiden door de 'vooruitgang'. Zij volgde een lerarenopleiding in Norilsk, de stad die is opgericht voor de tachtigduizend mensen die werken in 's werelds grootste nikkelmijn aan de andere kant van Tajmyr. Die is berucht om zijn vervuiling die het bos over honderden kilometers rondom heeft gedood. Een witte koepel van dampen hangt 'als een paddenstoel' boven de stad en smaakt 'als het gas waarop we koken'. Het gaat in je mond zitten, 'alsof je krijt eet', zegt Anna. Ze kreeg er hoofdpijn van en haatte het. De helikoptervlucht erheen was duur. Ze zag er het nut niet van in. Nu werkt ze liever niet op een kantoor en komt ze zo vaak mogelijk naar de schone, sprankelende toendra. Het is goed voor haar kinderen, zegt ze.

'Toen wij nog kinderen waren, waren er geen telefoons, onze ouders waren de hele tijd op de toendra...' Ze vertelt over Alexej die weigert zijn kinderen naar school te sturen, de Sovjetautoriteiten die hen op de toendra opjaagden en haar uiteindelijk toch naar Khatanga brachten. Ze is teruggekeerd naar haar vaders wereldbeeld, en hij is daar duidelijk blij mee. Maar met hun frequentere terugkeer als gezin naar de toendra hebben ze ook de veranderingen opgemerkt. Zij hebben geen enorme veranderingen in temperatuur of vegetatie gezien, maar wel kleine dingen, alsof de aarde beeft van iets dat er nog aankomt. De eerste bevingen van het ontwaken van Siberië uit zijn bevroren winterslaap van het Holoceen manifesteren zich als ongewone waarnemingen van vogels, insecten en vlinders en vreemde luchtbellen onder het ijs.

Na het eten kijkt Tanja naar TikTok-video's waardoor de batterij van haar moeders smartphone leegloopt, terwijl Anna haar haren kamt en vlecht bij het vuur. Ze lijkt haar dochter dicht bij zich te houden, denkend aan de seizoenen die voorbijgaan. Dit wordt Tanja's laatste jaar op de basisschool. Daarna zal ze zich bij haar broers en zussen voegen op de kostschool in Khatanga.

'Afgelopen voorjaar was echt vreemd,' zegt ze. 'We hadden enorme vlinders, een nieuwe soort die we nog nooit eerder hebben gezien. De kinderen waren ze aan het vangen.'

Er verschijnen madeliefjes, zwaluwen en libellen op de toendra, en vorige zomer zwommen de mensen twee weken lang in zee. Meestal duurt de zomer maar een paar dagen. De bessen worden groter, en het zee-ijs in de baai van Syndassko doet er 's winters langer over om dicht te vriezen. En de kust bij het meteorologisch station verzakt steeds verder en stort in zee! Anna zegt dat ze ook andere dingen hebben opgemerkt: nu zijn er ineens raven en kraanvogels. Dat zijn beide vogels die ze vroeger nooit zagen en die normaal veel zuidelijker broeden.

'Wat ze zegt is waar,' zegt Alexei. 'De meeuwen komen eerder, en vervolgens ook de ganzen en de eenden, want de meren zijn ijsvrij. En het vogeltje dat *kystaatch* heet – dat betekent in het Dolgan "degene die in de winter blijft", dat blijft niet meer.'

Anna grist de telefoon weg van haar dochter en stuurt haar nog een laatste keer naar buiten voor ze naar bed gaat.

De lucht is helder. Het maanlicht op de sneeuw verandert de toendra in een gloeiende zee van melk. Tanja is in haar bont gewikkeld en springt van sneeuwjacht naar sneeuwjacht in de richting van een bevroren rivier. Ik loop de andere kant op naar een lichte helling om een plasje te doen in de sneeuw. Op de door mij gekozen plek schiet een *ptarmigan*, een soort korhoen met een zwarte staart en besneeuwd lichaam, kakelend uit zijn hol de avond in. Daarachter ligt een uitgestrekte vlakte. Ik volg voetsporen naar een diep gat met een stalen pin vastgevroren op zijn plaats. Het gat is puur ijs. Ik sta op een meer. Als ik de sneeuw wegveeg verschijnt er een grijs gemarmerd oppervlak. Breuklijnen die de duistere diepte in snijden. Dit is waar het water voor onze thee vandaan komt. Diep in het ijs zijn kleine bevroren belletjes te zien, als parels die in het donker drijven. Als je de kaart later bekijkt, lijkt de toendra in twee dimensies een net of een Zwitserse kaas, vol gaten. In de zomer bestaat ze voor 80 procent uit water.

'Elke poel op de toendra heeft zijn eigen naam,' zegt Alexei als ik weer binnenkom. 'Die heet Oetsjoektai in het Dolgan.' Dat betekent het 'slapende' of 'dromende meer'. Hij kent het verhaal erachter niet, maar meestal is er wel een.

Het meer slaapt inderdaad. De benthale laag, het organisch materiaal op de bodem, wordt door de kou en het gebrek aan zuurstof in een toestand van schijndood gehouden zonder te ontbinden. Bevroren toendrabodems vormen enkele van de grootste opslagplaatsen van organische koolstof op aarde – levende materie, planten en dieren die nog niet volledig zijn weggerot of zo langzaam rotten dat ze bewaard zijn gebleven of gefossiliseerd zijn. Daarom gaan Kolja en Kolja elke zomer graven naar mammoetslagtanden in de toendra van Tajmyr: de dooiende permafrost maakt de zoektocht naar prehistorisch ivoor tot een soort goudkoorts.

Als de temperaturen stijgen en de permafrost begint te ontdooien, komt bij anaerobe afbraak methaan vrij. Tegenwoordig verschijnen er methaanbellen in de poelen op de toendra en in het zee-ijs in de riviermonding. Die parels zijn een teken dat het slapende meer ontwaakt.

Misja komt binnen met een vlaag bevroren mist, zijn lippen bevroren, zijn ogen toegeknepen van de kou en een frons op zijn jeugdige gezicht. Zes uur in het rond rijden, maar hij kon zijn rendieren niet vinden. Hij lijkt ongelukkig. Alexej werpt hem een blik toe en mompelt iets in zichzelf.

Misja's falen kan van alles betekenen. De in Cambridge gevestigde antropoloog Piers Vitebsky schreef over de naburige Evenynomaden, verwante inheemse rendierhoeders die één tijdzone ten oosten van hier de toendra bewonen, en hun gevoel van *bayanay*, de afstemming van een persoon op het landschap, de enorme wereld van een gedeeld bewustzijn dat de levende wereld en de mensen daarin omvat.[11] Misja komt maar zo zelden naar de toendra en daarom is misschien niet in staat geweest om er goed op af te stemmen. De volgende ochtend zal Alexej zich met zijn sneeuwscooter in de verblindende sneeuw storten, maar ook hij zal onverrichter zake terugkeren.

'Vissen is veel gemakkelijker!' zegt Anna, die van haar plaats aan het vuur de boel probeert te sussen. Misja trekt zijn wenkbrauwen op maar glimlacht niet. Niets is nog eenvoudig. Methaan bemoeilijkt de wintervisserij, zegt hij. Je moet voorzichtig zijn, want de bellen maken het ijs zwak.

'Het begint gevaarlijk te worden!'

In de jaren 1970 waren de Kara-, Laptev- en Oost-Siberische Zee slechts gedurende twee maanden ijsvrij – in augustus en september. In 2020 begon de dooi al in april en was de zee aan het eind van het jaar nog steeds niet volledig bevroren. Op 18 mei 2020 verliet de Sovcomflot, een Russisch schip, de haven van Sabetta aan de andere kant van het Jamal-schiereiland dan Tajmyr en sloeg rechtsaf richting China, om op 10 juni aan te meren in de Chinese haven van Jingtang. Het was de vroegste reis ooit op een noordelijke zeeroute die de laatste jaren slechts bevaarbaar was geweest van juli tot november.

Het Siberisch plat, dat de zeebodem vormt voor de kust van Tajmyr, betekent dat de oceaan naar de Noordpool toe ondiep is. Aan het eind van de laatste ijstijd was dit toendra. Toen de gletsjers smolten, overstroomde het land en kwamen alle half vergane aarde en vegetatie terecht onder een koude zee die het grootste deel van het jaar bevroren bleef, waardoor methaanhydraten ontstonden, ijsstructuren die het gas vasthouden. Maar nu de reflecterende deken van zee-ijs bijna verdwenen is, absorbeert de donkere zeebodem tot 80 procent meer straling van de zon, warmt het ondiepe water snel op en blijft het hele jaar door warm. De permafrost op de zeebodem smelt, waardoor de hydraten vrijkomen die olie- en gasbedrijven zo enthousiast maken en klimaatwetenschappers in paniek brengen. Een paar zomers geleden verscheen er een booreiland in de baai van Syndassko, op zoek naar de zachtere zeebodem.

Het meer doet me denken aan een gesprek dat ik voor mijn bezoek aan Siberië had met dr. Ko van Huissteden, een zachtaardige en bedachtzame Nederlandse wetenschapper, een van 's werelds meest vooraanstaande autoriteiten op het gebied van permafrost. Het is moeilijk om het vrijkomen van methaan te meten, vertelde hij me. Wetenschappers hebben het pas onlangs leren vastleggen. Sentinel, een EU-satelliet, kan methaanconcentraties in de atmosfeer meten, maar het is niet zo eenvoudig te bepalen waar het vandaan komt. Volgens sommige studies zou een instabiele zeebodem 500 tot 5000 gigaton methaan kunnen 'boeren', het equivalent van tientallen jaren broeikasgasemissies, en zo kunnen bijdragen tot een abrupte temperatuursprong die de mens niet meer zal kunnen tegenhouden.[12] Ko weet het niet zeker, maar dat, benadrukt hij, is nu net het punt.

Er zijn slechts vier meetstations op het vasteland in Siberië die trachten gegevens te verzamelen over het vrijkomen van methaan en kooldioxide uit de permafrost. De ontdooiende zeebodem wordt niet permanent bewaakt.

'Je hebt minstens tien jaar aan gegevens nodig om iets te ontdekken. En wat neem je als uitgangspunt?'

De meeste Europese onderzoekers verzamelen zich op Spitsbergen, omdat het moeilijk is om in Siberië te komen. De bureaucratie is een ramp, vertelde hij me.

'Niemand heeft enig idee van wat er aan de hand is!' Er is tweemaal zoveel broeikasgas – kooldioxide, methaan en distikstofoxide – opgeslagen in de permafrost als er momenteel in de atmosfeer zit, genoeg om de opwarming van de aarde exponentieel te versnellen en effectief een einde te maken aan het leven op aarde zoals wij dat kennen, als het allemaal in één keer zou vrijkomen. Toch houden de meeste klimaatmodellen geen rekening met permafrost omdat er te weinig gegevens voorhanden zijn, ook al wordt verwacht dat 40 procent van de permafrost tegen het einde van de eeuw verdwenen zal zijn.

Dit alles maakt dat Ko gefrustreerd is over de regeringen omdat ze niet in het verzamelen van gegevens investeren: 'Het is ontstellend hoe weinig geld eraan wordt besteed.' En over de media: 'Het grote publiek denkt nog steeds dat de klimaatverandering geleidelijk zal verlopen. Zij beseffen niet dat het een abrupt proces zal zijn en wat dat betekent in termen van klimaatrampen en het lijden van hun kinderen.' Andere wetenschappers hebben de bevroren broeikasgassen van de permafrost een 'verborgen monster' genoemd. Ko noemt Siberië een 'slapende beer'.

In de baloch steken grote fonkelende scherven van het mooie, maar plotseling sinistere meer uit de ketel, en nog meer kristallijnen blokken ontdooien in een emmer die boven het vuur hangt. Terwijl Misja stoofpot eet en Alexei zijn krant leest, spelen moeder en dochter domino en zingen zachtjes, nu de telefoonbatterij leeg is, even genietend van de oude manier van doen, tot morgenochtend, wanneer we over de bevroren toendra terugvliegen naar die laatste buitenpost van de menselijke beschaving, Syndassko, als astronauten die terugkeren naar hun ruimtestation na een wandeling buiten, in het niets.

Vier maanden later, in juni 2020, zal een recordhitte de thermometer in Syndassko voor het eerst in de geschiedenis boven de 30 graden brengen. Het historisch gemiddelde voor de maand is 10 tot 12° Celsius. De bosbranden in de regio zullen tien keer groter zijn dan in het voorgaande jaar waarin ook al records werden gebroken. Het verdwijnen van de permafrost zal gedeeltelijk verantwoordelijk zijn voor het scheuren van de olietanks in Norilsk, waardoor 21.000 ton diesel aan de voet van het schiereiland Tajmyr terechtkomt, in het Pyasina-meer en -rivierenstelsel dat vanuit de ruimte rood zal lijken, als aderen die door het land lopen. De *Siberian Times* bericht dat de temperaturen in Tajmyr 'alle klimaatrecords hebben gebroken en oudjes hebben verrast', en citeert een ambtenaar die zegt dat, terwijl de sneeuw gewoonlijk in juli smelt, er nu al 'geen sneeuwvlokje meer in de toendra ligt en witte hazen verbijsterd rondhuppelen in het groen.'[13] Wetenschappers wereldwijd zullen volkomen over hun toeren raken van de extreme opwarming van het Noordpoolgebied. Wanneer ik Ko in Nederland bel om te vragen naar zijn visie op wat er gebeurt in de buitengewone zomer van 2020, met 40° C in Europa en vergelijkbare temperaturen in Siberië, zegt hij dat het een ramp is en dat, 'de slapende beer zich roert.'

Ary Mas, Rusland
72° 28' 07" N

Deze keer treffen we, wanneer we de rivier weer afvaren naar Novoribyne, de Nganasanen-familie wel thuis. Het heeft uren geduurd, een hele dag rijden vanaf Syndassko, langzaam stroomopwaarts langs de steeds nauwer wordende riviermonding, een grote witte veeg onder een gebogen blauwe hemel die nu en dan wordt onderbroken door het vierkant van een baloch van grijs canvas, midden op het ijs geplant: ijsviskampen van de Dolgan. Zwarte Kolya stopt bij verschillende ervan omdat hij de jerrycan wodka wil ruilen voor bevroren vis, maar ze zijn verlaten, de gaten zijn dichtgevroren, netten en vangst geconserveerd in het frazil ijs – bijna-ijs – onder het bevroren oppervlak van de rivier. Het is inmiddels donker wanneer we de bomen van Novoribyne weer zien, korte stekelige schaduwen van lariksen die de rand van de wereld afbakenen, zwart tegen het diepe blauw van de nachtelijke hemel.

We kloppen aan in een bevroren houten portiek en stappen naar binnen, sneeuw valt op de vloer. Een oudere vrouw in een velours kamerjas, pantoffels en een heel dikke bril waardoor ze ons verbaasd aankijkt, gebaart ons de keuken binnen te gaan. Ze lijkt Dima's uitleg over waarom we hier zijn niet te begrijpen en stuurt een van de vele kinderen die naar ons staren de nacht in om een buurman te halen.

Enorme blauwe pijpen zo dik als mijn middel lopen langs de binnenkant van de muur. Op de achtergrond sudderen stoofpotten zachtjes op een fornuis, gestookt op hout, kolen of turf. Ze zet ons aan een houten tafel en schenkt taigathee in: wilgenkruid en munt.

'*Grande Bretagne*?' roept ze in gebrekkig Frans naar mij, via Dima, dan weer in het Russisch. 'Is Bush je president of is het de vrouw? Heb je Poetin gezien in Moskou?'

Zij heet Maria. Ze wijst naar zichzelf. Terwijl we wachten op de buurman, komt Maria's man binnen.

'Yevstappi.' Ze wijst. 'Dzjasta!'

Dzjasta is lang, en zijn krachtige schouders zijn duidelijk zichtbaar onder zijn geruite shirt. Zijn witte haar is kortgeknipt en zijn lichte ogen fonkelen als de sneeuw en het ijs van de toendra. Maria en Dzjasta wonen pas de laatste tien jaar in een houten huis in Novoribyne. De eerste zestig brachten ze door in een tent op de toendra of in het bos van Ary Mas. Novoribyne lijkt mij een van de meest afgelegen plaatsen op aarde, maar voor Maria en Dzjasta vertegenwoordigde het altijd de beschaving – de plaats met de school, de kliniek, het regeringskantoor – een plaats die ze zoveel mogelijk vermeden.

Vroeger, voor de Tweede Wereldoorlog, staken de meeste Nganasanen nooit de Khatangarivier, de zuidelijke grens van het schiereiland, over.

Generatie na generatie leefde en stierf hier bovenop de wereld, boven de 72ste breedtegraad, ver van de gebeurtenissen op de rest van het continent, met hun traditionele manier van leven, grotendeels vrij van de invloed van tsaren, Kozakken, Sovjets of wie dan ook. Ze verplaatsten zich naar believen over de toendra op sleden gemaakt van larikshout, in de door het seizoen bepaalde achtervolging van de overvloedige wilde rendierkudden van Tajmyr die in grote jaarlijkse herhalende patronen heen en weer trokken over het schiereiland – zoals Sovjet-antropoloog Popov het beschreef. Alles wat ze nodig hadden was te vinden ten noorden van de golf van de Khatangarivier. En er was veel te vrezen in het zuiden.

Moderne prioriteiten hebben die oude geografie echter overhoop gehaald. Vanuit het oogpunt van bestuur en communicatie is de Golf van Khatanga geen grens, maar de belangrijkste bevaarbare snelweg waarlangs bonthandelaren, belastinginners en de gevangenen die door Stalin naar de Goelag werden gestuurd, reisden. Toen de staat zich vestigde in de twee seizoensgebonden vissersdorpen van de nomaden, Novoribyne en Syndassko, werkten de Dolgans mee. De Nganasanen van Tajmyr niet. In de daaropvolgende campagne tegen 'dorpen zonder vooruitzichten' werden veel mensen onder dwang verplaatst en werd er feitelijk een einde gemaakt aan de oude manier van leven.

Dzjasta's ouders behoorden tot de lastige nomaden die naar een stad ten zuiden van Khatanga werden gestuurd. Ze wisten echter te ontsnappen en keerden zo dicht mogelijk terug naar de wilde vlakten van Tajmyr waar ze geboren en getogen waren op het moment van Popovs fatale bezoek. De dichtstbijzijnde officiële nederzetting die ze konden vinden was het Dolgan-vissersdorp Novoribyne.

'Ik ben hier geboren,' zegt Dzjasta, terwijl hij nadrukkelijk naar de linoleumvloer van de keuken wijst, en zijn stem klinkt uitdagend. 'Op de identiteitskaart die ik heb gekregen, staat dat ik in 1951 ben geboren.'

Dzjasta spreekt in het Nganasan tegen Maria, die half Dolgan is, en zij vertaalt in het Dolgan. Anna, de buurvrouw die Dolgan is, is gekomen om naar het Russisch te vertalen voor Dima, die haar woorden vervolgens voor mij in het Engels vertaalt. In het begin lijkt Dzjasta terughoudend om met ons te praten.

'Ik ben gewoon een wilde man, een wilde. Ik weet niet veel, ik ben niet naar school geweest!' Maar steeds als het ook maar even over de toendra lijkt te gaan, lijkt zijn geheugen te worden ontgrendeld.

'Voor de Sovjets was dit alles' – hij wijst op de wereld buiten het raam – 'ons gebied. Tajmyr!' Hij zegt de naam met gevoel.

'Het is uitgestrekt! Je kunt er jagen! De bomen, daarentegen, waren een soort plaag, alleen nodig om te overleven. Hij vond ze maar niks. Het bos was donker en benauwend. Ze gingen elke winter naar Ary Mas omdat de rendieren dat nu eenmaal deden. Het bos was meer beschut, er was brandhout en er waren korstmossen voor de dieren om te eten. De Nganasanen volgden een jaarlijkse maancyclus verdeeld in twee 'jaren', het zomerjaar en het winterjaar, in overeenstemming met de seizoensgebonden migraties van een breed scala van dieren waarnaar zij hun maanden noemden – 'elandenmaand, maand van het hoornloze hert, maand van de ruiende gans, maand van het ganzenjong' – en de cycli van de bomen. *Sjesusena kiteda*, 'berijpte-bomen-maand', is de tweede helft van februari en de eerste helft van maart, en *feniptidi kiteda*, 'zwart-wordende-bomen-maand', is wanneer de takken vrij raken van sneeuw in de tweede helft van maart en de eerste helft van april, wat aangeeft dat het binnenkort tijd is om de beschutting van het bos te verlaten. Dan, in de zomer, de hoogvlakte! Vis, gevogelte, hazen, elanden, rendieren. Als hij niet tien jaar geleden een beroerte had gehad, zou hij nog steeds daarbuiten zijn, wonend in een *chum*, een tent die veel lijkt op de laavo van de Sami. Zijn tien kinderen zijn geboren in een chum, net als hij. Maria knikt plechtig.

Het Sovjetkolonialisme na de revolutie van oktober 1917 had een ander karakter dan zijn West-Europese tegenhanger. De USSR onteigende de inheemse bevolking van het noorden niet – men was niet in de eerste plaats uit op land, want daar was genoeg van – maar trachtte hen 'productief' te maken, in de communistische economie op te nemen. Men beweerde hen te bevrijden van primitieve gewoonten en de feodale verhoudingen van het verleden. Toen hij terugkeerde naar het noorden, sloot Dzjasta's vader zich aan bij de Novoribyne sovkhoz, die zich in dit deel van het Sovjetrijk bezighield met rendieren hoeden. Overal in Siberië werden rendierhoeders in de Sovjeteconomie opgenomen in 'brigades', met leiders, routes en gebieden, gebaseerd op hun traditionele praktijken en migraties, maar vaak zonder de flexibiliteit en familiestructuren van de oude aanpak. Net als andere onderdelen van het Sovjetsysteem hadden de brigades doelstellingen en quota, en reikten ze prijzen uit aan hoeders die hun quota overschreden. En de sovchoz had zijn hoofdkwartier in een stad, met een kantoor, het contactpunt tussen het geherconfigureerde nomadenleven en de industriële infrastructuur van de twintigste eeuw. Novoribyne was het hoofdkwartier van de brigade die Dzjasta's vader leidde en die hij op zijn beurt ook zou leiden.

Hun familie was beroemd in de stad. Eén keer per jaar kwamen ze naar het kantoor van de sovchoz en de rest van het jaar trokken ze zich terug op de toendra en in het bos. Dzjasta stond, net als zijn vader, bekend om zijn kracht. Hij kon in zijn eentje een rendierkarkas van vijftig kilo aan zijn hoeven optillen. Zijn moeder was een felle traditionaliste, die het Nganasan-taboe op geweven kleding handhaafde en alleen Nganasan sprak. In Novoribyne konden ze haar niet verstaan. Zij droeg haar hele leven rendierhuiden en werd in 1990 op het kerkhof van de stad begraven met haar slee en haar drie leidende rendieren, geofferd aan de rand van het graf. Dzjasta is de laatste Nganasan-spreker in de stad en toch is hij vreemd genoeg nuchter over het dreigende uitsterven van zijn cultuur.

'Er zijn veel heilige plaatsen in de toendra en het bos. Als je er een passeert, moet je stoppen en een offer brengen. Maar mijn kinderen kennen die plaatsen niet omdat ze niet migreren. Niemand kent deze plaatsen nog, en niemand zal het nu nog weten omdat we gestopt zijn met hoeden.'

De mythische wereld van de Nganasanen was verdeeld in drie

niveaus. Lariks, de 'wereldboom' die in het hele inheemse Siberische sjamanisme voorkomt, is een vrouwelijke godheid die Moederboom wordt genoemd en die de drie werelden met elkaar verbindt: de boven-, midden- en onderwereld. Het noorden, het onderaardse en het dikke ijs vormen het rijk van de doden, waar ziekte en geesten wonen. In het zuiden is het warme huis van de god van de donder. De helden leven in de bovenwereld, en opmerkelijke punten in het landschap – de beken, bomen, bossen, holten en rotsen van Tajmyr – vormen doorgangen tussen de drie. Men moet zeer voorzichtig zijn om de wezens die bij deze poorten kunnen leven niet te beledigen. Dit zijn de heilige plaatsen die niemand meer bezoekt.

De lariks verbond de niveaus. De etnologie van Popov verklaart de centrale rol van de lariksboom als volgt:

> Op de zevende dag bereikte Dyuchade het hoogste niveau van de hemel. Een lange paal werd in het midden van de tent geplaatst. De sjamaan klom omhoog en stak zijn hoofd uit het rookkanaal. De paal symboliseerde de boom die in het midden oprees. Boven in de boom leefde een godheid met een vlekkerig gezicht... Toen werd hij naar de oevers van de negen meren gedragen. In het midden van een van die meren lag een eiland. Op het eiland stond een boom, een lariks die tot in de hemel reikte. Het was de boom van de Meesteres van de aarde... Toen hoorde hij een stem: 'Er is besloten dat je een trommel krijgt van de takken van deze boom.'

De taak van de sjamanen was te bemiddelen tussen de niveaus en ervoor te zorgen dat het evenwicht en het respect bewaard bleven. Met tromgeroffel en gezang communiceerden zij met de levende wereld die al het leven in stand hield. Elk levend wezen, ook de mens, had zijn eigen unieke autobiografische lied dat essentieel was om het leven tot stand te brengen of in rituelen aan te spreken. Dzjasta herinnert zich sjamanen in Ary Mas, en hoe zij wat afgezonderd leefden van de rest van de tenten, in hutten van lariksstammen en aarde. Als kind werd hem opgedragen niet te schreeuwen of lawaai te maken in hun nabijheid, schuin te passeren en nooit rechtstreeks naar de sjamanen en hun woningen te kijken.

'Heb je Kosterkin gekend?' vraag ik. Kosterkin was een beroemde sjamaan, de laatste sjamaan van de Nganasanen, die in de jaren 1980 overleed. Hij stond ooit toe dat zijn seances van een week en zijn onderricht in de Nganasan-animistische geloofsovertuigingen werden gefilmd door een Estse televisiemaatschappij.[14] Dit is een van de enige verslagen van de traditionele Nganasan-sjamanistische praktijk. De mythische wereld van de Nganasanen was zeer geavanceerd. Er bestond geen onderscheid tussen geesten en de fysieke wereld, en het bezielende leven in elke plant, rots, persoon of dier was een geest die niet gebonden was aan de fysieke vorm van het betreffende ding. Elke groep geesten had een code van acht regels, gewoonten, taal en kleding. Afgezien daarvan was geur van cruciaal belang. Als je te lang aan de geur van iets wordt blootgesteld, loop je het risico de eigenschappen van dat ding te absorberen. Dus een mens die lange tijd naast een boom zit, kan ervoor zorgen dat die boom menselijk wordt. Maar Dzjasta wordt boos als ik het over de sjamaan heb.

'Ik heb wel gehoord van Kosterkin, maar hem nooit ontmoet. Dat soort dingen is nu allemaal verleden tijd. De Russen!'

Als ik vraag naar de traditionele geneeskunde krijg ik dezelfde afwijzende reactie.

'Wij hadden de beste dierenartsen en dokters. De Sovjets brachten ze naar de toendra in helikopters!'

Er lijkt een soort oorlog plaats te vinden in de lichamen van die ouderen die vroege herinneringen hebben aan een manier van leven die sinds de ijstijd onveranderd was gebleven, maar die als volwassenen een ervaring hebben van razendsnelle vooruitgang die hun leven gemakkelijker heeft gemaakt, ook al is daarbij nog zoveel verloren gegaan. Ze zijn gekoloniseerd door het koolwaterstofdenken en moeten het Faustiaanse contract en de omstandigheden van hun nakomelingen aanvaarden, hoe pijnlijk die ook zijn. Alexej doet geen moeite om te verbergen dat het hem verwart, en beweegt heen en weer tussen een verlangen naar wat verloren is gegaan en de aanvaarding van de prijs die moest worden betaald. Maar Dzjasta is eerder star en houdt vast aan het vooruitgangsverhaal van de Sovjetstaat, ondanks de consequenties die dat heeft voor zijn erfgoed.

Als ik vraag naar zijn dertien kleinkinderen en drie achterkleinkinderen die de Nganasan-taal nooit zullen spreken, haalt Dzjasta zijn schouders op, alsof hij wil zeggen: 'Nou en?' Door de deur van de slaapkamer zijn ze nog net zichtbaar, de kleine gezichten van de nakomelingen van de trotse boswachters van Ary Mas, verlicht door de blauwe gloed van een televisie die in het Russisch pruttelt.

Dzjasta's houding herinnert aan een studie over de Nganasan-cultuur die ik heb gelezen en waarin professor Helimski uit Hamburg verwijst naar de 'bevroren cultuur van de Nganasan' als een overblijfsel dat bewaard is gebleven in de permafrost, een uitgebreide mondelinge cultuur die zich ontwikkelde gedurende de vele lange maanden van de winter en waarin het vertellen van verhalen, grammaticale precisie en metaforische vaardigheid hoog in het vaandel stonden. Helimski citeert ouderen die niet tegen de stroom van de verandering op willen zwemmen en die over hun kinderen zeggen: 'Laten ze onze taal maar beter helemaal niet spreken dan haar te verbasteren.'[15]

Op het eerste gezicht lijkt het een vreemde houding, maar er zit iets in de trotse weigering om compromissen te sluiten, iets nobels, maar ook een andere verhouding tot de sterfelijkheid. Voor inheemse volken die dicht bij de onmetelijke en onvoorspelbare krachten van de wilde natuur leven, is de dood altijd aanwezig. Misschien gaat er een zekere vrijheid uit van de aanvaarding die de geest helpt verder te reizen dan het benauwde kader van een enkel leven of een enkele soort, waardoor men zichzelf volledig kan laten opnemen in een schitterend, alomvattend geheel: we zijn niets, maar we zijn alles. Het is een geweldig, uitdagend vooruitzicht. Dzjasta's gevoel voor tijd stamt van een soortgelijk perspectief. Het is geologisch, en het is een gevoeligheid die de rest van ons misschien nog snel van pas zal komen.

'De bomen rukken op naar het noorden, zeg je? En beweren de wetenschappers niet dat er hier vroeger bossen waren?'

Dat is zo, al zijn ze het niet eens over het tijdsbestek. Een verband kunnen aantonen tussen Dzjasta's mondelinge overlevering en de geologische gegevens zou de echte wetenschappelijke hoofdprijs zijn, hoewel ik vermoed dat de kans op een dergelijk gesprek klein is. Mensen zijn maar een stipje op die tijdlijn, en Dzjasta is er weinig nostalgisch over. Hij aanvaardt het harde regime van de natuur volledig. Dat geeft hem een nederigheid die moedig is in de verwachting dat het niet eenvoudig zal zijn, en compromisloos in de afwijzing van elk sentiment.

'Opwarming van de aarde? Vertel dat maar aan mijn kleinkinderen, tegen die tijd ben ik er niet meer.'

Na het interview besluiten Kolja en Kolja dat als we Ary Mas bij daglicht willen zien, we 'vroeg' moeten vertrekken.

'Om vier uur 's nachts misschien? Drie uur?' vraag ik hoopvol.

'Nee, om middernacht.'

En dus gingen we na opnieuw een maaltijd van ijskoude vis, mosterd en chilipoeder met Anna en Konstantin, 's nachts op weg langs een andere bevroren rivier, de Novaya, een zijrivier van de Khatanga, noordwaarts naar het hart van het schiereiland. Ik zie niets, ben me van niets bewust, behalve van de blauwe plekken op mijn lichaam, terwijl de Trekol ons door elkaar schudt als erwten in een rammelaar.

We komen aan op onze bestemming terwijl de maan ondergaat, negen uur later. De bleke maanschijf, zwevend in een indigo hemel, verschilt in tint nauwelijks van de besneeuwde toendra eronder. Donkere grasvlekken en af en toe een boom markeren de grond, zodat we enig idee van de schaal krijgen. Zonder dat zijn de witte golven van het landschap desoriënterend en strekken zich in alle richtingen uit, als een soort witte Sahara. We zijn op zoek naar een bos in dit enorme, eindeloze landschap. Waar zijn de bomen? Ze zouden hier moeten staan volgens Kolja.

Kolja staart naar een klein gps-apparaatje dat van plakband aan elkaar hangt en dat hij in zijn ene hand houdt, terwijl hij met de andere het stuur van onze vreemde terreinwagen vast heeft.

De maan werpt een griezelige gloed terwijl de terreinwagen voortjankt, de loop van de rivier volgend, en we turen door de wazige voorruit naar de plooien en richels van de sneeuw die langs de oever opgestapeld ligt. Dan, plotseling, doemt het bos op, alsof het oprijst uit de toendra, de dalen en troggen van de vallei overspoelend. Het is wat merkwaardig, want hoewel we op een bevroren rivier rijden, bevinden we ons hoger dan het bos. Toch zijn er maar weinig dingen die werkelijk lijken te kloppen zo ver noordelijk, vlak voor zonsopgang op 11 februari 2020, bij 44 graden Celsius onder nul. Ik heb de hele nacht heen en weer gerold achterin de terreinwagen, tegen dieseltanks, gereedschapskisten, reserveonderdelen en een jerrycan wodka van vijf liter aan stotend zonder een oog dicht te doen. Maar nu ben ik klaarwakker en kijkt met een glimlach naar de dageraad. De ontberingen van de reis zijn vergeten. We zijn er eindelijk.

De bomen verdwijnen een tijdje uit het zicht, maar na een volgende bocht in de rivier hebben ze een bergkam beklommen. Rang na rang torenen de spichtige stammen boven ons uit, tegen de verlichte achtergrond van een gelig, nevelig ochtendgloren. Uitsluitend lariksen. De dunne takken en tere naalden geven de berijpte Larix gmelinii een frêle aanblik, maar dat is misleidend. Eigenlijk zijn het de taaiste bomen van de taiga, en dus van de hele wereld. Ze vormen de enige soort die geëvolueerd is om zo ver noordelijk te overleven, in deze extreme koude, waar de permafrost meer dan 200 meter diep is, en de temperatuur gedurende negen maanden van het jaar altijd onder het vriespunt is gebleven.

Ik haast me naar voren, opgewonden om het bos te zien opdoemen uit het vaalblauwe licht van voor zonsopgang. Maanden lang heb ik over dit hoogtepunt van de boomgrens gelezen en gedroomd. Russische popmuziek blijft klinken, en het deinen van de Trekol voelt nu bijna triomfantelijk terwijl we onze bestemming naderen. Blonde Kolja begreep niet waarom we het bos zouden moeten bezoeken en probeerde me verschillende keren deze omweg te ontraden. Maar nu glimlacht hij ook.

Het bos gaat links van ons verder en houdt ons gezelschap op de oplopende zuidelijke oever van de rivier. We rijden verder, in westelijke richting, tot er aan de noordelijke oever meer bomen verschijnen, en een handjevol besneeuwde hutten, een waslijn, een weerstation met een antenne en een in de grond geslagen matmetalen bord waarop in het Russisch staat: Ary-Mas: het noordelijkste bos ter wereld.

Blonde Kolja grijpt naar de moersleutel die als versnellingspook dient en zet de terreinwagen in neutraal, maar laat de motor draaien. Die heeft vier dagen onafgebroken gedraaid. Hij zet de muziek uit die al de hele avond krassend uit zijn telefoon klinkt, leunt achterover in zijn stoel en ademt luid uit. Hij heeft geen moment geklaagd, maar de tocht over de spoorloze, bevroren toendra met slechts één slechte koplamp en heel weinig slaap is zelfs voor iemand met zoveel ervaring als hij een beproeving geweest. Hij legt zijn voorhoofd op het stuur, op enkele centimeters van het dashboard met zijn ondiepe bak met daarin sleutels, isolatietape, veiligheidsspelden, lucifers, aanstekers, een usb-stick, vijf kogels en een flessenopener en reikt in de zak van het bestuurdersportier naar een gehavend pakje sigaretten. Hij steekt er een op, opent de deur, een ijzige bries binnenlatend, en wendt zich tot mij op de passagiersstoel met zijn speelse halve glimlach.

'Ary Mas! Oké? Oké Ary Mas!' Hij spreekt geen Engels en ik geen Russisch, maar we begrijpen elkaar perfect. Wat hij bedoelt is, 'Ben je nu tevreden?'

We trekken onze sneeuwlaarzen, mutsen, twee paar handschoenen, bivakmutsen en gevoerde jassen aan en stappen uit de terreinwagen. Dat is nog niet zo eenvoudig. Je moet je vasthouden aan de deur terwijl je eerst op een van de enorme ronde rubberen wielen van de Trekol stapt en dan anderhalve meter naar beneden springt op het bevroren oppervlak van de rivier.

De rivieroever loopt steil omhoog naar het wetenschappelijk

station. De sneeuw kleurt crèmekleurig oranje, net als de lichter wordende hemel, en hier en daar steken er bevroren en kristalheldere grassen en zaadkoppen uit die in de zachte lucht hangen. De bevroren rivier buigt af naar het westen, waardoor dit kleine eiland van bomen op de noordelijke oever helemaal alleen achterblijft. Een eiland binnen het eiland van bos. Zo'n 15.611 hectare bomen is aan alle kanten omgeven door toendra. Niemand weet waarom dit bos het hier heeft overleefd. De meest gangbare theorie is dat de laatste ijstijd bijzonder agressief was en grote hoeveelheden water op aarde in ijs opsloot, waardoor het zeeniveau zo sterk daalde dat de kust van de Noordelijke IJszee honderden kilometers noordelijker kwam te liggen. Daardoor raakten de vlakten van het Tajmyr-schiereiland maar ongelijkmatig met gletsjers bedekt, en Ary Mas zou een overblijfsel zijn uit de vorige ijstijd.

Anderen menen dat de bomen relatieve nieuwkomers zijn, die profiteren van gunstige bodemstructuren en heel langzaam op weg zijn, nog verder naar het noorden. Ze groeien en sterven echter zo langzaam dat geen van beide theorieën makkelijk te bewijzen is op een menselijke tijdschaal.

Dima en ik knarsen door het glinsterende oppervlak van de sneeuw. De hutten zijn verlaten en er is hier de hele winter niemand geweest. De bomen staan stil en er is geen zuchtje wind. De waslijn hangt slap. De maan is nu achter de horizon verdwenen en de zon is zojuist opgekomen. De sneeuw glinstert roze en de naalden van de bomen lijken in brand te staan. De lariks laat in de winter zijn naalden vallen, maar de eerste vorst kwam duidelijk voordat de bomen er klaar voor waren, en de dode, uitgedroogde naalden zijn aan de tak bevroren. Ik strijk langs een van de lariksen, en de naalden tinkelen op de grond door mijn aanraking. De slanke takken zijn bedekt met zeer fijne trachoomhaartjes die lijken op die van de zachte berk, een bontjas om warmte vast te houden en de kou te temperen. Ze breken als balsahout omdat er geen vocht in de twijgen zit. Dit is de reden waarom de lariks in de winter zulk goed brandhout levert en waarom hij überhaupt bij deze temperaturen kan overleven: de boom heeft een mechanisme ontwikkeld om de fatale vorming van ijskristallen in levende cellen te voorkomen.

De belangrijkste lariksspecialist van Ary Mas, Nadezjda's vriend Aleksandr Bondarev, was jaloers dat wij het bos in de winter bezochten. Hij doet, net als de meeste andere wetenschappers, alleen onderzoek in de zomer. 'Mijn bomen! Ze zullen zich mij herinneren! Doe ze de groeten!' had hij me aan de telefoon op het hart gedrukt. Zijn enthousiasme voor de Aziatische lariks is ongewoon, geboren uit twintig jaar steeds weer hernieuwde kennismakingen. 'Het is een heel slimme boom. Slimmer dan jij!'

Larix gmelinii is een wonder van de natuurlijke wereld. Wanneer de winter nadert, begint de boom water vanuit het xyleem, de haarvaten in zijn stam, naar de schors en alle andere ruimten buiten de levende cellen van de boom te verplaatsen. Hierdoor kan het plasmamembraan van de cel leeglopen en vormt het ijs zich buiten de cel, zonder deze te kunnen beschadigen. Als de luchttemperatuur daalt tot -5 of -6, blijft de temperatuur binnenin de stam op nul omdat de boom langzaam afkoelt. De temperatuurgradiënt tussen de vloeistof in de cellen en het ijs buiten de cellen maakt verglazing mogelijk – het stollen van water zonder dat het in ijs verandert. Dat is wat er gebeurt als je een boom in vloeibare stikstof legt: door de superkoeling verandert het water in iets wat meer op glas lijkt dan op ijs. IJs bestaat uit kristallen die de cellen beschadigen, wat leidt tot een toestand die vorstschade wordt genoemd. Verglaasd water is daarentegen gelijkmatig en vast. Door deze langzame afkoeling kan het water uit de levende cellen worden gezogen. Ondertussen vinden er talloze andere veranderingen plaats. De boom vult zijn cellen met abscisinezuur dat de doorlaatbaarheid van de celmembranen voor water verhoogt, waardoor ze kunnen 'lekken'. Suikers en eiwitten veranderen bij lage temperaturen in gedepolymeriseerde suikers die zich aan het bevroren water hechten zodat de boom bestand is tegen uitdroging. Naarmate het kouder wordt, produceert de lariks chloroplastlipiden om vet af te zetten en de plasticiteit van zijn celwanden te vergroten, waardoor het watergehalte nog verder afneemt. Op het hoogtepunt van de winter zit er zo weinig vocht in een overwinterende lariksboom dat onmogelijk vast te stellen is of hij dood is of leeft.

Het is dit vermogen om vocht in de vorm van water en ijs te beheren dat de lariks in staat stelt te gedijen onder de relatief woeste omstandigheden van Siberië. In de winter kunnen hun wortels dan misschien vastgevroren zijn, maar zelfs het winterse licht van een korte dag dat op de uiteinden van hun takken valt, kan de wortels activeren, waardoor vocht uit de ijzerharde grond omhoog wordt gezogen naar de takken en naalden. Bij lage temperaturen is vocht schaars, maar ijs – in de vorm van permafrost – is er in overvloed. De Aziatische lariks houdt zo van de kou dat onderzoekers denken dat hij mee-evolueerde met de verspreiding van de permafrost. Het is geen verrassing dat dit cryolithische bos, het bevroren bos van de noordelijke taiga, wordt gedomineerd door de soort die het ijs het beste heeft leren waarderen.

Voorbij de spaarzame gebouwen van het wetenschappelijk station, waar de blonde Kolja klauwsporen onderzoekt op een ingebeukte deur, blijkbaar het werk van een veelvraat, zijn de bomen gestuit in hun groei, staan ze steeds verder uit elkaar en verdwijnen uiteindelijk helemaal te midden van de kniediepe sneeuw. Ik staar weg van de opkomende zon naar de toendra die oprijst uit de dageraad, de prachtige, onvergetelijke, kraakheldere rand van de beboste wereld. Het is een abrupte boomgrens. In de lange schaduwen van de dageraad lijken de bomen tot stilstand gekomen figuren in groepjes van twee en drie, met enkele eenzame koplopers een paar honderd meter verder, alleen in de toendra, strompelend op weg naar de pool. Wanneer de zon boven het bladerdak van het bos verschijnt, lijkt ze de korte takken van de piekerige lariksen in brand te steken, en plotseling zijn er oranje en rode vlammen die over de paarsachtige sneeuw flakkeren tegen de zachte roze-blauwe lucht.

Het patroon van bomen in het vroege ochtendlicht lijkt op taigapioniers die op weg zijn naar de Noordelijke IJszee en scouts vooruit hebben gestuurd om het terrein te verkennen, maar door mijn gesprek met Aleksandr kijk ik nu anders naar dit deel van de boomgrens en het bos van Ary Mas.

Aleksandr begon in 1995 de bomen van Ary Mas te bestuderen, maar na een jaar of vijf, zes werd hij naar een ander deel van Siberië overgeplaatst om leiding te geven aan de natuurbeschermingsinspanningen in het Altai-gebergte. Na een onderbreking van bijna twintig jaar keerde hij in 2019 terug om vast te stellen dat zijn geliefde lariksen zich niet hadden bewogen en niet waren gegroeid.

'Dat was een bijzonder vreemde ervaring voor me,' zei Aleksandr.

De maximale toename in diameter was twee millimeter, en voor de meeste bomen waar hij in boorde en kernmonsters van nam om de ringen te tellen, was het zelfs nog minder. De bomen waren nog even hoog en het uitzicht was nog precies hetzelfde als al die jaren geleden.

Aleksandrs bevindingen waren in tegenspraak met alle modellen voor het oprukken van de boomgrens en strookten niet met het beeld van de zich noordwaarts haastende bossen waarmee ik mijn onderzoek begon, en dat door simplistische modellen uitsluitend op basis van de temperatuur wordt voorspeld. Toen een vanuit Cambridge geleid onderzoek al het materiaal over de boomgrens van de afgelopen twintig jaar samenbracht, lieten de in 2020 gepubliceerde resultaten[16] een gemengd beeld zien van soorten die verschillend reageren in verschillende ecosystemen. Aleksandrs waarnemingen komen overeen met twee andere rapporten – uit West-Siberië en Oost-Alaska – waar de boomgrens stabiel leek te zijn of zich zelfs aan het terugtrekken was. Bomen zijn geen eenvoudige machines die meer kooldioxide fotosynthetiseren en meer groeien, alleen omdat het warmer is. Het zich aanpassende DNA van de lariks zou wel eens een andere reactie kunnen conditioneren. Overleven in deze extreme omgeving wordt niet bepaald door groei, grootte of de hoeveelheid zaad, maar door strategisch denken. Het is, zoals Aleksandr zegt, een erg slimme boom.

Er is nog geen duidelijk aanwijsbaar spoor van opwarming in

de dicht opeengepakte boomringen van de lariksen van Ary Mas. De winters zijn warmer geworden en de gemiddelde zomertemperaturen zijn langzaam omhoog gekropen, maar de winden die over het zee-ijs komen aanwaaien, hebben de zomertemperaturen tot voor kort altijd laag gehouden. Ook al zou het uitblijven van een opmars van de boomgrens verklaard kunnen worden door andere factoren, zoals de slechte kwaliteit van de bodem, het gebrek aan beschikbare voedingsstoffen of een ontoereikende populatie mycorrhizaschimmels om voor een toename van het aantal bomen te zorgen, dan nog had Aleksandr een betere opvulling, meer successie binnen het bos verwacht. Daar was echter geen sprake van. De onderlaag was nog net zo als twintig jaar eerder en er was heel weinig dood hout. Hij schreef dat toe aan de nomadische hoedersbrigade van Dzjasta, die het bos pas niet meer mocht betreden en kappen toen het in 1979 tot nationaal reservaat werd verklaard.

'Zij waren uitstekende bosbeheerders!'

Toch was de ondergroei ongewoon dun.

'Het was een raadsel. Ary Mas is een zeer interessant bos,' zei hij.

Het bos is hier open. Zonder de sneeuw die tot mijn knieën reikt en me afremt, zou ik gemakkelijk tussen de korte, krummholz-bomen kunnen wandelen. Het is geen bos met een gesloten bladerdak in de traditionele zin – de takken van de bomen raken elkaar niet. Maar op een andere manier is het wel een gesloten bladerdak: ondergronds. De afstand tussen de bomen wordt bepaald door hun wortels die verspreid liggen in de zeer ondiepe actieve laag grond boven de permafrost, de dertig centimeter die elke zomer zo'n honderd dagen lang ontdooit. Er is maar een beperkte hoeveelheid grond die moet worden gedeeld, en de lariks lijkt te voorkomen dat andere struiken kunnen wortelen tussen de bomen. Bij het onderzoeken van deze strategie ontdekte Aleksandr nog iets anders unieks aan Ary Mas.

Verder naar het zuiden in de taiga hebben andere larikssoorten relatief beperkte wortelstelsels en meer fytomen (levende cellen) boven de grond. Maar bij Ary Mas zit bijna de helft van de fytomen van de plant onder de grond en de andere helft erboven. De met sneeuw bedekte grond is isolerend in de winter en beschermend, uit de wind, zodat een groter deel van de boom onder de grond zit. Die zit daarmee ook dichter bij de permafrost, de bron van voedingsstoffen en vocht. Bij het onderzoeken van de relaties die deze vreemde ondergrondse boom aangaat, merkte Aleksandr dat de lariksen van Ary Mas zich vegetatief voortplantten onder de bemoste laag van niet verteerde naalden en korstmossen – zonder bestuiving. De wortels krijgen uitlopers en nieuwe scheuten boven de grond zijn verbonden met de wortels en stronken van oudere bomen. Alle bomen lijken samen te werken als in een orkest.

Bovendien merkte Aleksandr op dat alle volwassen bomen dezelfde maximale hoogte van vijf meter lijken te hebben, ongeacht hun leeftijd. Er zijn geen hogere exemplaren. In de zuidelijker gelegen lariksbossen zijn gemengde hoogten en opstanden de norm. Als je een lariks van bovenaf bekijkt, heeft hij een kurkentrekkerachtige vorm, waarbij de takken spiraalsgewijs langs de stam naar beneden uitwaaieren. Zo kunnen ze zoveel mogelijk licht vangen zonder andere in de schaduw te stellen. We weten het niet zeker, maar het lijkt erop dat in Ary Mas de gelijkmatigheid van de hoogte en de ruimte tussen de bomen het mogelijk maakt dat de maximale hoeveelheid licht, zelfs onder een lage hoek, het bos binnendringt en zo elke boom bereikt. Wanneer de toppen van de bomen het roze ochtendgloren vangen op hun ijzige naalden, lijkt het patroon van het bomenlandschap te suggereren dat er een collectieve intelligentie aan het werk is. Het bos hier heeft er zeer lang over gedaan om te ontstaan en het heeft zich op unieke wijze aangepast en een systeem geëvolueerd dat aansluit op deze extreme omgeving. Het lijkt volkomen redelijk dat dit intelligente verspreide organisme oppast geen plotselinge bewegingen te maken.

De temperatuuranomalieën voor Siberië in 2020 zijn schrikbarend: ze liggen vier keer hoger dan het wereldgemiddelde en zijn daarmee de extreemste ter wereld. Boven de 75ste breedtegraad is het Noordpoolgebied als geheel in 2020 nog sneller opgewarmd, namelijk zes keer zo snel als het mondiale gemiddelde.[17] Het uitgangspunt van die opwarming is echter zo laag dat het soms nauwelijks wordt opgemerkt. Vandaag is het -44, net binnen het normale bereik voor februari van -40 tot -60, maar, zoals de Dolgans en anderen die elke dag buiten leven heel goed weten, zijn temperaturen onder de -40 tegenwoordig een zeldzaamheid. Grote land- en watermassa's hebben veel tijd nodig om op te warmen. Terwijl de klimaatcrisis het eerst wordt gevoeld in maritieme zones met een grote gevoeligheid voor fluctuerende weerpatronen, zoals Noorwegen, of, zoals we hierna zullen zien, Alaska, gebeurt alles veel langzamer in de diepvries die Siberië heet.

En dus is het gemakkelijk om, zoals Dima mijn tolk dat doet, te beweren dat de opwarming van de aarde een leugen is, bedoeld om het koolwaterstofrijke Rusland economisch lam te leggen. Daar hoor je vaak: 'Olie is onze vader en gas is onze moeder!'

'Greta [Thunberg] is gewoon een marionet, ze wordt gestuurd, toch?'

Er is niets in het ongerepte uitzicht deze ochtend dat erop lijkt te wijzen dat er gevaar dreigt. De dageraad is volkomen stil. Het delicate korstoppervlak van de sneeuw is bedekt met een fijn vlechtwerk van sporen. De wind veegt hier elke nacht het toneel schoon. Wat in de sneeuw geschreven staat is het nieuwe drama van één enkele morgen. Een poolhaas heeft hier gegraven naar bevroren bessen en de sneeuw bespat met wat scharlaken bloed lijkt. Hij ging ervandoor in de richting van de rivier toen andere dieren verschenen: een stel poolvossen, sneeuwhoenders en een enkele wolf. De pootafdrukken van de wolf zijn enorm en zeker. Lange tenen, bijna zo groot als mijn handpalm, drukten de sneeuw ongeveer een centimeter diep samen. Hij had geen haast. Een hele bossamenleving met verschillende wezens was hier slechts momenten eerder nog aanwezig. Ze zijn vast nog dichtbij, verborgen tussen de bomen, en bekijken me van daar. De gedrongen gelederen van de lariks zijn niet passief. Het is een woud van ogen. Ik voel me als een indringer in een privéwereld en de roze sneeuw, de roerloze bomen, de armzalige door mensen gebouwde hutjes lijken bijkomstig.

'De taiga is machtig en onoverwinnelijk,' schreef Tsjechov. 'De uitspraak "De mens is de heerser over de natuur" klinkt nergens zo bedeesd en vals als hier.'[18]

Wanneer de Trekol een paar uur later stroomafwaarts rijdt, kleurt de lucht oranje aan het einde van deze korte winterdag. Wanneer we Khatanga weer naderen, worden de rookpluimen van de centrale hoog in de atmosfeer verlicht en geven hun gouden en violette strepen de hoogte van de temperatuurinversie aan, geschilderde luchtlijnen van een halve mijl hoog. Bij de eerste aanblik van deze vertrouwde vervuiling raakt de blonde Kolja opgewonden, doet het raam open en steekt een sigaret op.

'Welkom in mijn prachtige moderne stad!' zegt hij, sputterend van het lachen.

Dima stelt triomfantelijk vast dat de bomen van Ary Mas niet in beweging zijn, alsof dat bewijst dat mijn beweringen over het veranderende klimaat inderdaad een complottheorie zijn.

'Zie je wel?'

Ik heb er genoeg van om hem nog langer te proberen te overtuigen en dus glimlach ik maar wat. Maar als we de volgende dag ons laatste bezoek van de reis brengen aan Bondarevs vriend op het kantoor van het Tajmyr Nationaal Park in Khatanga, is Dima ongewoon stil. De bomen zijn misschien traag, maar er zijn andere signalen van de opwarming, andere soorten die sneller kunnen bewegen, met poten of vleugels.

In een slecht verwarmd houten kantoor boven een zaal vol natuurhistorische artefacten ontmoeten we Anatoly Gavrilov, de laatst overgebleven wetenschappelijk medewerker van het Tajmyr Nationaal Park, nadat de regering de kosten had 'geoptimaliseerd' en het aantal wetenschappers had teruggebracht van 67 tot dertien, toen elf, toen één. Dat men voor Anatoly koos, is veelzeggend. Hij is ornitholoog.

Tajmyr is de noordelijkste continentale landmassa en het punt waar vijf van de acht grote migratieroutes van de planeet elkaar kruisen – trekroutes voor vogels. Vogels die overwinteren in Australië, westelijk en zuidelijk Afrika, het Verenigd Koninkrijk, het Middellandse-Zeegebied, India, China en Centraal-Azië, komen allemaal naar de top van de wereld om te broeden. Het boreale gebied herbergt vijf miljard vogels en Tajmyr heeft de hoogste concentratie vogelsoorten ter wereld. Elke zomer brengt Anatoly zestig dagen door in de houten hutten die we in Ary Mas hadden bezocht (en waar hij Bondarev had leren kennen), om het bos en de toendra af te speuren naar vogels. Elk jaar registreert hij tientallen nieuwe soorten die hij nog nooit eerder heeft gezien. Op zijn bureau ligt de veer van een raaf, een nieuwkomer op het schiereiland. Maar dat is inmiddels alweer oud nieuws. In de afgelopen jaren heeft hij veel meer verrassende waarnemingen gedaan. Meer en meer zuidelijke soorten duiken op in het bos en de toendra ten noorden van Ary Mas.

'Het bos wordt drukker!' En nieuwe grassoorten trekken nieuwe insecten aan die op hun beurt nieuwe vogels aantrekken. Tropische soorten uit China, bijvoorbeeld, nieuwe soorten meeuwen uit de Atlantische Oceaan. Het hardst schrok hij van de hop die hij zág, een soort die thuishoort in de gematigde bossen van de Middellandse en de Zwarte Zee.

'Ik kon het niet geloven! Dat had ik nooit verwacht.'

De bomen staan dan misschien stil, maar de rest van het bos schuift op naar het noorden. Anatoly haalt nog steeds kaarten tevoorschijn en is op zoek naar de Engelse namen van soorten wanneer Dima ons verontschuldigt – ons vliegtuig vertrekt zo. Anatoly lijkt het echt jammer te vinden dat we al moeten gaan, alsof hij niet veel professionele bezoekers meer krijgt. Er is maar weinig publiek voor zijn boodschap: de vogels waarschuwen ons.

'Ik ben hier een eenzame roepende in de woestijn! In Rusland hebben de mensen het merkwaardige idee dat hun daden weinig aan de wereld kunnen veranderen.'

Dima vertaalt die laatste zin en kijkt dan schaapachtig weg. Eenmaal op het vliegveld vraagt hij: 'Dus hoe erg is het nou eigenlijk?' Ik leg uit dat we het niet goed weten.

'Waar moet ik heen verhuizen?'

'In dezelfde richting als de vogels gaan, naar het noorden.'

Het vliegtuig heeft vertraging, en we zitten vast in de ijskoude blikken doos van het luchthavengebouw terwijl een hond met vastgevroren stront aan zijn achterste eindeloos om ons heen draait. Ik voel me misselijk, maar niet alleen vanwege de geur. Luchthavens zijn als de Nganasan-poorten tussen werelden, waar de contingentie en de dreiging van ons fragiele leven duidelijk worden: de toekomst kan talloze verschillende kanten op. Dmitry's vraag en mijn antwoord geven het gewicht van de feiten waarvan we getuige zijn geweest een persoonlijke lading. Dit is geen proces dat we van een afstand gadeslaan. Wanneer we thuiskomen, zullen we niet veilig zijn. Ik voel een lichtheid in mijn ledematen en de beklemming in mijn borst die ik ken van het werken in oorlogsgebieden. Zo voelde ik me ook toen de raketten over gierden of het schieten te dichtbij kwam, toen die militieman bij de controlepost zijn hand opstak om ons tegen te houden. Mijn instinct zegt me te vluchten, maar waarheen?

Tsjerski, Rusland
68° 44' 23" N

In de zomer van 2018 veroorzaakte een onconventionele aardwetenschapper met baret, baard en sigaret, Sergej Zimov, die er eerder uitzag als een linkse filosoof dan als een natuurkundige, een schokgolf in de wetenschappelijke wereld. In het tijdschrift *National Geographic* stonden foto's van een grijnzende Sergej aan de bediening van een pneumatische boor, die door de permafrost aan het boren was in zijn onderzoeksstation in Tsjerski, in de uiterste noordoosthoek van Siberië.[19] Tsjerski ligt op de boomgrens, in de zone van ononderbroken permafrost, vier tijdzones ten oosten van Tajmyr. Hier stroomt de beroemde goudhoudende Kolymarivier, een van de bolwerken van de Goelag, de oostelijkste van de grote rivieren van Siberië, uit in zee in een brede vlakke delta van toendra, permafrost en lichte boomgroei. Op dezelfde lengtegraad als Kamtsjatka en Nieuw-Zeeland, één tijdzone verder naar het oosten, ligt de Beringstraat.

Het was niet de boor die de schok veroorzaakte – Sergei staat bekend om zijn unieke onderzoeksmethoden – maar wat hij vond. Na ongeveer een meter vaste grond was de grond eronder dunne modder, precies zoals hij voorspeld had: de permafrost smolt zowel van onder als van boven. Bijna iedereen was ervan uitgegaan dat de permafrost geleidelijk van bovenaf zou smelten, als gevolg van de warmere luchttemperaturen die de actieve laag van niet-bevroren grond bovenop zouden verdiepen. Maar Sergejs bevindingen wijzen op een andere toekomst: een snel verdwijnen van de permafrost. Dat betekende dat elk bevroren ecosysteem op basis van de permafrost ernstige problemen zou krijgen, om nog maar te zwijgen van de niet te kwantificeren uitstoot van methaan en koolstof die het gevolg zou zijn.

De Aziatische lariks houdt er niet van om natte voeten te krijgen. Hij steekt zijn wortels horizontaal uit in de ondiepe grond bovenop de permafrost, en onttrekt het vocht van onderen. Hij verdraagt water gedurende korte perioden, wanneer de actieve laag, de bovenste 30-100 centimeter, in de zomer gedurende ongeveer tachtig dagen ontdooit, maar de wortelactiviteit van de lariks vereist zuurstof, en een langdurig onder water staan van de wortels betekent de dood voor de boom. IJs daarentegen brengt, dankzij de luchtbellen die door bevriezing in de bodemstructuur vrijkomen, leven. In de diepvries van Tajmyr is de permafrost intact en de lariks stabiel, maar in het uiterste oosten van Siberië, waar de opwarmende stromingen van de Stille Oceaan het Noordpoolbekken binnendringen en warmere circulatiepatronen meebrengen, is de boomgrens die helemaal vanuit Tajmyr langs de Laptevzee loopt, dwars over de uitgestrekte stroomgebieden van de Lena, de Yana, de Kolyma en de Indigirka, zich in feite aan het terugtrekken.

In sommige gevallen, wanneer de permafrost smelt, loopt het

water weg en zakt de bodem in, waardoor grote zinkgaten ontstaan, een beeld dat nu overal in Siberië te zien is, waarbij de grotere lijken op kraters die door reusachtige meteorieten zijn geslagen. In lager gelegen gebieden kan het water echter nergens heen en stijgt de grondwaterspiegel. Zoals de wetenschappers van het Soekatsjev-Instituut hebben vastgesteld, is een waterpeil van 1,5 meter of hoger fataal voor de lariks. De verzadiging van de bodem met water in de grond 'verdrinkt' de bomen. Zonder de permafrost is de lariks kwetsbaar en wordt hij weggeconcurreerd. Langs de oevers van de Kolymarivier, waar de permafrost het sterkst ontdooid is, winnen wilgen, populieren en berken terrein.

Sergej Zimovs zoon Nikita leidt nu het Noordoostelijke Wetenschappelijke Station. Nikita had beloofd me later in de zomer mee te nemen in een boot om de dooi met eigen ogen te zien, samen met andere wetenschappers die de uitstoot meten van methaan en koolstof uit de permafrost en de hoeveelheid organische koolstof die door de rivieren wordt meegevoerd naar zee. De installatie van de Zimovs is een van de vier door de Nederlandse permafrostdeskundige dr. Ko genoemde installaties die proberen het vrijkomen van methaan te kwantificeren. Maar Rusland heeft nu alle vluchten opgeschort vanwege de Covidpandemie en de luchthaven in Tsjerski is hoe dan ook buiten gebruik – bosbranden hebben de regio in rook gehuld. Wanneer ik Nikita eindelijk te spreken krijg, is dat op het scherm.

'Lariks? Ik heb de pest aan de lariks! Je hebt de verkeerde gebeld,' zegt Nikita lachend. 'Die is heel geschikt voor de kachel.'

Nikita en Sergei geven niets om het redden van het bos, ze maken zich eerder zorgen om de permafrost. En vreemd genoeg lijkt de beste manier om de dooi te vertragen en misschien sommige delen van de taiga te behouden, het kappen van de bomen te zijn.

Terwijl hij praat, draait Nikita heen en weer in een grote stoel met leren rugleuning in zijn kantoor met houten lambrisering in de onderzoeksfaciliteit die Sergei en zijn collega's in de jaren 1970 hebben gebouwd. Aan de muur achter hem hangt de schedel van een bizon met intacte hoorns, terwijl tegen de deurpost een hele slagtand van een mammoet leunt, langer dan hij. Hij draagt een 'Florida State'-baseballpet op zijn ronde dos muisbruin haar en een rood Nike T-shirt. Het is juni 2020. Siberische bosbranden halen de wereldwijd de krantenkoppen en Nikita's video's, genomen vanaf een nabijgelegen heuvel, tonen branden die over de hele horizon razen, een ononderbroken band van rook over de stad leggen en de normaal 24 uur per dag zichtbare zomerzon op de Noordpool bedekken. Nikita is in zijn eentje in lockdown in het onderzoeksstation. Zijn vrouw en dochters zijn 'op het vasteland' in Novosibirsk in het zuiden van Siberië. Zijn vader is in de buurt van Moskou. Er moet toch iemand zorgen voor de atmosferische metingen en de langlopende experimenten, en het onderzoeksstation is hun familiebedrijf in het Rusland van na de Sovjet-Unie. Normaal in deze tijd van het jaar zijn er tientallen gastwetenschappers.

Nikita werd in 1982 geboren en groeide op in het onderzoeksstation, in het gezelschap van wetenschappers uit de hele wereld. De winters in zijn jeugd waren kouder, en het ijs in de riviermonding viel altijd tussen 1 en 10 juni uiteen en dreef af naar zee. In 2020 werd een nieuw record gevestigd: toen gebeurde dat al op 24 mei. In de Sovjettijd vormden de wetenschappers een elite. Posten in Tsjerski waren felbegeerd en werden goed beloond, en de school in de stad was goed. Maar na de perestrojka en de ineenstorting van de USSR ging het bergafwaarts, en Nikita voltooide zijn opleiding op het station waar hij scheikundeles kreeg van de vrouw van een van zijn vaders collega's. Hij kreeg een beurs voor de universiteit in Novosibirsk en studeerde wiskunde, maar dat beviel hem niet. 'Er zijn 27 wiskunderichtingen aan de universiteit, en 26 zijn er al te veel.'

Hij begon wiskundige modellen te gebruiken om ecosystemen en milieuveranderingen te bestuderen, en zijn vader overtuigde hem om terug te komen naar het familiebedrijf. Twintig jaar later is hij er nog steeds en zet hij Sergejs visie en wetenschappelijke agenda voort, hoewel hij betwijfelt of zijn dochters de traditie in ere zullen willen houden.

Sergej Zimov vertrok in 1977 van de Universiteit van het Verre Oosten in Vladivostok om het Noordoostelijk Wetenschapsstation in Tsjerski op te richten. Nikita vertelt dat hij naar het noorden ging om in de natuur te zijn, de Sovjetbureaucratie te ontvluchten en zijn passie voor de jacht uit te leven. 'Maar tegen de tijd dat hij besefte dat Tsjerski geen goede plek was om te jagen, was het al te laat.'

In een artikel in *Science* uit 2006 waarschuwde Sergej Zimov als een van de eerste wetenschappers ter wereld voor de hoeveelheid koolstof en methaan die is opgeslagen in de bevroren Yedomabodems van Siberië en de gevoeligheid van die bodems voor opwarming.[20] Yedoma is permafrost die gedeeltelijk vergane grond bevat: het bladafval van het bos dat zeer langzaam of helemaal niet is verrot door het gebrek aan warmte en schimmels om het af te breken. Yedoma bevat vijf keer meer koolstof dan de bodem van het regenwoud. En de permafrost bedekt een veel groter deel van het aardoppervlak dan het regenwoud. Totdat hij achteruit begon te gaan, bedekte de permafrost een kwart van het landoppervlak van de planeet, waarvan meer dan de helft in Siberië, en hij smelt veel sneller dan de modellen voorspelden.[21] Het belang van bomen is hier niet alleen de zuurstof die ze produceren en de emissies die zij vastleggen, maar ook de rol die ze spelen bij het vertragen of versnellen van het ontdooien van de permafrost.

Sergei maakte naam met gedurfde praktische experimenten, zoals het met een bulldozer verwijderen van de actieve laag van een hectare permafrost om te zien hoe die achteruit zou gaan. Een decennium later is dat stuk land nu een kuil met enorme pilaren van modder – het enige wat er overblijft als het water en de grond wegsmelten. En hij heeft een aantal radicale ideeën over de lariks van het boreale woud naar voren gebracht die aanvankelijk als controversieel werden beschouwd, maar inmiddels tamelijk gangbaar zijn geworden.

Voortbouwend op de inzichten van Soekatsjev van bijna honderd jaar geleden, suggereerde Sergej dat er 20 miljoen jaar geleden een ecologische revolutie moet hebben plaatsgevonden.

Hoge planten – de voorouders van de huidige bomen – leerden zich tegen de begrazing te verdedigen door gifstoffen te produceren. Ondertussen vormden de grassen een bondgenootschap met de herbivoren. Alle herbivoren zijn afhankelijk van grassen, die geëvolueerd zijn om afhankelijk te zijn van herbivoren voor bemesting en voortplanting – de verspreiding en ontkieming van hun zaden. Dit driehoekige ecosysteem – bos, gras en grazende dieren – was miljoenen jaren lang productief en duurzaam. Geologisch bewijs suggereert dat er 15.000 jaar geleden tien keer minder bomen waren in Siberië. Zoals de Afrikaanse ervaringen met de Serengeti en andere Europese experimenten op het gebied van biodiversiteit, zoals die in de Oostvaardersplassen in Nederland en het Knepp Estate in het VK lijken aan te tonen, is een bos met een dicht bladerdak vaak niet het climax-ecosysteem, maar heeft de jacht op megafauna – olifanten, mammoeten, elanden, wapiti's en oerossen – een mozaïek van gemengd bos- en grasland doen ontstaan. Zimov suggereerde dat de taiga in feite een savanne was geweest. Toen verscheen er een superroofdier, *Homo sapiens* genaamd, dat te veel herbivoren in de keten uitschakelde – mammoeten, bizons, elanden, paarden enzovoorts – en zonder hen werd het gras weggeconcurreerd door struiken en bomen, vooral door de lariks, die zich zo succesvol had ontwikkeld om te gedijen op permafrost. Het is een interessante theorie: dat de schijnbaar tijdloze larikstaiga in feite een geologische nieuwkomer is – een onkruid dat door menselijke activiteit is ontketend.

'De mensen zien de taiga als een wild ecosysteem, maar voordat de eerste mensen kwamen, waren bomen op deze plek zeer zeldzaam. De lariks is een nutteloos ecosysteem. Niemand eet lariks. Alleen knaagdieren eten de zaden,' zegt Nikita.

Latere onderzoeken bevestigden Soekatsjevs inzichten over de relatief korte voorgeschiedenis van de taiga en Sergejs meer algemene theorie over wat eraan vooraf was gegaan. Sinds het einde van de laatste interglaciale periode heeft het cryolithische lariksbos zich in dialoog met de permafrost ontwikkeld, zijn horizontale wortels in de actieve laag boven de bevroren massa eronder uitzettend, naar het noorden kruipend om een eensoortig bos te vormen, van de Siberische grens met China, 3200 kilometer zuidelijker, tot helemaal aan de noordelijke boomgrens. Dit is een gevaarlijke, kwetsbare en door de mens veroorzaakte situatie, aldus Sergej en Nikita.

Met lariks erbovenop is de permafrost veel kwetsbaarder voor opwarming, aangezien de lariks sneeuw vasthoudt. Nikita houdt dagelijks de temperatuur bij op het station, en zet het werk voort dat Sergei begon toen hij nog een kind was. Tijdens Nikita's leven is de temperatuur van de permafrost gestegen van -6 naar -3 graden Celsius. Tegelijkertijd is de gemiddelde luchttemperatuur gestegen van -11 naar -8.

'Die opwarming van de bodem met 3 graden wordt veroorzaakt door sneeuw,' legt Nikita uit. De winterkou kan niet in de grond doordringen vanwege het sneeuwdek.

Sergei geloofde dat de verdwenen dieren van de savanne de sneeuw zouden hebben vertrapt om het gras te bereiken of het helemaal hadden weggeveegd, waardoor de isolerende eigenschappen ervan aanzienlijk afnamen en de koude lucht de bodem kon afkoelen. De wind zou, zoals ik al had vastgesteld in de Finnmark in Noorwegen, hetzelfde doen – als er geen bomen waren. Sergei veronderstelde dat permafrost onder een bosbedekking enkele graden warmer was dan permafrost onder een savanne. Hij had alleen een manier nodig om het te testen. Daarom verwierf hij in 1988 van de Russische regering 62 vierkante kilometer struikgewas en toendra aan de boomgrens om het Pleistoceenpark te vestigen, een experimenteel safaripark net buiten Tsjerski.

In het park zijn zes soorten grote herbivoren (paarden, elanden, rendieren, muskusossen, wapiti's en bizons) uitgezet om de begrazing van de savannekuddes uit het Pleistoceen na te bootsen en aan te tonen dat de omvorming van de taiga tot toendra-steppe de beste manier is om de ontdooiing van de permafrost te vertragen en zo de mensheid ietsje meer tijd te geven om een catastrofale opwarming van de aarde af te wenden. Zoals verwacht verpletterden de dieren struiken, mos en zaailingen en stimuleerden ze de aanwas van gras, en uit gegevens bleek dat de bodem van het park inderdaad tot 2 graden kouder was dan die van het bos. En die 2 graden kunnen het verschil maken.

In 2018, het jaar van het experiment met de pneumatische boor, is de actieve laag helemaal niet opnieuw bevroren. In 2019 heeft ze zich hersteld, maar het scheelde niet veel.

'Dit heeft ingrijpende gevolgen voor onze regio. Er zal een massaal en plotseling verval van de permafrost plaatsvinden, die, hoe kan ik dat eens zeggen? Niet echt geweldig is,' zegt Nikita grinnikend.

Alle steden, wegen en pijpleidingen in Siberië zijn gebouwd op de permafrost, en ze zijn nu al aan het verzakken. Het leven in Siberië zoals het momenteel is opgebouwd, zal onmogelijk worden. Er zal een compleet nieuwe infrastructuur nodig zijn. Modderlawines slepen huizen en hele stukken land mee naar de rivieren. Al die ontdooiende grond in de rivieren verandert de hydrologie, met alle gevolgen van dien voor het waterleven. De vismigratie is gestopt, de inheemse witvis is vrijwel geheel verdwenen uit de Kolyma, en er zijn enorme aantallen zeehonden verschenen. En het is niet alleen het leven van de rivieren dat verandert. De rivieren van Siberië lozen 15 procent meer water in de oceaan dan tien jaar geleden, en dat percentage neemt elk jaar toe. Daardoor lijkt het zoutgehalte van de Noordelijke IJszee te veranderen, en dat kan op zijn beurt de pompende werking van het poolgebied beïnvloeden. Dit is het proces waarbij zout water naar de bodem zinkt, waardoor een cyclus ontstaat waarin het diepere water zich mengt met voedingsstoffen van de zeebodem en weer naar de oppervlakte stijgt om daar het fytoplankton te voeden. Dit proces van de primaire productie, waarbij voedingsstoffen worden omgezet in plantaardig en dierlijk materiaal, vormt de basis van de oceanische voedselketen. Deze stimulering van de planktongroei is ook de reden waarom de toegangspunten tot de Noordelijke IJszee – de Beringstraat en de Barentszzee – behoren tot de rijkste voedselgebieden op aarde voor zeedieren en vogels.

Nikita heeft ook de bittere kijk van zijn vader geërfd op de conclusies die hun onderzoek heeft opgeleverd. 'Persoonlijk zal ik geen traan laten om het einde van het moderne leven, maar het zal jammer zijn als de vissen er niet meer zijn.'

Het onderzoeksstation is gebouwd op een voormalige steengroeve, een eerbetoon aan de vooruitziende blik van zijn vader. Nikita zal zich wel redden.

'Maar als het dorp hier onder mijn raam voorbij komt glijden, is dat wel triest.'

Sergej verwacht de ineenstorting van de menselijke beschaving op korte termijn, omdat hij niet ziet hoe de opwarming zal stoppen.

'Maar ik denk niet dat hij daardoor gefrustreerd is,' zegt Nikita. 'Hij hoopt dat het zo snel mogelijk gebeurt, om zijn hypothese te bewijzen. Hij is een wetenschapper!'

Anders dan je zou verwachten vanwege hun ogenschijnlijke misantropie, zijn de Zimovs niet cynisch en hebben ze het nog niet opgegeven. Nikita is van plan om later in het jaar samen met een Franse televisieploeg een schip te charteren en naar het afgelegen wildreservaat op het eiland Wrangel in de Beringstraat te gaan om daar muskusossen te gaan vangen voor het Pleistoceenpark. En Sergei is in Moskou, waar hij een andere bezoekersattractie opzet, Wild Field genaamd, om te trachten mensen voor te lichten en hun houding te veranderen. Ondanks het wetenschappelijke succes van de Zimovs heeft het voorbeeld van het park nog niet geleid tot grootschalige noodprogramma's om de afkoelingseffecten te evenaren. Nikita is niet verrast: 'Als het al moeilijk is in Rusland, waar de regering alles bezit, dan moet het in andere landen pas echt ingewikkeld zijn!'

En miljoenen hectaren bos kappen om ze te vervangen door gras is intuïtief zo'n tegenstrijdige oplossing voor de opwarming van de aarde dat ze waarschijnlijk geen ingang zal vinden in een wereld die tracht de ontbossing een halt toe te roepen door meer bomen te planten.

Toch hebben we de uitdaging die van dit soort wilde ideeën uitgaat hard nodig om het dreigingen en de mogelijkheden van dit moment het huidige moment te kunnen begrijpen: wij hebben dit tot stand helpen brengen, en dat betekent dat wij het ongedaan kunnen maken of vernieuwen. Uit het werk van de Zimovs blijkt dat de mens net zo'n belangrijke rol heeft gespeeld in de ecologische successie van de taiga als de lariks – en misschien wel een grotere. Zoals met Schotland of de herinneringen van de Nganasan, moeten wij leren kijken en zien met oude ogen. De landschappen waarin wij zijn opgegroeid en die wij gedurende een paar korte generaties als vanzelfsprekend zijn gaan beschouwen, zijn helemaal niet tijdloos, maar een door mensen gevormd moment in een voortdurende dynamiek van veranderende kleuren van blauwe oceaan, wit ijs en groen bos op een stenen bal, omgeven door gas, die rondtolt in de ruimte.

4.

De grens

Witte spar, *Picea glauca*

Zwarte spar, *Picea mariana*

Fairbanks, Alaska
64° 50' 37" N

Slechts zo'n 90 kilometer ondiep water scheidt Rusland van Alaska. Tijdens het laatste glaciale maximum, 20.000 jaar geleden, toen een groot deel van het water op aarde was opgesloten in gletsjers, lag het zeeniveau honderd meter lager en was de Beringstraat droog land. In de geologie staan Alaska en de Yukon bekend als Oost-Beringië – en worden ze in wezen beschouwd als het verlengde van Oost-Siberië. Toen de landbrug nog intact was, bewogen planten, dieren en mensen vrij rond in een toendrasteppe-ecosysteem dat gedomineerd werd door grassen en alsem met verspreide populierenbosjes, en toen het ijs over Eurazië in zuidelijke richting opschoof, trokken honderden soorten, waaronder ook vroege mensen, van west naar oost over deze laagvlakten, in de fuik van Alaska en de Yukon. Gletsjers in de Brooks Range, de bergen ten zuiden van Alaska en de Canadese Rockies, hielden een verdere trek landinwaarts tegen, waardoor Alaska en de Yukon tegenwoordig enkele van de meest biodiverse gebieden van de Arctische toendragordel zijn, met meer dan zeshonderd soorten, terwijl Tajmyr er 118 kent.

Toen het warmer werd en de zee de landbrug tussen de Stille Oceaan en de Noordelijke IJszee afsneed, werd de ecologische geschiedenis van de planeet voorgoed veranderd. Tientallen soorten kwamen aan weerszijden van de Beringstraat voor. Als tweelingen deelden deze twee afzonderlijke ecosystemen veel gemeenschappelijke kenmerken, maar in een opwarmend klimaat is er slechts een verschil van één of twee soorten nodig om systemen in opvallend verschillende richtingen te doen evolueren. Alaska kent twee belangrijke soorten die Noordoost-Siberië niet heeft: sparren en bevers.

Alaska lijkt de Zimovs gelijk te geven. Hun theorie dat het lariksbos van de taiga een jonge geologische formatie is, waarschijnlijk als reactie op het uitroeien van de megafauna door de mens, wordt ondersteund door de afwezigheid van de lariks aan de andere kant van het water, die van verder zuidelijk moet zijn gekomen, op het moment dat de zee al door de Beringstraat was gebroken. In het bos aan de kant van Alaska is geen lariks te vinden. In plaats daarvan wordt het gedomineerd door sparren (*Picea glauca/mariana*) waarvan de oorsprong ook verder naar het zuiden schijnt te liggen, hetgeen een verbinding met de binnenlanden suggereert.

Sparren zijn winterharde coniferen met taaie wasachtige naalden, hoge spitsen met korte zijtakken en ondiepe wortelstelsels die vocht kunnen onttrekken aan zelfs de schraalste bodem of moerassige, drassige omstandigheden kunnen doorstaan en daarmee tot de grote overlevers van de planeet behoren. Ze doen denken aan gedrongen centurions. Het geslacht *Picea*, daterend uit het Krijt, heeft extreme hitte en koude doorstaan en een grote verscheidenheid van atmosferen, van zuurstofarm tot kooldioxiderijk. Het lijkt de laatste ijstijd in refugia in de Rocky Mountains te hebben doorgebracht en zich naar het noorden te hebben verspreid toen de planeet weer opwarmde.

Zowel in Siberië als in Alaska bereiken noch de spar noch de lariks de Noordelijke IJszee. De massa zee-ijs heeft tot nu toe de bodem en het weer te koud gehouden. De 10°-juli-isotherm die de gemiddelde zomertemperatuur aangeeft, beweegt ver naar het zuiden voorbij de Beringstraat, en beschrijft een brede waaier in de noordelijke Stille Oceaan die ooit de grens van het winterse zee-ijs was. Het ijs hield de kustvlakten koel en de bomen in toom, vooral aan de Russische kant, waar de Oyashio-stroming vanaf de Noordelijke IJszee naar beneden stroomt, waardoor de kust afkoelt en Vladivostok de meest zuidelijke haven is die in de winter ijsbrekers nodig heeft. Daarom maakt de boomgrens in het hart van het schiereiland Tsjoekotka, het oostelijkste district van Rusland, dat als een pijl richting Alaska wijst, een bocht van negentig graden naar het zuiden en baant zich een weg langs de binnenkant van de vinger van Kamtsjatka rond de rand van de Zee van Ochotsk. De klimaatverandering overbrugt de toendrakloof aan de Russische kant niet. In plaats daarvan dwingt, zoals we al zagen, de waterverzadiging van de grond de lariks om zich terug te trekken. Aan de overkant van de Beringzee is het echter een ander verhaal.

De boomgrens van Alaska bestaat uit een mengeling van zwarte en witte sparren. De een houdt van goed gedraineerde, droge grond (wit), terwijl de ander de voorkeur geeft aan de waterrijke moerassen van de valleibodems (zwart). Deze brede ecologische niche verleent de spar een opmerkelijk aanpassingsvermogen. Het sparenduo kruipt langs de Yukondelta en over het schiereiland Seward, altijd op een respectvolle afstand van de kust, volgt de inhammen, schiereilanden en riviermondingen van westelijk Alaska, en buigt pas af naar het binnenland bij de rivieren de Kobuk en de Noatak, waar het bos op de ondoordringbare muur van de Brooks Range stuit. Vanaf de Kobuk-waterkering volgt de boomgrens de zuidkant van de bergen helemaal tot aan de Canadese grens.

Niemand kent deze hele grens zo goed als Ken Tape. Gedurende verscheidene jaren heeft hij zijn winters doorgebracht met zich een weg banen door de sneeuw langs de FTE – de Forest-Tundra Ecotone – op het Seward-schiereiland, om het einde van de Brooks Range heen, op de Noatak River boven Kotzebue tot aan Point Hope, Barrow en Deadhorse op de North Slope, om een transect, een dwarsdoorsnede door de sneeuwlaag, te maken teneinde de eigenschappen ervan te kunnen bestuderen.

Ken is destijds afgestudeerd aan de Universiteit van Alaska in Fairbanks, waar hij onderzoek deed naar de isolerende eigenschappen van sneeuw onder leiding van dr. Matthew Sturm. Hij hielp Sturms hypothese te bewijzen dat de struiken op de toendra bij warmere temperaturen meer sneeuw vasthielden die vervolgens de bodem isoleerde, de vorst vertraagde en de biologische activiteit in de grond stimuleerde. Hierdoor kwamen voedingsstoffen beschikbaar voor planten, die de groei van struiken stimuleerden, enzovoorts – een vegetatieve terugkoppelingskringloop die de modellering van de klimaatverandering zou kunnen veranderen.[1] Het was een controversieel idee en het kostte tijd om het te bewijzen. In 1999 stuitten ze op het equivalent van een wetenschappelijke schatkamer, big data van vóór het tijdperk van de satellieten die het mogelijk maakten de uitgangswaarden van het onderzoek verder naar het verleden te verschuiven: een bewaarplaats met foto's genomen door de US Geological Survey in de jaren 1940.

Dit gedetailleerde onderzoek van de gehele North Slope van Alaska was uitgevoerd toen men de regio in kaart wilde brengen, op zoek naar olievelden. Door het gebied opnieuw vanuit de lucht te fotograferen, konden Matthew en Ken de twee reeksen foto's vergelijken en de verschillen meten. In vijftig jaar tijd was overal op de toendra struikgewas verschenen. Het artikel dat zij in 2001 in *Nature* publiceerden werd wereldwijd gelezen. Het vormde het eerste significante wetenschappelijke bewijs van een proces waarover de Inuit-oudsten het al tientallen jaren hadden gehad: het Noordpoolgebied was aan het vergroenen.

Wanneer ik hem twintig jaar later aan de telefoon spreek, klinkt Ken nog steeds als de jeugdige promovendus die al die jaren geleden deze belangrijke doorbraak bereikte. In de winter doet hij geen veldwerk meer, en hij woont tegenwoordig met zijn kinderen in Fairbanks, maar hij voelt nog steeds het verlangen en de opwinding van de ontdekkingsreiziger. Ik bel op een belangrijk moment. Hij staat op het punt weer een baanbrekende studie te publiceren die, voor de tweede keer in zijn leven, wereldwijd de voorpagina's zal halen.

Hij vertelt het verhaal alsof hij nog steeds verbaasd is over zijn eigen ontdekkingen, met een stem waarvan je – zelfs aan de telefoon – kunt horen dat die klinkt uit een mond die elk moment in een glimlach kan schieten. In de decennia na die eerste baanbrekende ontdekking bleef Ken de dynamiek van de struiken bestuderen en veranderingen op de toendra observeren. Maar, zegt hij, hij bracht zoveel tijd door met zijn 'hoofd tussen de pollen' dat hij aanvankelijk het overzicht verloor: 'de vreemde dingen die onverwacht gebeuren. Je moet je ogen open houden.'

Alaska is het meest bestudeerde deel van het Noordpoolgebied, want de VS beschikken over de middelen en het wetenschappelijk vermogen waaraan het andere naties ontbreekt. Het is daarnaast beduidend anders dan Siberië, dat een meer geïsoleerde continentale landmassa is. Zoals we in Ary Mas hebben gezien, heeft die vele jaren nodig om op te warmen. Blootstelling aan de warme stromingen van de Stille Oceaan heeft geleid tot het verlies van zee-ijs in de Beringstraat, meer abrupte temperatuursprongen en duidelijkere effecten in Alaska. Bovendien beschikt de staat over goed uitgeruste veldstations en lijnvluchten. In Alaska zijn de gevolgen van de klimaatverandering al langer merkbaar en grondiger gedocumenteerd dan waar ook ter wereld. Deze meest noordelijke staat vormt als het ware de grens van ons begrip van wat er werkelijk aan de hand is, zowel in geografisch als in wetenschappelijk opzicht. Het grootste wetenschappelijke programma om de veranderingen in de boreale zone te bestuderen wordt uitgevoerd door de Amerikaanse National Aeronautics and Space Administration (NASA) en heet het Arctic Boreal Vulnerability Experiment (ABOVE). Het is erop gericht bekend onderzoek op alle niveaus van de aardsystemen te integreren in een poging de veranderingen die gaande zijn te modelleren.

'En toch weten we nog maar zo weinig,' zegt Ken. Met *remote sensing* heb je maar beperkte mogelijkheden. Dat moet worden aangevuld met 'grondwaarheid'. Toch is het soms gemakkelijker om gegevens uit de ruimte te krijgen dan waarnemingen op de grond. En wat we zien vanuit het ene gezichtspunt kan er heel anders uitzien vanuit een ander.

'Het is moeilijk om een onderzoeksproject op te zetten dat niet vanuit een veldstation wordt uitgevoerd.' Toolik Lake ligt in de Brooks Range op de North Slope en is, samen met een andere faciliteit in Nome, de plaats waar het meeste Arctische onderzoek plaatsvindt en waar Ken vroeger veel tijd doorbracht. In Toolik bestudeerde hij andere wilde dieren die vanuit het bos naar de toendra waren getrokken door de toename van het struikgewas en langere zomers als gevolg van de opwarming: de Amerikaanse haas en de veranderingen in de sneeuwhoenderpopulaties. Toen begon hij zich af te vragen wat er nog zou komen: elanden, beren... bevers.

'Toen had ik zo'n eureka-moment dat me zei dat we deze veranderingen misschien met satellieten konden waarnemen.' Bij ecologie is het meestal moeilijk om de dieren te vinden en te tellen, maar bevers laten zulke nadrukkelijke sporen na in het landschap dat je ze vanuit de ruimte kunt zien. 'Ik dacht, we kunnen deze jongens volgen. Tjonge, dit zou wel eens wat kunnen worden! Maar ik ben niet zo'n beverman.' Er was echter niet veel voor nodig. Ken sprak met een collega die hem in contact bracht met een deskundige, en al gauw waren ze op Google Earth aan het surfen om de bevervijvers op de toendra te tellen.

Hij keek opnieuw naar de oude luchtfoto's uit de Tweede Wereldoorlog, maar vond geen bevervijvers. De verandering was onmiskenbaar en schokkend. Collega's in Duitsland bestudeerden de veranderingen in de circum-Arctische thermokarstmeren – meren die niet bevriezen als gevolg van het methaan dat erin is opgelost – en brachten de toenemende wateroppervlakte in kaart, maar zij hadden er niet bij stilgestaan hoe de plassen tot stand waren gekomen. Zij waren ervan uitgegaan dat het smeltwater was. Niemand had zich gerealiseerd dat er slechts één soort was die het landschap zo ingrijpend kon veranderen.

'Ze waren stomverbaasd en vroegen zich af hoe ze dat over het hoofd hadden kunnen zien,' aldus Ken.

Het onderzoeksstation bij Toolik Lake is te bereiken via de Dalton Highway, ook wel de *haul road*, de vrachtweg, genoemd, de enige verharde weg in het noorden van Alaska. Die wordt gebruikt door het bedrijf Trans-Alaska Pipeline: van Prudhoe Bay via de Brooks Range en Fairbanks in het midden van de staat tot helemaal aan de haven van Anchorage in het zuiden. De overgangszone van toendra naar bos langs de weg in de bergen is erg smal, eerder enkele meters dan kilometers breed. De boomgroei stopt aan één kant van het dal en keert niet meer terug. De helling is steil. Er is geen brede, gevarieerde interactie tussen bos en toendra zoals in Siberië of Canada of de toendravlakten van westelijk Alaska die tegenover Rusland liggen, aan de andere kant van de Beringstraat. Er is een boom die de 'laatste spar' wordt genoemd en die iemand langs de kant van de weg op de noordelijke helling met een bord heeft gemarkeerd, maar het is een buitenbeentje, waarschijnlijk afkomstig van een zaadje dat is meegelift op een olietruck.

'Het effect van de bevers was niet echt zichtbaar vanaf de haul road, daarom hadden we het niet opgemerkt.'

Maar toen Ken nadrukkelijk begon te zoeken, zag hij overal bevers. Hij telde negentig bevervijvers op het Baldwin-schiereiland, terwijl er twintig jaar eerder maar twee dammen waren geweest. In totaal vond hij twaalf- tot dertienduizend beverdammen op de toendra die er in 1950 nog niet waren geweest. Ken heeft modellen gemaakt die hebben geleid tot een hypothese en een wetenschappelijk artikel dat op dat moment werd herzien en dat, toen het een paar maanden later werd gepubliceerd, in kranten wereldwijd werd overgenomen. Bevers, zo blijkt, hebben in Alaska meer invloed op het oppervlaktewater dan het klimaat. Ze zouden tot 66 procent van het oppervlaktewater op de toendra kunnen controleren, en zo de weg vrijmaken voor bomen.[2]

Bevers hebben geen volwaardig bos nodig om te gedijen. De toegenomen struikgroei op de toendra van de laatste dertig tot veertig jaar en de dwergwilgen en elzen zijn voor hen voldoende om dammen te bouwen en vijvers aan te leggen. Water geleidt warmte beter dan land, dus als je meer water creëert en het dieper maakt, maak je de omgeving warmer, en breng je de warmte dichter bij de bodem, bij de permafrost. Bevervijvers bieden een houvast voor meer bomen en voor andere soorten die van deze vijvers afhankelijk zijn: amfibieën, insecten, vissen en vogels. Bevers zijn geo-engineers van de eerste orde.

Het ecotoon van bos en toendra in Alaska heeft er dus een belangrijke nieuwe soort bijgekregen, de *Castor canadensis*. De Noord-Amerikaanse bever is veel talrijker dan zijn Euraziatische tegenhanger, *Castor fiber*. De Euraziatische bever was bijna uitgestorven in Europa en Azië toen de Sovjetregering het dier in 1922 op de lijst van beschermde soorten zette, en zelfs nu hebben geherintroduceerde populaties slechts kleine aantallen opgeleverd in zuidelijk Siberië en ten oosten van de Oeral. De Noord-Amerikaanse soort daarentegen is weer opgeveerd, telt nu meer dan vijf miljoen exemplaren en neemt nog steeds toe.

Ik vraag Ken om tips over waar en hoe ik zelf het 'bever-effect' kan zien. Hij stelt voor te kijken naar de toendra aan de andere kant van de boomgrens, ten westen van de Brooks Range. Er zijn nog geen bevers gezien aan de North Slope, hoewel ze in de bergen en in sommige bergpassen die naar de andere kant leiden, wel voorkomen. Het zal niet lang meer duren. De toendra van westelijk Alaska is een voorproefje van hoe de North Slope eruit zal zien als ze zich ook daar vestigen.

Ken is zelf van plan later in de zomer van 2020 een onderzoek te starten. Dit is het eerste volledige veldseizoen van het project en zijn team staat klaar om camera's te installeren en gegevens te verzamelen over vis, kwik, de voedselketen in het water en de gevolgen voor de inheemse zelfvoorzieningsjacht en -vangst. Ik ben opgewonden over de mogelijkheid om aan deze baanbrekende reis deel te nemen, hoewel Ken nog geen toezeggingen heeft gedaan. Hij stelt voor dat ik rond de Kobuk River ga kijken, en noemt een schrijver, Seth Kantner uit Kotzebue, die aan de rivier is opgegroeid. Met hem overleg ik via het beeldscherm over toegang, hoe er te komen, de moeilijkheidsgraad (en kosten) van vluchten naar deze wildernis. Noord-Alaska is, afgezien van de Dalton Highway, een land zonder wegen. We spreken af elkaar te ontmoeten als ik in Fairbanks ben. Maar een paar maanden later slaat de coronapandemie toe.

Kotzebue, Alaska
66° 53' 53" N

Ik bel Seth Kantner en vraag of het mogelijk is om Kotzebue te bezoeken.

'Ah, dat weet ik niet hoor,' zegt Seth. 'Wat voor een type ben jij? Ik bedoel, ben jij een blanke?' Hij lacht een beetje. Ik lach ook.

'Nou, dan zou het wel eens moeilijk kunnen worden.'

De laatste keer dat er een wereldwijde pandemie door Alaska trok, in 1919, werden de inheemse Inuit-, Iñupiat- en Athabaskanbevolking er bijna door uitgeroeid. Er zijn oude verhalen, schrijft Seth in zijn memoires *Shopping for Porcupine*, over 'hongersnood en griep – teams van reizigers met hondensleeën die half uitgehongerde kinderen aantreffen in iglo's vol bevroren dode mensen.'[3] De geschiedenis van het Wilde Noorden bepaalt nog steeds het heden: de angstige raden van de inheemse bevolking, de plaatselijke gemeentelijke autoriteiten, hebben hun eigen strengere lockdowns en beperkingen ingesteld voor bezoekers, en dus ook voor wetenschappers en journalisten, en nu zit ik dus met het dilemma van de afstandssensor: hoe kan ik begrijpen wat er op aarde gebeurt als ik het alleen vanuit de ruimte kan bekijken?

Seth zelf is blank, maar, zegt hij, en iedereen weet dat, slechts bij wijze van spreken. De regels zijn op hem niet van toepassing. Seth ontwikkelde zich als kind, zoals hij het zelf zegt, 'inheemser dan veel inheemse kinderen' in een door zijn ouders gebouwde iglo van zoden aan een prachtige bocht van de Kobuk River, ver van enige andere nederzetting. Het uitzicht omvatte de bosrand in het zuiden, een boomgrens van uitgespreide, spichtige, stuntelige sparren als strepen in de sneeuw. Hier verruilden zijn ouders Howard en Erna Kantner in 1965, net van de universiteit en erop gebrand om reguliere banen te vermijden, de banaliteiten van een conventioneel modern leven voor de wildernis en een zelfvoorzienend bestaan, levend van het land.

De Kantners maakten deel uit van een beweging van mensen uit de 'lagere 48' op zoek naar een eenvoudiger leven, een beweging waarover de New Yorker journalist John McPhee schreef in zijn boek uit 1976, *Coming into the Country*. Seth en zijn broer volgden correspondentielessen uit boeken die via hondensleeën in hun iglo aankwamen vanuit het postkantoor in Ambler, enkele dagen reizen verderop. Hun werkelijke leerschool was echter de strijd om te overleven, om zich aan te passen aan de seizoenscycli van het land. Vissen in de zomer en vallen zetten in de winter. Ze leerden visnetten en vallen maken van sparrenwortels en wilgenbast, sleden en sneeuwschoenen van berkenhout. Ze wisten waar ze in de herfst bessen konden vinden en leerden kariboes, elanden, beren, vossen, muskusratten en wolven op te sporen, te schieten en te villen, en hoe ze kleding konden maken van vachten, huiden en pezen. Seth ontdekte dat de beste manier om een geschikte kampplaats te vinden was door vossensporen naar de wilgen te volgen. Inmiddels breek je er je nek over de wilgen, en niet alleen in de kreken.

In 1975, toen Seth opgroeide aan de Kobuk, peddelde John McPhee met een kano de Salmon River op, een zijrivier die een eindje stroomafwaarts van Seths ouderlijk huis in de Kobuk uitmondt. Hij vergezelde functionarissen van de National Park Service, het Bureau of Land Management en de Sierra Club die het land onderzochten na de invoering van de Alaska Native Claims Settlement Act (ANCSA) om het natuurbeschermingspotentieel ervan te beoordelen voor opneming in een reeks voorgestelde nationale parken. Het waren, schreef McPhee, 'legionairs uit een andere wereld... Romeinen die het trans-Alpijnse Gallië inspecteerden.' De vraag waarmee zij en McPhee zich bezighielden was:

'Wat zal het lot zijn van al dit land?'

Vijftig jaar later lijken we langzaam het antwoord op die vraag te hebben gevonden. ANCSA kende de oorspronkelijke bewoners van Alaska een miljard dollar en bijna 18 miljoen hectare land toe in ruil voor het afzien van verdere aanspraken op land. Dat maakte de weg vrij voor de Trans-Alaska Pipeline en de afbakening van nog eens 32 miljoen hectare als gebieden van 'nationaal belang' die moesten worden bestudeerd om vast te stellen wat de mogelijkheden waren voor natuurbescherming, hetgeen uiteindelijk resulteerde in 13 miljoen hectare nieuwe nationale parken, een gebied zo groot als de staat New York en meer dan alle andere nationale parken van de VS bij elkaar. Toen President Richard Nixon de ANCSA in 1971 ondertekende, was dit waarschijnlijk het grootste, meest progressieve akkoord met de inheemse bevolking ooit en een poging om de tegenstrijdige eisen van de twintigste eeuw in evenwicht te brengen: olie, natuurbehoud en het einde van het koloniale tijdperk. Alaska is daarom een microkosmos van de tragedie van de moderne industriële samenleving. Ondanks de inspanningen van het rijkste land ter wereld om het juiste te doen op het gebied van natuurbehoud en de rechten van de inheemse bevolking, ondermijnt de voortdurende toewijding aan de derde vraag – die naar koolwaterstoffen – de haalbaarheid van de rest.

McPhee heeft het niet over klimaatverandering maar, zoals we nu weten, waren de processen al in volle gang. Seth is vijftig jaar oud en de opwarming van de aarde vormt zijn hele leven al het decor.

'De oude Eskimo's zeiden al dat je niet al te ver ten noorden van ons huis kon kamperen,' vertelt hij me aan de telefoon. Om te kamperen had je twee wilgen nodig om naar elkaar toe te buigen voor een schuilplaats, en hout om te verbranden. Er waren nooit veel wilgen ten noorden van Paungaqtaugruk, hun bocht in de rivier, en nauwelijks sparren. In *Shopping for Porcupine* bezoekt Seth zijn ouderlijk huis van vroeger en stelt vast dat het pad zestig centimeter lager is komen te liggen en dat de gehele voorzijde van de heuvel lager is geworden als gevolg van het ontdooien van de permafrost. Het uitzicht op de toendra is diffuus, dus gaat hij in laden op zoek naar een oude foto om te vergelijken hoe het er vroeger uitzag. Die foto staat in het boek. Het laat Seths ouders en hun vrienden zien in 1965: roodharige, idealistische pioniers, en de eindeloze vlakke toendra die zich uitstrekt tot grijze, stemmige bergen in de verte. Ernaast staat een andere foto – van hetzelfde landschap veertig jaar later, een golvende massa groene vingers die naar de hemel reiken, een veld vol '*happy spruce*', blije sparren, zoals Seth ze noemt. De klimaatverandering is net zo oud als hij, ouder eigenlijk.

'Witte sparren komen op als gras... je kijkt even weg en ze hebben zich verplaatst!'

De plotseling hevig opkomende vegetatie maakt het navigeren op eerder nog bekend terrein moeilijk, zelfs voor doorgewinterde jagers en pelsjagers die op het land zijn opgegroeid, zoals Seth.

'Je rijdt langs een rivier en je weet bijna niet meer waar je bent,' zegt hij.

'We zijn allemaal geschokt. We dachten hier altijd dat we ons aan de boomgrens bevonden.' Hij grinnikt even. 'De zogenaamde boomgrens.'

De bomen brengen andere diersoorten met zich mee: vogels, elanden, beren en buitengewoon veel vis, op de vlucht voor warmere wateren elders. De zalm is compleet op hol geslagen. Seth is al beroepsvisser sinds hij negen was. De zaken zijn een heel eind uit balans geraakt. Drie jaar geleden vingen de vissers 100.000 zalmen op de Kobuk, twee jaar geleden 200.000 en vorig jaar 500.000. De zalm is een vluchteling geworden. Maar soms is deze gewoonlijk koude rivier nog altijd niet koel genoeg voor zalmen die een veilig heenkomen zoeken om te paaien. In 2014 en 2019 telde de rivier meer dode vissen dan levende. De watertemperatuur bleef een maand lang boven de 21° Celcius. Een vliegtuig van het Alaska Department of Fish and Game dat over een afstand van 200 mijl langs de rivier vloog, maakte foto's van de opgeblazen lichamen van zalmen die zich als drijfhout in het ondiepe ophoopten, en van de beren die zich tegoed deden aan de zalm. De oevers lagen vol met karkassen, kuit en bloed, verspreid over het grind als strepen oranje en rode verf. De populatie bruine beren breidt zich snel uit, en de voedselketen verandert mee naarmate de beren andere roofdieren verdringen.

Het hele ecosysteem ondergaat al meer dan vijftig jaar een transformatie in slow motion, en toch gaan de mensen die van dat ecosysteem afhankelijk waren, niet de straat op om te protesteren. In plaats daarvan passen ze zich aan.

Seth woont niet meer stroomopwaarts, maar in de haven van Kotzebue die op een smalle landtong ligt, een paar meter boven de zeespiegel in het midden van een enorme baai die Kotzebue Sound heet. De stad ligt rond de eroderende kustlijn van de landtong. Kleine hutjes, steigers en tot boven de waterlijn getrokken boten bevolken het kiezelstrand voor de 34 miljoen dollar kostende zeewering die Shore Avenue overeind houdt. Het plaatsje kijkt in noordwestelijke richting uit op zee, richting de rijke visgronden van de Beringstraat, waar de inheemse Iñupiat van oudsher hun voedsel vandaan halen. Witte walvissen vormden duizenden jaren lang een hoofdbestanddeel van hun dieet naast zeehonden, maar de overvloedige aantallen van deze dieren in de Kotzebue Sound zijn inmiddels niet meer dan een folkloristische herinnering. Niemand weet waarom deze zeer intelligente dieren niet meer terugkeren.

'Twintig jaar geleden was het politiek gevaarlijk om over de opwarming van de aarde te praten,' vertelt hij, 'maar tegenwoordig accepteert iedereen het, het is gewoon een feit.' De veranderingen zijn nu zo duidelijk dat het zinloos is ze te ontkennen. Het ijs in de Kotzebue Sound is in de herfst en de lente niet langer betrouwbaar. Meer dan tien jaar geleden, nadat verschillende gezinnen geliefden hadden verloren omdat sneeuwscooters door het zee-ijs zakten in perioden van het jaar waarin het ijs vroeger sterk was, hield men op de oude winterroutes te gebruiken. Het is misschien een glimp van het komende tijdperk van de klimaatpolitiek op andere plaatsen. Ons evolutionaire succes is ook onze strategische zwakte.

In Kotzebue leven de mensen al zo lang met de achteruitgang

van hun leefmilieu dat ze het niet echt meer opmerken. Omdat ik Kotzebue niet kon bezoeken, las ik in plaats daarvan de stapel mediaverslagen van twee decennia over het klimaat ter plaatse en werd getroffen door het overweldigende gevoel van berusting, de Iñupiat die rouwen om het verdwijnen van een manier van leven, hun eigen machteloosheid accepterend met een hartverscheurende gratie. Wanneer de walvissen er niet meer zijn, jagen ze op zeehonden. Wanneer ook die verdwijnen, halen zij hun schouders op en wenden zich in plaats daarvan voor hulp tot de regering wier makkelijk verdiende oliegeld zowel de bron van het probleem als de kortetermijnoplossing is.

In de olieboringscontracten is ook een dividend voor inheemse bedrijven opgenomen, en de structuur van het oude leven van Alaska is, net als de permafrost, fataal ondermijnd. Zelfvoorzienend leven, het ideaal waarvoor Seths ouders naar de Kobuk-vallei waren verhuisd, is niet langer een haalbare kaart. Dat is niet omdat de natuur zou zijn gestopt met geven – nog niet – maar omdat de mensen zijn gestopt met oogsten. De principiële houding van Seths ouders die geen voedsel uit de voedselindustrie in de winkel kochten, heeft de overgang naar de volgende generatie niet overleefd. In plaats daarvan hebben de olie en de geïmporteerde consumptiegoederen ervoor gezorgd dat de kosten van levensonderhoud omhoog zijn geschoten en dat de mensen afhankelijk zijn geworden van bijstandscheques, gratis huisvesting en munitie voor hun jachtgeweer, en nu zelfs stimuleringsdollars. Dit, en de 'ziekte' zoals een van de ouderen van Kotzebue het typeert, van de sociale media, hebben de oude gewoonten ingehaald. De koolwaterstofcultuur heeft de scherpe schoonheid van het overleven, gedreven door honger, verstikt. Niemand mist de honger, en nu is er geen weg meer terug. De kennis over hoe te overleven is er nog, nog net, bewaard door mensen wier leven ingrijpender veranderingen heeft ondergaan dan dat van vrijwel ieder ander. Maar ze gaat verloren.

'Bijna alles komt nu uit vliegtuigen,' zegt Seth, en er klinkt teleurstelling in zijn stem. Ogen en oren die vroeger de toendra afspeurden naar sporen van kariboes, ganzen, wolven of een hondenteam wachten nu op het gezoem van propellers en de ping van een telefoon voor hun voedsel en voor nieuws.

Agashashak River,
Kobuk Valley National Park, Alaska
67° 34' 92" N

Vanuit de ruimte bevestigden satellieten Ken Tapes idee dat Alaska steeds groener wordt. In de afgelopen twee decennia heeft dit geleid tot modellen en voorspellingen over de noordelijke boomgrens die zich naar het noorden haast. Toch loopt het niet helemaal zoals verwacht.

Seth brengt me in contact met een paar wetenschappers die hij in de loop der jaren heeft leren kennen en die elke zomer door Kotzebue komen op weg naar de binnenlanden, waar ze de groei van de witte spar in het oog houden. Als ik bel, zijn Roman Dial en zijn collega Paddy Sullivan nogal gefrustreerd. Al vijftien zomers zijn ze steeds teruggekeerd naar dezelfde plek aan de boomgrens, een afgelegen vallei aan de Agashashak-rivier, een zijrivier van de Noatak, in het Kobuk Valley National Park. In 1979 ging Roman bergbeklimmen in de Aregache Peaks en kampeerde hij boven de boomgrens. Daar stuitte hij op een botanicus van de Colorado State University, David Cooper, die op zoek was naar witte sparren, honderden meters hoger dan waar ze hadden moeten staan. Roman deed mee en wilde gelijk niks anders meer. Dat was het begin van zijn levenslange obsessie voor de boomgrens.

Het ABOVE-project van Paddy en Roman is een van de langstlopende ecologische experimenten in het Noordpoolgebied en heeft waardevolle gegevens opgeleverd over de veranderende vegetatiedynamiek, met name over het lot van de spar in Alaska. Maar deze zomer kunnen ze niet gaan. Zo missen ze een heel jaar aan gegevens, en dat brengt het wetenschappelijk gehalte van hun onderzoek in gevaar.

Wat Paddy het meest dwarszit, is kunstmest. Elk jaar bemest hij in Agashashak een perceel witte sparren met voedingsstoffen. Ernaast ligt een controleperceel dat hij niet bemest. Het doel is te begrijpen wat de groei van bomen op extreme breedtegraden en hoogten beperkt. Een van de blijvende mysteries van de veranderingen in de boomgrenszone is waarom het bos zich op sommige plaatsen naar het noorden lijkt te haasten (honderd meter per jaar in Scandinavië) en er op andere plaatsen de tijd voor neemt (minder dan tien meter per jaar in Midden-Canada). Computermodellen die alleen op temperatuur zijn gebaseerd voorspellen op de meeste plaatsen een snelle opmars van de bossen, maar de werkelijkheid is subtieler omdat verschillende soorten op verschillende manieren op de opwarming reageren. Alaska bevat voorbeelden van zowel het oprukken als de stilstand binnen één soort, en dit is wat Paddy en Roman bestuderen.

Ten oosten van de vrachtweg lijken de witte sparren nergens naar op weg te zijn, maar in het meer maritieme laagland ten westen daarvan haasten ze zich met grote snelheid de toendra in, alsof ze rennen voor hun leven voor de bosbranden en de droogte verder zuidelijk. Als Paddy's team de beperkende factoren van deze indicatieve soort kan vaststellen, kunnen ze beter voorspellen hoe het landschap er in de toekomst uit zal zien, hoeveel koolstof het zal kunnen vastleggen en hoeveel straling het zal kunnen absorberen. Nu hij een jaar geen kunstmest kan strooien zal dat de metingen verpesten.

Terwijl ik me van een afstand een beeld van de Agashashakvallei vormde, 'vloog' ik stroomopwaarts van Kotzebue als een sjamaan uit de oude wereld die het landschap in een droom doorkruiste. Achter de landtong waar Kotzebue aan ligt, verliezen de Kobuk en de Noatak zich in de Kotzebue Sound in het vlakke doolhof van een delta. Hier stuit de boomgrens op het zoute water in een griezelig landschap van geel zand dat meer op de Sahara lijkt dan op de Noordpool. De zuidelijke oever van de Kobuk-delta bestaat uit 200.000 hectare zand, de overblijfselen van gletsjermorenen die de beschutte vallei zijn ingewaaid. Poedervormig goudkleurig eolisch zand komt veel voor in het hoge noorden. Hier ontmoeten de twee geologische krachten die sinds de laatste ijstijd aan het werk zijn elkaar: terugtrekkende gletsjers en oprukkende bomen. De beschutte plek die een gunstige plaats vormt voor bomen is ook een plaats waar de wind het zand kan afzetten dat hij over de vlakten heeft meegevoerd. Het duinlandschap is spookachtig: enorme golvende gele en paarse schaduwen die associaties oproepen met hitte in plaats van koude, met vetplanten en kamelen zoals je die in de woestijn ziet, niet met af en toe een bloem van het roze vuurkruid die uit het zand steekt of een onvolgroeide spar die er verbaasd bij lijkt te staan tegen een immense achtergrond van duinen. Het is bijna alsof ze weten dat ze daar niet thuishoren.

Boven de rivierdelta komen de dunne lijnen van kreken op weg naar zee uit de modder- en zandvlaktes te voorschijn om samen te smelten in de hoofdstroom en hun meander te beginnen die de ritmische opeenvolging van het bos bepaalt. Vanuit de lucht volgen groene strepen de bochten van de rivier als uitwaaierende rimpels. Het bos lijkt in S-bochten steeds weer op de vlakte te zijn geschilderd, en onder een lagere hoek worden de verschillende hoogten en dichtheden van de bomen zichtbaar, elke streep, elke lijn anders, waardoor een effect ontstaat als van weefsel, van draden die steeds weer zijn ingeweven en strak tegen elkaar zijn getrokken.

Terwijl de stroming van de rivier steeds de buitenste oever van de bochten uitslijt, leggen ze ook de grond bloot onder het gemengde sparrenbos – witte en zwarte sparren, oude groei die inmiddels honderdvijftig tot tweehonderd jaar oud is in wat een climaxtoestand wordt genoemd. Langs de binnenoevers legt het water een spoor van grind neer dat langzaam wordt gekoloniseerd door wilgen, gras en mos. Daarachter ligt een bocht met hogere wilgen, elzen en berken die de rivier lijken te volgen, en achter deze strook jong bos ligt een meer open bos dat voornamelijk bestaat uit de smalle spitsen van zwarte sparren en een enkele, hogere, witte spar. De zwarte verkiest de vochtige drassige grond van de riviervlakte, terwijl de witte houdt van het gesteente van de valleikanten.

Naarmate de meanders zich een weg banen door de vallei, rukt het bos parallel eraan op. Het is een beeld dat in de loop van duizenden jaren heel langzaam is geschilderd met de weloverwogen penseelstreek van de rivier.

Onderin de vallei zijn de goed afwaterende gronden gunstig voor de bomen, maar aan de rand, achter de rij sparren die de vallei begrenzen, belemmert de permafrostlaag de afwatering en bloeit de laaglandtoendra: korstmossen, mossen, bessen, en het stilstaande water van meren en poelen in een mozaïek van pollen. Nog hoger, waar het gesteente door een dun laagje grond steekt, nemen de sparren het weer over. Het is wat men noemt een omgekeerde boomlijn. Het dichte bos boven, de alpine toendra onder en een strook bos die de route van de rivier volgt. De laatste tijd verschijnen er populieren die als struiken beginnen en in de herfst als vlammen uit de valleien omhoog schieten.

'Ja, de populieren slaan op hol!' zegt Roman. Maar jaar na jaar dezelfde plaats bezoeken is niet genoeg. Dat is nu precies het probleem voor iedereen die probeert af te stemmen op de boomtijd, of de aardetijd. 'Het is alsof je een kind ziet opgroeien – je merkt het niet,' zegt Roman, die binnenkort grootvader hoopt te worden.

Ze bekeken eerdere foto's. Toen zij hun percelen vergeleken met luchtfoto's uit de jaren 1950, stelden ze vast dat het bos zich slechts weinig had uitgebreid, niet zo veel als de modellen voorspelden. De echte schok was dat een voorheen marginaal ecosysteem – hoge struiken met hier en daar wat bomen zoals de populieren – met 400 procent was toegenomen. Door de opwarming verschuift het evenwicht van de ecosystemen aan de boomgrens, waarbij de overgangszone zich lijkt uit te breiden ten gunste van struikgewas in plaats van bos.[4]

De vergroening leidt niet tot het opschuiven van de boomgrens, maar tot het ontstaan van een landschap dat compleet nieuw is voor Alaska. Bovendien raakt de toendra in haar geheel overgroeid met vegetatie. Het is geen kwestie van een versnelde opmars van een boomgrens of van bepaalde soorten. Wanneer je een stuk papier aansteekt met een lucifer, kruipt er een gloeiende rode sintel over de bladzijde, maar wanneer je een vel papier in een oven legt, ontbrandt de hele boel in één keer. 'Toendra' zal binnenkort een historische term zijn in Alaska. Boreale vogelsoorten en struiken zijn nu al te vinden in het Arctic National Wildlife Refuge aan de North Slope, aldus Roman.

Elke onderzoeksvraag leidt weer tot een volgende vraag. Paddy en Roman wilden weten wat er aan de hand was met de struiken: wat hadden de wilgen en de elzen dat de sparren niet hadden? Kan het antwoord op die vraag misschien helpen het verschil te verklaren tussen de sparren in het oosten en het westen van de Brooks Range?

'We hebben maar 78 datapunten,' zegt Paddy, die uitlegt hoe weinig ze weten over waarom sommige bomen het goed doen en andere afsterven als gevolg van de opwarming. 'We weten niets.'

Met de hulp van een deskundige op het gebied van de bosondergrond, Rebecca Hewitt, begonnen ze de schimmelassociaties van sparren te onderzoeken.

De spar is sterk afhankelijk van mycorrhizanetwerken en van korstmossen om hem van stikstof en mineralen te voorzien, zoals de meeste planten. Meer dan 90 procent van alle plantensoorten is afhankelijk van schimmels om te overleven. Een uiteinde van een schimmelvezel nestelt zich in of rond een boomwortel. Het andere uiteinde van de schimmel, een draad die *hypha* wordt genoemd, kan vijftig maal dunner zijn dan de dunste wortels en honderden malen langer. Hierdoor wordt de reikwijdte van de boomwortel in feite vergroot. Wereldwijd maken deze draden van mycorrhizaschimmels tussen een derde en de helft van de levende massa in de bodem uit.[5] De bodem is in feite een enorme, fragiele kluwen van kleine met elkaar verbonden draadjes.

In de oostelijke Brooks Range, in het drogere, koudere, continentale klimaat, stelden Paddy en Roman vast dat de schimmelactiviteit hoog was, zelfs in zeer koude bodems met continue permafrost. Ten oosten van de Dalton Highway groeiden de bomen niet, en rukte ze ook niet verder op, maar investeerden in plaats daarvan zwaar in hun schimmelpartners, om zo te overleven. In de westelijke Brooks, waar de maritieme invloed van de Beringstraat zorgt dat het warmer en natter is, waren er minder schimmelassociaties maar waren de groei en de opmars meer uitgesproken. Ze gingen er daarom van uit dat de bomen hier niet zo veel hoefden te investeren in schimmelrelaties om toegang te krijgen tot de voedingsstoffen die ze nodig hebben.

Rebecca Hewitt heeft opvallend rood haar en blauwe ogen met het nooit dovende vuur van een zoekende. Als geduldig woordvoerder legt ze mij tijdens ons videogesprek langzaam en in begrijpelijke termen uit hoe planten stikstof nodig hebben om hun fotosynthetische machinerie op te bouwen, dat de toendra en het boreaal gebied maar over een beperkte hoeveelheid stikstof beschikken en hoe, wanneer dit kritische element wel beschikbaar komt, de toendra wordt overweldigd door vegetatie. Zij heeft planten op de toendra geobserveerd die stikstof uit de diepe ondergrond lijken te halen en die vervolgens, via complexe symbiotische relaties die door schimmels worden bemiddeld, de stikstof en diverse mineralen met andere soorten delen. De stikstof vastleggende planten zelf vertonen geen tekenen van toegenomen groei, terwijl andere, zoals wilgen, het zeer goed doen. Waar komt het stikstof vandaan? Zouden de planten het uit de afbrekende permafrost halen? Wie deelt wat met wie in deze kluwen van uitwisseling onder het bodemoppervlak? En wie beslist er over het evenwicht van de beschikbare middelen, het machtsevenwicht?

Wij weten dat schimmelnetwerken koolstof, water en mineralen kunnen transporteren tussen bomen en andere planten, zelfs van de ene naar de andere soort. Het idee van een 'woud wijd web', dat voortkomt uit het baanbrekende onderzoek van de ecologe Suzanne Simard naar het delen van koolstof tussen de berk en de douglasspar in de noordwestelijke regio van Noord-Amerika, heeft aan bekendheid gewonnen.[6] Onderzoek heeft sindsdien aangetoond dat er honderden kilo's koolstof binnen één enkele hectare via schimmelnetwerken tussen bomen worden overgebracht. Het concept van schimmelnetwerken als passieve geleiders van materiaal en informatie is volgens mycoloog Merlin Sheldrake echter een zeer 'plantcentrische visie'. De schimmels hebben immers, zo merkt hij op, ook hun eigen belangen. Volgens hem kunnen we de rol van mycelium in de bodem beter vergelijken met die van een makelaar. Maar als ik Roman en Paddy hoor praten over de explosieve reactie van het struikgewas op de opwarming, ten koste van de bomen, schiet mij een andere analogie te binnen. Als de schimmel nu eens eerder lijkt op een boer (van koolstof en suiker) die zijn gewassen diversifieert vanwege een onzeker klimaat?

Het is niet ondenkbaar dat processen van ontbinding, bodemvorming en schimmelmigratie net zo belangrijk zijn als temperatuurstijging bij het aansturen van de grootschalige vegetatieverschuivingen die momenteel de oppervlakte van de aarde veranderen. Het zou zowel in spiritueel als in biologisch opzicht voor de hand liggen: dat het patroon van het leven bepaald wordt door het patroon van leven dat eraan voorafging.

We beginnen nog maar net onder het oppervlak van de bosbodem te kijken en hebben nog maar nauwelijks een idee van daar zoal gaande is. Wat we wel weten is dat het bos, net als al het leven, een symbiotisch systeem is, een dynamisch proces, niet een verzameling van dingen of afzonderlijke wezens. En hoe nauwkeuriger we het onderzoeken, hoe mysterieuzer het wordt. Ergens daar beneden, tussen het web van schimmels en wortelpunten en de permafrost, kan de grens van het bos zijn. Het lijkt erop dat de sleutel om te begrijpen waar en wat de boomgrens is en hoe deze zal reageren op opwarming en dooi, niet te vinden is tussen de groen wordende toppen van de ijverige sparren boven de grond, maar in de vochtige zwarte organische laag eronder.

De vergroening van de toendra is echter maar de helft van wat de satellietfoto's laten zien. Verder naar het zuiden wordt het bos bruin.[7] Rebecca's vriend en collega Brendan Rogers ontwikkelt klimaatmodellen voor de Woods Hole-installatie in Massachusetts en is betrokken bij veel van de ABOVE-projecten, met name bij de raming van de koolstofvoorraden in bodems en bossen. Aan de telefoon legt hij uit dat aanvankelijk op kleinschalige satellietbeelden niet te zien was dat individuele bomen in gezonde bosbestanden bruin werden, maar dat het beeld tegen 2010 begon te veranderen en dat er tegen 2020 duidelijk een wijdverspreide achteruitgang van de bossen op gang leek te zijn gekomen. Satellietfoto's van het Noord-Amerikaanse boreaal tonen inmiddels groene valleien, zwarte brandlittekens en hele stukken bruin – door hitte gestreste of door insecten beschadigde sparren. In plaats van een gelijkmatig tapijt van pulserend, levendig groen, lijkt de aarde nu een huidziekte te hebben.

In zekere zin houden het groener en het bruiner worden verband met elkaar, zegt Brendan. Verwacht werd dat de opwarming de productiviteit van het bos zou verhogen, omdat de groeiseizoenen langer zouden worden en de planten meer zouden fotosynthetiseren. Het zogenaamde kooldioxide-bemestingseffect was echter van korte duur.[8] NASA-wetenschappers ontdekten dat de fotosynthese niet alleen werd bepaald door de temperatuur, maar ook door vocht en voedingsstoffen. Warmere lucht houdt meer waterdamp vast, waardoor het dampdruk-deficiet, het mechanisme dat planten ertoe aanzet water te laten verdampen en aan de atmosfeer af te geven, toeneemt. Het komt erop neer dat warmere lucht meer vocht uit de bladeren zuigt. Om geen vocht te verliezen bij hogere temperaturen, sluiten bomen hun huidmondjes en stoppen ze met de fotosynthese. Zelfs als er voldoende water in de grond zit, zal een boom, als de snelheid waarmee hij water verliest groter is dan de snelheid waarmee hij het kan opnemen, het verstandige doen en zijn groei stopzetten, waardoor zijn vermogen om bladeren te maken en koolstof op te slaan wordt beperkt.[9]

Sparrennaalden zijn opgerolde bladeren die bedekt zijn met een wasachtige cuticula die overmatig vochtverlies voorkomt, en elk huidmondje is bovendien aangepast om water te bewaren. Deze veerkrachtige naaldboom van de noordelijke wouden is geëvolueerd om te overleven met zeer weinig vocht, maar hij kan niet helemaal zonder water.[10] Het is een verbijsterend hoe weinig we weten over het sterven van bomen. Wanneer de fijne naalden aan de uiteinden van de takken van de spar bruin worden en afvallen, zoals elke zomer in toenemende mate gebeurt, zou een lijkschouwer moeite hebben om de doodsoorzaak vast te stellen. Is het watertekort, vasculaire schade of een gebrek aan koolstof?[11]

Sparren zijn taai, hun xyleem is weinig gevoelig voor waterstress, en daarom worden ze gewaardeerd om hun pulp. De kleine tracheïden die als leidingen door de groeiende boom lopen en deze voeden, zijn sterk en dikwandig. Ze zijn de vezels in papier. Maar extreme hitte zet zowel witte als zwarte sparren onder druk. Winter- of zomerdroogte is hetzelfde: gebrek aan water in de boom verhoogt de druk in de kolom. De spar heeft een uniek mechanisme ontwikkeld voor het bepalen van deze druk die kan oplopen tot wel 63 bar – een autoband haalt een maximum van 2,76. Hij heeft een soort kleine voorkamers tussen de cellen die met elkaar in verbinding staan en de samenhang van het geheel handhaven, terwijl de vochtsamenstelling binnen elke cel flexibel kan worden aangepast. Er lijkt geen ondergrens voor bevriezing te zijn, maar bij warm weer heeft zelfs de spar een punt waarop hij in de problemen komt. Zonder water in de wortels veroorzaakt de verdwijnen van het water dat langzaam in de boom wordt verbruikt een onderdruk, waardoor het water vanuit de wortels omhoog wordt gezogen door het xyleem. Uiteindelijk trekt het xyleem luchtbellen door de celwanden naar binnen, waardoor het indeukt. Wanneer die bellen samenkomen, heeft het veel weg van een embolie in de aderen van een mens, zoals een duiker die caissonziekte krijgt.

Net als de meeste noordelijke soorten heeft de spar zich ontwikkeld om het grootste deel van het jaar slapend door te brengen en te profiteren van het korte groeiseizoen om reserves op te bouwen voor de strenge winter. Maar als hij ook de zomer slapend moet doorbrengen om de hitte- of droogtestress te overleven, heeft hij weinig kans om te groeien. Gelegenheid tot groeien tijdens de zomer is inmiddels steeds vaker een luxe.

Tegelijkertijd betekent deze versnelling van de watercyclus dat er meer transpiratie is van alle vegetatie, waardoor de convectieve energie in het systeem toeneemt. Dat leidt tot meer stormen, meer donder en bliksem die tot meer bosbranden leidt, een verdubbeling van de omvang van het verbrande gebied en een exponentiële toename van de emissies, bijna elk jaar weer. In 2019 stootten de bosbranden in Alaska volgens Brendan 70 teragram koolstofdioxide uit, evenveel als de menselijke activiteit in de staat Florida.

Sparren hoeven niet dood te zijn om goed te branden. De zwarte spar wordt door brandweerlieden 'benzine op een stokje' genoemd vanwege zijn ontvlambare gom. Het bladafval van sparren bevat kamfer – dat wordt gebruikt in vuurwerk. Dat komt doordat de zwarte spar zich pas na een brand vernieuwt: zijn kleverige zwarte hars-achtige kegels sluimeren totdat de gom is gesmolten en de zaden vrijkomen. Maar nu elk jaar steeds grotere gebieden in brand staan, zoals in Rusland, worden de traditionele opvolgingspatronen verstoord en regenereren de zwarte sparren niet langer.[12]

'Het boreale woud valt uit elkaar,' zei een onderzoeker uit Alaska al in 2016. 'Met de sparren verlies je ook alles wat in die sparren leeft, en dat is in feite het boreale woud.'[13] Dat is niet alleen een probleem voor de bewoners van dat woud, maar voor ons allemaal. De terugkoppelingen en onderlinge relaties tussen bosbouwsystemen, watercycli, atmosferische circulatie, koolstofopslag en het smelten van de permafrost zijn complex en verstrekkend, te complex om in één enkel computermodel te vangen.

'Het enige wat we met zekerheid kunnen zeggen is dat er veel meer klimaatverstoring zal komen,' zegt Brendan. Om een glimp te kunnen opvangen van wat er zou kunnen veranderen als we een bos verliezen, moet je eerst begrijpen welke rol het bos speelt bij het handhaven van de huidige toestand.

Een intact sparrenbos is, zoals elk bos, in de eerste plaats bezig met het tot stand brengen en in stand houden van zijn eigen habitat. We weten dat bomen regen maken. Sparren zijn hier bijzonder goed in, met krachtige vluchtige organische verbindingen die zich binden aan de moleculen van waterdamp, waardoor ze condenseren tot water en zwaarder worden, zodat ze als regen vallen. Bovendien hebben de bomen de waterdamp daar toch al veroorzaakt. Elke boom is een kleine onafhankelijke regenmakerij. Bomen nemen veel meer water op en geven veel meer water af dan ze voor de fotosynthese gebruiken, tot wel 90 procent van het water dat ze opnemen, wordt niet gebruikt. Waarom doen ze dat? Zoals wetenschappelijk journalist Fred Pearce het formuleert: 'Bomen geven vocht af om een wereld te maken die geschikt is voor meer bomen,' en voor ons.[14]

Vijftig procent van de regen die op het land valt, is afkomstig van de evapotranspiratie van bomen. En aangezien bomen water blijven opnemen en uitstoten en de regen die zij maken recycleren, lijken aaneengesloten stukken bos belangrijke verkeersroutes te zijn voor regen en wind. De regen die op het bos valt wordt getransporteerd en valt vervolgens weer als regen op de continenten, als in een soort pomp die wel ook wel 'vliegende rivieren' wordt genoemd.[15] In ander onderzoek spreekt men over dit fenomeen als 'teleconnecties' tussen bossen op verschillende continenten, zoals het verband tussen het regenwoud van de Amazone en de West-Afrikaanse moesson. De sparrenbossen van Alaska en Noord-Canada lijken direct van invloed te zijn op de regenval in de zogenaamde 'Graanschuur van Amerika', de grote vlakten van het Amerikaanse Midwesten.[16] Het onderzoek naar teleconnecties is nog maar net begonnen, maar hetzelfde lijkt te gelden voor de Russische taiga en de tarwevelden van de Oekraïne.[17]

Bossen helpen ook wind te maken, al is men het er nog niet over eens hoe dat precies werkt. Het polaire front is de abrupte overgang tussen de koude luchtmassa boven de Noordpool en de warmere lucht van de gematigde breedten. Het beweegt met de seizoenen mee. In de winter daalt het vaak af naar lagere breedtegraden en brengt ijs en sneeuw met zich mee, maar in de zomer is het meestal stabiel en neemt een positie in die min of meer parallel loopt met de boomgrens. Tot in de jaren 1990 werd aangenomen dat de positie van de bomen werd beïnvloed door de wind, maar onderzoek door Roger Pielke en Piers Vidale, twee wetenschappers uit het Verenigd Koninkrijk, suggereerde dat juist het omgekeerde waar zou kunnen zijn: dat de bomen de positie van het front bepalen.

Sparren zijn donkergroen door het sterk geconcentreerde mesofylweefsel in hun naalden dat straling absorbeert. Zoals bij de hoge dennen van Schotland kan deze kleur zo dicht zijn en de wasachtige schublaag op de naalden zo dik dat de naalden blauw of bijna zwart lijken. Wanneer het zonlicht de naalden van de spar raakt, kaatst de microstructuur van de boom – de stammen en naalden – de straling tussen de bomen heen en weer, waardoor de kortgolvige straling wordt geabsorbeerd en de golven langer worden, zodat zoveel mogelijk fotonen worden verzameld. Omdat de bomen het licht absorberen, wordt er minder infrarode straling terug de atmosfeer in gestuurd om door de kooldioxidedeken te worden gevangen en te worden omgezet in warmte die de opwarming van de aarde voedt. De grote sparrenbossen van Noord-Amerika produceren niet alleen enorme hoeveelheden zuurstof en absorberen koolstof, maar koelen de planeet tegelijk ook af. Eén boom levert gedurende de zomer 70 kilowatt koeling per 100 liter water, hetgeen overeenkomt met twee normale airconditioners.[18]

In de winter is dit vermogen om straling te absorberen de reden waarom sneeuw rond de stammen van sparrenbomen zal smelten. Ze verwarmen de bodem rondom en dragen bij tot een gunstig leefmilieu voor insecten, knaagdieren en schimmels in het ondergrondse. De temperaturen tussen de takken van de sparren en onder de bomen kunnen aanzienlijk hoger zijn dan de lucht elders, omdat de boom de uit het licht geabsorbeerde energie naar beneden uitstraalt in de richting van de sneeuwlaag. Daarom kamperen de menselijke bewoners van de noordelijke bossen vaak onder sparrenbomen en beschouwen ze grote exemplaren als heilige toevluchtsoorden.

In de zomer leidt de donkere kleur van de bomen echter tot een enorm verschil tussen het reflecterend vermogen, het albedo, van de toendra en het albedo van het bos. Omdat het boreale woud zoveel straling absorbeert, warmt het op zoals een zwart wegdek in de zon dat doet. De toendra even verderop kaatst daarentegen het grootste deel van de straling weer de ruimte in. Het verschil tussen de twee is zo groot dat er een enorm temperatuurverschil ontstaat tussen de toendra en het bos. Dit verschil, zo opperden Pielke en Vidale, brengt de winden op gang en bepaalt de positie van het polaire front.[19]

Later onderzoek heeft echter uitgewezen dat temperatuurverschillen niet het hele verhaal zijn. Meer dan tien jaar geleden kwam de Russische natuurkundige Anastasia Makarieva met een nieuwe theorie die tegen de tijd van de ABOVE-conferentie in 2020 meer en meer aanhangers had gekregen.

Makarieva was geïnteresseerd in het vacuüm dat ontstaat wanneer de waterdamp die vrijkomt bij verdampende bomen afkoelt en condenseert tot waterdruppels. Als natuurkundige ging ze uit van het principe dat water, een vloeistof, veel minder ruimte inneemt dan waterdamp, een gas. De omzetting van gas in vloeistof creëert een gedeeltelijk vacuüm, een drukafname, waardoor meer vochtige lucht van onderen wordt aangezogen. Deze opstijgende vochtige lucht wordt dan lager vervangen door lucht die horizontaal over het bladerdak van het bos stroomt. Makarieva en haar collega Viktor Gorshkov noemden hun theorie de biotische pomp. Het proces van het maken van regen pompt ook lucht over het bos om de regen te doen voortbewegen. Deze wind zal blijven waaien zolang er waterdamp condenseert, dus zolang de bomen transpireren.[20]

Het concept van een biotische pomp zou kunnen helpen verklaren waarom de positie van het polaire front en de boomgrens in de zomer (wanneer de bomen transpireren) samenvallen, maar niet in de winter (wanneer ze in rust zijn). De geest van de noordenwind – BOREAS in het Grieks – zou dus wel eens kunnen huizen in de noordelijke bossen, de boreale. Makarieva vertelde Fred Pearce dat bossen 'niet alleen de longen van de atmosfeer zijn, maar ook het kloppend hart. De biotische pomp is de belangrijkste motor van de atmosferische circulatie op aarde.'[21]

Als Makarieva gelijk heeft, moeten bossen worden beschouwd als natuurlijke rijkdommen van het allergrootste belang, die niet alleen van essentieel belang zijn voor de instandhouding van menselijke habitats op de plaatsen waar ze zich bevinden, maar ook als biologische motoren met geopolitieke relevantie, over grenzen en continenten heen. Zou het, naarmate er meer aandacht wordt besteed aan de wetenschap van de klimaatverandering en naarmate er meer vragen worden gesteld zodra de 'ecosysteemdiensten' die wij als vanzelfsprekend hebben beschouwd, beginnen te haperen, dan zo kunnen gaan dat natiestaten belangstelling beginnen te krijgen voor de ontbossing in het buitenland, en in plaats van legers te sturen om de oliestroom op gang te houden, een land binnenvallen om de bossen te beschermen die de regen maken en die naar hun eigen land sturen?

De biotische-pomptheorie lijkt ook de veranderingen te verklaren die nu in de bossen van Alaska plaatsvinden. Naarmate bossen minder water uitstoten, valt er minder regen en is er minder wind, wat op zijn beurt leidt tot hetere en drogere omstandigheden die gunstiger zijn voor droogte en brand. De zomerwinden in Alaska lijken al af te zwakken, waardoor langdurigere, drogere hogedruksystemen blijven hangen en de verdroging vervolgens versnelt.[22] Het boreale woud is van fundamenteel belang voor het klimaatsysteem van de laatste paar miljoen jaar, en naarmate de bomen naar zee oprukken, uitdrogen of worden weggevaagd door een struikachtige massa van groen wordende toendra's, zullen de stabiele winden die bovenop de wereld rustig het noordelijk halfrond reguleerden, op hol slaan – zo ver is het al.

Huslia, Koyukuk, Alaska
65° 42' 7" N

'Solastalgie' is een neologisme dat we tegenwoordig steeds vaker horen. Het beschrijft een gevoel van heimwee dat je voelt terwijl je nog thuis bent. Het is een gevoel van verlies, maar ook een gevoel van verwarring: de planeet waarop wij dachten te leven, bestaat niet meer. In een opwarmende wereld raken woorden los van hun betekenis. De kloof van de antropoloog tussen de betekenaar en het betekende wordt gevaarlijk breed. 'Toendra' beschrijft niet meer precies wat de toendra inmiddels is geworden. 'Lente', 'winter' en 'herfst' zullen binnenkort in grote delen van de wereld omstreden begrippen zijn. De meesten van ons zullen dit binnenkort zo ervaren, maar zij die dicht bij het land stonden, leven er al bijna een eeuw mee.

In de toekomst zal de geschiedenis van de oliewinning in Alaska misschien worden gezien als een pijnlijke ironie. Het was uiteindelijk de olie die John McPhee en zijn collega's in 1975 de Salmon River deed afvaren op hun zoektocht. De ontdekking van olie leidde tot de Alaska Native Claims Settlement Act. En het was de verontwaardiging over de oliepijpleiding die leidde tot de opname van bepalingen over land van 'nationaal belang' en de National Parks Service om rangers en verkenners uit te zenden die het land van de Noordelijke IJszee tot de Stille Oceaan en alle grote rivieren en bergen daartussenin onderzochten en in kaart brachten.

Een belangrijk onderdeel van het programma van de National Park Service was de Cooperative Park Studies Unit, opgericht aan de Universiteit van Alaska in Fairbanks, onder leiding van de antropoloog Zorro Bradley. Bradley verzamelde een team van onderzoekers om uitgebreid de 'levenswijzen' te documenteren van inheemse bevolkingsgroepen in gebieden die in aanmerking komen voor de status 'van nationaal belang'. De NPS was vastbesloten toekomstige nationale parken te beheren in overeenstemming met de culturele en sociaaleconomische belangen van de mensen voor wie deze habitat thuis is. Het was een baanbrekend programma dat een zeer uitgebreide inventarisatie opleverde van wat, veertig jaar later, gestaag verloren gaat als gevolg van enorme tegemoetkoming die werd gedaan aan het privébezit en de op koolstof gestookte consumptiedrang waar de ANCSA voor stond. De inspanning was echter ook waardevol om een andere reden: het vastleggen van de wijsheid en het wereldbeeld van de inheemse bevolking vanwege de dorst naar olie, biedt ook veel aanknopingspunten voor een mogelijke uitweg uit het doolhof van verwarring en ontkenning dat door die olie is ontstaan.

Aan de bovenloop van de Kobuk houdt het stroomgebied op bij een continentale scheidslijn, een lage bergrug van blauwe heuvels die noordwaarts loopt tot hij stuit op de wand van de Brooks Range. Regen die aan de ene kant van de bergkam valt, stroomt via de Kobuk naar Kotzebue en de Tsjoektsjenzee. De regen die aan de andere kant valt voedt de Alatna, vervolgens de Koyukuk en uiteindelijk de Yukon, en bereikt de Stille Oceaan enkele duizenden kilometers verder zuidelijk. Toen Seth, de schrijver die opgroeide in een iglo aan de oevers van de Kobuk, jong was, was de continentale scheidingslijn het begin van het eigenlijke bos. Het volk van de Koyukuk-rivier, bekend als de Koyukon, is in tegenstelling tot de Iñupiat die hun ogen op de zee gericht houden, volledig op het bos ingesteld. In hetzelfde jaar dat McPhee de rivier afzakte, in 1975, trok een 35-jarige antropoloog met zijn hondenslee het Koyukon-gebied binnen, dwars door verse lentesneeuw. Dat leidde tot een ontmoeting met ingrijpende gevolgen voor zowel de antropoloog als het Koyukonvolk.

Richard K. Nelson had op 22-jarige leeftijd voor het eerst kennis gemaakt met Alaska toen hij bij de US Air Force in Wainwright werkte. Daarna had hij antropologie gestudeerd en was hij op Hawaï gaan doceren over het leven op de Noordpool. In 1974 greep hij zijn kans om te werken voor Zorro Bradleys nieuwe Cooperative Park Studies Unit, en keerde terug naar Alaska. Bradley stuurde hem naar Ambler en Shungnak, Seths oude werkterrein in de Kobuk-vallei. Na verloop van tijd trok hij naar het oosten, de binnenlanden in, naar de Koyukuk om een jaar in Huslia door te brengen, een jaar dat na verloop van tijd zou leiden tot een van de belangrijkste werken van de naoorlogse etnografie, een klassieker die de inspiratie vormde voor een televisieserie en die nog steeds opnieuw wordt uitgegeven: *Make Prayers to the Raven: A Koyukon View of the Northern Forest* (1983).

Nelsons belangrijkste inzicht en prestatie was dat hij de 'manier van leven' van de Koyukun, hun wereldbeschouwing, respecteerde en vervolgens in zijn eigen woorden beschreef. *Make Prayers to the Raven* is, zo schreef hij, 'een inheemse natuurgeschiedenis die buiten het domein van de westerse wetenschap staat.' Het boek bevat uitgebreide appendices met Koyukon-namen voor soorten en begrippen, op zich al een belangrijke bijdrage. Daarnaast laat Nelson zien hoe de Koyukon-kijk op de natuur tastbaar en bovenal reëel is, ook al gaat ze ons emotionele begrip te boven. Hij schreef:

> 'Het Koyukon volk leeft in een wereld die toekijkt, in een woud van ogen. Iemand die zich door de natuur beweegt – hoe wild, afgelegen, ja zelfs desolaat de plek ook is – is nooit echt alleen. De omgeving heeft een bewustzijn, neemt waar, heeft een persoonlijkheid. Ze voelt. Ze kan worden beledigd. En ze moet steeds met gepast respect worden behandeld.'[23]

Voor de Koyukon is dit wereldbeeld bepalend voor hoe zij leven en overleven op het land. Het biedt een glimp van wat het zou kunnen betekenen om echt te leven als onderdeel van een ecosysteem:

> 'Ideologie is een fundamenteel onderdeel van het bestaan... de meeste interacties met natuurlijke entiteiten worden op de een of andere manier beheerst door een morele code die een juist spiritueel evenwicht bewaart tussen het menselijke en het niet-menselijke.'

Zoals voor zoveel inheemse gemeenschappen zijn voor de Koyukon de mensheid, de natuur en het bovennatuurlijke verenigd in één morele orde in 'de wereld die Raaf heeft gemaakt'.

Dat is een inspirerend uitgangspunt dat ons misschien zou kunnen helpen om van onze afhankelijkheid van koolwaterstoffen af te komen. Door dit boek begon ik landschappen anders te zien. Nadat ik het had uitgelezen, en gewapend met een heleboel vragen, ging ik op zoek naar Richard K. Nelson, die na zijn tijd in Huslia een gezien schrijver was geworden, gezien als de held van Alaska en vaak te horen was op de National Public Radio van de Verenigde Staten, met een langlopende serie over *soundscapes* en de natuur die de toepasselijke naam *Encounters* droeg. Helaas vernam ik dat hij net een paar weken daarvoor was overleden, terwijl ik zijn boek aan het lezen was. Hij had gevraagd om nadat zijn beademingsmachine was uitgeschakeld, alleen te worden gelaten met een opname van de roep van een raaf.

Dus ging ik op zoek naar zijn belangrijkste Koyukon-lerares, Catherine Attla, maar vernam dat zij een paar jaar daarvoor was overleden. Ook zij was een begrip bij de publieke omroep van Alaska, waar ze een programma presenteerde dat verhalen en kennis van de inheemse bevolking verzamelde en deelde onder de naam *Raven Time*. Het archief van deze opnames aan de Universiteit van Alaska in Fairbanks is een rijke bron voor een nieuw type geschiedschrijving, de orale geschiedenis van de opwarming van de aarde.[24]

K'ititaalkkaanee, zoals Catherine in de Koyukon taal heet, verschijnt op het scherm, een donkerharige vrouw die buiten zit, gekleed in een warme parka met een kraag van wolfsbont. Boven haar omlijsten enkele berkentakken een lichtblauwe lucht. De zon staat op haar gladde gezicht, glinsterend op de stalen poten van haar bril. Ze glimlacht alsof ze plezier heeft om haar eigen verhaal.

'Shhh!' zegt ze, giechelend. 'Dat zeiden ze vroeger ook: "Je moet stil zijn in de aanwezigheid van het ijs. Je moet respect betonen."'

Het is lente. Het ijs verdwijnt uit de rivier: grote grijze schuivende platen die met een snelheid van één knoop stroomafwaarts schuiven, kraken en tuimelen, voorbij aan het dorp Huslia. De zon schijnt op spichtige berkenbomen, de toppen van bronzen sparren en vierkante huizen met lage daken, gemaakt van sparrenstammen. Een groep verzamelt zich aan de oever van de rivier met petten, zonnebrillen en bontparka's om christelijke gebeden te bidden en traditionele liederen te zingen, als dank aan het ijs: 'Moge hetzelfde aantal van ons u volgend jaar weer zien bewegen, o rivierijs.'

Catherine vertelt dat, als zij en haar zus stokken in de bevroren rivier gooiden, de oudsten haar terechtwezen. Er zit een geest in het ijs en die is krachtig. Er werd hun altijd gezegd dat ze hun mond moesten houden en niet moesten spreken over 'grote dingen die je niet begrijpt, daar is je mondje te klein voor!' Het was hen verboden te praten over de zon, de maan, de hemel, de dieren. De wereld leeft en kan je horen. En als een dier het niet prettig vindt dat er over hem wordt gesproken, zal het je ongeluk bezorgen.

'Ik kan niet wachten om groot te zijn,' zei haar zus altijd, 'dan kan ik net zo praten als zij!'

Catherine spreekt vrijuit, lacht en deelt de verhalen over de ouderen en haar eigen verwarring. In 1950 bezocht ze de pastoor en zei: 'Vader, ik word verscheurd door twijfel. Ik ken de overlevering van mijn voorouders en ik ken de leer van Jezus, maar ik weet niet welke van die twee boodschappen waar is.'

'Ze zijn allebei waar, ' was zijn antwoord, 'en je moet ze allebei volgen.'

'Daarna voelde ik me zo veel beter, zo opgelucht!' zegt ze, en ze lacht weer.

Dat was in 1986. Catherine spreekt voor de camera in het kader van een televisiedocumentaire, gebaseerd op Nelsons boek.[25] Zij nam Nelson in het voorjaar van 1975 in huis omdat ze geloofde in het delen van de wijsheid van de ouderen die zij had mogen ontvangen en omdat zij het Engels machtig was en het zo kon overbrengen. Catherine werd in 1927 geboren in Cutoff, het dorp dat na overstromingen werd vervangen door Huslia. Als tiener leerde ze Engels door de etiketten op conserven en andere producten van de kolonisten te lezen en werd ze bedreven in het bemiddelen tussen de instanties van de koloniale macht, de federale regering van de VS, en haar volk, de Koyukon.

Na het vertrek van Nelson ging zij in dezelfde geest door met spreken en het delen van haar kennis en herinneringen op de radio. In één episode beschrijft Catherine hoe ze in 1937 op tienjarige leeftijd met een jachtgeweer naar 'een goede ganzenplek', Willow Lake, ging en hoe de lucht 24 uur lang, dag en nacht, 'zwart' van de vogels was. 'Zoveel vogels waren er. Maar nu,' in de jaren 1990, 'zijn er eigenlijk geen vogels meer, als je het vergelijkt.' Zelfs in de jaren 1970 schreef Nelson al over ouderen die klaagden dat de dageraad zo stil was geworden, met zo veel minder vogelgezang, en over het opdrogen van het water in meren die vroeger vol zaten met wilde vogels.

In een andere aflevering vertelt ze hoe zij in de jaren 1930 met haar grootmoeder ging vissen en hoe ze geleerd had het weer te voorspellen aan de hand van de vlekken op de snuit van een vis: witte vlekken betekenen dat er koud weer op komst is. Of hoe een enkele meeuw ver landinwaarts een slecht visjaar voorspelt, terwijl een hele zwerm een goed jaar aankondigt. 'Elk dier weet veel meer dan jij.'

In die tijd aten ze weinig vis omdat ze hun eigen netten moesten maken, en katoenen garen ging niet lang mee. Netten maken van schors of pezen kostte veel tijd. Haar stem is zacht en laag en legt geduldig het ingewikkelde geheel van rituelen, taboes en gebruiken uit: de routines van het viskamp, de juiste manier om een bever te slachten of een gans te plukken, hoe gedode dieren een nacht moeten rusten om de geest de kans te geven het lichaam te verlaten en hoe de poten van een beer worden afgehakt om te voorkomen dat zijn geest blijft ronddwalen. Bepaalde dieren zijn steeds voorbehouden aan bepaalde mensen om te eten, aangezien de kenmerken van het dier besmettelijk zijn. Zo zouden alleen ouderen de gavia (een watervogel die in Europa ook wel 'duiker' wordt genoemd, zoals de parelduiker van Loch Maree) mogen eten, omdat consumenten van zijn vlees het risico lopen net zo onhandig te worden als de vogel, en ouderen zijn dat toch al. Dit geldt ook voor andere entiteiten: met water moet spaarzaam worden omgegaan om te voorkomen dat de gulzige drinker net zo zwaar wordt als het water zelf.

De vorm en het patroon van de natuurlijke wereld geven vorm aan het landschap van het voorstellingsvermogen en de sociale verbanden van de mensen die erin leven. Tegen de natuurlijke wereld ingaan wordt ondenkbaar, een soort ketterij, en in de Koyukon-traditie hangt daar een prijskaartje aan. In de televisiedocumentaire wordt een begrafenis getoond van een jongen die zichzelf van het leven heeft beroofd. Moeders staan te wenen rond een vuur en branden offergaven, een reusachtig wit sparrenkruis wordt door zijn leeftijdsgenoten op zijn verse graf gezet, en Catherine schudt haar hoofd.

'Te veel ongelukken,' zegt ze. Dat komt omdat we de *hutlanee*, de traditionele rituelen en taboes van het bos, niet respecteren. Voor het televisiepubliek zegt ze het op een andere manier: 'Het Hooggerechtshof zou een wet moeten maken die mensen verplicht de aarde te benaderen zoals ze een ander mens zouden benaderen.'

De laatste opname van Catherine die ik kan vinden is een radioprogramma dat is geproduceerd door studenten van de Jimmy Huntington High School in Huslia in samenwerking met het Wereld Natuur Fonds. Die stamt uit 2005. Haar haar is inmiddels wit, ze draagt een bril en een vest, en spreekt langzamer.[26]

'Ze moeten niet met de maan rommelen, weet je. Onze ouderen zeiden dat er iets zou veranderen als je een man op de maan zou zetten. De maan houdt verband met het weer. Zie je nu wat er is gebeurd?'

De andere ouderen in de kring knikken instemmend. De studenten hebben opgemerkt hoe de sparren lijden onder de hittestress, en Rose Ambrose zegt: 'Het weer wordt te oud om zichzelf in de hand te kunnen houden. Het water van de Koyukuk River staat hoger dan de oever, het is verschrikkelijk, verschrikkelijk.'

Virginia McCarthy is het ermee eens: 'Dit is niet meer het land waarop wij zijn opgegroeid.'

Marie Yaska zegt: 'Alle vogels zingen iets voor ons. Het enige lied waarvan we merken dat het echt veranderd is, is dat van het roodborstje. Dat zingt maar een half deuntje en dan gaat het van "Ha ha ha." Ik vraag me af waarom.'

Ik wil weten hoe het nu met de Koyukon gaat. Ik bel de burgemeester van Huslia, Carl Burgett. Terwijl we op een zonnige ochtend in juni met elkaar praten, komt de wereld die Nelson en Catherine beschrijven in mijn gedachten tot leven.

'Wij zijn een tamelijk onaangetast volk,' zegt de stem aan de andere kant vriendelijk lachend. Er is 320 kilometer stroomop- en afwaarts geen ander dorp te bekennen. Alleen de Eskimo's wonen noordelijker.'

Carl vertelt me dat hij buiten de hut staat die hij aan het bouwen is van sparrenhout. Ik heb een foto gezien van Huslia, het onregelmatige cluster van stevige houten hutten met bijgebouwen en de hoger gelegen voorraden erachter, gelegen tussen verspreide berkenbomen, op enige afstand van de wijde bocht van de Koyukuk-rivier, die zich uitstrekt naar het westen. In de verte breekt de vlakte op in onregelmatige patronen van muskeg, een soort veenlandschap, en bos tot de vlakte de donkere lijn van de Brooks Range in het noorden ontmoet, het geheel doorsneden door de enorme slingers van de glinsterende rivier. In de Koyukon-taal is de naam van de plaats *Tsaatiyhdinaadakk'onh dinh* – 'waar het bos de heuvel verbrandde tot aan de rivier'. *Huslia* is een variant op de inheemse naam van de beek, de Huslee.

Op deze ochtend in juni is de sneeuw bijna gesmolten en het laatste ijs van de rivier verdwenen, zegt Carl. Het 'groener worden' – het ontluiken van de bomen – en het 'breken' – het afbreken van het ijs – zijn voorbij, en de nacht zal zich zeker tot in augustus niet meer vertonen. Carl is in een goede bui.

'Dit is een prima moment om te bellen, ja, een prima moment,' zegt hij, opnieuw lachend. Zoals de meeste Koyukon leeft hij niet met de klok. Hij eet als hij honger heeft en slaapt als hij moe is. Tijdens de poolzomer kan het bijhouden van de tijd er wel eens bij inschieten. Kinderen spelen buiten om drie uur 's nachts, mensen blijven wakker om bij elkaar op bezoek te gaan en gaan pas naar huis om te slapen als het gesprek is geëindigd. Het is net voor de middag in Huslia, en Carl gaat naar de rand van het dorp om hout te hakken. Ruim zestig kilometer in de ene richting staat er niets dan *ts'ibaa t'aal* (zwarte spar) en zestig kilometer de andere kant op alleen *ts'ibaa* (wit). De zomer is de tijd voor houtkap, in voorbereiding op de winter. In de extreme kou is warmte belangrijker om te kunnen overleven dan voedsel. Een goed gevulde houtopslag geeft aanzien.

Dat kan ik in Huslia niet alleen zien, maar vooral ook horen. Nelsons boek staat vol met stemmen als die van Carl, met een nederige, open, melodieuze grammatica die evenzeer deel lijkt uit te maken van de natuurlijke klanken van het land als de wind die door de sparren zingt of de berken doet ratelen, het gezang van vogels, het plonzen van de zalm in de rivier of het geluid van een peddel op het meer. Nelson citeert een vrouw, wellicht Catherine Attla: 'Sommige mensen zullen op de duiker jagen, maar ik dood hem niet graag. Ik luister liever zo veel mogelijk naar hem en probeer de woorden op te pikken die hij kent.'

Natuurlijk is het lawaai van kettingzagen, sneeuwscooters, buitenboordmotoren en propellers tegenwoordig een vast onderdeel van het leven in Huslia. Carl vertel me met enige trots dat het dorp groeit: inmiddels wonen er driehonderdvijftig mensen en de school heeft honderden leerlingen. Maar zonder wegen en binnen de beschermde enclave van het Gates of the Arctic National Park, waar commerciële houtkap verboden is, heeft de rest van de wereld maar weinig interesse in de Koyukon. De wasserij-annex-cafetaria van de gemeenschap (vanwege de permafrost is er geen stromend water) is pas sinds kort uitgerust met wifi.

'Het is een *fly-in*,' zegt Carl, 'en dat betekent isolement, traditioneel leven, wild eten.' Door de Covid-pandemie zijn de vluchten onderbroken, maar meer dan de helft van het voedsel van de gemeenschap komt van het land, dus als er helemaal geen vliegtuigen meer zouden komen, zouden ze het toch wel redden. 'Onze kennis, onze cultuur is nog sterk,' zegt hij.

Ik vraag hem of Nelsons boek heeft bereikt waar de auteur op had gehoopt, namelijk de Koyukon zelf een houvast bieden bij de instandhouding van hun cultuur.

'Welk boek?' zegt hij. Ik herinner hem aan Nelson en Attla.

'Ah, die kerel.' Hij grinnikt. 'Mensen stellen zich gewoonlijk niet open voor buitenstaanders, maar die kerel, op een of andere manier is het hem wel gelukt.'

Carl ontwijkt mijn vraag over klimaatverandering en wijst in plaats daarvan op de geweldige regen die ze hebben gehad. In het hoge noorden van Alaska viel vaak minder dan 38 centimeter regen per jaar, maar dit jaar is er veel gevallen. En er is veel stuifmeel. De regen komt al maandenlang vanuit de bergen over Huslia gewaaid. Drie keer meer dan normaal. De bomen vinden het geweldig. Tijdens ons gesprek verwarmt de zon de harsachtige gom van de blondbruine zaadkegels van de witte spar. Wanneer de hars zachter wordt, springen de als een veer gespannen schubben van de kegels allemaal tegelijk open. Als je tijdens het openklappen van de dennenappels uitkijkt over de vallei, lijkt het wel of er in de verte een veldslag woedt. In het bos klinkt een kraken als van geweerschoten, en wolken geel stof drijven op de thermiek boven het bladerdak. Op al het stilstaande water, de meren rond Huslia en het oppervlak van de rivier, zijn lange gele strepen stuifmeel te zien.

'De mensen zijn blij,' zegt Carl. Al tien jaar drogen de meren steeds verder uit en de bosbranden beginnen steeds ernstiger uit de hand te lopen. 'Het wordt een goed jaar voor bessen – het bos zou het dit jaar goed moeten doen,' zegt hij hoopvol.

Maar het extra water heeft ook andere gevolgen. De dynamische meanders van de rivier zullen nog grotere happen uit de rivieroever nemen dan gewoonlijk en meer huizen zullen moeten worden verplaatst. De gemeenschap verhuist elke lente vier of vijf huizen, maar soms zijn ze niet snel genoeg.

'Ja, dat is gewoon geworden,' zegt Carl, 'tegenwoordig.'

Misschien zullen we ons uiteindelijk allemaal op dit soort manieren moeten aanpassen. De ouderen van Huslia klagen niet langer over de onnatuurlijke overstromingen, zoals Virginia McCarthy en Rose Ambrose dat nog wel deden in de radio-interviews tien jaar eerder. In plaats daarvan is het onnatuurlijke natuurlijk geworden, het apocalyptische gewoontjes, een permanent gebeuren dat zich op de achtergrond afspeelt. Dat is misschien een van de aspecten van die nieuwe realiteit van de klimaatcrisis: dat we ons niet kunnen veroorloven erom te rouwen. Het dagelijks leven houdt ons zo zeer bezig dat er geen ruimte is om erbij stil te staan of er afstand van te nemen. Er is altijd werk aan de winkel.

'De negatieve gevolgen van de klimaatverandering doen zich voor in de natuur, niet voor mensen, omdat wij ons aanpassen. Als de ene soort lijdt, bloeit de andere,' zegt Carl nuchter.

Carl maakt zich minder zorgen over de geleidelijke ecologische veranderingen die worden veroorzaakt door de olie die hij vijftien jaar lang heeft helpen winnen toen hij aan de North Slope werkte, dan over de plotselinge veranderingen die door de mens worden gepland. Krachtens de ANCSA berustten alle land- en mijnbouwrechten bij een twaalftal inheemse ondernemingen. De Koyukon bezitten geen olieconcessies, maar hebben, net als alle inheemse groepen in Alaska, de materiële vooruitgang van de laatste veertig jaar te danken aan de olie, en zijn daarom niet snel bereid de industrie te bekritiseren.

Zoals Roman het zegt: 'Natuurlijk veranderen er dingen. Nu staan er kersenbomen in Fairbanks. Maar iedereen krijgt 500 dollar per maand. We hebben al dertig jaar geen inkomstenbelasting meer betaald en er is geen werkloosheid. Het ziet er nog steeds behoorlijk rooskleurig uit.' Het is dezelfde spagaat waarin alle moderne samenlevingen zich bevinden, hoewel de rol van fossiele brandstoffen in de economie van Alaska wel veel duidelijker is. De inwoners van Alaska weten beter dan de meesten dat actie tegen klimaatverandering ingrijpende gevolgen heeft voor hun comfortabele manier van leven. En voor menigeen is dat onaanvaardbaar. Het 'koolwaterstofcompromis', zoals Roman het noemt, bestaat grotendeels nog altijd.

Afgelopen najaar, in oktober 2019, daagden Nanieezh Peter, vijftien jaar oud, en Quannah Chasing Horse Potts, van zeventien, twee tienermeisjes, de oudsten tijdens de Alaska Federation of Natives Convention uit om een resolutie door te drukken waarin de noodtoestand werd afgekondigd in verband met de klimaatverandering.[27] Maar de meerderheid van de inheemse bedrijven is nog steeds pro-olie. Twee weken later ging het Bureau of Land Management over tot de veiling van 1,6 miljoen hectare boorrechten aan de North Slope, terwijl Conoco Phillips een project van 5 miljard dollar met de naam 'Willow' presenteerde. Naast de warmte en de bevers zullen wilgen binnenkort de ontdooiende toendra overheersen, waar het bedrijf inmiddels de permafrost koelt om te voorkomen dat de op ijs gebouwde infrastructuur instort.

In plaats van zich zorgen te maken over de toenemende hoeveelheid kooldioxide in de atmosfeer, maakt Carl zich zorgen over een meer zichtbare, minder verraderlijke vijand: de Amerikaanse overheid. Hij vreest dat de federale regering de lockdown in verband met de pandemie zal gebruiken om impopulaire plannen door te drukken voor de aanleg van een 350 kilometer lange weg door het Gates of the Arctic National Park, om zo de Dalton Highway te verbinden met een controversiële mijnbouwconcessie aan de Kobuk River bij Ambler. Een weg zou het de Koyukon moeilijker maken om te bepalen wie ze toelaten. Erger is echter dat de voorgestelde weg de waterhuishouding van het stroomgebied in de war zal sturen, de afwatering en daarmee de structuur van het bos en de ecosystemen erin zal veranderen. De afgelopen twee jaar hebben Seth, Roman, Paddy, Carl en honderdduizend anderen een petitie ondertekend tegen de Ambler Road. Tijdens drukbezochte openbare bijeenkomsten in Anchorage werden de voorstellen boos van de hand gewezen, maar terwijl wij elkaar in 2020 spraken, versnelde de regering Trump het goedkeuringsproces.

'Ik zou graag willen dat die jongens van de wegenbouw hierheen kwamen om te zien wat ze van plan zijn te vernietigen,' zegt Carl. Het lachen is hem vergaan.

Wat zij voorstellen zou alles vernietigen waar de wereld van de Koyukon op berust. Nelson heeft een van de scheppingsverhalen van de Koyukon opgetekend:

> Lang, lang geleden doodde de Raaf een walvis in een meer en reeg zijn ingewanden langs de oevers. Sindsdien hebben de sparren die langs de oevers van het meer groeien vaak lange, magere wortels. De Mink-man ging naar de boomvrouwen en vertelde hen dat hun echtgenoot de Raaf was omgekomen. Toen een vrouw het verhaal hoorde, huilde ze en kneep in haar vel. Toen veranderde ze in de spar met zijn ruwe bast die eruitziet alsof erin is geknepen. Toen een ander het hoorde, huilde ze en sneed zich in haar huid met een mes. Ze werd een populier met zijn diep ingesneden schors. Toen een derde vrouw het verhaal te horen kreeg, huilde ze en kneep zichzelf tot bloedens toe. Ze veranderde in de els, waarvan de schors wordt gebruikt om rode verfstof te maken.

Het land vormt de basis van het wereldbeeld van de Koyukon. Het is niet alleen een provisiekast, maar ook een woordenboek en een bijbel, de bewaarplaats van verhalen, geschiedenis en cultuur, iets dat zo heilig is dat het nooit kan worden vervangen. Elke plek en elke soort heeft een rol in het verhaal van de wereld die de Raaf heeft gemaakt. Mijnbouw maakt echter geen deel uit van dat verhaal.

Het mijnbouwproject heeft tot dusver drie naamsveranderingen ondergaan en als een hydra blijft het zich omvormen om in leven te blijven, hoewel de verwachte belastingopbrengsten van de mijn die door de weg zou worden bediend in het niet vallen bij de 500 miljoen dollar die de weg om het koper, zink en goud te vervoeren, zou kosten. Voordat Carl later die ochtend een spar omhakt, richt hij zich daarentegen tot de boom, bedankt hem en legt uit waarom hij dat doet, want volgens de Koyukon-traditie mogen bomen nooit zonder reden worden omgehakt, omdat ze zoveel geven.

Behalve vanwege hun praktische gaven van warmte en onderdak, worden de bomen ook gerespecteerd om hun magisch-medicinale werking. De grote oude sparren van het woud zijn vaste kampeerplaatsen en, zo geloven de Koyukon, beschermen iedereen die eronder slaapt. De actief delende cellen (meristemen) helemaal bovenin elke boom zijn de plaats waar de kracht en het medicijn van de boom worden verzameld. De top van de spar is de borstel van de sjamaan, die wordt gebruikt om ziekte weg te nemen. De dreigende kracht van de meren van Hudo' Dinh en Hunoo' Dinh bij Huslia kan worden geneutraliseerd door bij het oversteken ervan de top van een sparrenboompje bij je te dragen.

De westerse wetenschap is het daarmee eens. De spar bevat tussen de 21 en 25 geneeskrachtige biochemicaliën. Die zijn geconcentreerd in de groeitoppen van de boom en in de harsachtige gom die een beschermend omhulsel vormt over de ontspruitende bladeren. Deze gom is een cardiotonicum dat helpt bij de zuurstofsaturatie van het bloed, de bloeddruk verlaagt en helpt bij het reguleren van aritmie in het hart. De dispergeringsmiddelen die deze biochemische stoffen de atmosfeer in jagen hebben antibiotische en antiseptische eigenschappen – dezelfde chemicaliën die het werk doen wanneer je een op dennen gebaseerd desinfectiemiddel in het huishouden gebruikt. De meristemen van de sparren in het noorden steriliseren met hun miljarden in feite de lucht die wij inademen.[28]

In een verrassende symbiose vermenigvuldigt de spar deze antibiotische functie door de korstmossen die tussen zijn takken leven aan te moedigen hetzelfde te doen. Uit de naalden van de spar komt een alkaloïde vrij, ethanolamine genaamd, die rond de kruin van de boom cirkelt en de aanmaak van antibiotica door korstmossen op gang brengt. Deze liften dan mee op de andere aerosolen van de sparren en komen, gedragen door de winden die door het bos worden gepompt, naar beneden om de luchtwegen van het noordelijk halfrond te ontsmetten.[29] Onder de cocktail van vrijgekomen aerosolen bevindt zich een kleverige verbinding, betafellandreen genaamd, die werkt als een lijm. De antibiotica die door de boom worden vrijgegeven hebben hun eigen kleefstof die aan blootgestelde huid blijft kleven, vanwaar zij in de bloedbaan worden opgenomen. Dit alles wordt meegedragen in de geur van de boom. Geen wonder dat het Japanse 'bosbaden' in naaldbossen ook werkelijk een positief effect blijkt te hebben op de gezondheid en de ademhaling.[30]

De spar doet dit niet alleen voor mensen. De biochemische stoffen in de boom trekken ook insecten aan die zijn gom gebruiken om hun nesten te bouwen en te ontsmetten en uit zijn stuifmeel eiwitten halen voor hun lichaam. Stuifmeel is rijk aan essentiële aminozuren die insecten nodig hebben, en de honingdauw die door insectenschade aan de boom wordt geproduceerd levert gemakkelijk toegankelijke oplosbare suikers voor de insectenwereld. De insecten vormen weer het voedsel voor dieren hogerop in de keten, met name voor de zwermen trekvogels die naar het boreale gebied komen om te broeden. De vogels verzorgen op hun beurt de boom door de insecten weg te nemen.

Dit is de morele orde waartoe de Koyukon behoren, waarin alle levende wezens een plaats, een stem en een ziel hebben, en waarmee mensen een individuele relatie hebben. Dat is de orde die de Ambler Road in de weg staat. Nelson citeert een oudere:

'Heel Alaska is alsof het zich in de hand van een stekelvarken bevindt.'

Op 23 juli 2020, terwijl de pandemie Amerika teisterde en gemeenschappen in heel Alaska vanwege de lockdown thuisbleven, gaf het US Bureau of Land Management een doorgangsvergunning af, waarmee het tracé van de weg door federaal beschermd land werd goedgekeurd. Negen milieugroeperingen hebben een rechtszaak aangespannen bij de districtsrechtbank van Alaska, waarbij ze aanvoerden dat het bureau de Clean Water Act, de National Environmental Policy Act en de Alaska National Interest Lands Conservation Act had overtreden door het project voort te zetten.[31]

Terwijl de regering-Biden de olie-exploratie in Alaska herzag, ging zij wel door met het Ambler-mijnbouwproject en de controversiële weg. En dus is het nu de laatste hoop van de Koyukon en de tegenstanders van de weg dat de natuur zal ingrijpen en de verzakkende permafrost het hele project onbetaalbaar zal maken. De Amerikaanse regering onderkent eindelijk het probleem van de koolstofuitstoot, maar ze moet nog laten zien dat ze ook begrijpt dat de crisis in de natuur niet alleen te maken heeft met de opwarming van de aarde. Ze heeft geluisterd naar de leidinggevenden in de olie-, mijnbouw- en financiële sector, maar niet naar de stemmen die Richard Nelson heeft getranscribeerd: de stemmen die weerklinken uit de uithoeken van de koude noordelijke bossen met de grammatica van een andere wereld: 'Het land weet het. Als je er verkeerde dingen mee doet, voelt het wat er gebeurt. Ik denk dat alles op een of andere manier met elkaar verbonden is, ondergronds.'

5.

Het bos in de zee

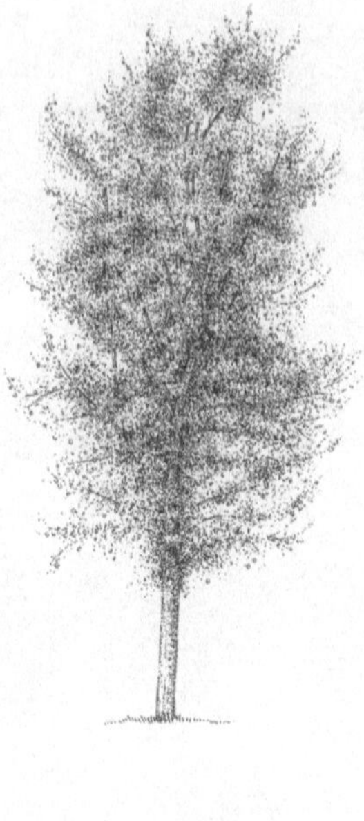

Balsempopulier, *Populus balsamifera*

Merrickville, Ontario, Canada
44° 55' 06" N

Vanaf de Brooks Range in Alaska snijdt de boomgrens dwars door de Canadese Yukon, de voorste witte sparren volgen de contouren van de noordelijkste delen van de Northwest Territories. Ze lijken op weg naar Nunavut – de provincie van Baffin Eiland en Canada's Arctische archipel – maar komen er nooit aan. In plaats daarvan strompelen de bomen op dramatische wijze zuidwaarts als een soort grote groene waterval door Alberta en Manitoba om in de Hudson Bay de zee te bereiken bij een plaats die Churchill heet.

Churchill ligt op 59 graden noorderbreedte, op dezelfde breedtegraad als John O'Groats, het noordelijkste puntje van Schotland, maar de gemiddelde jaartemperatuur is er een stuk lager. Het gemiddelde dagelijkse minimum in januari is -30. In de winter vriest de Hudson Bay bijna helemaal dicht, tot twee meter dik, en pas in augustus is de baai weer helemaal vrij van zee-ijs, waarna het in november weer begint te vriezen. De Hudsonbaai is de grootste baai ter wereld die water uit de Stille Oceaan en de Noordelijke IJszee vermengt met een derde van de zoetwaterafvoer van Canada en het via de Hudsonstraat langs de kust van

Labrador en Groenland weer naar de Atlantische Oceaan stuurt. Het is deze lange ijzige greep van de Noordelijke IJszee die tot in het hart van het Noord-Amerikaanse continent reikt en zo de temperatuur drukt en de boomgrens terugdrijft.

Bij Churchill komen drie ecosystemen samen: de zee, de toendra en de bomen. Dit driezijdige ecotoon heeft geleid tot de reputatie van de stad als de ijsbeerhoofdstad van de wereld. Beren verlaten het uiteenvallende zee-ijs in de zomer om op land te foerageren en op de toendra en in het bos een hol te zoeken om in te schuilen, waar ze in de herfst bevallen voor ze naar het ijs terugkeren wanneer dat weer opvriest.

Hier, zo bedenk ik me, is een belangrijk punt op de boomgrens, een ideale plek om de veranderingen te komen observeren.

'Nee, nee, nee,' zegt de stem met een zacht Iers accent aan de andere kant van de lijn. 'Je kunt het niet alleen van één kant bekijken. Je kunt de relatie tussen de bomen en de oceaan niet begrijpen zonder het hele stroomgebied te hebben gezien. Je moet stroomopwaarts gaan.'

Zes maanden voor de pandemie toesloeg, in de zomer van 2019, maakte ik een pelgrimstocht naar Canada, voor een bezoek aan een van de meest vooraanstaande geleerden van het boreale woud. Wanneer ik haar eindelijk ontmoet, is Diana Beresford-Kroeger bezorgd. De zomer is te heet. Het heeft al maanden niet meer geregend in Ontario. De bomen in haar tuin lijden eronder. Haar moestuin kan ze tenminste nog water geven, maar buiten het autoraampje op de weg van het vliegveld staan rijen en rijen strak opgestelde maïsstengels in verwelkte groene jassen zo ver het oog reikt. Toen ze hier veertig jaar geleden kwam wonen, waren veel van deze oceaanvelden bebost.

Aan de overkant van de weg komt een grote industriële gewasbesproeier ons tegemoet geraasd op wielen zo hoog als een huis, zijn lange stuiterende armen achter zich gevouwen, giftige pesticide druppelend op het asfalt. Diana deinst zo abrupt terug dat het haast lijkt alsof ze uit het raampje wil springen.

'Verdomme!' spuwt ze. 'Pesticiden. Net waar de planeet op dit moment behoefte aan heeft, meer kanker. Het is de dood, op maat ontworpen voor planten, dieren en ons.'

De zon staat al laag wanneer we aankomen in Merrickville, een schilderachtig koloniaal stadje met stenen winkels, een enorm blokhuis en slaperige dwarsstraatjes op de splitsing van de Rideau River en het Canal. Hier stonden een oude zagerij, een wol- en graanmolen en was het eindpunt van de weg voor de maagdelijke boomstammen die de rivier af dreven. Die laatsten gingen van hier op weg naar Quebec en Montreal.

De helft van Canada bestaat uit bos. Dat gold vroeger ook voor het grootste deel van de andere helft, maar de zuidelijke strook van de boreale zone die honderden kilometers noordelijker wordt begrensd door de Hudson Bay is geleidelijk opgeslokt door landbouw, industrie en de steden en voorsteden van Oost-Canada. Het huidige tempo is 1 procent ontbossing per jaar. De 65 hectare die Diana en haar man Christian sinds de jaren 1970 hebben onderhouden vormen een van de weinige overgebleven stukken oerbos van ceder.

Als we haar oprijlaan opdraaien, staat de zon op de kruinen van de rode dennen en sparren die aan één kant van de weg staan. Amerikaans vogelkers en witte eik staan aan de andere. De zonsondergang is een prachtige karmozijnrode waas die de omtrek van de bomen doet vervagen, maar Diana vindt het maar niks.

'De deeltjesvervuiling is dit jaar met honderd procent toegenomen. Honderd procent! Wist je dat? Dat is omdat de bomen verdwijnen.' Ze legt uit dat alle bomen, vooral loofbomen zoals esdoorns, aan de onderkant van hun bladeren trichomale haren hebben die deeltjes uit de lucht kammen die vervolgens naar de grond worden gespoeld wanneer het regent.

Diana Beresford-Kroeger is een van die zeldzame mensen die je manier van kijken kunnen veranderen. Zij heeft de manier veranderd waarop veel mensen, ook bosbouwdeskundigen en vooraanstaande academici wereldwijd, naar een bos kijken. Het personage Patricia Westerford in Richard Powers' roman *Tot in de hemel* is gedeeltelijk gebaseerd op haar leven en werk. Zij doet baanbrekend onderzoek naar de manier waarop bomen door middel van chemie communiceren in de vorm van aerosolen – organische verbindingen die als kleine vliegers in de lucht worden losgelaten – en via hun wortelnetwerken en interne schimmelrelaties. De fictieve Patricia is een wereldberoemde geleerde en bestsellerauteur die hele generaties latere onderzoekers heeft geïnspireerd. Het onderzoek van de echte Diana heeft inderdaad de manier veranderd waarop bomen worden gezien en bestudeerd, maar ze heeft niet de erkenning en het succes gekregen dat men zou verwachten. Dat heeft te maken met het uitgangspunt van haar unieke wetenschappelijke perspectief. Ze weigerde een hoogleraarschap aan de universiteit omdat ze vond dat ze buiten de instelling meer kon doen om de bewustwording en oplossingen voor de klimaatverandering te bevorderen. Ze noemt zichzelf een 'afvallige' wetenschapper, iemand die buiten de kaders denkt en verbanden legt die anderen over het hoofd zagen.

Diana's opvoeding in het naoorlogse Ierland was nogal ongewoon. Haar beide ouders stierven toen ze acht was en ze stond op het punt om naar de beruchte Magdalene Laundry van Sunday's Well in Cork te worden gestuurd. Maar de rechter, die hoorde van Diana's aristocratische connecties in Engeland en Ierland, stelde voor dat zij bij haar oom Patrick zou gaan wonen. Hij was een verstrooide veelzijdige geleerde die vaak vergat te eten, maar haar wel van uitgebreide geestelijke voeding voorzag uit zijn aanzienlijke bibliotheek. Eén gesprek aan het haardvuur is haar altijd bijgebleven. Dat ging over temperatuur. Als de gemiddelde mondiale temperatuur met 1 graad Celsius zou stijgen, zou dat hongersnoden veroorzaken. Gewassen zijn zo geëvolueerd dat ze rijpen binnen smalle temperatuurmarges: te warm en koelgematigde gewassen zullen verwelken, te koel en tropische gewassen zullen bederven.

Diana bracht haar zomers door in West Cork, in de kleine vallei van Lisheens bij Bantry Bay, waar kennis van de oude Keltische wereld bewaard was gebleven. De Brehon-wet (oude inheemse

Ierse wet) stelt dat 'een wees ieders kind is'. Diana werd opgevoed als beschermeling van de Brehon-wet: de heilige kennis van de Keltische drie-eenheid van lichaam, geest en ziel, eindigend met de wetten van de bomen, moest de hare worden om die uiteindelijk met de wereld te delen. Er werd haar verteld dat zij hun laatste beschermeling zou zijn die werd onderwezen in de oude wetten. Na haar zouden er geen meer volgen. Ze heeft die verantwoordelijkheid gedragen als een heilige opdracht.

Diana leerde dat de eerste dauw op de klaver heilig is voor de jonge vrouwen van Lisheens. En ze leerde vele andere rituelen waarvan ze de onderliggende biochemie later in het lab zou aantonen. Ze had de vrijheid en het vertrouwen om grote vragen te stellen. Toen ze voor het eerst hoorde over de fotosynthetische reactie, besefte ze dat die het omgekeerde was van ademen. Dezelfde elementen en chemicaliën verbonden planten en dieren als het ware in spiegelbeeld: kooldioxide en zuurstof. Zij leerde ook dat bijna alle bomen en bossen in Ierland waren vernietigd.

Toen vroeg ze zich af: wat zou er gebeuren als de planten – laten we zeggen bossen – van de planeet worden verwijderd? Het antwoord ligt voor de hand. Dan zou al het leven verdwijnen. Het is het omgekeerde van het beroemde experiment met de stolp.

Voor haar masterscriptie aan University College in Cork in 1965 bestudeerde ze hoe planten zouden reageren op een opwarmende planeet. Voor haar doctoraat aan de Carleton University in Ottawa vergeleek ze de functie van hormonen in planten en mensen. Bij de mens genereren de tryptofaan-tryptaminebanen alle neuronen in de hersenen. Diana bewees dat bomen deze ook hebben en ze gebruiken om dezelfde chemicaliën aan te maken – een sucrose-versie van serotonine bijvoorbeeld – die wij in onze hersenen hebben. Haar werk maakte het vervolgens denkbaar dat bomen het neurale vermogen hebben om te luisteren, te denken, te plannen, te beslissen, wellicht in de cambiumhuid, de binnenste laag van de schors. Later deed ze aanvullend doctoraal onderzoek dat draaide om de zuurstofvoorziening van het kloppende hart. Als het zuurstofgehalte te laag is, ontstaat er hartschade. Zij vervaardigde een nieuwe, niet specifieke bloedgroep om deze situatie te corrigeren met behulp van een proces dat 'hemodilutie' wordt genoemd. Tegenwoordig wordt dit kunstbloed gebruikt bij transplantatietherapie en bij de toediening van medicinale biochemie in het lichaam om kankers te stoppen.[1] Het blad en het hart zijn de twee belangrijkste organen voor het menselijk leven op aarde, en Diana's leven is gewijd aan het begrijpen en het beschermen van het verband tussen die twee.

Haar ideeën waren controversieel en werden door het wetenschappelijke establishment van de jaren 1960 bijna als ketters beschouwd. Toen zij in haar volgende stap de cel van een plant onderzocht onder een door haarzelf gemodificeerde elektronenmicroscoop en zo de bioluminescentie ontdekte, een verschijnsel in de kwantumfysica dat 25 jaar later een Nobelprijs zou opleveren voor een team van drie wetenschappers, weigerden de verantwoordelijken van haar universiteit in Canada haar werk nog langer te financieren.[2] Drie mannen in pak achter een sobere houten tafel zeiden haar met zoveel woorden: 'Ga naar huis, ga trouwen en kinderen krijgen.'

Diana keerde de gevestigde wetenschap de rug toe, kocht samen met haar man Christian een boerderij, bouwde een passief zonnehuis dat microgolven weerkaatst en verloor zich in het bos, waar ze haar eigen onderzoekstuin en microscopie opzette. Het biodiverse bos van Ontario was haar troost en haar redding. De ongerepte botanische wonderen van Canada waren nogal overweldigend voor een jonge vrouw uit Ierland die – dankzij de zeer effectieve Britse ontbossing van haar geboorteland, waardoor veel Ieren geen idee hebben van de ecologische geschiedenis van hun eigen land – nog nooit de anatomie en de enorme afmetingen van een maagdelijk oerbos had gezien. Ze deed experimenten, verzamelde zeldzame en bedreigde soorten uit heel Noord-Amerika en legde een arboretum aan. Ze knoopte betrekkingen aan met de inheemse volkeren van Canada, wier plantenkennis en wijsheid ze enorm respecteerde.

Ze combineerde wat zij wist uit de plantkunde, de organische scheikunde en de kernfysica met wat zij haar vertelden, en voegde zo iets toe aan de Keltische wijsheid. De resultaten publiceerde ze in twee baanbrekende, door wetenschappers serieus genomen naslagwerken, *Arboretum America* en *Arboretum Borealis*, waarin in detail wordt uitgelegd welke kritieke rol het noordelijke bos speelt bij het reguleren van het water, de lucht, de bodem, het klimaat en de voedingsbodem van de oceanen en waarin ze het enorme, nog onontgonnen potentieel van bomen om de moderne wereld van voedsel en geneesmiddelen te voorzien, laat zien. Bij de inheemse volkeren van de Mohawk en de Cree staat ze bekend als de bewaarster van medicijnen. Er bestaat geen grotere autoriteit op het gebied van het boreale bos. Ze is een profeet voor onze tijd.

We hebben net ontbeten in het huis van wit dennenhout dat Christian en zij bouwden.

Diana, in korte broek en een geel Australisch T-shirt met het opschrift 'Surf Patrol', veegt ongeduldig wat weerbarstig zilverkleurig haar uit haar gezicht. Ze wijst indringend naar de kokende ketel die stoomspiralen naar de dakspanten stuurt. 'Dat dus!' Ze wijst. 'Zie je dat?' Ik knik. 'Daar zie je de simpele fysica van de opwarming van de aarde! Het is een basisprincipe van de wetenschap. Hoe hoger de temperatuur, hoe sneller de reactie verloopt.'

Ze probeert me uit te leggen waarom alle bossen bedreigd zijn, maar vooral de boreale. Hogere temperaturen leiden tot meer verdamping, hetgeen weer leidt tot meer neerslag, maar die regen blijft niet op de grond. De warmte versnelt de cyclus van verdamping en condensatie, waarbij een groter deel van het water wordt omgezet in atmosferische waterdamp. Dit is waarom opwarming zo gevaarlijk is. Niet dat het de mensen zal doden doordat de planeet nu te heet wordt voor menselijke bewoning, maar de versnelling van de watercyclus zal droogte en overmatige bodemvochtigheid veroorzaken, waardoor de bossen en bomen en de wortelstelsels van alle planten die nodig zijn om de atmosfeer van zuurstof te voorzien, onder druk zullen komen te staan.

Diana is al sinds 1963 geobsedeerd door de klimaatverandering. 'Ik wil gewoon niet dat mensen, dat kinderen lijden,' zegt ze. 'Vooral de kinderen niet.'

Tegen de tijd dat ik haar bezoek, heeft de mens inmiddels gezorgd voor een toename van de kooldioxide in de atmosfeer tot 415 ppm. En terwijl de mens prima kan overleven bij 1000 ppm, zijn de opwarmingseffecten van zo'n dikke deken die straling vasthoudt op de planeet precies datgene waar zij zich zorgen over maakt – de invloed van hittestress op het zuurstofleverend vermogen van het plantenrijk op het land en in de zee. Enorme sterfte van plankton of bomen, het einde van de regenwouden en de verwoestijning van de tropen zouden kunnen leiden tot een versnelling van de daling van het zuurstofgehalte in de atmosfeer die inmiddels al is ingezet. Bomen zorgen voor ongeveer de helft van de zuurstof in de atmosfeer, fotosynthetiserende algen in de oceaan zorgen voor de andere helft. Beide zullen naar verwachting minder goed functioneren naarmate de planeet opwarmt.

'De zieken, de jongsten en de ongeborenen zullen het eerst sneuvelen,' stelt ze: degenen wier hart het bij iets lagere zuurstofconcentraties begeeft: baby's, die in de eerste levensjaren veel zuurstof nodig hebben om te groeien en foetussen, die via de placenta superzuurstofrijk bloed nodig hebben.

'De vrouwelijke mens is geëvolueerd om 38 weken zwanger te zijn, niet 40 of 42. Een menselijke foetus heeft een bepaalde hoeveelheid zuurstof nodig, en die krijgt hij niet in 38 weken tijd. Ik verwacht problemen met de voortplanting, de vruchtbaarheid, miskramen, dat soort dingen. En dat zou best al snel het geval kunnen zijn. Zo niet tijdens mijn leven, dan toch vrijwel zeker nog tijdens het jouwe.'

Diana rommelt wat in haar keuken, pakt boeken en tekent schema's op velletjes papier om de chemische reacties en ecologische processen waarover zij spreekt te illustreren.

'De mensen moeten het fundamentele belang van bomen begrijpen en stoppen met die waanzin van het kappen.'

Populus balsamifera, die moet je hebben,' zegt ze. 'Die moet je echt eens bekijken.'

Het boreale is het 'laatste woud', aldus Diana. Volgens haar is het Amazonegebied waarschijnlijk ten dode opgeschreven, zelfs als er onmiddellijk een einde zou worden gemaakt aan de ongebreidelde ontbossing. De branden en de uitdroging zullen daar binnen vijftig jaar voor zorgen.

Andere tropische regenwouden zijn ernstig aangetast, vooral in West-Afrika, Maleisië en Indonesië, hoewel de ontbossing wereldwijd de laatste jaren wel is vertraagd, en het verlaten van landbouwgrond in Rusland en Europa de vernietiging elders compenseert. Het boreale gebied is het grootste en belangrijkste intacte bioom dat zich over een groot temperatuurbereik uitstrekt, en het heeft daarom een goede kans om zich aan te passen.

De belangrijkste soort in het Canadese boreale woud is volgens Diana die welke het ecosysteem en zijn relatie tot andere ecosystemen als het ware verankert, de balsempopulier. Het is een heilige boom voor de inheemse volkeren en levert een sterk medicijn, het sterkste van alle noordelijke boomsoorten. De geneesmiddelen van het noorden zijn het krachtigst vanwege de extreme omstandigheden van droogte en koude, die de bomen ertoe brengen deze chemicaliën te produceren voor hun eigen bescherming. Het volk van de Cree noemt de balsempopulier de lelijke boom vanwege zijn bobbelige schors en dikke bladeren, maar dat zijn tegelijk ook de fysiologische kenmerken die hem zo waardevol maken – een schatkist vol geneesmiddelen – en hebben geleid tot zijn andere bijnaam – de balsem van Gilead. De diepe scheuren in de schors vangen regen op en leiden water naar de wortels van de boom. Zijn grote plaatvormige bladeren met hartvormige uiteinden en een heldergroen wasachtig oppervlak zitten vol oliën en harsen. En zijn grote uitwaaierende takken, die zich in een schijnbaar willekeurig patroon uitstrekken en uitspreiden, zorgen voor weldadige schaduw voor het complexe leven van de boreale ondergroei. Ze ziet er misschien wat lomp en onhandig uit, maar is de betrouwbare verpleegster van het bos.

De chemicaliën worden onder druk opgeslagen in de boom, in de bladeren en de schors, en Diana maakt een gebaar van wanhoop wanneer ze uitlegt hoe weinig we erover weten. Tientallen laboratoria en teams van wetenschappers zouden aan deze ene boom kunnen werken. Diana heeft in elk geval een eerste aanzet gegeven. Ze heeft de lentezon de knoppen zien verwarmen die de vrouwelijke balsempopulier in de vorige herfst had gevormd, vóór de extreme vorst van de winter. Als de hars die de knop de hele winter heeft vastgehouden, begint te smelten, brengt dat de schubben die de bladeren beschermen ertoe uit te zetten. Als het warmer wordt, verhit de zon de harsmoleculen en stijgen ze als esters en terpenoïden op in de lucht. Dit zijn aerosolen, en deze golf van tonnen oleohars die miljoenen populieren in het boreale gebied elk voorjaar weer in de atmosfeer loslaten werkt als een gezondheidsbeschermend schild voor al het leven op de planeet. De aerosolen, zo heeft ze ontdekt, zijn slijmoplossend, ontstekingsremmend, antibacterieel en schimmelwerend. Maar dat is nog maar het begin. De oleoharsen bevatten ook dihydrochalconen, andere flavonen en zuren die essentieel zijn voor de ontwikkeling van de hersenen, de lever en de klieren bij de mens. Ze zijn de bouwstenen van de hersenen en ze vormen het bruine vet in het lichaam dat essentieel is voor de mens om kou te kunnen weerstaan door te rillen. De rillingsreflex metaboliseert het vet als brandstof. De boom die geleerd heeft de kou te weerstaan, helpt ons om onder dezelfde omstandigheden te overleven.

Ook aanwezig zijn de prostaglandinegroep, betrekkelijk nieuw voor de wetenschap, die prostacycline omvat, een vaatverwijdende stof die de primaire functie van het hart helpt en de slagaders opent en reinigt, en andere oxytocines die de vrouwelijke vruchtbaarheid bevorderen en de bloeddruk verlagen. De Cree-volkeren gebruikten het sap van de populier om diabetes te behandelen, wat volkomen logisch is, aangezien Diana populine met glucosiden in de boom aantrof. Het helpt de maag en het spijsverteringskanaal om de maagsecretie te vertragen en het metabolisme van de vetafbraak te reguleren.

Diana is in het bijzonder geïnteresseerd in de bomen van het noorden omdat ze zich onder de moeilijkste omstandigheden hebben ontwikkeld. Daar hebben ze van geleerd. Ze bevatten hormonen en hebben overlevingsstrategieën die andere planten vanwege de klimaatverandering nog zullen moeten leren. Daarnaast bevatten ze chemicaliën die essentieel zijn voor de mens. Nu moest de wetenschap nog eens de tijd en de middelen vinden om ze fatsoenlijk te onderzoeken. Dan, zegt ze, zouden we misschien anders gaan denken over hoe we bomen oogsten – hout is misschien wel het minst waardevolle wat het bos heeft te bieden.

De balsempopulier maakt deze chemicaliën uit de mineralen die hij diep onder de grond wint. In tegenstelling tot coniferen met hun ondiepe wortels heeft hij een diepe penwortel die als kanaal fungeert tussen de benthale en permafrostlagen in de bodem. Die zuigt mineralen op en concentreert ze in de bladeren. Een ander verschil met coniferen is dat hij zijn grote bladeren in de winter verliest. Een enkele boom kan tot twee hectare bladeren produceren als je ze allemaal naast elkaar legt. Dit enorme volume aan bladafval maakt hem tot een hoeksteen voor de rest van het boreale gebied en daarbuiten. De grond rond balsempopulieren is zeer donker omdat hij rijk is aan fulvine- en humuszuren, met grote moleculen die verwant zijn aan melanine en melatonine, de chemische stoffen die in het menselijk lichaam huidskleuren veroorzaken. Pigmenten nemen spoorelementen mee naar de bodem. Ze kunnen metalen uit de rottende bladeren aantrekken en insluiten, met name ijzer – de essentiële katalysator bij organische groei. Deze zuren logen uit in de bodem en het grondwater en vinden uiteindelijk hun weg naar zee. In zout water zijn zij de katalysator voor de basis van de voedselketen in de oceaan.

De mineralen in de balsempopulier zijn geconcentreerd vanwege de kou. Ongebruikelijk voor een bladverliezende boom is hij geëvolueerd om te gedijen op noordelijke breedtegraden, misschien als reactie op stress of opeenvolgende periodes van klimaatverandering – ijstijden enzovoorts – waarbij hij in warme perioden naar het noorden trok en vervolgens, duizenden jaren later, vast kwam te zitten toen de temperatuur daalde.

Een van de gevolgen van dit aanpassingsvermogen is dat de populier in staat is om zich vegetatief voort te planten. Zowel mannelijke als vrouwelijke bomen kunnen ondergronds zijwaarts wortelknollen uitzenden, vaak over een flinke afstand, die vervolgens uitlopen tot nieuwe bomen die somatische klonen van het origineel zijn. De populier kan helemaal alleen een bos stichten dat verbonden is door een ondergronds netwerk van wortels die voedingsstoffen opslaan en berichten, voedsel en koolstof transporteren tussen alle bomen in een voortdurende uitwisseling waarvan onderzoek inmiddels laat zien dat ze verdacht veel lijkt op massale berekening. Wat jonge bomen lijken, zijn vaak slechts takjes van een veel groter en ouder wezen – vooral als ze in groten getale aanwezig zijn. Bossen van de balsempopulier en zijn sierlijker neefje, de Amerikaanse ratelpopulier, *Populus tremuloides*, zijn meestal een teken dat je met een oerbos te maken hebt op het noordelijk halfrond. Het oudste levende organisme dat tot nu toe is ontdekt, is een groepje espenbomen in Utah die allemaal met elkaar verbonden zijn over een oppervlakte van 32 hectare en het DNA delen van één enkele voorouder die dateert van het smelten van de ijskap in het Pleistoceen, 1,6 miljoen jaar geleden.[3]

Maar dit is slechts een van de drie bossen die de balsempopulier in stand houdt. Het tweede bos is het kreupelhout – de struiken, meestal bessendragende struiken die van cruciaal belang zijn voor vogels, zoogdieren en mensen in het boreale gebied en die de schaduw die de populier biedt evenzeer nodig hebben als de mineralen die hij opzuigt om te overleven. Het derde is het bos in de zee.

Jaren geleden, toen Diana in Cork zeewiermonsters aan de kust verzamelde, vroeg zij zich af waarom de riviermonding zo'n rijk en gevarieerd leven kende – zeevogels, walvissen, zeehonden en nog veel meer. Kwam dat enkel doordat zoet water meer zuurstof bevatte dan de zee? Of was er nog iets anders aan de hand? Bij toeval ontmoette ze vervolgens professor Katsuhiko Matsunaga, een Japanse wetenschapper van het eiland Hokkaido, die zich dezelfde vraag had gesteld en met een antwoord was gekomen.

Matsunaga was geïntrigeerd door het klaarblijkelijke verband tussen het kappen van een bos voor landbouw in een provincie van Hokkaido en de gelijktijdige ineenstorting van de voedselketen in de oceaan voor de kust. Zijn onderzoek toonde aan dat de primaire productie in de oceaan – de groei van minuscule eencellige wezentjes, diatomeeën en sieralgen genaamd, die de massa vormen van het fytoplankton, de basis van de voedselketen in de oceaan – afhankelijk is van voedingsstoffen en mineralen die niet van nature in de oceaan voorkomen in een vorm waar het fytoplankton gebruik van zou kunnen maken. Dat heeft fosfor, stikstof en ijzer nodig om te fotosynthetiseren en zich te delen, en krijgt deze chemicaliën van de bomen.[4] Fytoplankton leeft in grote kolommen in de zee. Zonlicht activeert hun chloroplastische structuren en ze gebruiken de fotonen van de gammastralen van de zon om in kooldioxide de koolstof van de zuurstof te splitsen. Het is een mysterieus proces. We weten nog steeds niet precies hoe fotosynthese werkt, maar de fotonen moeten worden geconcentreerd of vergroot zoals in een laser, zodat ze een stevig gebonden molecuul kunnen splijten. 's Nachts zet het fytoplankton die koolstof om in eiwitten met behulp van stikstofhoudende enzymen en ijzer. IJzer is het belangrijkste, schaarse, ingrediënt dat dient als katalysator. Zonder ijzer kan het plankton zich niet delen. De hydroxylgroepen van het humuszuur dat door rottende bladeren wordt gevormd maken dat het zich aan dingen kan hechten: aan watermoleculen, aan de onderkant van het zee-ijs bijvoorbeeld, vandaar het groene waas onderaan ijsbergen – dat zijn algen die het zuur oogsten. Zonder het kapsel van het humuszuurmolecuul zou het zware ijzeratoom rechtstreeks naar de bodem van de zee of de rivier zinken en zou het zelfs nooit in het water zijn terechtgekomen. Het humuszuur voert het ijzer naar de zee, waar het door het plankton wordt gebruikt om te groeien.

Als er eiwitten beschikbaar zijn, gebruikt fytoplankton ijzer om zich voort te planten en te delen. Zoöplankton eet het fytoplankton. Schaaldieren, witvissen, weekdieren en mijten eten het zoöplankton. Vissen eten ze, en grotere vissen... enzovoort. IJzer dat door bomen beschikbaar wordt gesteld, vormt de basis van de voedselketen in de oceaan.

Hongersnood op het land veroorzaakt hongersnood in de zee, en bovendien een enorme afname van de hoeveelheid zuurstof. Blauwalgen nemen meer dan 50 procent van de fotosynthese op aarde voor hun rekening en vormen een vitale bron van zuurstof. Droogte is niet het enige probleem, want ook een overstroming kan dodelijk zijn. Een toevloed van voedingsstoffen van het land – te veel nitraten en fosfaten, weggespoeld uit de landbouw – kan een anoxische zone in de oceaan doen ontstaan. Algenbloei – de overproductie van fytoplankton die de hogere voedselketen niet kan consumeren – zet aan tot uitbraken van bacteriën die de algen opeten maar daarbij alle zuurstof in de oceaan verbruiken, waardoor dode zones ontstaan. Als vissen door een dode zone zwemmen, sterven ze.

Zo blijkt er toch meer schuil te gaan achter het oude Japanse gezegde: 'Als je een vis wilt vangen, plant je een boom.' Bomen reguleren de atmosfeer door hun eigen activiteit en door hun rentmeesterschap van de primaire productie in de oceaan. En toch, zegt Diana vol ongeloof: 'Is het niet raar dat niemand tot nu toe het humuszuurmolecuul heeft beschreven?'

De balsempopulier is de mineraalwinner bij uitstek en veruit de grootste loofboom van het boreale woud. Hij is gewoonlijk geen soort voor aan de boomgrens, maar hij kan overleven bij -67° Celsius en is bestand tegen extreme hitte. 'Qua klimatologisch bereik en productie van organisch materiaal kan geen van de evergreens eraan tippen,' zegt Diana.

Om te begrijpen wat er gebeurt in de oceaan bij Churchill, waar de bomen, de toendra en het bos elkaar ontmoeten, raadt ze mij aan eerst een plaats te bezoeken die Poplar River heet, een reservaat van de inheemse bevolking dat deel uitmaakt van het stroomgebied van de Hudson Bay dat uitmondt in de rivieren de Nelson en de Churchill. Het is een van de laatste intacte stroomgebieden waar men de onbelemmerde werking van de natuur kan observeren.

'De mensen daar zullen je alles kunnen vertellen over de heilige betekenis, de medicijnen en nog veel meer – meer dan ik kan weten. Maar je moet voorbereid zijn op een andere manier van denken. Ze zien de dingen anders dan jij gewend bent, als je begrijpt wat ik bedoel.'

Ik leg uit dat ik vele jaren in Afrika heb gewoond bij inheemse volkeren, het Swahili heb bestudeerd en de geestenwereld heb ervaren, als dat is wat zij bedoelt. Ze lacht en stuurt me op weg: 'O geweldig, dat is dan in orde. Je komt goed beslagen ten ijs.'

Poplar River, Manitoba, Canada
53° 00' 07" N

De bestemming begint altijd bij de eindhalte. Je krijgt een idee van de wereld aan het eind van de treinreis of de vlucht door de mensen die in de rij staan, de namen van de haltes, de inhoud van de gesprekken. In Winnipeg begint de reis naar het reservaat met de pendelbus naar St. Andrews Airport. Ik kende de moeilijke geschiedenis van de inheemse bevolking in Canada en in grote lijnen ook het verhaal van de koloniale onteigening, maar ik was er niet op voorbereid hoe actueel de strijd nog is, hoe vers de wonden zijn en hoe hoog de emoties nog oplopen.

De chauffeur is een man genaamd Murdoch, een Schotse naam. Hij heeft een kaalgeschoren hoofd en een bril. Hij is trots op het feit dat hij een selfmade man is en schrijft dat toe aan zijn onafhankelijkheid, van jongs af aan. Hij werd bij zijn moeder weggehaald toen hij tien was. 'Het beste wat me ooit is overkomen… Ik heb al mijn geld zelf verdiend. Niet zoals deze indianen.' Ik wacht af wat er komen gaat. Ik neem aan dat ik nu een preek krijg, omdat de enige bestemmingen waar je vanaf St. Andrews naartoe kunt vliegen de reservaten van de inheemse bevolking in het noorden zijn. Murdoch wil een punt maken, maar het is me niet geheel duidelijk welk.

'Wat het is met deze indianen,' mijmert hij, 'ze willen alleen maar meer geld, meer geld, meer geld. Hoelang blijven we ze nog betalen? Ja, we hebben hun land lang geleden gestolen, maar hoe lang gaat dat nog zo door? Wat mij betreft komt daar nu een einde aan.' Het verwart me. Hij is merkwaardig beslist in wat hij zegt. Ondanks zijn Schotse naam blijkt Murdoch een 'verdragsnummer' te hebben, wat betekent dat hij de vierde generatie is die afstamt van de inheemse bevolking en dus aanspraak kan maken op huisvesting, belastingvermindering en diverse andere sociale voordelen die zijn beloofd aan Canada's inheemse bevolking in de reeks verdragen die hun leiders hebben ondertekend met de Britse en Canadese regeringen.

'Het is absurd. Ik hoefde geen belasting te betalen op mijn nieuwe auto! En als je er iets van zegt, maken ze je uit voor racist.'

Nu wordt duidelijk waar Murdoch naartoe wil. Hij wil erkend worden als een onafhankelijk mens, niet als iemand die afhankelijk is van wat hij krijgt, maar erg stevig staat hij niet. De geschiedenis is niet erg helder en hij weet zelf ook niet zo goed hoe hij zich ertoe moet verhouden. Zo riskeert hij wat absurd over te komen: een man van gemengd ras die zijn eigen achtergrond verwerpt.

Buiten zie ik steriele vierkanten in geel, groen en bruin, een doosvormig licht-industrieel landschap van wegen, voorsteden, drive-throughs, de hemel boven de prairie en schuren met plastic gevelbekleding. Er is nauwelijks een boom te zien in wat ooit bekend stond als Elm City. Dit is wat de blanken, waaronder ook Murdochs voorouders, hebben gedaan met het land dat ze stalen. Dit is de 'beschaving' waarmee Murdoch geïdentificeerd wil worden in plaats van het reservaat of de majestueuze savanne die hier iets meer dan een eeuw geleden nog was.

Hij is nieuwsgierig en wil weten waarom ik naar wat hij noemt een 'godvergeten' reservaat ga. Ben ik op vakantie? Het gesprek komt op klimaatverandering en de dood van Lake Winnipeg door landbouwvervuiling. Murdoch is pessimistisch. 'We kunnen er niets aan doen. Er komt een nucleaire oorlog. De helft van de wereldbevolking uitroeien en dan opnieuw beginnen – dat is wat ik denk. Ik hoop dat je me niet te negatief vindt!' Ik beweeg me wat ongemakkelijk in mijn stoel.

Er stappen nog twee passagiers in de minibus: een weldoorvoed echtpaar dat in het noorden van Canada supermarkten beheert voor de Northern Company – wat vroeger de Hudson Bay Company heette, een erfenis van de oude koloniale netwerken.

Murdoch voelt zich wat zekerder met deze nieuwkomers, met wie hij zijn vooroordelen deelt terwijl ze me de les lezen over wat ik kan verwachten.

'Ik hoop dat je geen whisky in je tas hebt, anders ga je naar de gevangenis!'

Zij maken grappen met Murdoch over de zelfopgelegde regels die alcohol in de reservaten verbieden en over het welig tierende alcoholisme en drugsmisbruik dat er in feite heerst. Ze klagen over de kwaliteit van het eten daar en zijn zich blijkbaar niet bewust van de ironie dat ze zelf een voedselwinkel runnen die daar wat aan zou kunnen verbeteren. Ze voelen zich kennelijk niet bezwaard over de exorbitante prijzen die aan klanten worden gerekend. Leden van de inheemse bevolking in afgelegen reservaten die vaak over de weg niet te bereiken zijn, worden geconfronteerd met hoge luchtvaarttarieven om ergens anders te komen. Zij redeneren dat de bewoners federaal uitkeringsgeld uitgeven en toch geen belastingen betalen. In zekere zin is hun terloopse racisme, dat wordt afgedaan als plaatselijke wijsheid, een noodzakelijke kortzichtigheid waardoor zij zich goed kunnen voelen over hun werk, over hun rol in een systeem van koloniaal winstbejag dat feitelijk nog altijd bestaat.

De luchthaven lijkt hetzelfde verhaal van uitbuiting en misbruik te vertellen, zij het van de andere kant. Hier klinkt niet de taal van rechtvaardigingen en irrationele argumenten, maar staat het geschreven in mensen: een trotse cultuur die worstelt onder het gewicht van wezensvreemd consumentisme, lichamen die zijn vervormd door industrieel voedsel, gepropt in synthetische kleding en petten die buitenlandse honkbalteams aanprijzen, een taal sprekend die is ingesnoerd en uitgehold door het gekef en geblaf van het Engels en dezelfde trage, achterdochtige blik van gematigde verwachtingen, niet nagekomen beloften en cynische vijandigheid die ik zo goed heb leren kennen in veel andere voormalige koloniën.

Tegen de tijd dat ik aan boord ben van de tweemotorige Cessna naar Poplar River, dreigt de koloniale mentaliteit mijn eigen blik te kleuren. De enige andere passagiers zijn twee gebroken uitziende inheemse mensen, een man en een vrouw, onderuitgezakt in hun stoelen in besmeurde kleren, snurkend in een alcoholische roes nog voor we zijn opgestegen. Ontdaan van enige zeggenschap, in de wereld van de blanken, worden zij gemakkelijk gezien als slachtoffers van een lange geschiedenis van Europees geweld in Noord-Amerika, mensen om medelijden mee te hebben of aan de schandpaal te nagelen, afhankelijk van je politieke standpunt. Maar over een uur zullen ze weer nuchter zijn, uit het vliegtuig stappen en hun rol hervatten als ouders, broers en zussen, leden van de gemeenschap of ouderen in het reservaat, behoeders van ecosystemen die alle Canadezen ten goede komen en oude wijsheden doorgeven waar wij allen spoedig acht op zullen moeten gaan slaan.

Na twintig minuten passeert het kleine vliegtuigje een grens ver onder ons. De grote stukken landbouwgrond waar de natuur is gemanipuleerd, gesnoeid, onderdrukt, vergiftigd en bespoten, zijn plotseling verdwenen. In het oosten kabbelt het modderige water van Lake Winnipeg, het op negen na grootste zoetwatermeer ter wereld, over een strand dat groen is gekleurd door algen. Onder ons is het verschijnen van het bos als een enorme zucht frisse lucht. Het volgende uur vertoont de grond onder ons willekeurige stroken kleur – het gevlekte oranje van veenmos, ongelijke stroken gele espen en zwarte sparren, ontelbare groene veelhoeken van moerasgras, wervelingen van bos en de ragfijne draden van beekjes bezaaid met heldere parels van water in het muskeg: de Hudson Bay Lowlands, 300 duizend vierkante kilometer, 's werelds grootste wetlands. Ze markeren het begin van Canada's legendarische maar vaak over het hoofd geziene noorden – zo'n groot deel van de identiteit van het land en toch zo weinig be- of onderzocht.

Het is verleidelijk om je te verliezen in de immense horizon, overweldigend voor zowel het oog als de geest: een ongerepte habitat zonder enig teken van de mens. Maar ook dat is een koloniale manier van kijken. Geen enkele 'ongerepte wildernis' is werkelijk ongerept of wild voor wie er thuis is. Een lid van de inheemse bevolking is in deze natuur nooit echt verdwaald en altijd thuis. Het land onder ons is gevormd door duizenden jaren van menselijke beschermers, en de meest recente zijn mijn snurkende medepassagiers.

Het is een landschap dat inspireert tot nederigheid, eerbied en dienstbaarheid. Je zou je makkelijk kunnen voorstellen dat het grenzeloos is, en onoverwinnelijk. Het idee van de wildernis, de opwinding en de mogelijkheden die deze biedt, hangen af van het uitwissen van de menselijke bewoners. De savannes en bossen waar de vroege kolonisten zo blij mee waren, waren voor het grootste deel eerder al beheerde landschappen, verlaten door inheemse bevolkingsgroepen die door vroegere golven van indringers sterk waren uitgedund.[5] Dat uitwissen is nog steeds aan de gang, aangezien de mensen – en hun vermogen om daarvoor de wet te gebruiken – de voornaamste hinderpaal vormen voor de eindeloze honger van het kapitalisme naar bossen. En in deze strijd zijn stereotypen – de ontaarde inboorling, de ongerepte wildernis – de wapens. Beide zijn het noodzakelijke leugens die Canada's zelfbeeld van de redelijke welvaart schragen.

De website van Natural Resources Canada beweert dat het ontbossingspercentage van het land 0,4 procent bedraagt, maar gaat er gemakshalve van uit dat alle kaalkap in het boreale gebied uiteindelijk wel weer aangroeit en dus niet meetelt. Eenmaal verstoord kan een kostbaar ecosysteem zoals dat waar ik nu overheen vlieg, dat zich in 30 duizend jaar heeft ontwikkeld en nog steeds blijft ontwikkelen, in feite nooit meer worden vervangen. Een zevende van Canada's boreale bossen is sinds 1990 gekapt, en een stuitend groot deel daarvan wordt gebruikt als pulp voor toiletpapier.[6] Wij zijn in feite ons achterwerk aan het afvegen met de laatst overgebleven bomen die het verschil uitmaken tussen leven en dood voor de mens op de planeet aarde. Het Canadese percentage van bosverstoring (een betere maat) bedraagt 3,6 procent en is het hoogste ter wereld, zelfs hoger dan dat van Brazilië. De vraag naar pulp, papier en hout, en de uitgestrekte gebieden die worden kaalgekapt om de lucratieve teerzanden onder Alberta te bereiken, maken dat Canada in één keer bovenaan de tabel staat. De druk op en de stimulansen voor de inheemse bevolking die haar handtekening zal moeten zetten voor houtkap en mijnbouw in haar gebied, zijn immens geweest.

Het laatste half uur vlogen we echter over land waar de bedrijven niet langer aan kunnen komen. Dit is een van de plaatsen waar de ogenschijnlijk onverbiddelijke aantasting van het milieu omwille van de winst op miraculeuze wijze een halt is toegeroepen. Vier inheemse gemeenschappen onder leiding van de Poplar River First Nation hebben zich verenigd om iets opmerkelijks presteren: in 2018 werd hun traditionele grondgebied aangewezen als UNESCO Werelderfgoed. Het gebied van bijna 30 duizend vierkante kilometer dat door de inheemse bevolking wordt beschermd en beheerd, is het grootste beschermde bosgebied in Noord-Amerika, met een oppervlak zo groot als Denemarken.

De status als UNESCO Werelderfgoed werd niet alleen toegekend vanwege de betekenis van het land voor het milieu, maar – en dit is een belangrijk precedent – ook vanwege de culturele band die de Anishinaabe ermee hebben. Want de inheemse volkeren die hier hebben geleefd sinds het land volgens hun scheppingsmythe uit het water oprees, zo'n achtduizend jaar geleden, gelijktijdig met het Stenen Tijdperk in Europa, stellen zich de mens niet voor als los van het land, maar als deel van een totaal systeem, één organisme. Zoals alle andere inheemse menselijke bewoners van de noordelijke wouden menen ze dat de rotsen, het water, de bomen, de dieren, de planten, de wind, de regen en de donder allemaal bezield zijn met geesten met wie zij het land delen en met wie ze moeten onderhandelen over de beperkte natuurlijke middelen. Het is precies deze relatie die nu erkend en beschermd wordt.

Onder ons verschijnen uiteindelijk een boot, een radiomast, een flits van ijzeren dakbedekking, clusters van gebouwen langs de kaken van een rivier die schoon water in het vervuilde Lake Winnipeg stuwt en het litteken van de landingsbaan die in het bos is vrijgemaakt. Wat ooit voor een bepaalde groep Anishinaabe een eenmalig visserskamp voor de zomer was en in 1806 door de Hudson Bay Company voorgoed op een Engelse kaart werd vastgepind, is door zijn natuurlijke haven en de vestiging van een handelspost uitgegroeid tot een permanente nederzetting van 1400 mensen.

Tegen de omheining van de landingsbaan staan vrijstaande houten huizen op open plekken, omringd door ruige grasvlakten. Een stoffige grindweg slingert zich tussen de bomen door. Bij de poort staat een twaalftal gehavend uitziende pick-ups bedekt met wit stof in een rij te wachten op de post. Achter de voertuigen lees ik op een enkel oud gebouw, dat al lang niet meer in gebruik is, een tekst in groene letters: '*Poplar River, elevation 760 feet*' (Poplar River, 232 meter boven zeeniveau). Mijn medepassagiers pakken hun tassen, omhelzen de mensen die hen tegemoet zijn gekomen en rijden weg. Net als Huslia, is Poplar River een gemeenschap die je alleen per vliegtuig bereikt. De weg door de muskeg is alleen begaanbaar als die 's winters bevroren is, en zelfs dat is steeds onzekerder.

Dit piepkleine, barre plaatsje wijst ons niettemin de weg naar de toekomst en toont ons de enige haalbare en realistische afslag van de doodlopende weg naar de onvermijdelijke klimaatverandering waarop we ons nu bevinden. De vierduizend bewoners van het grootste beschermde landschap in Noord-Amerika laten zien hoe een harmonieuze relatie tussen mens en moeder aarde kan worden hersteld. Ze proberen ons te herinneren aan enkele fundamentele waarheden. Zij noemen hun traditionele grondgebied *Pimachiowin Aki* – 'het land dat leven geeft'.

'Als het land ziek wordt, worden wij ook ziek,' zegt mijn gastvrouw, Diana's vriendin Sophia. Het lijkt zo voor de hand te liggen, zo simpel. Hoe hadden we dat ooit kunnen vergeten?

Een van de stoffige pick-ups bij de landingsbaan is van Ray en Sophia Rabliauskas, leiders en activisten van de gemeenschap, die mij komen ophalen. We rijden al rammelend en schuddend over het grindpad van de landingsbaan door de stad. De hoofdgebouwen van Poplar River bestaan uit kubussen van verschillende grootte, bekleed met wit plastic. De grootste is de supermarkt die door Northern wordt gerund, daarna komen de school, het buurthuis en de brandweerkazerne. Als we het centrum achter ons laten, komen de bomen dichterbij. Plukken Amerikaanse ratelpopulier van vijftien meter hoog staan langs de weg – de Anishinaabe spreken van *poplars* in het Engels, maar *auhsuhday* in hun eigen taal. Af en toe staat er in een opening tussen de bomen een huis. Door de bladeren flitst de rivier met haar zilveren huid en verstrooit het licht. Het plaatsje, de huizen in de schaduw van de opdoemende bomen, lijken overgeleverd aan de genade van de natuur: auto's, boten, barbecues die op het erf worden achtergelaten, lopen het risico binnen een paar seizoenen door het bos te worden verzwolgen.

Een enorme vrachtwagen waarin de radio kennelijk hard staat, raast voorbij en blaast stof door onze open ramen naar binnen. We passeren het keurig omheinde terrein van de Royal Canadian Mounted Police, daarnaast het 'groepshuis' waar pleegkinderen verblijven die bij hun familie zijn weggehaald, en het kantoor van de gevreesde Children and Family Services. Aan het einde van het afgebakende reservaat, waar de weg eindigt in een gemengd bos van Amerikaanse populieren, balsempopulieren, berken en wilgen, in een bocht van de rivier, staat de blokhut van Sophia en Ray. In hun prachtige huis, versierd met inheemse kunst, racet een kleinzoon met een auto over de vloer van de woonkamer. De ramen bieden een magisch uitzicht op de rivier met wilde rijst, moerasgras en de zon die schittert op het water.

We praten over de CFS. Het lijkt misschien vreemd, maar de wortels van de pogingen om hun land te beschermen die tot Pimachiowin Aki hebben geleid, liggen daar, in de kantoren van de regering, waar de echo van het geweld dat vroegere generaties is aangedaan, nog steeds doorklinkt. De staat die het land en vervolgens de kinderen van inheemse families heeft gestolen en hen uit naam van de 'beschaving' naar kostscholen heeft gestuurd, haalt nog steeds kinderen bij hun families weg, maar nu om ze te 'beschermen'. Werkloosheid, alcoholisme, drugsverslaving en sociale achterstand zijn endemisch in de inheemse gemeenschappen van Canada, met enkele van de hoogste percentages in Noord-Amerika. Het reservaat is de dupe omdat de door de staat beloofde gratis huisvesting alleen hier beschikbaar is. Er zijn niet genoeg huizen. Veel families wachten nog steeds. Ondertussen zijn de banen in het reservaat dun gezaaid. Opleidingsmogelijkheden zijn er bijna niet, en voor middelbaar onderwijs moeten de kinderen naar Winnipeg. Zelfs loodgieters en elektriciens worden ingevlogen. Een gebrek aan eigenwaarde en aan zinvol werk kan hard aankomen.

Er is geen gezin in het reservaat waar de Children and Family Services niet hebben ingegrepen. Sophia schudt haar hoofd, haar ogen neergeslagen. Met haar lange zwarte haar lijkt ze niet oud genoeg om grootmoeder te zijn. Zij en Ray hebben jarenlang geprobeerd te zorgen voor nichtjes en neefjes in haar eigen familie die leden onder ouders die hen volgens de Canadese overheid verwaarloosden of mishandelden. Meestal kregen ze daar echter geen toestemming voor. Als een kind eenmaal in het systeem zit, is het bijna onmogelijk om het eruit te krijgen.

Ray en Sophia vroegen zich af wat er aan de hand was en zagen een verband. In de begindagen van de koloniale overheersing werden inheemse kinderen aangemoedigd naar school te gaan. Toen de missiescholen zich uitbreidden en het macht van de staat groter werd, veranderde die aanmoediging in een plicht. Maar omdat veel gezinnen rondtrokken of ver verwijderd waren van de buitenposten van de regering, moesten de kinderen naar kostscholen, vaak tegen hun wil. Ray en Sophia merkten dat de kinderen die naar deze scholen werden gebracht en vervolgens werden geslagen, kaalgeschoren, mishandeld, hun mond uitgespoeld kregen met zeep omdat ze hun 'vuile indianentaal' spraken en andere gruwelen meemaakten, zelf problematische ouders werden. De gemeenschap besprak dit en zij en andere ouderen deden een voorstel hoe dit probleem te verhelpen: de slachtoffers van de kostscholen en de latere generaties die onder hun erfenis hadden geleden, zouden moeten terugkeren naar het land, opnieuw kennismaken met hun traditionele ceremonies en opnieuw hun moedertaal moeten leren. Wanneer taal en cultuur zijn afgeleid van het land, is de weg naar genezing de terugkeer naar dat land.

De kerk, de staat en de school hadden Sophia's ouders verteld dat de oude manier van leven zondig was, heidens en verkeerd, maar Sophia's vader was haar 's avonds verhalen blijven vertellen. Hij was een wijs en – belangrijker – koppig man. Hij liet zijn dochter naar de universiteit gaan, maar waarschuwde haar wel: 'Als je niet weet wie je bent en waar je vandaan komt, heb je niks aan die kennis.' Gelukkig had ze zich dat wel herinnerd.

'We waren vergeten de geesten te eren,' zei ze. Wij staan niet los van het land, wij maken er deel van uit. Dat heeft de schepper ons geleerd. Zelfs aan de rivier zitten werkt al helend, als je je hart, je geest, maar openstelt voor het land.'

De gemeenschap startte een programma van genezingskampen. Zij kozen een plek, honderdzestig kilometer stroomopwaarts, waar families vroeger in de herfst en de lente gingen jagen. Ze zamelden geld in om tipi's en voorraden voor langdurig verblijf per vliegtuig naar die plaats te laten brengen. Ver van enige weg of pad, vroeger alleen bereikbaar per kano, was dit een heilige plaats aan de oevers van wat de blanke man Weaver Lake noemde, maar dat de Anishinaabe nu pas weer leren noemen bij de naam die hun voorouders het gaven: *Pinesiwapikung Saagaigun* – *Thunder Lake* in het Engels.

Veel mensen waren er nog nooit geweest. Sophia zelf was er niet meer geweest sinds haar kindertijd, toen haar vader haar had meegenomen. De jongeren kenden de oude ceremonies of de taal niet en wisten zelfs hun eigen traditionele namen niet.

'Wij gebruiken het woord "verloren" niet,' zegt Sophia trots. 'Ze is hier – de kennis – in het land. Klaar om aan ons worden geopenbaard als we maar luisteren en onze traditionele ceremonies uitvoeren.' Het land is geheugen en archief. Als je lang genoeg naar de dieren zit te kijken, kom je iets te weten van wat zij weten. Je ziet de paarden bijvoorbeeld de bladeren van de balsempopulier eten om koliek te voorkomen. Of je kan de bever de populieren zien opeten om zijn pels te laten glanzen. Sophia lacht om *Canada's Food Guide*, een handboek over voeding, geproduceerd door de overheid. 'Dat is totaal ongepast.' Traditioneel aten de Anishinaabe geen koolhydraten en zuivelproducten. Velen van hen verdragen niet eens lactose. Maar hun werd verteld: 'Dit is een gezond dieet,' terwijl in hun eigen wilde voedsel feitelijk veel beter voor hun gezondheid was.

'Als wij de bever eten, krijgen we alle medicijnen die de bever at: de populieren, de wilgen, de berken, de waterlelies.'

De genezingskampen waren een enorm succes. Ze werden jaar na jaar georganiseerd, met gespecialiseerde kampen voor kinderen met gedragsproblemen, mensen met diabetes – aangezien chronische emotionele pijn hand in hand gaat met wat men eet – en kampen voor ouderen die op de kostscholen waren misbruikt. De terugkeer naar de traditionele ceremonies, voedsel en taal gaf de gemeenschap het vertrouwen om kritiek te leveren op wat hen over hun eigen cultuur was verteld en om hun rechten en verantwoordelijkheden met betrekking tot het land op te eisen. Het proces zette als het ware een deur open. Het leidde tot de campagne voor de oprichting van het beschermde gebied Pimachiowin Aki en een Goldman-milieuprijs voor Sophia.

Inmiddels runt de school daar een boskamp voor de kinderen en geeft Sophia op de lagere school les in het Anishinaabeg, de inheemse taal. De eerste keer vroeg ze aan de klas: 'Wie hier is

Anishinaabe?' en slechts twee kinderen staken hun hand op, hoewel ze het allemaal waren. Wanneer ze nu die vraag stelt, weten ze allemaal waar ze het over heeft.

Het is niet altijd gemakkelijk om die cultuur en het moderne leven met elkaar te verzoenen. Aidan, hun oudste kleinzoon, komt de kamer binnen waar wij zitten te praten, ploft met een iPad op de bank en begint onmiddellijk een gewelddadig computerspelletje te spelen.

'Kun je op zijn minst de herrie uitzetten?' smeekt Sophia.

Toch heeft de gemeenschap van Poplar River een manier gevonden om te leven. Ze hebben nu iets waar ze alles aan kunnen toetsen: het land. Zo vaak ze kunnen, nemen Ray en Sophia en anderen ouderen mee op het land om herinneringen op te halen, hun woordenschat uit te breiden en het vertellen van verhalen aan te moedigen.

De volgende dag zullen ze een boottocht maken op de rivier naar Lake Winnipeg, en ze nodigen me uit mee te gaan.

Ik houd Abels hand vast om hem te helpen terwijl hij uit de oranje glasvezel speedboot op de gladde keien stapt. Zijn zwarte schoenen hangen even boven de waterlijn terwijl hij zijn stok van mij terugneemt, maar dan loodst hij zijn lichaam de helling op alvorens het op een bed van korstmossen te laten zakken. Het kleine eiland is begroeid met het gebruikelijke struikgewas van het boreale gebied – jeneverbes, wilgenroosje, moerasrozemarijn en lisdodde. De onvolgroeide struikdennen (*Pinus banksiana*) klampen zich vast aan de schaarse spleten in de rotsen. Het voorkomen van een bodem is een luxe van oudere landschappen, en het relatief jonge Canadese Schild kent pas sinds een paar duizend jaar vegetatie.

Abels zwarte ogen kijken mij aan en richten zich dan op een van de ontelbare kleine eilandjes die de kustlijn van Lake Winnipeg vormen aan de monding van de Poplar Rivier. Het is alsof het land aan stukken is geslagen en vervolgens in het water is geland. Zijn gladde bruine huid gloeit in het warme middaglicht en vertoont grijze stoppels. Naast hem zit zijn neef. Albert is iets ouder dan Abel, maar zijn haar is net zo zwart en zijn geest net zo scherp. Hij draagt een bomberjack en een baseballpet die hij laag over zijn bril heeft getrokken.

'*Manitoo*,' zegt Albert langzaam. 'Dat is de schepper... *Manitoopa*, dat betekent "waar de schepper zit".'" Hij wijst naar het meer rondom ons met een opwaartse beweging van zijn vierkante kin. De Anischinaabe zijn niet de enigen die God in alles zien. Nog niet zo lang geleden was dat in de meeste menselijke samenlevingen een uitgangspunt. Het is moeilijker om een bos om te hakken of een stuk weideland af te graven als je gelooft dat God daar woont.

De Ojibwe-volken, waartoe ook de Anishinaabe behoren, geloven dat het land in het begin uit het water werd opgetild en aan de mens werd gegeven als een geschenk voor zijn voortbestaan. In ruil daarvoor moest de mens voor dat land zorgen. Toen de Laurentide-ijskap zich elfduizend jaar geleden terugtrok, onthulde die een gletsjermeer genaamd Lake Aggasiz, veel groter dan het huidige Lake Winnipeg. Zo'n tienduizend jaar geleden lag het hele land van Pimachiowin Aki nog op de bodem van het Aggasiz-meer, maar een paar duizend jaar later was het land, dat niet langer omlaag werd gedrukt door het enorme gewicht van het opgehoopte ijs, opnieuw opgeveerd en kwam de rots waarop wij nu zaten boven water. In het begin werd de rots ontgonnen door korstmossen, mos, struikdennen en sparren. Vervolgens, ongeveer vijfduizend jaar geleden, kregen deze vroege pioniers gezelschap van berk en populier. De *mashkeek* (moeraslanden) van Pimachiowin Aki zijn sindsdien relatief stabiel gebleven, tot nu.

'De elanden vertrekken, de vogels vertrekken, de konijnen vertrekken, de kariboes zijn al bijna verdwenen.' Abel is neerslachtig. 'We zien de jongeren niet langer gaan jagen, vallen zetten en vissen.' Volgens hem ligt het probleem in het niet oogsten van de dieren die de schepper ter beschikking heeft gesteld. Het oogsten van de dieren is een eerbetoon aan hen en hun geest. 'Als we ze oogsten, zullen ze ook weer terugkomen.'

Het is een controversieel idee dat weinig populair is bij natuurbeschermers, maar als de hazelaar reageert op snoeien voor hakhout door krachtiger te groeien en veenreukgras reageert op plukken, waarom zou dat dan niet ook voor dieren gelden? Botanicus en docent Robin Wall Kimmerer schreef over een pelsjager die, door selectief mannetjes te vangen, de marterpopulatie in zijn jachtgebied wist te vergroten. Het vraagt om een gedetailleerd begrip van de ecologie, hoewel Albert en Abel dat woord nooit zouden gebruiken. In plaats daarvan praten zij over heilige ceremonies en geesten.

'Voordat we iets doden, eten of plukken, danken we en geven we tabak aan de schepper.' Abel tilt zijn stok op en zwaait hem in een wijde boog. 'Alles wat je ziet is medicijn. Ik ken 24 soorten medicijn.' Abel is een van de medicijnmannen van de Anishinaabe gemeenschap van Poplar River. Een van de bomen die hij kreeg was *muhnuhsuday*, de balsempopulier, die de Anishinaabe in het Engels *black poplar* noemen. Het is een heilige boom, zoals alle bomen met essentiële gaven, en dat zijn de meeste bomen.

Als kind had ik nooit tandpijn,' vertelt Abel. 'Mijn vader plukte een takje zwarte populier voor me en dan viel zo'n tand er gewoon uit. Zonder pijn.' Zijn glimlach vormt het bewijs.

De geneeskundig effecten van balsempopulier voor het hart, waar Diana het over had, zijn bekend bij de Anishinaabe-oudsten: je snijdt ter hoogste van je hart een stuk uit de schors, zo groot als je hart, en kookt het in water om de cardiotonica vrij te doen komen. Men heeft ontdekt dat het ook tegen kanker kan werken, en Diana is het daar mee eens. Een van de vele souvenirs die Ray me per se mee wil geven wanneer ik Poplar River weer verlaat, is een potje zalf, gemaakt van balsempopulierknoppen dat volgens hem een wonderzalf is tegen elke huidaandoening.

De witte spar wordt gebruikt voor de bouw, voor tipi-palen en als winterbed, legt Abel uit. Kornoelje wordt gebruikt voor het maken van manden en medicijnen, populier wordt gebruikt voor strikken, wilgen worden gebruikt om zweethutten te maken. De lijst is bijna eindeloos.

'We zouden de hele dag en avond kunnen doorpraten over alle dingen die ik weet,' zegt Abel. Dan zwijgt hij even, om vervolgens abrupt van onderwerp te veranderen.

'Die kostschool, daar zat ik vier jaar op. Daar zijn zoveel erge dingen gebeurd. Ik werd seksueel misbruikt door mijn leraar. Ja. Ik ben verkracht. Elke dag werden we geslagen. Mijn moeder had mijn lange haar gevlochten en zei me dat ik het nooit mocht afknippen, maar toen ik daar aankwam, knipten ze het af. Die school was in Cross Lake. Ik denk er nog vaak aan terug en heb er nog steeds nachtmerries over. Soms sla ik met mijn vuisten tegen de muur. En toen ik weer thuiskwam, wist ik niet meer wie mijn moeder was. Wie was mijn vader? Ik wist niet meer wie dat waren. Ik wist niet meer hoe ik moest lachen of glimlachen. Mijn gevoelens waren afgestompt. Voorheen kon ik nooit tegen kietelen. Dat was wel anders nu. Mam heeft me nooit verdedigd. Ze zei tegen me: 'Geen dingen meebrengen naar huis. Breng dat maar terug naar waar je vandaan komt."'

We kijken uit over het meer. Pelikanen patrouilleren ver weg rond wat rotsen. Zeearenden cirkelen rond de dennenbomen op een ander eiland. Canadese ganzen zweven sereen voorbij alsof ze alle tijd van de wereld hebben.

Zestig jaar lang heeft Abel nooit iemand verteld over wat er met hem is gebeurd op de kostschool van Cross Lake. Hij werd feitelijk ontvoerd door missionarissen toen hij een jaar of acht, negen was. Maar sinds zijn ervaringen in het genezingskamp is het vaak het eerste wat hij mensen vertelt.

'Ja, zo doet hij dat,' zegt Ray. 'Abel praat tegenwoordig graag. Het is alsof hij het kwijt moet.

De genezingskampen stelden Abel en de anderen die geleden hadden, in staat om erover te praten. En dat praten was een eerste stap op weg naar het begrijpen van de ernst van wat er was gebeurd en wat er verloren was gegaan en kapotgemaakt. Er was zoveel energie gestoken in pogingen om te assimileren, te ontkennen, serieus genomen te worden en te slagen op de voorwaarden van de blanke en in zijn steden. Door erover te praten kregen ze een glimp van mogelijke gerechtigheid, ook al was het nog niet duidelijk hoe die precies kon worden verkregen.

Er zijn tienduizend inheemse kinderen omgekomen op de kostscholen. De Canadese staat probeerde Abel en Albert en de anderen los te maken van hun geschiedenis, hun cultuur en hun taal, in feite om te veranderen wie zij waren. Als wie je bent slechts één wezen is dat is ingebed in een ecosysteem samen met talloze andere, dan betekent genezing dat je in die rol die je had geërfd wordt hersteld, dat je verbinding met het land wordt hersteld, hoewel het woord 'land' eigenlijk tekortschiet. Pimachiowin is alles, het systeem van een wereld. Zelfs 'natuur' is een misleidend begrip, omdat het iets is gaan betekenen dat losstaat van de menselijke sfeer. Pimachiowin is een perfect voorbeeld van wat antropoloog Eduardo Kohn een 'antropologie voorbij de mens' noemt – een geheel van tekens, symbolen, relaties en betekenissen dat groter is dan het bereik van het menselijk bewustzijn en waarvan de mens slechts een deel uitmaakt.

We zijn hier om uit te kijken naar elanden en de omvang van de populatie in te schatten, zodat we kunnen bepalen hoeveel er 'verantwoord kunnen worden afgeschoten'. Hoewel ze ooit een belangrijk deel van het leven vormden in Poplar River, zijn elanden inmiddels steeds zeldzamer geworden. Niemand weet precies waarom, maar de veranderende structuur van het bos, een verdichting als gevolg van brand en opwarming, waardoor het ontoegankelijker wordt, lijkt iets te maken te hebben met de afnemende populatie. De elanden trekken naar het noorden.

De verouderde glasvezel speedboot met witte kunstlederen zitjes wordt bestuurd door Eddie Hudson, gemeenteraadslid en bestuurslid van de Pimachiowin Aki Corporation. Eddie leunt achterover in zijn stoel, zijn geruite hemdsmouwen opgerold, een elleboog op het gangboord, zijn cowboylaarzen uitgestrekt. De zon staat op zijn gebruinde gezicht en de wind speelt met de grijzende lok haar die over zijn voorhoofd hangt. Hij bewondert het licht dat de fijne zandstranden van de kust oranje en roze kleurt.

'Als ik bomen zag, zag ik geld.' Hij studeerde economie, maar de ouderen leerden hem het landschap waaruit hij stamde toch weer anders te zien.

Alle ogen speuren de dichte bosrand op het vasteland af. Eddie duwt de boot een ondiepe baai van drassig gras en rotsblokken in om een nieuwe beverdam van dichtbij te bekijken die is verschenen sinds hij hier voor het laatst was. Geen eland te bekennen.

De wind zweept het oppervlak van het bruine meer op tot steeds hogere golven waarop poedersuiker lijkt te zijn gestrooid. We leggen de boot vast aan een andere rots en verzamelen jeneverbesstruiken voor een vuur om thee te maken. Twee zandhoenders die aan de overkant voedsel aan het zoeken waren, stijgen klapperend op tegen de roze lucht en maken een geluid dat erg lijkt op de naam die ze van de Anishinaabeg kregen: *oocheechuhg*. Net als we op de rotsen neerstrijken om thee te drinken, tuimelen een vrouwtjesbeer en haar jong uit het bos op het vasteland om te gaan zwemmen. We kijken hoe ze over het strand ravotten.

'We waren het bijna kwijt!' zegt Eddie, terwijl hij erbij zit als een tevreden koning die zijn domein overziet. 'We kunnen het nog steeds verliezen! We hebben ons land verkocht aan de kroon!' Iedereen lacht en kijkt naar Albert. Het was zijn betovergrootoom die namens de gemeenschap zijn kruisje zette onder Treaty 5, het verdrag waarmee ze dit land in 1875 aan koningin Victoria afstonden.

Maar alle kruisjes zien er hetzelfde uit,' voert hij aan als excuus. Opnieuw lacht iedereen.

'Nu hebben we er tenminste weer iets over te zeggen en kunnen we het beschermen,' zegt Eddie. Een van de voorwaarden voor de beschermde status was dat de gemeenschap met een 'landbeheerplan' moest komen. Dat hebben ze veranderd in een 'landgebruiksplan'. 'Ze zeggen dat het land beheerd moet worden. Onzin. Laat het bos zichzelf beheren, laat de dieren zichzelf beheren.' Nu lacht Eddie ineens niet meer. 'We moeten het in de taal van de blanke man zeggen, zodat hij het kan begrijpen.' Het verschil tussen beheer en gebruik is belangrijk: het eerste impliceert heerschappij, het tweede suggereert respect, toestemming en dankbaarheid.

Naast de elandentelling is er een meerjarig onderzoek om de uitdroging van de veenmoerassen te meten – de moerasgebieden van de mashkeek, waarvan het Engelse woord muskeg is afgeleid. Uit een in opdracht van de gemeenschap uitgevoerde koolstofstudie is gebleken dat een hectare muskeg achttien keer zoveel koolstof bevat als een vergelijkbare hectare bos en dat in de hele Pimachiowin Aki 444 miljoen ton koolstof ligt opgeslagen. Koolstofboekhouding zou wel eens de nieuwe economie van Poplar River kunnen worden.

De voorwaarden van het landgebruikplan en wat de Anishinaabe verschuldigd zijn aan hun schepper, zijn dezelfde. Het land moet worden gebruikt. De geesten moeten worden geëerd. De heilige plaatsen moeten worden bezocht en de schepper moet om advies worden gevraagd. Tabak moet worden verbrand en vis gevangen. Voor het weekend is er een expeditie gepland naar Thunder Lake. Dat is gelijk ook een goede gelegenheid om de jongere generatie eens van hun telefoons los te weken.

Het wordt al laat. De zon raakt bijna het geribbelde bruine oppervlak van Lake Winnipeg, en de wind jaagt ons naar huis terwijl we ons een weg banen tussen de chaotische rotsblokken, maar Abel en Albert zijn nog maar net op gang gekomen. Albert is van de steurenclan en Abel is van de wolvenclan, leggen ze uit.

'Het dier is je voorouder, je beschermer. Je moet het verhaal van die geest, dat dier leren kennen en het respecteren,' zegt Albert.

Hij vertelt hoe de haas aan zijn lange oren kwam, over de jager die werd bedrogen door de wolf die in een vrouw veranderde, en wijst dan naar een heilige plaats aan de oever.

'Daar stond onze beeftent. Dat was onze telefoon. Kinderen werden niet toegelaten. We feestten de hele nacht door en communiceerden met andere stammen tot in Brits Columbia, zelfs Nunavut, tot de kerk het verbood.'

Zelfs nadat we de boot weer aan het ponton hebben vastgemaakt, ons weer in Ray's truck hebben gehesen en hem bij zijn huis hebben afgeleverd, praat Albert nog steeds alsof er levens van zijn kennis afhangen, wat natuurlijk ook zo is, vooral dat van hemzelf.

'Alle bomen in de wereld stammen af van één boom, een ceder, die nog steeds leeft. Die ceder is heilig, en de populier, want de populier onderhoudt de rivier...'

We hebben geen elanden gezien.

De volgende ochtend staan Sophia, Aidan en ik in de zon waar de weg zachtjes bergafwaarts het water in loopt en stopt. Dit is het einde van het korte pad door het reservaat en het begin van de wildernis. Het is de plaats waar al duizenden jaren kano's te water worden gelaten voor tochten stroomopwaarts. Aan weerszijden van de rivier wuiven stengels wilde rijst in de stroom. De zon breekt door boven de bomen en baadt de tegenoverliggende oever in een goudkleurig licht dat glinstert op het oppervlak van miljoenen kleine gelede populierenblaadjes. Eenden duikelen in het ondiepe water, een zeearend vliegt met een kreet weg van een stronk op de oever en landt boven het bos aan de verre overkant, en op het wateroppervlak wervelt een bruisende massa insecten als rook. Daarachter, in het noordoosten, markeert een breed spiegelend stuk rivier dat het bos doorklieft de weg die wij moeten volgen, de route van onze pelgrimstocht naar de bron.

De geur is bedwelmend: jeneverbes, munt, gentiaan, populier, sparren. De lucht, weet ik nu van Diana, is gevuld met pineen en andere aerosolen die de atmosfeer zuiveren en elke ademhaling steriel en medicinaal maken.

Twee kano's worden in het water geschoven en er worden buitenboordmotoren aan bevestigd. We wachten op een derde. Er worden tassen ingeladen, peddels, brandstof, koelboxen, een hengel, een bijl, een kettingzaag, een geweer.

Het is warm. Warmer dan ooit, zegt Sophia. Vroeger kwamen de zomertemperaturen nooit boven de 25°C, maar nu is er elk jaar een hittegolf. Canada als geheel warmt tweemaal zo snel op als het wereldgemiddelde, en in het noorden gaat het zelfs nog sneller. Sophia knielt om te bidden en tabak te offeren aan de voet van de boom waar de zeearend had gezeten.

‘Nu zal hij ons volgen, het hele eind stroomopwaarts. Dat is een goed teken.’

De laatste kano arriveert en we zijn vertrokken. Ik ben in een slank grijs exemplaar gezet dat er gloednieuw uitziet. Deze is van Roger, die het roer met enig gezag vasthoudt.

‘Denk om de lak, Roger!’ roept een stem vanaf de oever. ‘Die kano kost zo zesduizend dollar!’ Ooit werden kano’s uitgehold uit stammen van de balsempopulier – vanwege de diameter en het feit dat het hout droogt zonder te splijten. Tegenwoordig worden nieuwe esdoornen kano’s ingevlogen vanuit Winnipeg.

Ik zit op het middelste zitje. Clint, door de corporatie aangesteld als bewaker van het land – een soort parkopzichter, zit voorin. Honderdzestig kilometer lang zie ik van hem alleen zijn rug. De drie kano’s trekken brede voren in het bruine water. We varen in formatie en zeggen weinig, want het gedrein van de buitenboordmotoren maakt het moeilijk om te praten. Het bos glijdt vorsend aan ons voorbij, machtig en stil, en neemt de mensen in zich op. Balsempopulier, ratelpopulier, spar en struikden staan hier door elkaar. De overheersende soort is echter de populier – het is één enorm dicht struikgewas. De oevers en de inhammen en kreken die uitmonden in de Poplar River zijn bezaaid met beverdammen.

De brede loop van de rivier is een eindeloos, onveranderlijk vergezicht, tot we een onheilspellende verbrande zone binnenvaren. De verschroeide oranje naalden van de sparren zitten nog aan de takken en de stammen zijn zwart. Dunne staken populier staan hier en daar nog overeind, maar de meeste bomen zijn omgevallen. De ondergroei is zich alweer aan het herstellen: wilgenroosje, vuurkruid, wilgen en populier, het bos komt terug, veel dichter dan voorheen. Af en toe blaast de bries een mineraal vleugje houtskool naar ons toe. De wortels en uitlopers van de ratelpopulier reageren krachtig op vuur. Net als de balsempopulier kan hij zich via uitlopers voortplanten en zichzelf klonen. Het zou me niet verbazen als heel Pimachiowin Aki één boom was. Raak een stam aan in Poplar River en het kan 'gevoeld' worden door een stam duizend kilometer verderop, aan de andere kant van het reservaat.

Eddie herinnert zich dat toen hij een kind was, je door het bos kon kijken en een eland tussen de bomen kon zien staan. De populieren stonden aan de rand van hun noordelijke verspreidingsgebied en verdrongen de ondergroei niet. Maar nu is de samenstelling van het bos aan het veranderen. Het kreupelhout is dicht, moeilijk voor elanden om door te komen. Geen gevlekte schaduw meer van de populieren en de struikdennen, maar donker struikgewas.

Na een uur komen we bij de eerste stroomversnelling. De kano's moeten worden uitgeladen en dan over een ladder van rechte sparrenhouten palen naar boven worden gesleept, de rots naast de waterval op.

Dat is zwaar werk.

'Trek!' roepen twee mensen net niet helemaal tegelijk.

'Er zijn hier te veel opperhoofden!' roept Clint, en iedereen schatert het uit.

De koelboxen, tassen, vishengels, kettingzaag, bijl en geweer worden weer in de kano's geladen en we springen er weer in.

'Nog maar twaalf stroomversnellingen te gaan!' grijnst Roger. Het wordt een lange dag.

In 1794 werd John Best van de Hudson Bay Company vanuit de York Factory aan de baai naar het zuiden gestuurd om het gebied van Pimachiowin Aki te verkennen. Het kostte hem drie weken en zevenenvijftig keer kano dragen om Lake Winnipeg te bereiken. Dit was voldoende om zijn collega's weg te houden, en de Anishinaabe-gemeenschappen bleven nog honderd jaar gespaard van de bonthandel.

In de voorste kano zitten George, Errol en Aidan, Sophia's kleinzoon. Aidan vindt het geweldig, al dat duwen en trekken en de grappen van de volwassen mannen. Errol is een jongen uit een probleemgezin, maar hier is hij een leider, die bij elke stroomversnelling uit de kano springt, het ding trekt met de kracht van twee en iedereen aan het lachen maakt. George is de meest ervaren riviervaarder van de groep. Hij loodst zijn glasvezel kano met elegante vaardigheid door het ondiepe en gaat recht op de kleine stroomversnellingen af, surfend over de hekgolven.

De middelste kano wordt bestuurd door zijn neef Guy, een oudere man die zijn zonnebril drie dagen lang niet afzet en die weinig zegt, behalve dan dat hij de clou van een mop van een ander verklapt. Eddie en Sophia zitten bij hem in de kano. Zij zijn de oudsten van de groep en hoeven niet te helpen wanneer de kano's voorbij stroomversnellingen worden gedragen.

Bij de derde stroomversnelling stapt de rest van ons uit op de platen gesteente aan de rand van de rivier, die door de lage waterstand zichtbaar zijn geworden. Dunne aarde, bedekt met een lichtgroen, bijna spookachtig korstmos, vormt een korst op de geologische schildformatie die een tiental meters hoger begint. We hijsen de kano's uit het water, zwoegen, vloeken, zweten en slepen ze over rollende boomstammen op een pad door het bos, waarbij we abrupt in een andere wereld worden ondergedompeld.

Weg zijn het verblindende licht van de rivier en de weidse vergezichten op het bos. Korstmossen, waarvan de bleke stekelige bladen als koraal in de lucht prikken, verschijnen en verdwijnen weer uit het zicht tussen de knoestige takken van de struikdennen. Bendes populieren steken hun rechte grijze staken als geweerlopen de lucht in. Zonlicht bereikt de grond in linten en vlekken, of anders in glijdende stralen waar een omgevallen boom een gat in het bladerdak heeft gescheurd, alsof we onder water zijn. Maar in dit koraalwoud is er lucht, en wat voor een lucht! Geurig en zwaar, als in een parfumerie. Plots besef ik hoe zeldzaam deze ervaring is, hoe weinig mensen een zevenduizend jaar oud bos hebben geroken en aangeraakt. Dus dit is wat 'oude groei' betekent.

Perspectieven openen en sluiten zich weer. Onder de struikdennen is de bosbodem sponzig van mos en korstmos, als een strak geweven stof waarvan de draden aangetrokken zijn. De onderlaag is dun. Je zou een eland kunnen zien aankomen, of een beer.

Onder de populieren is de grond zachter en zwart. Gebleken is dat populieren- en espengrond een veel rijker mycorrhizaal leven kent dan berkengrond, de grond onder de andere belangrijke bladverliezende pionier, die meer verwant is met dennen- en sparrengrond, zijn groenblijvende buren. Het chemische milieu leidt tot meer mineraaluitwisseling, een verhoogde pH-waarde van de bodem en een hoger vochtgehalte van de bodem. De grotere bladeren geven meer schaduw, wat beter is voor de bessen.

De bladeren van dit jaar zijn net begonnen te vallen, te vroeg, en bedekken de dikke onderlaag met knapperige grijze vlokken. Bosbessen, vogelkers, wilde frambozen en nog veel meer andere bessen verdringen elkaar in de schaduw van de populieren, en aan het eind van het pad ligt de grootste traktatie: mollige, fluweelachtige bessen, 'saskatoons' genaamd, die het gezichtsvermogen in het donker verbeteren. We leggen de kano even neer en grijpen een handvol bessen voor de laatste keer trekken en sleuren. Dan gaat het verder naar een andere ladderachtige structuur van sparrenhout, en de kano's gaan met een zoevend geluid weer het water weer in.

Niet weer het touw loslaten, Clint! Iedereen lacht.

Urenlang stroomt het eindeloze bos voorbij. De buitenboordmotoren janken door. Honderdzestig kilometer zonder een glimp van een ander mens. Alleen de regelmatige aanblik van onze vriendelijke zeearend, die in een bocht op een tak zit en onze vorderingen in de gaten houdt.

Er zijn dertien stroomversnellingen waar we omheen moeten, sommige met een groter verval dan andere. Nadat de laatste is gepasseerd bij het licht van de ondergaande zon, wordt de rivier plotseling breder en gaat over in een breed meer met beboste oevers die zich uitstrekken onder een perfecte magentakleurige lucht.

'Gehaald!' roept Roger.

Aan de oever markeert een grote dode dennenboom de toegang tot het meer, en boven op de hoogste tak zit een uitkijk, een grote zeearend, die met zijn witte kop knikt als we voorbij varen. Sophia strooit tabak op het water.

Thunder Lake is enorm, bijna een zee. De wind is gaan liggen als we eindelijk een eiland bereiken en de kano's op een zacht glooiende rotsgesteente laten glijden waarop de sporen van honderden kielen die hier in de loop van duizenden jaren tegenop zijn geschoven duidelijk zichtbaar zijn. In een ondiepe poel aan de rand van het meer zie ik een kleine gespikkelde bruine kikker. De boreale kikker kan de hele winter overleven met 75 procent van haar lichaamsmassa bevroren, terwijl zich ijs vormt in haar vetcellen, en ze als het ware al het leven terugtrekt tot een klein deel van haar lichaam rond het hart. Als de lente aanbreekt, komt ze uit haar cryogene toestand. Ik hoop dat ze het zachte water lekker vindt. Het voelt en ziet eruit als lauwe thee.

Bovenop de rotskoepel van het eiland staat Guy's hut. De achterwand hangt vol met geweien van elanden. Buiten, tussen de dennen, liggen generatoren, oude kano's, platen aluminium, propaantanks, een trimmer, verfpotten en zelfs een koelkast. Binnen is een slaapkamer volgestapeld met matrassen en er is een keuken met een tafel, een gietijzeren fornuis en een moderner gasfornuis. De gootsteen loopt uit in een emmer, de kasten zijn volgepropt met een jaarvoorraad ingeblikt voedsel, en er ligt scherpe munitie in de besteklade. Aan de muur hangt een afbeelding van een wolf en een klok die stilstaat op 6.44 uur.

De vijf Anishinaabe mannen slapen in de ene slaapkamer. Sophia en haar kleinzoon, Eddie, en ik zetten onze tenten op op het kleine eiland. Wij trekken aan het kortste eind. Ik slaag erin een relatief vlak stuk te vinden met lichtgroen korstmos tussen onvolgroeide struikdennen. Het kraakt en knispert als oud brood onder mijn voeten. Wanneer we naar bed gaan en elkaar goede nacht wensen, waait er een koude wind door de dennenbomen. In de lucht boven het bos op de andere oever is een vlek die donkerder lijkt dan de rest. Dan een onmiskenbaar gerommel.

'Dondervogels!' zegt Eddie, lachend. 'Die weten dat we hier zijn.' Vuur is de motor van het leven in het boreale gebied. Het landschap en het bos zouden er heel anders uitzien zonder het vuur, en ook de evolutie van de soorten hier zou anders verlopen.

De drie loofbomen van de regio – de ratelpopulier, de balsempopulier en de papierberk – zijn alle drie goed aangepast aan het vuur. De populieren (zowel ratel- als balsem-) zien er misschien kwetsbaar uit met hun lichtgrijze schors en zweepachtige scheuten, maar wanneer vuur het bos en zelfs de bodem verteert, overleven hun penwortels. Drie tot vier weken later beginnen er uitlopers te verschijnen – de witgrijze scheuten van de ratelpopulieren en de bleekgroen-rode van de balsempopulier. Ze gedijen goed in de mineraalrijke grond die na een brand is blootgelegd. Dat geldt ook voor de zaden van de struikden, die zonder vuur helemaal niet zouden ontkiemen.

De dennenappels van de struikden zijn zo hard als steen, hun schubben zitten aan elkaar vast met een hars die de kracht van superlijm heeft, om de zaden tegen knaagdieren te beschermen. Bij 50 graden Celsius smelt de hars en wakkert het vuur aan, waardoor de kegel verandert in de lont van een kaars die negentig seconden brandt, genoeg om de kegel te doen opengaan als een bloem. De struikden regelt dus eigenlijk het vuur, en zorgt ervoor dat zijn zaden precies lang genoeg de juiste hoeveelheid warmte krijgen. De kegel laat zijn zaden vervolgens pas los als ze weer koel zijn, want tegen die tijd is de grond inmiddels ontdaan van de concurrentie en kunnen de zaden ontkiemen in de zanderige minerale bodem waar ze dol op zijn.

De reactie van deze boomsoorten op brand is van cruciaal belang voor de levenscyclus waarvan de Anishinaabe afhankelijk zijn. In de eerste jaren na een brand is het opengelegde bos een toevluchtsoord voor elanden en hazen die graag van de jonge scheuten en gerookte bladeren eten. Gedurende een twintigtal jaren zijn dergelijke plaatsen de vaste voederplaatsen voor elanden, en geschikt om vallen te zetten voor marterachtigen en lynxen die er komen voor de hazen. Na vijftig jaar beginnen de hazen af te nemen als de struikdennen te hoog worden. Uilen nestelen in de verbrande stammen en tegen die tijd raakt de grond bedekt met vedermos dat meer vocht vasthoudt voor bessen en struiken. De populieren stoppen met zich voort te planten na een jaar of zestig en dan begint het aantal elanden af te nemen. Het mos maakt na 75 jaar plaats voor korstmossen, en er verschijnen kariboes om het te begrazen. De balsemzilverspar en andere naaldbomen wortelen dan in de dieper wordende zwarte grond – *okataywikamik* genoemd door de Anishinaabe – ontstaan uit het rottende bladafval van de populieren. Inmiddels is het bos voor mensen niet langer een goede plaats om voedsel te vinden, en ze beginnen te bidden dat het maar snel weer mag branden.[7]

Vuur is een scheppende levenskracht, en de balsempopulier was altijd de bron van vuur voor de inheemse bevolking van het woud. Het is het beste hout voor de vuurboor die wordt gebruikt om door wrijving een vonk te produceren, en niets werkt zo goed als de binnenbast van balsempopulier om de door de boor gegenereerde sintel te voeden. Verrot kernhout van populieren, zowel balsem als ratel, dat zacht en lichtontvlambaar is en langzaam gloeit, werd gebruikt om vuur te vervoeren. En soms veroorzaakte de mens zelf de brand als de bliksem niet kwam of om de regeneratie in bepaalde gebieden aan te moedigen. De Anishinaabe doen dat niet meer, omdat niemand weet waartoe het kan leiden.

Het bos is droger. De vuren branden heter en langer. Meer van het veen en organische grond verbrandt, en de soorten die profiteren van de sterk verbrande gebieden – het wilgenroosje en de wilgen – zijn dikker en agressiever dan de tere ondergroei van bessen en rozemarijn. De struikden wordt aangevreten door de *Choristoneura fumiferana*, een worm, en de populieren domineren. Het is nu juist de jonge struikden die de hazen het liefst eten. De populier beschikt over spoorelementen die hij gebruikt om de bladeren van zeer jonge bomen slecht te laten smaken voor de hazen. Wat zullen de hazen dan eten? En wat zullen de carnivoren eten? En...

Niemand heeft ooit een dondervogel gezien. Die verbergen zich achter donkere wolken, maar op afbeeldingen zien ze eruit als vogels met bliksemschichten uit hun ogen en vuur dat uit hun vleugels stroomt. 85 procent van alle branden is het gevolg van blikseminslag, de rest van gecontroleerde of toevallige branden die door de mens zijn veroorzaakt. Dondervogels zijn daarom de belangrijkste wezens in de kosmologie van de Anishinaabe. Thunder Lake is naar hen genoemd. Het is een plek waar dondervogels zouden nestelen.

Deze nacht zijn ze nogal onrustig. Ik word om middernacht wakker van een vreselijke knal die de nachtelijk hemel doet beven. De struikdennen slaan tegen elkaar en de golven op het meer rijzen op als schuimbekkende honden, hun tanden flikkerend in het licht. De bliksem doet de hele hemel draaien en flikkeren alsof de wereld zich in een stroboscoop bevindt. Ik ben dankbaar dat er geen balsempopulieren op het eiland zijn – de stammen van groene balsempopulieren met hun hoge vochtgehalte zijn uitstekende bliksemgeleiders. In plaats daarvan maak ik me zorgen over de metalen palen van mijn tent die op een beboste rotskoepel zes meter boven het meer staan. De rest van de nacht lig ik onrustig, soms kort wat wegdommelend, terwijl de wind aan mijn tent rukt en het verschrikkelijke gerommel langzaam naar het noorden verdwijnt.

De ochtend breekt aan in stilte en de hemel is weer helder en wolkenloos. De lucht is vochtig en fris, de geuren van het bos zijn geactiveerd door de regen. De aarde ruikt zoet en het korstmos, dat de nacht tevoren stijf en broos was, heeft al het water als een spons opgezogen. Mos dat dood en bruin leek, is plots pulserend groen. De dondervogels hebben het dorstige bos eindelijk wat te drinken gegeven.

Later die ochtend varen we met onze drie kano's aan de overkant van Thunder Lake een andere rivier op. Oudere dennen en grote populieren staan aan oevers. Langs een kant is er een rotswand. Roger matigt de snelheid van onze kano. Het graniet is okerkleurig gestreept. We leggen onze kano's op een rij dicht bij de wand onder een gevaarlijk uitziende overhang. In een klein hoekje liggen de resten van kaarsen, sigaretten, plastic voorwerpen, munten en takjes. Roger staat op, neemt twee sigaretten uit zijn pakje en legt ze op de stenen richel. Clint doet hetzelfde.

'Grootvaderplek,' zegt Roger formeel, bij wijze van uitleg. Zelfs rotsen hebben in de Ojibwecultuur iets van leven in zich. En de okerschilderingen zijn het werk van *memegwesiwag*, halfmenselijke holbewoners die de Anishinaabe leerden hoe ze pijlen en pijpen van steen konden maken. Roger en Clint lachen wanneer ze deze dingen uitleggen, maar ik twijfel er niet aan of ze het geloven.

Verderop gaan we met de kano's aan land bij een brede poel net onder een stroomversnelling. George en Errol pakken hengels en zwiepen spinners in de stroming. Binnen enkele minuten halen ze wit-groen gestreepte vissen met een stekelige rugvin binnen – breedbekbaars of kettingsnoek.

'We doen boodschappen!' zegt George. 'En dit is onze supermarkt.' Wanneer hij het doet lijkt het ook net zo eenvoudig als blikjes in een winkelmandje gooien.

Clint en Eddie slepen dode boomstammen uit het bos en maken een vuur met gedroogd gras en berkenbast als tondel. De Anishinaabe maken alleen vuur met dood hout en hakken nooit een levende boom om.

Terwijl de ketel kookt, gaan Eddie en ik zitten onder een grillig uitziende dennenboom. Eddie draait een van de bollen van de boom en snijdt hem doormidden met zijn mes. Binnenin zit een kleverige oranje smurrie met daarin vijf of zes roomwitte wormen – larven – ongeveer zo lang als een mier. *Choristoneura fumiferana*. Ik kijk nog eens goed naar de boom. Die is verwrongen en vervormd. De vliegende insecten leggen hun eitjes in de knoppen van de den, en deze voeden zich met het sap om een grote bol, hun nest, te vormen. Alle bomen zijn geïnfecteerd. Gedurende de rest van de reis zie ik niet één gezonde struikden meer. Elke boom langs de rivier heeft het kromme uiterlijk van een voorovergebogen bejaarde, en de naalden vallen voortijdig.

'Maken jullie je zorgen over de opwarming van de aarde?' vraag ik.

Eddie strekt zijn in cowboylaarzen gestoken benen uit en vertelt over een van de ouderen.

'Hij zei dat het klimaat aan het veranderen was en dat de

mensen zich zouden moeten aanpassen. Ook al regent het meer, het extra water zal de uitdroging van het land niet tegenhouden. Het wordt warmer en het droogt uit. Tegenwoordig brandt het turf – dat deed het vroeger nooit. De soorten zullen veranderen, er zullen nieuwe soorten komen. De vissen gaan naar diepere plekken in het meer, waar het koeler is. Uiteindelijk zullen ze sterven, soorten zoals de breedbekbaars zullen stikken. En dan zullen er nieuwe vissen komen...' Eddie is even stil, alsof hij zich bezint op wat hij heeft gezegd. Dan haalt hij zijn schouders op en slaat zijn ene been over het andere.

'Ik maak me geen zorgen. We zullen ons aanpassen, precies zoals ze ons gezegd hebben. Ik zou een langere zomer niet zo erg vinden.' Hij grinnikt.

Plotseling heeft iedereen verhalen over veranderingen, over sneeuw die zwaarder en natter wordt, over de ijswegen die smelten, over de textuur en de kleur van het ijs op het meer, over soorten als eksters en gieren die zijn verschenen, marters en stinkdieren, over bessen die anders smaken, het plukseizoen dat korter wordt, te weinig sneeuw voor het zetten van vallen in de winter, het grotere aantal bosbranden, het waterpeil van het meer dat daalt, de oude krassporen van kano's die twee meter hoger op de rotsen staan.

'Kijk eens naar de bladeren van de populieren,' zegt George. 'Die zijn verschroeid.' Het is waar. Aan bijna elke boom zijn bladeren die nog groen en gezond zouden moeten zijn, twee maanden te vroeg verschroeid, oranje gekleurd door de hittestress wanneer het sap zich terugtrekt uit niet-levensvatbare bladeren.

'En de spar?' vraag ik, terwijl me voor het eerst al die lichtbruine kruinen van de kerstbomen tussen de bosopstanden opvallen. Die lijken ook uit te drogen.

'Yep,' zegt Guy.

Nu vestig ik mijn blik op wat anders. De ongerepte omgeving vol leven, ogenschijnlijk onaangetast en niet bedorven door de industrialisatie, lijkt plotseling te zijn aangetast met een eerste voorteken van de dood. De bomen zijn het onschuldige slachtoffer van processen die zich ver van hier afspelen. Ziekteverwekkers zoals de Choristoneura fumiferana kunnen hele ecosystemen uitroeien. Maar de ineenstorting van ecosystemen wordt meestal pas achteraf gedocumenteerd. Een bos kan de ondergang lange tijd verhullen omdat de achteruitgang van de belangrijkste soorten en natuurlijke processen pas op de lange termijn zichtbaar worden. Natuurbeschermingsgroepen hebben het al over de 'transformatie' van het Canadese boreale woud, nu de hele structuur ervan door de opwarming wordt 'geherconfigureerd', maar 'ondergang' is misschien een beter woord.[8]

Het onderzoek naar de 'de-megafaunicatie' van bossen – het verdwijnen van grote dieren zoals elanden, kariboes en beren wanneer zij naar het noorden trekken, en de gevolgen daarvan voor de biodiversiteit – is nog maar net begonnen. Als de struikden verdwijnt en de ratelpopulier wordt gehinderd door de hitte, kan de balsempopulier alle andere soorten verdringen. Er zijn nu al wetenschappers die naaldbos in het noorden als iets uit het verleden beschouwen.

'Dennen worden om de twee jaar of zo ziek, het is een cyclus. Ze zullen terugkomen,' zegt Eddie, zich herstellend. De anderen knikken omdat ze hem graag willen geloven.

'Hoelang zijn ze al zo?' vraag ik.

'Vijf jaar nu,' zegt Guy.

'Het komt wel goed,' zegt Eddie. 'We passen ons wel aan.'

De toekomst is geen veilige plaats voor de geest om te vertoeven.

George verbreekt de ongemakkelijke stilte door ostentatief een blikje Cola light te openen met een luid gesis.

'We leven van het land!' lacht hij, terwijl hij het blik ironisch opheft, en iedereen lacht met hem mee.

Die avond, nadat we gegeten en gedankt hebben voor de vijftien breedbekbaarzen die we met z'n negenen hebben opgegeten, zet Roger de kettingzaag in een verrotte stronk van een struikden en maken we een kampvuur. De weerkaatste vlammen dansen op het oppervlak van het zilveren meer, vlak en kalm in het maanlicht. Net als iedereen klaar is om naar bed te gaan, verschijnt er een glinstering recht voor ons. Het meer en de lucht houden samen een lichtshow. Achter wolken die de vorm hebben van vliegende adelaars, beginnen lichtbundels in een vage groenachtige kleur te pulseren. De gloed wordt sterker en onttrekt zich aan de wolken om zich vervolgens over de hele noordelijke hemel te verspreiden. Groen licht stroomt als water over galactische kiezelstenen, kabbelt over het zwart, en achter dit alles wordt een soort immanentie voelbaar.

De Anishinaabe zeggen dat de aurora borealis het geluid heeft van een ratel, en als je klapt verdwijnt ze. Eddie probeert dat, maar het werkt niet. Sophia maakt haar kleinzoon wakker om het mee te maken, en wij staren allen als gehypnotiseerd naar het verschuivende, pulserende schouwspel. Iets in het licht en het moment beweegt mijn metgezellen om in hun moedertaal te spreken. De frequentie van het lachen neemt toe. Aidan kan het meeste van wat zijn grootmoeder zegt niet verstaan, maar daar gaat het niet om. Zij wil dat hij dit ervaart, dat hij het opneemt in zijn herinnering aan wie hij is en waar hij vandaan komt. Het is onmogelijk onze ogen af te wenden van deze bezielde aanwezigheid die alleen maar in kracht toeneemt. Tegen één uur 's nachts vult het noorderlicht de halve hemel, en het ritmische pulseren weerspiegelt in het meer.

'De geesten van onze voorouders zijn nog steeds sterk in dit gebied,' zegt Sophia. 'Ik wil dat mijn nakomelingen hier op dezelfde plek kunnen zitten en genieten zoals ik dat vandaag doe.' Ze weet dat de klimaatverandering eraan komt, ze weet dat die de dingen zal aantasten waarvan zij het meest houdt en die zij het meest koestert, maar haar troost en haar oplossing is het land.

'Als het eenmaal zover is, kunnen we overleven van dit land dat ons is gegeven', zegt Sophia. Ik denk dat ze gelijk heeft: de bevolking van Pimachiowin Aki behoort tot het best voorbereide deel van de mensheid wat betreft de opwarming van de aarde.

Zelfs nu de soorten veranderen en er nieuwe bijkomen, zijn hun reservaten afgelegen en ontoegankelijk. Ze hebben de controle over 30.000 vierkante kilometer land dat hen zeker kan voeden, kleden en huisvesten, al is dat dan misschien niet op de manier die ze gewend waren. Het bos is als een reddingsvlot. En de kennis van hun voorouders die hen de weg zal wijzen, is vooralsnog springlevend.

Maar Pimachiowin Aki is niet alleen voor de Anishinaabe. 'Wij geloven dat we een sterke bijdrage leveren aan de rest van de planeet,' zegt Sophia. De meeste inheemse wijsheid gaat over evenwicht, over vuur en water en de heilige relatie tussen die twee. Dit is de kennis, de boodschap, de heilige plicht die Pimachiowin Aki vertegenwoordigt.

De Anishinaabe hebben het in dat verband over de Profetie van het Zevende Vuur. Hun voorouders benoemden de tijdperken van de Anishinaabe-beschaving aan de hand van vuren. Het eerste verwijst naar hun begin aan de kust van de Atlantische Oceaan, het tweede naar hun verhuizing naar het westen, het derde spreekt over hun noodzaak om te verhuizen naar waar het 'voedsel op het water groeit' (de wilde rijst van Pimachiowin Aki), het vierde naar de komst van de vreemde mensen uit het oosten (de Europese kolonisten), het vijfde beschrijft hun bijna-vernietiging door toedoen van zwart geklede mensen met zwarte boeken (de missionarissen) en het zesde het moment waarop 'de beker van het leven bijna de beker van het verdriet zou worden.'[9] Dat is de tijd die net voorbij is.

Het volk van het zevende vuur moet een keuze maken. Het kan de vuurstok die het heeft gekregen gebruiken als scheppende kracht, om het pad van genezing en natuur te kiezen dat niet vooruit leidt maar terug, om de heilige wijsheid van de voorouders, de geesten en het land opnieuw te leren. Of het kan voortgaan op dit pad naar de vergetelheid. Alleen als het de juiste keuze maakt, mag het volk van het zevende vuur het achtste ontsteken. Een vuur van vernieuwing in een nieuwe wereld die anders zal zijn dan de oude. De Anishinaabe van Pimachiowin Aki en andere bewaard gebleven inheemse culturen zijn de vuurwachters van onze aarde, niet alleen bewaarders van hun eigen tradities en waarden, maar van een manier van kijken en handelen die respectvol is en in harmonie met de levende wereld.

Aidan is op de rots in slaap gevallen. Het is tijd om naar bed te gaan. Wanneer de zon weer opkomt op het zuivere koperkleurige water van Thunder Lake, zal het tijd zijn om het effect van het heilige werk van Pimachiowin Aki te volgen, om de invloed van het stroomgebied – stroomafwaarts – te volgen.

De kano's stuiteren op de golven, op weg naar het westen. Iedereen dompelt zijn waterflessen onder in het meer, dat volgens hen zuiverder is dan de rivier thuis, hoewel beide schoon genoeg zijn om van te drinken. Eddie vertelt me dat de zwarte spar een chemische stof bevat die zowel de lucht als het water zuivert, en dat wanneer het sap in de winter daalt, dat iets doet met de grondwaterspiegel waardoor de vissen onder het ijs kunnen overleven. Alweer een oude wijsheid die de wetenschap zou moeten onderzoeken.

Aan het eind van het meer, wanneer we de bovenloop van de Poplar Rivier opvaren, steekt Clint zijn neus in de lucht. 'Ruik je dat? De geur van thuis!' roept hij. Clint beweert dat hij net als een zalm zijn thuisrivier kan herkennen aan de unieke chemische samenstelling van het water. Wanneer er bomen worden gekapt of vervuiling optreedt, verandert de samenstelling van een rivier of raakt deze onherkenbaar in de war en keert de zalm niet meer terug. Het is een hele prestatie dat een rivier zijn geur kan behouden tot aan de oceaan, of toch in elk geval genoeg ervan om herkenbaar te zijn, ondanks de industriële catastrofe die Lake Winnipeg is. De scherpe tonen van die rijke zwarte grond moeten heel sterk zijn. Honderden kilometers stroomafwaarts, in de ijzige wateren van de Hudson Bay, kan de zalm of de walvis die terugkeert naar de monding van de Churchill nog steeds de bomen van het Thunder Lake proeven.

Churchill, Manitoba, Canada
58° 46' 06" N

De plaatsen in Canada's afgelegen noorden worden bediend door vliegtuigen alsof dat een soort peperdure bussen zijn. Het vliegtuig van First Air dat mij vanuit Winnipeg naar Churchill brengt, moet eerst naar de kale nederzetting Rankin Inlet op de noordwestelijke oever van Hudson Bay vliegen, alvorens te keren en weer zuidwaarts te vliegen. Het vliegtuig is in tweeën gedeeld – passagiers zitten achterin, terwijl de voorste helft is gereserveerd voor vracht. De omweg geeft me vanuit de lucht een goed overzicht van het taiga-toendra-ecotoon die zich uitstrekt van Churchill helemaal tot aan de Arctische Oceaan. Terwijl bijvoorbeeld op Groenland de poolwoestijn en de boomgrens griezelig dicht bij elkaar liggen, is het ecotoon hier 650 kilometer breed. De struikgrens loopt helemaal door tot in het uiterste noorden van de Arctische archipel van Nunavut.

Dan is dit het moment om te discussiëren over de definitie van 'boomgrens'. Volgens één opvatting beschrijft die het noordelijkste punt waarop er nog bomen groeien van meer dan vijf meter hoog. Toch lijkt dat een beetje gemeen tegenover de winterharde en vastberaden, onvolgroeide sparren die dit land bedekken met ware verschansingen van krummholz. Deze bomen zijn xerofyten: ze zijn aangepast aan een xeretisch landschap waarin het water en de temperaturen zeer beperkt zijn en ze maar in beperkte mate worden blootgesteld aan fotonen. Ze vormen een steunpunt tussen de toendra en de boomgrens. Volgens een andere opvatting is de boomgrens de noordelijke grens van de bos-toendrazone voorbij het aaneengesloten bos waar het evenwicht tussen bos en toendra doorslaat ten gunste van de toendra. Die lijn vastleggen op een concreet punt ergens tussen Churchill en Rankin Inlet zou onmogelijk zijn zonder gedetailleerd onderzoek van satellietbeelden. Vraag het echter aan een kariboejager van het inheemse Sayisi-Dene-volk, en hij zal het instinctief weten.

De *Sayisi-Dene* – bij de Europeanen bekend als Chipewyan,

de naam die hun buren, de Cree, hen gaven – noemen zichzelf het 'volk onder de zon' en verwijzen naar hun traditionele leefgebied als 'het land van de kleine stokjes', de vlakke krummholzgebiedentussen taiga en toendra. Het is een groot gebied. Aan het noordelijke uiteinde ervan, bij het Great Slave Lake in de Northwest Territories, overlapt hun grondgebied dat van de Inuit. Voordat de Hudson Bay Company hen naar zich toetrok in het kader van de bonthandel, volgden ze de kariboes van de rand van het boreale woud naar hun kalvergebieden op de toendra in de zomer en weer terug in de winter. De scheidslijn tussen de leefgebieden bepaalde hun agenda en hun manier van leven.

Een verhaal dat de Sayisi-Dene elkaar vertellen vertelt over hoe mensen en kariboes lang geleden samenleefden, maar dat dit veranderde toen enkele vrouwen probeerden zich de kariboes toe te eigenen door met messen merktekens op hun huid en oren aan te brengen, zoals de Sami doen. De kariboes werden boos en renden weg. Toen ze uiteindelijk werden overgehaald om terug te komen, waren ze voortaan veel meer op hun hoede voor mensen. In veel onderzoeken worden ze dan ook een 'signaalsoort' genoemd, een die het gevoeligst is voor verstoring. Kariboes in heel Canada worden nu ernstig bedreigd. Slechts enkele van de resterende kuddes worden geacht zichzelf in stand te kunnen houden. Er zijn inmiddels andere soorten verschenen in het ecotoon.

'Elanden zijn tegenwoordig op de taiga net als vee,' zegt Dave Daley, een inheemse jager uit Churchill. Dus daar zijn de elanden van Pimachiowin Aki allemaal naartoe! En hier in het stroomgebied van Hudson Bay is het bos tenminste nog intact genoeg zodat ze door een ononderbroken corridor kunnen trekken. Dergelijke corridors worden steeds belangrijker, want naarmate de opwarming van de aarde de habitats verder naar het zuiden aantast of het er gewoon te warm maakt, wordt het vermogen van dieren om zich te verplaatsen nu al een zaak van leven of dood.

'De zwarte beren zijn er ook al, verdorie,' zegt Daley. 'Het klimaat is geschikt voor het dier, ook al moet hun normale habitat van bomen nog volgen. Wetenschappers schatten dat de boomgrens hier met ongeveer een meter per jaar naar het noorden opschuift, maar over zo'n uitgestrekt en gevarieerd terrein is het bijna onmogelijk om daar zeker van te zijn. Er vinden grote veranderingen plaats in de uitgestrekte vlakte met zijn plukjes sparren en streepjes water, die zich onder het vliegtuig, op drieduizend meter, ontvouwt. De huid van de aarde smelt, microbieel leven ontwaakt na duizenden, mogelijk miljoenen jaren bevroren te zijn geweest. De bodem transpireert – je zou ook kunnen spreken van afscheiden, aangezien er meer vocht wordt afgegeven dan opgenomen – en de dieren en planten nemen er nota van. Dit is een nieuwe wereld en intelligent leven – de slimme genen – snuffelt eraan, stuurt uitlopers, zaden en verkenners op pad, op weg naar het noorden, in voorbereiding op wat er komen gaat.

'Die zouden hier niet moeten zijn.'

'Wie? De bomen?'

'De balsempopulieren. Die horen hier helemaal niet thuis!' roept LeeAnn Fishback uit, een wetenschapper van het Churchill Northern Studies Center.

We rijden in LeeAnn's truck over een esker – een grindrug die door de terugtrekkende Laurentide-ijskap is ontstaan. Smeltwater onder het ijs heeft de morene uitgeslepen tot linten die het landschap rond de stad Churchill bepalen. Het is een van de jongste landschappen van de planeet dat nog steeds verandert. De laatste ijstijd heeft een lange staart. Het volume en het gewicht van het ijs veroorzaakten een depressie in de aardkorst van ongeveer 270 meter diep. Toen de ijskap smolt, liep het water niet meteen naar zee, maar bleef het op de laagvlakte van de Hudson Baai liggen en vormde zo de binnenzee van Lake Agassiz. Uiteindelijk, zo'n 8000 jaar geleden, loste de ijskap die het smeltwater tegenhield op, waardoor het grootste deel van de 841.000 vierkante kilometer van Lake Agassiz in twee opeenvolgende golven door de Hudson Strait de oceaan in kon stromen. Wetenschappers schatten dat deze 150.000 kubieke kilometer water de wereldwijde zeespiegel met een meter heeft doen stijgen en de inspiratie heeft gevormd voor legendes over overstromingen in laaggelegen gebieden en het scheppingsverhaal van de Ojibwe-volken over een land dat uit het water oprijst.[10]

Ontdaan van al dat gewicht, stijgt het land nog steeds met een snelheid van ongeveer drie meter per eeuw in een proces dat post-glaciale rebound wordt genoemd. Het effect is het duidelijkst zichtbaar aan de kustlijn. In de verte beukt de grijze branding op het grind langs de vlakke rotskust. Het strand wordt elk jaar een paar meter breder omdat de bodem stijgt en het water zich terugtrekt. De wind draagt regenvlagen over de sombere toendra die als een soort littekens de sporen draagt van gravelwagens en de toendrabuggy's waarin de toeristen op ijsbeersafari gaan. Ze ziet eruit als een maanlandschap en als de permafrost niet zou ontdooien, zouden de sporen op deze tere grond bijna net zo lang blijven staan als sporen op de maan.

De weg over de esker voert ons in een kaarsrechte lijn landinwaarts, in de richting van de subglaciale rivieren die de route van de terugtrekkende ijskap in omgekeerde richting volgen. Verder van zee neemt de vegetatie toe. Het zijn meestal wilgen die op het blootliggende grind van de stuwwal staan. Op de lager gelegen moerassen aan weerszijden staan sparren en tamaracks (Noord-Amerikaanse lariks) bijeen op verhoogde heuvels, 'palsa's' genaamd. Deze ronde veenheuvels worden gevormd wanneer het veen uitzet en inkrimpt door dooi en bevriezing. Ze bevatten een kern van ijs die in vocht voorziet, maar het droge veen eromheen is beter gedraineerd en zorgt voor een minder waterrijke omgeving voor bomen. Dat verklaart dan ook het verschijnen van eilandjes bomen overal in de vennen. Dit zijn de gezonde bomen. In de moerassen staan tamaracks en sparren, die vroeger van de kortstondige vochtigheid van de zomer genoten als een verademing na de droge permafrostwinter, nu met hun wortels in het water, en sterven af door te veel dooi.

Het regent en het is koud. Twintig graden kouder dan Poplar River dat slechts een paar honderd kilometer zuidelijker ligt. Dit is de diversiteit van het temperatuurbereik waar Diana het over had en die maakt dat het boreale gebied zich zo makkelijk kan aanpassen. Het heeft al eerder extremen doorgemaakt.

Vanaf onze uitkijkplaats op de bergkam overzien we de ontelbare poelen die het toendra-veengebied bespikkelen - zwarte schijven water, afgezet met schuim als schimmige kappen, bekleed met vossenbont. Ze zijn LeeAnns specialiteit. Het verhaal van de veengebieden is aan de cycli van deze meertjes af te meten. Net als in Schotland stapelt turf zich hier al vierduizend jaar lang op de harde ondergrond op met een millimeter per jaar.

Het bos is hier één of twee keer gekomen en ook weer gegaan, en al die koolstof is in het veen opgeslagen: 1,1 triljoen ton ervan – meer koolstof dan de mens tot nu toe heeft uitgestoten door verbranding van fossiele brandstoffen.[11] Deze platte, miezerige vlakte die bezaaid is met sparren en tamarack en zich ononderbroken eindeloos in alle richtingen voortzet, was ooit een dicht woud. Spoedig na de terugtrekking van Lake Agassiz rukten de bomen op door een bres, tot 320 kilometer ten noorden van hier, helemaal tot aan Rankin Inlet. Toen, 5500 jaar geleden, werd het kouder en trokken ze zich terug naar hun huidige breedtegraad. Nu verzamelen ze zich voor een hernieuwde aanval op hun vroegere grondgebied, en bomen die al 5000 jaar dood zijn beginnen opnieuw te rotten. Dat is wat de opwarming van turf inhoudt: de tot stilstand gebrachte ontbinding, vastgelegde historische emissies, die allemaal tegelijk vrijkomen. En daarom is de opwarming van het boreale woud zo gevaarlijk. We moeten niet alleen bang zijn voor het haperende vermogen van het woud om koolstof te blijven vasthouden, maar ook voor het vrijkomen van alle koolstof die eerder door prehistorische bossen werd vastgelegd. Als Nadezjda in Rusland gelijk heeft en het omslagpunt al is gepasseerd waarop emissies van smeltende permafrost nu voor meer opwarming zullen zorgen, wat de mens ook doet, dan moeten we ons inderdaad grote zorgen gaan maken.

LeeAnn neemt een hand van het stuur en wijst naar een vlak stuk modder met een grasachtige rand. De meertjes drogen snel uit. De zwarte modder absorbeert meer straling, waardoor de grond nog verder opwarmt. De biologische activiteit in de meertjes neemt toe – vandaar het schuim – en wanneer de meertjes bevriezen, wat over enkele weken, eind oktober, het geval zal zijn, zullen er parelslierten in het ijs te zien zijn – kooldioxide, dat raadselachtige gas, eindelijk zichtbaar gemaakt. Die parels zijn een product van de laatste ontbindingen van de zomermaanden, omdat het afbreken van organisch materiaal de laatste zuurstof verbruikt. Wanneer het water vervolgens helemaal tot op de bodem bevriest, verschijnen er grotere bellen dieper in de ijsstructuur. Je kunt een naald in deze bubbels prikken en het gas in brand steken. Het is methaan, zoals in de Laptevzee ten noorden van Siberië, waar de anaërobe afbraak in het sediment is doorgegaan zonder zuurstof. LeeAnns studenten vinden dat een leuk experiment.

LeeAnn stopt de auto. De wind slaat de regen tegen het raam. Ze loopt met bakken tegelijk naar beneden.

'Zie je dat?'

Een zaailing van de balsempopulier, niet meer dan vijf jaar oud, knikt in de wind. Tussen de wilgen, sparren en lariksen is hij zeker de vreemde eend in de bijt, met zijn grote bladeren die vroegrijp in de windvlagen wapperen. Hij lijkt het goed te doen: zijn stam is groen en sterk, de bladeren hebben een gezonde kleur. Hij geniet duidelijk van het mineraalrijke grind van de esker, en is daarin niet de enige. Wanneer we verder rijden, zien we langs de weg steeds meer jonge balsempopulieren die met de wilgen concurreren om de carbonaatrotsen die uit de kalksteen van het Canadese Schild zijn geërodeerd. Over honderd jaar zal deze weg een laan zijn met tientallen meters hoge populieren, vergelijkbaar met een landweggetje in Zuid-Frankrijk.

De esker eindigt bij een kame – een voorgebergte waar twee eskers samenkomen en waar de terugtrekkende ijskap een ijsberg heeft achtergelaten die is gesmolten en een hooggelegen meer heeft gevormd. Het grind is hier gezakt en aan weerszijden van de weg strekt het water zich uit. De bewoners noemen de plaats Twin Lakes.

We stappen uit de truck de stormwind in. LeeAnn schuift

twee patronen in haar geweer en hangt het over de schouder van haar felgekleurde regenjas. Het is het ijsbeerseizoen in Churchill, wanneer de dieren door het terugtrekkende ijs op het land achterblijven en de wijfjes op de toendra hun jongen krijgen. Dit lage struikgewas met de ontdooiende permafrost waar makkelijk in te graven is, is een goede plek voor hun soort.

We banen ons een weg door de bessenstruiken die bijna de stronken van de in een recente brand verbrande sparren overweldigen om de bomen te bereiken waarvan LeeAnn zegt dat ze hier niet horen te staan. Op een kleine helling boven het meer staat een half dozijn indrukwekkende balsempopulieren. Ze zijn veel groter dan ik me had voorgesteld, meer dan twintig meter hoog, en de massa's bladeren boven me maken een klapperend geluid in de wind. Van dichtbij is de schors zeer ruw, gebarsten en gegroefd in diepe geulen, grijs en zwart en glibberig van mos en zwart korstmos. Schors van vijftien centimeter dik die niet verbrandt en niet bevriest. De binnenste schors heeft doorlaatbare membranen die een snelle verplaatsing van water uit het levende weefsel mogelijk maken, zodat zich geen destructieve ijskristallen in de cellen kunnen vormen. De stam van de grootste is breder dan mijn borstkas. Het bladafval is dicht, als een rottend tapijt, en als ik mijn handen in de donkere natte lagen steek, ruikt die ook zo. Dit is wat het kreupelhout voedt en het zo rijk maakt aan jeneverbes, wilgenroosje, moerasrozemarijn, bosbessen, roos, wilde kruisbessen, frambozen en rode bessen. LeeAnn kende de plek al, want dit is waar ze fruit komt plukken om jam te maken.

Het is schokkend om te zien dat populieren zo ver noordelijk in een heel ander gezelschap verkeren dan hun buren in het dichtbegroeide bos meer naar het zuiden. We begrijpen nog steeds niet goed hoe soorten zich verspreiden. Waarom staan sommige bomen hier en niet ergens anders? Hoe zijn ze hier gekomen? De witte spar, die door de wind wordt bestoven, zich gemakkelijk verspreidt en gemakkelijk ontkiemt, vormt als vanzelf de voorste rand van de boomgrens zoals die zich in de loop van eeuwen en millennia heeft verplaatst. De balsempopulier vindt seksuele voortplanting moeilijk. De kleine gele bloempjes die uit de olieachtige knoppen van de vrouwelijke bomen komen en er elk voorjaar uitzien als de ronde kopjes van rupsen die uit hun poppen breken, komen nog voor de bladeren zich hebben ontplooid. Ze trekken vogels en insecten aan die hongerig zijn naar de eerste nectar van de lente. Als de bloemen vallen, komt het hele katje los. De vrucht rijpt wanneer de bladeren volgroeid zijn en splitst zich in tweeën om de minuscule zaden vrij te geven, elk voorzien van een pluk lange, witte, zijdeachtige haren die de wind moet vangen. Dit 'katoen' waaraan de andere populieren hun bijnaam *cottonwood* ontlenen, werd vroeger door de inheemse bevolking gesponnen voor verband en om de wiegjes van zuigelingen mee te bekleden. Het pluis werd ook toegevoegd aan buffelbessen en tot schuim geklopt om er 'Indiaans ijs' van te maken.

Dat zaad moet vallen op een vochtige voedingsbodem, met gemakkelijke toegang tot minerale grond (recent verbrande plaatsen zijn het best), die vervolgens gedurende verscheidene weken bij de juiste temperatuur vochtig moet blijven om ontkieming mogelijk te maken. Maar de zaden overleven niet lang, en gezien de voorliefde van de balsempopulier voor rivieren, maken overstromingen vaak korte metten met fragiele zaailingen in oevergebieden. Het brandinterval zo ver noordelijk bedraagt meer dan vierhonderd jaar. Een zwervend, bevrucht populierzaadje zou, zelfs als het hier terechtkwam, precies moeten komen na een brand zoals die van een paar jaar geleden, wil het een kans maken. Vandaar de neiging van de boom om verder zuidelijk te blijven en vandaar ook LeeAnns verbazing over de aanwezigheid van balsempopulieren hier aan de boomgrens aan de kant van de Twin Lakes.

Steve Mamet, LeeAnns collega, heeft kernboringen gedaan in de plaatselijke sparren, tamaracks en berken en daarbij vastgesteld dat de oudste ongeveer vierhonderd jaar oud zijn. Dat heeft hij echter nog niet gedaan voor de balsempopulieren. Ik hoop dat hij dat nog gaat doen. Is hun verschijnen misschien een tamelijk recent en toevallig gebeuren? Zijn het vluchtelingen, de laatste achterblijvers van hun soort uit een tijd toen het woud nog noordelijker lag? Of zijn ze door mensen geplant en wachten ze sindsdien op een warme periode zoals de huidige om hun uitlopers langs de grindweg uit te zetten? De eskers van de Twin Lakes hebben aanzienlijke archeologische bewijzen opgeleverd van een Inuit-gerelateerde beschaving van meer dan duizend jaar oud, ouder dan de Inuit 'Dorset'-cultuur van de middeleeuwen.

'Het was een heilige boom, weet je nog,' zei Diana later. 'Misschien hebben ze hem meegebracht.' Net als de Kelten en hun heilige Schotse dennen. Waarom ook niet? De populier zou de habitat voor vissen hebben verbeterd, en het zout van de as van de populier werd gebruikt bij het conserveren en koken van vis. In dit deel van de wereld, net als elders – in Schotland, Rusland en Alaska – volgden bomen en mensen samen de terugtrekking van het ijs. Misschien hadden ze elkaar harder nodig dan wij beseffen.

Churchill is altijd een voorpost geweest. De stad werd gesticht als een versterkte haven voor de Britse handel met de inheemse bevolking en voor de winning van grondstoffen uit de waterscheiding van de Hudson Bay. Koning Karel II van Engeland verleende de Hudson Bay Company het eigendomsrecht op alle grond die zich afzette in de baai, een gebied dat bekend staat als Rupert's Land en zich uitstrekt tot in het huidige Minnesota en Noord-Dakota. Het lot van Churchill is altijd afhankelijk geweest van de grillen van mensen ver weg.

Het besluit om een spoorlijn aan te leggen van Winnipeg naar Churchill (waarover een trein reed met de onvergetelijke naam 'Muskeg Express') bepaalde de rol van de stad in de twintigste eeuw als een graanoverslagplaats die de oogst van de prairie naar de zee bracht, juist toen de Hudson Bay Company haar beste tijd had gehad. Het besluit van het Amerikaanse leger om onderzoek te doen naar het noorderlicht en de magnetosfeer van de aarde leidde er in de jaren 1950 en '60 toe dat veel wetenschappers naar de stad kwamen en er een erfenis achterlieten van betonnen lanceertorens midden in de toendra, met de brokstukken van mislukte lanceringen verspreid over het Wapusk National

Park. Wanneer ik de stad in 2019 bezoek, is men er nog steeds verbitterd over dat de eigenaar Omnitrax drie jaar eerder heeft besloten om de haven te sluiten.

In het stadhuis – een detonerend betonnen gebouw aan de monding van de Churchill met een overdekt basketbalveld, een gezondheidscentrum, een hockeybaan, een gesloten bibliotheek en een zwembad dat drie dagen per week open is – vertellen de drie medewerkers die hun kantooruren proberen door te komen dat de stad sindsdien in een shellshock verkeert. Het besluit is onlangs teruggedraaid en het eerste schip in jaren wordt binnenkort verwacht, maar de aarzeling van het bedrijf heeft veel banen en ten minste één onderwijzer op de school gekost. Over de opwarming van de aarde praten de mensen op het kantoor met dezelfde berusting en hetzelfde gevoel van onrechtvaardigheid: de zoveelste ellende die hun van veraf wordt aangedaan.

Verderop, in een houten hut die hij zelf heeft gebouwd van sparrenstammen die hij bij de Twin Lakes heeft gekapt, leunt David Daley achterover in een houten stoel. De sparren die hij gebruikte zaten vol met Choristoneura fumiferana – anders zou hij geen levende bomen hebben gekapt – en het eerste jaar in zijn nieuwe hut kwamen er voortdurend kevers tevoorschijn uit de stammen in de woonruimte. Hij is opgegroeid met jagen en vallen zetten in de omgeving van Churchill en hij heeft in die tijd grote veranderingen gezien: in de moerassen verliest de tamarack zijn schors en zet geen zaad meer af, de sparren zijn gedecimeerd door de Choristoneura fumiferana, de berk duikt overal op en de balsempopulier ontspruit overal langs de rivieroever.

‘De populieren zijn al zo groot sinds ik een klein kind was,’ zegt Dave. Hij vertelt hoe de bomen rond Churchill het jarenlang goed hebben gedaan, maar door het moeras worden overweldigd nu de permafrost smelt. ‘Je kunt zien wat er onder de grond gebeurt door wat er boven gebeurt.’

De populieren aan de Twin Lakes zijn echter tevreden, daar op de grindrug. Ze vinden het daar prettig, zegt hij. Grind vriest niet zo hard aan als aarde, het is warmer, minder aangetast door het veen. Mensen hielden ook van de grindruggen. Ze bouwden daar steeds weer hun nederzettingen. Dave heeft zeeschelpen, walvisbotten en tentringen gevonden in kuilen op de esker, niet ver van de populieren. Het ligt voor de hand, denkt hij, dat zijn voorouders van het Cree-volk, of misschien nog verder terug, een zaadje of een zaailing hebben meegenomen en zo honderden jaren van natuurlijke zaadverspreiding hebben overgeslagen. Met 'natuurlijk' bedoelen wetenschappers de verspreiding door andere dieren dan mensen.

We praten over de invasie van de balsempopulier langs de hele rivier, en over het mogelijk regenererende effect van de bomen op de visstand, maar Dave schudt zijn hoofd.

'Praat me niet van vis! Die is er niet!'

In dit geval is duidelijk wie de boosdoener is. Een ander bedrijf in de stad heeft zijn hoofdvestiging ver weg: een energiebedrijf genaamd Manitoba Hydro.

'Vroeger zette ik mijn net uit en kon ik mijn honden dagenlang zuigbaarzen voeren. Nu zit er niets meer. Manitoba Hydro heeft de rivier om zeep geholpen. Ze lieten het waterpeil zo laag zakken dat ze tot op de bodem bevroor, waardoor al het leven werd gedood. De dam houdt het sediment van de rivier tegen, en daarmee alle voedingsstoffen. Geen wonder dat de touroperators nu kunnen zeggen dat je de walvissen zo goed kunt zien zwemmen! Al het goede is uit het water gefilterd.

'En er zijn ook niet langer vogels op de rivier. Vroeger deed ik elk jaar voor Natural Resources Canada een telling op de rivier, maar nu is er niets meer te zien. Ik heb geklaagd bij Manitoba Hydro, maar die zeiden: "We gaan geen miljoenen dollars water verspillen zodat jij kunt gaan vissen."'

Manitoba Hydro laat om de zoveel tijd enorme hoeveelheden water ontsnappen, maar extreme wisselingen in het waterpeil dragen niet bij aan een stabiel ecosysteem. Telkens wanneer de verschillende lagen van de rivier juist weer tot leven zijn komen en er zich zaailingen van de balsempopulier aan de oever van de rivier vestigen, worden deze weggespoeld. Het volume van die overstromingen is overigens alleen nog maar toegenomen doordat de rivieren de Churchill en de Nelson met elkaar zijn verbonden. Inmiddels hebben de overstromingen die plaatsvinden wanneer de dammen hun water loslaten zelfs een naam. De lokale bevolking noemt ze *hydrotides*, waterkrachtgetijden. De Poplar River mondt uit in Lake Winnipeg, dat vroeger via de Nelson River de oceaan bereikte. Maar nu de twee rivieren zijn samengevoegd, worden de mineralen, voedingsstoffen en zuren van Pimachiowin Aki en de andere bossen in het stroomgebied, die de unieke chemische signatuur van de Poplar River vormen, in plaats daarvan via turbines geloosd in de Churchill of de Nelson, afhankelijk van hoeveel mensen in heel Manitoba die dag hun airconditioning aanzetten, waterkokers gebruiken of televisie kijken. Wie in Manitoba op een schakelaar drukt, denkt waarschijnlijk niet aan het water dat zijn comfort mogelijk maakt, en niet aan de signatuur van de bodem die de bomen van het stroomgebied verbindt met de vissen in de rivier en de walvissen in de zee.

Het positieve effect van de opwarming van de aarde is in Churchill duidelijk te zien: poolexpedities, ijszeevaarten, ijsberensafari's, toendrapubs, aurorahotels en talloze andere toeristische attracties met een noordelijk thema zijn zij-aan-zij te vinden aan de brede hoofdstraat van het Noord-Amerikaanse pioniersstadje, en de straat is bezaaid met roestende containers, dichtgetimmerde bedrijven en een enkele benzinepomp. Het enige verkeer bestaat uit af en toe een suv met knobbelige banden met diepe loopvlakken of een enorme 'argo' toendrabuggy met wielen die in een dagbouwmijn lijken thuis te horen, maar eigenlijk zijn ontworpen om toeristen door de wetlands te vervoeren.

Sinds de onduidelijkheid rond de sluiting van de haven heeft de stad moeite gedaan om zich als toeristische bestemming te profileren. De voor de hand liggende strategie was in te spelen op de groeiende belangstelling voor het kwetsbare landschap van het Noordpoolgebied dat mensen willen zien voordat het voor altijd verdwenen is, en Churchill heeft het geluk dat twee van de meest aansprekende soorten Arctische megafauna zich hier voortplanten: de ijsbeer en de witte dolfijn.

Ik stap voor het Polar Hotel op een bus met meer dan honderd andere toeristen uit de hele wereld: Californië, Maleisië, China, Ierland en Australië. We nemen de weg naar het oosten van de stad, langs de gemeentelijke stortplaats en graansilo's, zo lang en zo hoog als een gestrande olietanker. De betonnen torens steken boven de stad uit als een soort industriële dictator die de inwoners eraan herinnert dat ze in economisch opzicht gevangen zitten. Hoog in de lucht hangt een transportband boven de zee, klaar om het graan in het langverwachte schip te storten. De roestige stalen en afbrokkelende betonnen silo's, gebouwd in de jaren 1930, bepalen de aanblik van de oever van de riviermonding. Braakliggend terrein, wilgen, wilgenroosjes en oude gaashekken scheiden het terrein van de jachthaven waar de bus ons afzet aan het eind van een vierkant van drijvende pontons. We trekken reddingsvesten aan, luisteren naar veiligheidsinstructies en gaan dan aan boord van een vloot zwarte rubberboten die over het melkachtige water pruttelen. Het pas gesmolten zee-ijs geeft de riviermonding een ondoorzichtig glinsterende, mineraalblauwe kleur.

Het is hoogtij, en het water is doodstil. Aan de overkant komt nevel van de toendra naar de oever gerold. De hemel is hetzelfde rokerige grijs als de zee. De Churchill River is achthonderd meter breed, heeft een zwakke stroming en vloeit met een minimum aan inspanning in de zwoele zee. De rubberboten cirkelen aan de oppervlakte als vliegen op een vijver. Ik had verwacht dat het bij dit soort walvissafari's niet gegarandeerd was dat je er ook een te zien kreeg, maar mijn medepassagiers veren al overeind zodra we ons bij de hoofdstroom voegen: 'Daar! Daarginds! En daar...' Overal rondom ons breken witte ruggen als een soort klodders slagroom door het wateroppervlak. De rivier kolkt van de witte dolfijnen, *Delphinpterus leucas* – de witte dolfijn zonder rugvin.

Onze gids loodst onze opblaasbare boot in lussen rond de etende walvissen. Er is een school voor elke boot en nog veel meer. Ze zwemmen kriskras om ons heen, onder de boot, rollen zich op hun zij om deze vreemde toeschouwers bij hun middagmaal goed te kunnen zien. Van alle baleinwalvissen is de witte de enige met een flexibele nek. Omdat hij niet de vergroeide wervels heeft van zijn neven, kan hij draaien en keren, waardoor hij nog meer een antropomorfe uitstraling krijgt. Zijn kromme snuit wordt altijd getekend door een grijns, en door de echolocatie-apparatuur die hij heeft in een bol op zijn voorhoofd, de 'meloen', krijgt hij een groef in zijn voorhoofd die op wenkbrauwen lijkt. Dat geeft hem een gezicht als een soort nieuwsgierige nerd. Het zijn kleine walvissen, maar ze worden toch meer dan vier meter lang – forse, intelligente wezens, die langer zijn dan de boot en met tien keer zoveel als wij. Vijf of zes van hen blijven een poosje achter de rubberboot hangen, genietend van het zog. De gids weet niet zeker of ze dat nu doen vanwege de warmte van de uitlaat of vanwege het zuurstofverrijkende effect van de kolkende schroef, of misschien dat de frequentie van een Yamaha-motor van negentig paardenkrachten iets hypnotiserends heeft.

Het hoogtepunt van de tocht bestaat uit het laten zakken van een hydrofoon – een waterdichte microfoon – achter de boot. Uit de luidspreker op de bodem van de boot klinken plots piepjes en trillers, gefluit, langere uithalen en ritmisch klikken. De witte dolfijnen voeren daar beneden een verhit gesprek, en als ze hun eigen stemmen terughoren, worden ze nog drukker. Ze kennen twaalfhonderd verschillende geluidssignalen, een veel verfijnder alfabet dan *Homo sapiens*. Inmiddels is aangetoond dat witte dolfijnen hun stem verheffen om gehoord te worden, net als mensen, maar op een gegeven moment geven ze het op. Hun stressniveau hangt nauw samen met de mate van geluidsoverlast. De enorme toename van de scheepvaart in het noordpoolgebied, die naar verwachting het gevolg zal zijn van het verdwijnen van het zee-ijs, vormt wellicht de meest dodelijke bedreiging voor de dolfijnen die 'zien' met echolocatie en die in een bijna permanent web van geluiden leven. Ze zijn voortdurend met elkaar in gesprek: leven is kletsen. Er zijn letterlijk hele talen die de mens nog moet leren verstaan.

En er komen er nog meer die zich aan de achterkant van de

Zodiac verdringen om een blik te werpen op die drijvende mensen die hun gesprek papegaaien. Aan de rand van de school sluit zich een moederdier aan. Op haar rug zit een kalf, ongeveer zo groot als een volwassen mens, nog met de resten van zijn eerste oranje huid. De witte dolfijnen kalven in het ondiepe water van de riviermonding dat relatief warm is en meer zuurstof bevat dan de open oceaan. Vrouwtjes dragen hun jongen gedurende twintig maanden en voeden ze tot ze drie zijn, terwijl ze in de loop van de tijd en door de melk steeds witter worden. In gevangenschap geboren exemplaren hebben nooit langer dan dertig jaar geleefd, waardoor onderzoekers aanvankelijk dachten dat de levensduur van witte dolfijnen merkwaardig kort was, maar inmiddels wordt aangenomen dat ze meer dan honderd jaar oud kunnen worden. Dit kalf is hier waarschijnlijk twee jaar geleden verwekt. Witte dolfijnen keren, net als zalmen, altijd terug naar dezelfde rivier.

Het is logisch dat het thuisinstinct is geëvolueerd als een hormonaal-chemische reddingslijn, terug naar een veilige plaats waar de voortplanting in relatieve rust en met een overvloed aan voedsel kan plaatsvinden. Maar dat goed afgestemde en intelligente plan lijkt eerder een risico te vormen nu klimaatzones en oceaanstromingen onvoorspelbaar worden. Het opportunisme van de ontdekkingsreiziger of de kolonist is een andere vaardigheid, een andere mentale geografie dan de genetische roep van de thuishaven. Zullen de witte dolfijnen en andere dieren in staat zijn om in zo'n korte tijd te leren? Zal er eigenlijk wel een klimaatanaloog – de wetenschappelijke term voor een locatie die overeenkomt met hun huidige habitat en verspreidingsgebied – bestaan in een wereld die drie, vier of vijf graden warmer is? Terwijl alle boreale soorten verder noordwaarts trekken, kunnen de soorten op de hoogste breedtegraden, zoals de witte dolfijn en de ijsbeer, niet nog verder noordelijk gaan.

'Wat is er dan zo speciaal aan deze plek?' vraag ik onze gids. 'Waarom blijven ze hier terugkomen?'

'Er zijn verschillende theorieën,' zegt hij. 'Zo zouden ze vervellen op de rotsen in de rivier. Het is hier ondieper en de orka's kunnen niet in de riviermonding komen. Bovendien is er hier veel voedsel. Maar eigenlijk weten we het niet echt.'

Ik denk dat ik het misschien wel weet. De groep die ons volgt valt uiteen wanneer de hydrofoon wordt opgehaald, en de witte dolfijnen schieten in kleinere groepjes door het water, op jacht naar lodde, *Mallatus villosus*. De lodde is in deze tijd van het jaar zo overvloedig dat er massa's aanspoelen op de gletsjerstranden. Bewoners nemen emmers vol mee, en anderen klagen over de stank. Wat onze gids niet vertelt, is dat de lodde hier is vanwege het plankton, en het plankton en fytoplankton waarmee ze zich voeden leeft hier vanwege de *sweet spot* waar al het goede van het smeltende zee-ijs samenkomt met het goede van de bomen dat stroomafwaarts komt.

De witte dolfijnen wagen zich alleen naar het zuiden in de riviermondingen om te kalven tijdens de korte dooi in de zomer. De rest van de tijd leven zij aan de rand van het pakijs en ademen ze door de barsten die in het ijs ontstaan, de zogenaamde polinia's, en in de geulen. In noodgevallen kunnen ze met hun geharde bolvormige koppen door het ijs breken om adem te halen. De 'dolfijn zonder rugvin' evolueerde zo om onder het zee-ijs te zwemmen en zich te voeden op de lagere trofische niveaus van de voedselketen met voorns, jonge zalmpjes, garnalen, plankton en schaaldieren, die allemaal afhankelijk zijn van de voedingsstoffen die de rivier afkomen of langzaam uit het zee-ijs zakken als een soort onderwaterregen, waardoor de oceaan wordt 'bemest'.

De cruciale rol van het zee-ijs als platform voor het zeeleven aan de basis van de voedselketen is al bekend sinds de jaren 1960, en toch wordt het snelle smelten ervan door velen nog steeds beschouwd als niet meer dan het betreurenswaardige verlies van een pittoreske omgeving of, wat erger is, een kans voor nieuwe scheepvaartroutes. Maar het is in feite een catastrofale verzwakking van de voedselketen in de oceanen – het mariene equivalent van het verdwijnen van enorme hoeveelheden vruchtbare bodem op het land.

Tijdens de winter vloeit de zware (vloeibare) pekel uit het zee-ijs en zakt naar de oceaanbodem, waarbij het een circulatie van het oceaanwater veroorzaakt die voedingsstoffen naar de oppervlakte stuwt. In de zoetwaterkristallen van het zee-ijs bevinden zich door het zout vrijgemaakte kanalen waarin diatomeeën, micro-organismen die in het ijs zweven, kunnen beginnen te gedijen. Zodra de zon na de poolwinter op het pakijs schijnt, dempen de ijskristallen het licht en neemt plankton het door professor Matsunaga en Diana geïdentificeerde ijzer, dat in het humuszuur zit, op en begint zich te delen.

De hele lente door blijft het plankton zich delen in het ijs. Dat proces bereikt een hoogtepunt bij het breken van het ijs, wanneer het plankton, eindelijk bevrijd uit zijn kristallen cocon, door de injectie van zoet water en de cruciale lading ijzer in de zee, zich als een razende kan delen en een feestmaal vormt voor de lodde en andere jonge vis, de kleine zalmpjes en de andere, net uit het ei gekropen jonge vis. Het zal niemand verbazen dat dit vooral gebeurt aan de mondingen van de grote rivieren. De essentiële vetzuren in vis – oliezuren, die worden gebruikt voor de productie van eieren en melk – zijn afkomstig van fytoplankton, dat ze maakt met de mineralen die zijn opgelost in zoet water en die hun oorsprong vinden in het water dat uit afbrekende bladeren sijpelt. Een maand na de dooi en de planktonbloei arriveren de witte dolfijnen voor hun feestmaal.

Er moet nauwkeurig aan een aantal voorwaarden worden voldaan wil het feestmaal mogelijk zijn: zo moeten er genoeg bomen zijn in het stroomgebied, niet te veel landbouwvervuiling, en mag de zee niet te warm worden. Het onzichtbare woud van de oceaan – de algen onderwater en in het intergetijdengebied – heeft een kritiek temperatuurverschil met de omringende zee nodig (koud water ten opzichte van de warmte die in de plant wordt opgewekt) om zich te kunnen voortplanten.

Het verdwijnende zee-ijs zal dingen veranderen voor de witte dolfijnen. Het zou bovendien de circulatiepatronen van de oceaan kunnen veranderen. De geschiedenis laat zien dat stromingen al eerder zijn veranderd, en dat dit van het ene op het andere moment kan plaatsvinden. Diana citeert geoloog Alan Morgan van de Universiteit van Waterloo in Ontario, die stelt dat het in twee weken tijd gebeurd kan zijn. Plotseling, op een dag, kan de Golfstroom zich bijvoorbeeld omkeren. Er heerst momenteel chaos in de oceanen, dus niemand kan voorspellen hoe de temperaturen en stromingen en het bereik van die stromingen zullen verschuiven. Computers kunnen geen nauwkeurige modellen maken omdat er te veel variabelen zijn. De eventuele terugkoppeling tussen de opwarming van de vegetatie op het land en de chemie van de zoetwaterafvoer op de primaire productie in de oceaan is een grote onbekende factor.

De witte dolfijnen worden al heel lang de kanaries van de oceaan genoemd vanwege hun melodieus tsjilpende gezang. Maar net als de bomen waarmee zij verbonden zijn, zijn ze nu ook op een andere manier als kanaries. Wanneer de kritieke productieve relatie tussen de bossen op het land en het bos onder de zee uiteenvalt, zullen de witte dolfijnen de eersten zijn die dat voelen. Voorlopig zijn de wetenschappers die de witte dolfijn bestuderen nog tevreden. Er zijn er 57.000 in Hudson Bay, hun aantal is stabiel, en de grootste concentratie bevindt zich in de Nelson River, de belangrijkste uitstroom van Pimachiowin Aki.

Maar Dave Daley is daar niet zo zeker van. In zijn blokhut van door wormen doorzeefd sparrenhout perst hij zijn lippen op elkaar en schudt zijn hoofd. Hij weet wat er met de witte dolfijnen van Kotzebue is gebeurd: ze verdwenen van het ene jaar op het andere. ‘Ze zeggen dat de witte dolfijn zich staande houdt. Maar... de lodde die ze gewend waren te eten, is er niet meer. En deze dieren leven heel lang. Ik weet het niet hoor. Ik wacht het af.’

Deze gracieuze, speelse, vrolijke dieren die rond de boot cirkelen, weten veel beter dan wij wat er daar beneden gebeurt. Met infrageluid kunnen ze over duizenden kilometers communiceren. Zoals Albert met de mensen in Brits Columbia praat via de beeftent, zo praten alle witte dolfijnen in de zee misschien wel de hele tijd met elkaar. De ene dag houden ze een virtuele conferentie en de volgende dag zijn ze weg.

6.

Een laatste tango met het ijs

Groenlandse lijsterbes, *Sorbus Groenlandica*

Narsarsuaq, Groenland
61° 09' 41" N

Kenneth Høegh plantte zijn eerste boom toen hij dertien was. Op zaterdagen en na schooltijd had hij een bijbaantje op de kinderboekenafdeling van de plaatselijke bibliotheek in Narsaq, in het uiterste zuiden van Groenland. Naar eigen zeggen was hij een boekenwurm. Op een dag kwam hij in een wetenschappelijk tijdschrift voor kinderen een artikel tegen over experimenten met het planten van bomen in een beschutte fjord, verder naar het noorden.

'Toen ik op Groenland opgroeide, waren bomen iets onbekends, iets vreemds,' zegt hij.

Er waren er geen in het stadje Narsaq, dat overigens een schilderachtig samenraapsel van pastelkleurige huizen is op een groene heuvel rond een natuurlijke haven die tijdens de winter altijd dichtvroor. Tijdens zijn korte leven had Kenneth nog maar weinig bomen gezien. Hij wilde zelf ook wel eens een experiment doen en vroeg zijn ouders een zaailing voor hem te kopen, die per vliegtuig uit IJsland kwam en die hij in de tuin van zijn ouders plantte. Het was een Siberische lariks, *Larix sibirica*. Zijn ouders zijn verhuisd, en de tuin is nu van de buren, maar de lariks staat er nog altijd. Inmiddels is hij vijf meter hoog, en Kenneth is 53.

Kenneth ging agronomie studeren aan de universiteit en werd landbouwadviseur voor boeren in Zuid-Groenland, terwijl hij zijn passie voor het planten van bomen bleef uitleven. De probleem voor aspirant-bosbouwers aan het eind van de twintigste eeuw in Groenland was dat er bijna geen bomen waren. Er waren echter wel twee bosbouwdeskundigen. Sinds de jaren 1970 hebben ecologen Poul Bjerge en Dr. Søren Ødum experimenten uitgevoerd in de vallei van Narsarsuaq, om na te gaan welke boomsoorten in Groenland zouden kunnen groeien. Het artikel dat Kenneth had gelezen, ging over hun werk, en uiteindelijk zou hij ook met hun gaan samenwerken.

In de jaren 1980 en '90 reisden Poul, Søren en Kenneth naar talloze plaatsen langs de Arctische boomgrens om winterharde exemplaren van boreale soorten te verzamelen en mee te nemen naar Groenland. Zij reisden naar Alaska, Yukon, British Columbia, Hudson Bay, Quebec, Noorwegen en dwars door Siberië van de Oeral tot de Altai, naar Kamtsjatka en Sachalin, en stelden zo een van de meest uitgebreide arboretums van boreale boomgrenssoorten ter wereld samen. Met tot dusver 110 soorten evenaart het dat van het Soekatsjev-Instituut in Krasnojarsk. Het doel van de wetenschappers was een referentie voor Groenland vast te stellen. Naarmate de temperatuur wereldwijd stijgt, is het een belangrijke informatiebron die veel verder reikt dan de grenzen van deze smalle groep fjorden: het vervult een signaalfunctie voor het noordelijke bos en kan een toekomstig refugium zijn voor soorten die elders op het punt van uitsterven staan.

Kenneth hield van de wetenschap van het vergelijkend onderzoek en de langetermijnstudie van individuele soorten, maar hij hield ook gewoon van het planten van bomen: tienduizenden Siberische lariksen, Engelmansparren, fijnsparren, witte dennen, draaidennen, Douglassparren, balsempopulieren en vele andere. Het huidige nationale arboretum, het Arboretum Groenlandicum, *Kalaallit Nunaata Orpiuteqarfia* in het Groenlands, is een jong bos dat de helft van de vallei van Narsarsuaq beslaat met meer dan een kwart miljoen bomen.

Wanneer het vliegtuig zijn steile draai maakt naar de monding van de fjord, wordt het verblindende wit en blauw gescheiden door een dunne wig van groen en geel gloeiend bos met af en toe een uitbarsting van bloedrood-oranje. Het is augustus 2019. Het bladerdak van de late nazomer vormt een plotse flits van leven in een verder kaal landschap van rotsen en gras, ingeklemd tussen de ijskap en de zee.

Dezelfde topografische omstandigheden die Narsarsuaq tot een goede plaats voor het planten van bomen maken, maakten het tot een ideale plaats, bijna de enige in Zuid-Groenland die vlak genoeg is, voor een landingsbaan. Als het aan de Inuit lag, zou Narsarsuaq geen nederzetting zijn. Een brede, open vallei zonder natuurlijke haven, ver van het zomerse zee-ijs, is weinig aantrekkelijk voor een volk dat afhankelijk is van de zee. Maar de luchtmacht van de Verenigde Staten, die de landingsbaan aanlegde, bekeek het niet vanuit het oogpunt van levensonderhoud. In 1941 waren de Duitsers net Denemarken binnengevallen, en de Amerikanen zochten een tussenstop, een plaats om de vloten B-17 vliegtuigen bij te tanken die op weg waren van Georgia via Canada en de Deense kolonie Groenland naar Schotland om in Europa te vechten. Alle voorraden en bouwmaterialen werden verscheept of ingevlogen, inclusief de vijfduizend manschappen die tijdens de Koude Oorlog de basis zouden bouwen die bekendstaat als Bluie West One.

De Deense regering zag geen reden om te morrelen aan de infrastructuur die zij in 1958 van de Amerikanen erfde, en bijna zeventig jaar later is Narsarsuaq nog steeds de enige internationale luchthaven buiten de hoofdstad Nuuk, de toegangspoort tot wat de plaatselijke VVV 'Zonnig Zuid-Groenland' noemt. Bezoekers worden getrakteerd op een moment in de lucht dat doet denken aan de slotscène van Stanley's Kubricks film *Dr. Strangelove*: vliegtuigen die uit Europa aankomen scheren over de verblindende ijskap tussen gekartelde zwarte pieken, hangen in een hoek van negentig graden boven een turkooizen fjord, bezaaid met ijsbergen, en dalen dan steil af naar wat wel 's werelds gevaarlijkste landingsbaan wordt genoemd, met één uiteinde dat tot aan het water loopt en het andere dat eindigt op een klif boven een schuimende gletsjerrivier.

Ik krijg een berichtje binnen op mijn telefoon zodra we de angstaanjagende landing hebben overleefd en de vliegtuigtrappen zijn afgedaald, het asfalt op, rondom omringd door majestueuze bergen: 'Je vindt me in het restaurant van het hotel.'

Op de grond in de eenvoudige terminal met een defecte bagageband verdringen tientallen toeristen met grote felgekleurde rugzakken en anoraks elkaar. Ze willen graag door de wildernis trekken en het ijs zien voordat het verdwenen is. Dit is de laatste zomer voor de pandemie, en de zaken gaan goed: het jaar daarvoor waren er 92.677 vliegtuigpassagiers.

Sommige bezoekers wachten op helikopters die hen naar andere nederzettingen in het zuiden van Groenland brengen, anderen verlaten, net als ik, de Amerikaanse asfaltweg die naar de stad leidt, als je die zo kunt noemen: een handvol huizen, twee cafés en vier barakken die zijn omgebouwd tot door de regering gesubsidieerde woningen, geschilderd in het voor Groenland zo kenmerkende lichtblauw en felgroen. De weg loopt geleidelijk heuvelafwaarts naar de nederzetting en het fonkelende blauw van de fjord voor ons. De gebouwen staan onder een met jonge boompjes bezaaide heuvelrug die uitloopt op een voorgebergte dat wordt gedomineerd door een groep witte cilinders die als schildwachten boven een kleine haven staan en een modderig strand waarop donkerblauwe golven aanspoelen. Ze dragen de opschriften 'jet oil 1', jet oil 2', 'diesel' en 'kerosine' – nog zo'n Amerikaanse erfenis.

Op de trappen van een van de woonblokken maakt een man de loop van zijn geweer schoon. Hij kijkt me even aan en gaat dan verder met poetsen. Een oudere Groenlandse vrouw op pantoffels hangt in de zon de was aan de lijn. Twee kinderen rennen rond op een verlaten uitziende betonnen speelplaats. Op een grindterras boven hen staat een witte plastic doos zonder ramen waarin de supermarkt is ondergebracht. Buiten verkopen twee vrouwen in parka's keukengerei uit China en hotdogs gegrild op een gasbarbecue.

Naast de speeltuin vind ik waar ik naar op zoek was. Ook het Narsarsuaq Hotel is een militair gebouw dat een nieuwe bestemming heeft gekregen. Achter de open receptie kun je als het ware de Amerikaanse militairen nog zien rondhangen. Het is een roestvrijstalen kantine zonder ramen zoals je die overal ter wereld op militaire bases aantreft.

Aan een tafel, te midden van de overblijfselen van hun lunch, vind ik Kenneth, met kort zandkleurig haar, en Peter, een Deense wetenschapper met doordringende blauwe ogen en oplichtende oranje puntjes in een indrukwekkende baard. We gaan gelijk op pad, de achterdeur uit, in het verblindende zonlicht, langs de vuilnisbakken van het hotel en over een stuk braakliggend terrein dat ooit door de Amerikanen als grindgroeve werd gebruikt. De zon is heet en bijzonder fel. Een tiental mensen heeft zich verspreid over een karig grasveldje en is bezig met wat lijkt op raketwerpers die ze op de grond richten. Aan de ene kant staat een pick-up truck, half beladen met stapels kartonnen dozen. Een lange man met een plat hoedje met een brede rand waar exotische veren uit steken, een oranje baard en een blauwe zonnebril pakt een doos van de achterkant van de vrachtwagen en loopt naar het midden van de groep.

'Yo! Populieren, iedereen! Pak wat populieren!' roept hij met een Amerikaans accent.

De deelnemers verzamelen zich rondom hem, nemen een handvol zaailingen en lopen dan weg om ze in de open kamers van de bazooka's te steken. Ik laat mijn rugzak vallen, neem ook een handvol en zoek een partner. Als ik me omdraai, is Kenneth verdwenen. Al snel zit ik op mijn knieën zaailingen van de balsempopulier te planten, samen met een Spanjaard die Miguel heet. De zon is warm in mijn nek en mensen zweten en trekken hun jassen en truien uit. De grond is hard. De rotsachtige klip aan de rand van de vallei glinstert een beetje boven ons. Op de achtergrond is het geraas van de rivier nog net waarneembaar, alsof het geluid van een snelweg vanachter de heuvel klinkt. In het oosten staan bomen bovenop de heuvelrug, het begin van het arboretum. In het westen beginnen de huizenblokken.

'Niet te ver die kant op planten!' roept de man met zonnebril, die de leiding lijkt te hebben. Blijkbaar willen de bewoners van de huizenblokken niet dat er te veel bomen hun uitzicht bederven. De man met het geweer zit nog steeds op de trede, het wapen over zijn knieën. Een voorbijganger kijkt even onze kant op en loopt dan weer verder. Buitenlanders die als een bezetene bomen planten op braakliggend terrein aan de rand van de stad, het is blijkbaar een alledaags schouwspel. De plaatselijke bewoners zijn er echter niet bij betrokken. Bomen, ooit in de vorm van struikgewas en drijfhout essentieel om hier te overleven, zijn niet langer een bepalende factor in het leven van de mens. Veel belangrijker zijn nu de vluchten uit Denemarken, de schepen die voedsel, alcohol en brandstof uit IJsland en Canada aanvoeren, en de aanwezigheid van vis en wild om op te jagen. Een geweer poetsen is nuttiger dan een boom planten.

Miguel en ik planten een hele doos, vijftig bomen, terwijl de Amerikaan in het rond banjert en het hele gebeuren filmt met zijn iPhone. Miguel spreekt weinig Engels, maar ik heb begrepen dat hij werkt met toeristen en groepen naar de ijskap begeleidt. Onder onze medeplanters zie ik een man die me Japans lijkt, een vrouw en kind die uit het Midden-Oosten lijken te stammen, verschillende blanke mannen en een of twee Inuit. Uit Miguels pogingen om het me uit te leggen wordt me niet duidelijk wat dit nu precies is. De man met de iPhone draagt een T-shirt bedrukt met Groenlandse bomen. Hij verdwijnt plots achter de truck en komt net zo plotseling terug met nog een kartonnen doos.

'Oké, drinken! Limonade! Hallo allemaal, het is verdomde heet!'

De Amerikaan geeft me een cola en stelt zich voor. Hij is professor Jason Box, klimatoloog bij de Geologische Dienst van

Denemarken. Greenland Trees was zijn idee, vertelt hij me, hoewel hij er zelf niet veel schijnt te planten. In plaats daarvan praat hij, gesticuleert hevig en gebaart naar de bergen, de fjorden, de mensen die planten. Hij is een constante, wervelende bal van energie.

'Sommige mensen zeggen: laat maar zitten, laat de natuur haar gang gaan, je introduceert invasieve soorten. De ecologen mogen ons niet. Maar ik zeg: je kunt mijn rug op! We helpen de natuur een handje. Zaailingen vinden duurt hier lang, want er is geen natuurlijke bron van zaad... Peter en Kenneth vertellen ons waar we moeten planten.'

Jason begint nu iedereen aan te wijzen: Dirk en Maurice uit Nederland, Masahito uit Japan, Chris uit de Verenigde Staten, Fazia uit Iran, allemaal ervaren en gerespecteerde klimatologen die onderzoek doen voor het Intergovernmental Panel on Climate Change (IPCC) van de VN en die momenteel stoffige knieën krijgen terwijl ze zaailingen van de balsempopulier in de dunne grond drukken.

Het project is begonnen als een manier voor glaciologen die zich schuldig voelden om de uitstoot van hun onderzoeksprojecten te compenseren. Om elke zomer onderzoeksapparatuur en tonnen materiaal door de lucht naar de ijskap te brengen, zijn namelijk heel wat vliegtuigen, boten en helikopters nodig. Al vrij snel begonnen er echter ook andere wetenschappers mee te doen. Die waren zo geschrokken van het extreme smelten van het ijs dat ze zagen, dat ze iets tastbaars en directs wilden doen om kooldioxide uit de atmosfeer te halen. Ze zochten een plek waar ze bomen konden planten en herinnerden zich plots dat ze al tientallen jaren over het arboretum vlogen.

's Avonds, na het planten van 1300 bomen, worden alle vrijwilligers uitgenodigd voor een barbecue met rendiervlees en Groenlands lamsvlees. Hogerop in de vallei, voorbij de oude basis, aan de ingang van een kleinere vallei die de Amerikanen Hospital Valley noemden, staat een kleine houten hut die nu van Kenneth is, met een vlaggenmast die lang gelden al werd ontdaan van zijn *Stars and Stripes*. Kenneth heeft twintig jaar geleden de coniferen rondom de hut geplant, maar ze beginnen nu pas hun stempel te drukken op het vage blauw van de schemering. Als de zon eenmaal achter de berg is verdwenen, daalt de temperatuur plotseling tot dicht bij het vriespunt. Overdag kan het tot 25 graden worden, maar door de nabijheid van het ijs zijn de nachten op Groenland, zelfs in de zomer, altijd bijzonder fris.

De wetenschappers warmen hun handen rond het kampvuur en drinken bier. Ze zijn gekleed in de typisch dracht van hun beroep - technische expeditiekleding versierd met voorname logo's: *extreme ice survey*, *dutch arctic expedition*. De Nederlanders zijn onevenredig sterk vertegenwoordigd. Een kwart van Nederland ligt onder de zeespiegel, en smeltend gletsjerijs vormt de grootste bedreiging voor het land.

Peter is de enige die geen kleding met een logo erop draagt. Deze Deense klimatoloog bestudeert de historische patronen van de vegetatie. Hij ziet er eerder uit als een boswachter: hemd, broek, fleece en jas in contrasterende tinten groen. Hij zit er rustig bij terwijl de jongere wetenschappers aan de andere kant van het vuur zich zorgen maken over het weer. Bij dageraad zullen zij aan de rand van de ijskap met een boot en een helikopter samenkomen en met een BBC-filmploeg de stalen palen controleren die ze vorige zomer in het ijs hebben geplaatst. De diepte van de palen zal hen vertellen hoeveel de ijskap het afgelopen jaar is gesmolten. Het is het laatste weekend van augustus, meestal het einde van het dooiseizoen. Maar er wordt zware regen voorspeld, en ze zijn druk in de weer om de opties met een haast militaire precisie in kaart te brengen.

'Grondwaarheid' noemt Dirk, een Nederlandse glacioloog, het werk dat ze doen. Vliegtuigen van de Amerikaanse luchtmacht zijn met radar over de ijskap gevlogen om te proberen de ijsmassa en de smeltsnelheid te meten, maar die kunnen alleen in een rechte lijn meten. Satellieten met lasers zijn de ruimte ingestuurd om hetzelfde te doen, een NASA-project met de naam GRACE: *Gravity Recovery and Climate Experiment*. De NASA heeft het hoogteverschil tussen de aardkorst en het oppervlak van de ijskap gemeten en een schatting gemaakt van de ijsmassa. Elk jaar gaat er 300 kubieke kilometer verloren, en dat proces versnelt nog steeds.

Geen van de methoden is perfect en de schattingen moeten worden aangevuld met feitelijke metingen aan het oppervlak van het ijs. Sommigen komen hier al bijna twee decennia, voor anderen is het hun eerste reis. Het aantal projecten op Groenland – en het aantal wetenschappers – neemt snel toe.

Belangrijker dan boomringen is het klimaatarchief dat is ingesloten in het prehistorisch ijs en dat van cruciaal belang is voor ons begrip van de wijze waarop het klimaat op aarde in het verleden is veranderd. En de snelheid waarmee de ijskappen smelten is bepalend voor wat er vervolgens gaat gebeuren. Er zijn twee grote ijskappen op de planeet, op Antarctica en op Groenland, maar Groenland is veel gemakkelijker en goedkoper te bereiken. Het ijs smelt hier ook veel sneller dan op Antarctica. Op Groenland wordt baanbrekend werk verricht op het gebied van de glaciologie en de stijging van de zeespiegel, en de mensen rond het vuur zijn verantwoordelijk voor veel van wat we weten over hoe het verdwijnende ijs onze planeet zal veranderen.

Dirk bouwde het netwerk van meetstations voor de Antarctische ijskap en Jason deed dat voor Groenland. De gegevens worden gebruikt in de complexe klimaatmodellen die andere wetenschappers zoals Masahito opstellen. We praten wat over modellen. Dit is Masahito's tweede bezoek aan de ijskap dit jaar. Het is ver van Japan, waar zijn lab voortdurend werkt aan de verfijning van een van de meest geavanceerde modellen ter wereld, een model waarop het IPCC zich baseert. Hij erkent dat het model moeite heeft met de terugkoppelingslussen in het klimaat, en uit de manier waarop hij praat, snel, met wijdopengesperde ogen en opgetrokken schouders, blijkt duidelijk dat hij die gaten in het model dringend wil dichten. Wanneer ik zeg dat sommige ecologen geloven dat aardsystemen zo complex zijn dat ze onmogelijk in modellen kunnen worden gevat, stokt het gesprek.

Ooit waren modellen werktuigen voor wetenschappers, maar

tegenwoordig lijken mensen werktuigen van hun modellen te zijn geworden. Er worden onderzoeksbeurzen verstrekt voor projecten om meer gegevens te verzamelen waarmee de met supercomputers gebouwde modellen kunnen worden verfijnd. Maar modellen zijn gevaarlijk – ze kunnen zo worden aangepast dat ze het verhaal vertellen dat men graag wil horen. Het is bekend dat het vijfde IPCC-rapport van 2013 gebaseerd was op modellen voor de voorgaande tien jaar in plaats van op feitelijke waarnemingen die een veel pessimistischer beeld schetsten van het smelten van het Noordpoolijs.[1] Tegen echte gegevens valt weinig in te brengen.

Echte klimaatgegevens zijn op dit moment het waardevolste goed op aarde en deze wetenschappers zijn moderne schatgravers die gevaarlijk en roemrijk werk verrichten met helikopters en touwen, sleeën en de modernste technologie. Ze trotseren kloven en sneeuwstormen om onbetaalbare ijskernen mee terug te nemen waarin zij turen om onze toekomst te voorspellen. Maar het meten, waarnemen en onpartijdig uitleggen van de objectieve waarschijnlijkheid van het verdwijnen van de ijskappen en wat dat betekent voor het menselijk leven op aarde, leidt tot een emotionele tegenstrijdigheid. Wetenschappelijke onderzoeksprojecten worden altijd afgesloten met de vaststelling van gebieden die verder onderzoek verdienen om bij te dragen tot de totale som van de kennis. De westerse wetenschap is een product van haar eigen telos, een ideologisch idee van vooruitgang dat nu een achterhaalde futuristische cultus lijkt te zijn. Die gaat er immers vanuit dat er altijd meer tijd is.

Terwijl de jongere wetenschappers zoals Maurice gedreven lijken door een dringende zoektocht naar doorslaggevende feiten, zijn de ouderen cynischer. Jaar na jaar worden er steeds gevaarlijkere niveaus van dooi gedocumenteerd, terwijl het feit dat er geen actie wordt ondernomen, mensen steeds wanhopiger maakt. Dat was de reden waarom Dirk en zijn vrouw Fazia, ook een vooraanstaand glaciologe (die meer dan tien jaar eerder al de versnelling van de Kangerlussaq-gletsjer documenteerde), besloten de academische wereld te verlaten en zich in de plaats daarvan aan Groenlandse bomen te wijden.

Tegenwoordig kijken ze anders tegen Groenland aan. Eerder was Narsarsuaq de plaats om te wachten op een helikopter naar het ijs of om dronken te worden in de bar van het Narsarsuaq Hotel en beroepsroddels uit te wisselen met andere wetenschappers die op doorreis waren zonder ooit de plaatselijke bevolking te ontmoeten. In plaats daarvan zullen Dirk en Fazia morgen, wanneer Jason en zijn team naar de ijskap gaan, met Peter de boot naar het zuiden nemen om met schoolkinderen over het boomplantproject te praten. Vroeger zagen ze alleen het witte gedeelte van het eiland. Nu onderzoeken ze de mogelijkheid dat het groen zal worden.

De wetenschappers zijn teruggekeerd naar het hotel. Van het vuur is een handvol sintels over. In de schemering blijft een heldere gloed achter de donkere bergen hun contouren scherp aftekenen, en het verre gebrul van de rivier dat klinkt als een vliegtuig op afstand, brengt de nacht tot leven. De lucht is koud en fris. Groenland is een anomalie, zowel in de tijd als op zijn plaats. Op 61 graden noorderbreedte ligt Narsarsuaq een heel eind naar het zuiden, een breedte die vergelijkbaar is met die van de Shetlandeilanden, het midden van Noorwegen en Zweden of Anchorage in Alaska, stuk voor stuk subarctische boreale locaties. Maar de Oost-Groenlandstroom, die zee-ijs van de Noordelijke IJszee naar de kust brengt, en de koelende invloed van de ijskap, maken dat er een eigenaardig microklimaat heerst.

'Het is heel merkwaardig,' legt Peter uit. Hij heeft het over het feit dat de fjorden in het binnenland van Groenland een ideaal klimaat vormen voor boreale boomsoorten, maar dat er nauwelijks bomen zijn.

De gemiddelde jaartemperatuur ligt ruim boven het vriespunt en de laatste tijd ligt de zomertemperatuur boven de juli-isotherm van 10 graden, de traditionele definitie van de noordelijke boomgrens. Het nieuwe normaal voor juli is volgens Peter nu hoger dan 11 graden.

Maar de reden dat er geen bomen zijn op Groenland is niet

dat het te koud is geweest. Er was gewoon nooit zaad. Vegetatieve veranderingen duren duizenden jaren. Dit is wat ecologen *disequilibrium dynamics* noemen, een ecosysteem of een bioom dat bezig is zijn evenwicht te vinden. Net als bij de huidige opwarming van de aarde duurt het een tijd voor soorten en ecosystemen zich aan de veranderde temperaturen of stromingen hebben aangepast – in sommige gevallen wel duizenden jaren. Groenland is nog steeds bezig met een inhaalslag na de laatste ijstijd.

Het vorige glaciale maximum bedekte het hele eiland en nu heeft het ijs zich teruggetrokken tot ongeveer 80 procent. Ecologen schatten dat er zonder de invloed van de mens 'migratievertraging' in de vestiging van bomen kan optreden die duizenden jaren kan bedragen. Voor Groenland wordt dit nog gecompliceerder door de extreme hoogte- en topografische verschillen tussen de bergachtige fjorden. De soorten die zich er tot nu toe hebben gevestigd, zijn die welke door de lucht kunnen worden verspreid.

Zeer lichte zaden, zoals die van de katjes van de berk en de els in Labrador, zijn door de wind meegevoerd en neergeslagen in de fjorden. Hieruit, en uit de zaden in de bessen van lijsterbes en jeneverbes die door vogels worden verspreid, zijn de enige vier inheemse bomen van Groenland ontsprongen. De jeneverbes wordt overal in het boreale gebied gevonden. De berk en de els zijn Noord-Amerikaanse variëteiten die gemakkelijk kunnen worden getraceerd naar het naburige continent aan de overkant van de Davis Strait. Maar een soort lijsterbes, de *Sorbus groenlandica*, is een vreemde ondersoort waarvan wordt aangenomen dat hij Noord-Amerika tijdens het laatste interglaciaal vanuit Groenland heeft gekoloniseerd. Die heeft nu zijn weg terug gevonden vanuit een overzees refugium.

Hij blijft laag en is veel kleiner dan zijn Europese tegenhanger, de *Sorbus aucuparia*, of zijn twee Noord-Amerikaanse neven, de *Sorbus americana* en de *Sorbus decora*, met kleine versies van de lijsterbesbladeren en dezelfde zilverachtige schors en opvallende scharlakenrode bessen met een vijfpuntig pentagram onderaan de vrucht die geliefd is bij vogels en bij vroegere generaties mensen.

Het verhaal van de Sorbus groenlandica is een goed voorbeeld van speciatie, het mysterieuze evolutieproces dat wordt beheerst door het ritme van planetaire banen, van ijstijden en het onmerkbare voortschrijden van de geologische tijd. En het is een mythisch verhaal voor de boreale soorten, een voorbode van de uitdagingen die komen gaan.

Ergens tussen de eerdere ijstijden is een ondersoort van de Sorbus, de lijsterbes, in Groenland terechtgekomen en heeft zich in een plaatselijke populatie uitgezaaid. Lijsterbesvarianten komen overal in het boreale gebied voor, van Scandinavië tot Siberië, en hebben steeds blijk gegeven van een groot aanpassingsvermogen door krachtige hybridisatie. Het vermogen om te hybridiseren is een overlevingsstrategie, een nuttige vaardigheid voor het Antropoceen, en de lijsterbes is een overlever bij uitstek.

De schors is glad en zilverkleurig en weerkaatst zonlicht dat het onderkoelde sap zou kunnen ontdooien. De bladknoppen zijn donkerpaars om zonnewarmte vast te houden en in het voorjaar de eerste bloemen te produceren. De lijsterbes is een hermafrodiet. Elke roomwitte bloem met vijf bloemblaadjes bevat zowel mannelijke als vrouwelijke delen. De trossen kleine bloemen van de *Roseacae*, de rozenfamilie, zijn miniatuurreplica's van rozen. Ze bevatten zowel donker stuifmeel als een van de eerste nectars van het jaar, die grote en kleine insecten aantrekken. De lijsterbes kan het zich niet veroorloven kieskeurig te zijn over zijn bezoekers, want er zijn er zo weinig. Het sorbinezuur is in het voorjaar van cruciaal belang voor wespen, motten en andere insecten, en zangvogels komen in het najaar af op de suikerachtige sorbitol in de kenmerkende rode bessen. De lijsterbes markeert belangrijke momenten op de kalender, als een soort boreale klok: de witte bloesem is een voorbode van de lente, het rood worden van de bessen is het signaal dat de herfst is aangebroken en hun verdwijning een teken dat de winter is aangebroken.

Afgesneden van andere populaties, misschien door de zee of eerder nog door het ijs, hield de Groenlandse populatie zijn eigen ritme aan, evolueerde naar zijn nieuwe habitat, produceerde kleinere bladeren en werd minder ambitieus wat betreft hoogte. Dezelfde kenmerken van de topografie van Groenland die de verspreiding van zaden beperken, maken het ideaal als een eventueel microrefugium.

In het verleden hebben bergen en eilanden deze functie vervuld. Bergachtige gebieden met een gevarieerde topografie zoals Groenland kennen een grote variatie in habitats en kunnen bovendien inversies van de atmosfeer vertonen – waarbij warme lucht in de valleien gevangen wordt en op zijn plaats wordt gehouden door de koude winden op grotere hoogte. Geologische gegevens wijzen op dergelijke toevluchtsoorden in valleien waar het ijs niet kwam, waar soorten dicht op elkaar zijn gekropen in vreemde combinaties en met onvoorspelbare resultaten.[2] Geologen spreken ook wel over ijstijden als 'soortenpompen', vanwege deze cyclische dwang tot evolutie.

Toen het ijs zich terugtrok en de vogels hun weg over zee weer vonden, moest de Sorbus groenlandica bij terugkeer vaststellen dat de oorspronkelijke populatie onherkenbaar was geëvolueerd. Die had zich ontwikkeld tot een unieke ondersoort. In andere delen van de wereld zijn de verspreidingsgebieden van de soorten wel uiteen komen te liggen, maar nooit meer herenigd. In de Appalachen in de Verenigde Staten komen relicte boreale soorten voor die verwant zijn aan andere die nu in het hoge noorden van Canada groeien. In Tanzania bevatten inmiddels afgezonderd geraakte nevelwouden bovenop tropische bergen zoals de Udzungwa of de Usambara nu endemische soorten die zijn gestrand toen de bossen die eens de habitats met elkaar verbonden, zich terugtrokken en er savanne voor in de plaats kwam. De Himalaya is nog zo'n voorbeeld.

Welke soorten zullen er overblijven na de komende klimaatchaos, wanneer de aarde een nieuw evenwicht heeft gevonden? Het antwoord op die vraag zal worden bepaald door de refugia: of die al dan niet lang genoeg een toevluchtsoord kunnen bieden, en of ze al dan niet kunnen worden bereikt.

De harde mantra van een opwarmende wereld is: 'Aanpassen, wegwezen of ten onder gaan.' Sommige soorten kunnen zich echter gemakkelijker verplaatsen dan andere. De snelheid van de klimaatverandering is het tempo waarin een soort zich zal moeten verplaatsen om met zijn klimaatniche mee te migreren. Natuurbeschermers zullen harde keuzes moeten maken, zoals Noach destijds met zijn ark, hoewel hun ark bij lange na niet groot genoeg is. Dit is de relatief nieuwe discipline van de strategische ecologie. Aanplant die niet gebaseerd is op het huidige klimaat, maar op gissingen over de toekomst.

Op de evenaar zal de opwarming van de aarde de inheemse soorten van de nevelwouden uiteindelijk steeds hoger de berg op jagen, tot ze niet hoger kunnen en in de ijle lucht zullen uitsterven. Op het noordelijk halfrond neigen soorten nu al naar het noorden. Voor zoogdieren zoals de migrerende elanden, kariboes en beren van de noordelijke breedtegraden, of de vogels van het schiereiland Tajmyr is migreren geen probleem, mits er aaneengesloten corridors van habitat en voedselbronnen zijn, althans tot aan de Noordelijke IJszee. Maar wat als je op één plek geworteld bent? Wat als je een boom bent?

Grove dennen bijvoorbeeld brengen gewoonlijk nieuwe zaailingen voort op minder dan 200 meter van de moederboom, met hier en daar een zaadje dat nog verder weg groeit. Dennenbossen bewegen zich in roedels. Sommige soorten, zoals *Cerbera odollam*, soms de 'zelfmoordboom' genoemd, hebben slechts één individu als nageslacht, in situ, dat wordt gevoed door het rottende karkas van de moeder. Dergelijke gespecialiseerde soorten zijn nu al te traag om zich aan te passen aan klimaatveranderingen, wat betekent dat zij zonder hulp van de mens zullen uitsterven. Een gematigde of tropische boom die momenteel met hittestress te kampen heeft, kan zich misschien aanpassen aan het klimaat met een snelheid van enkele kilometers per jaar.[3] Als bomen hadden kunnen lopen, hadden we ze bij die snelheid kunnen zien bewegen.

Er zijn refugia in situ, die soorten op eigen kracht kunnen bereiken, en er zijn refugia ex situ – plaatsen die geschikt zijn om er te overleven, maar waar soorten eventueel naartoe moeten worden overgeplaatst – wat in de literatuur 'geassisteerde migratie' wordt genoemd. Dergelijke technische klimaattermen zullen tot het gewone taalgebruik doordringen – droge, klinische taal waarachter een impliciete capitulatie schuilgaat: we zijn er niet in geslaagd het proces te stoppen.

Toen Kenneth begon met het planten van bomen, dacht hij daarbij niet aan de aanstaande klimaatcrisis. Hij en zijn collega's begonnen met een zeer elementair inzicht: in Noord-Amerika is Sorbus groenlandica meestal helemaal geen boomgrenssoort, dus er moet op Groenland nog ruimte zijn voor andere soorten. Maar de vraag die zij stelden is in wezen dezelfde als de vraag die natuurbeschermers en strategische ecologen in de wetenschappelijke gemeenschap momenteel bezighoudt: wat is de klimaatanaloog van Groenland? Wat zou hier nog kunnen groeien, als het moest?

Ze waren niet de eersten die deze vragen stelden. In 1892 legde de Deense botanicus L.K. Rosevinge, in een van die typische koloniale experimenten om te zien welke rijkdommen konden worden gewonnen uit deze noordelijke kolonie van Denemarken, een proefplantage aan van zes grove dennen, hogerop in de fjord van Narsarsuaq.

De zee-engte heet *Qanasiassat* in de taal van de Inuit, en is ongeveer het maximum dat je landinwaarts kunt komen vanaf de open zee in de kustarchipel van Groenland. Een jollenman, Jiaggi genaamd, brengt me er vroeg in de morgen heen in zijn speedboot. De eerste sneeuw van de herfst is 's nachts gevallen en zalft de bergen die fronsend neerkijken op de boerderijen van die paar taaie mensen die op de steile hellingen van de schapenteelt proberen te leven. Rond de toppen hangen wolkenflarden en op het oppervlak van de fjord ligt een mist die op bont lijkt en de kleur heeft van vuile melk. De rivier die door de vallei van Narsarsuaq raast draagt sediment van de smeltende gletsjer met zich mee. Reservoirs van smeltwater hopen zich op onder de gletsjer, legt Jiaggi uit, en periodiek overstromen ze, waarna de rivier troebel ziet van de deeltjes.

De haven die de Amerikanen achterlieten is nog intact dankzij de enorme stammen van de Oregon pine die werden gebruikt, geteerd met pek en aan elkaar gesjord – het soort bomen dat ooit in de toekomst weleens op Groenland zou kunnen groeien. De zware boot snijdt een wit spoor in het perfecte oppervlak van de fjord. De zon staat nog steeds achter de heuvels, maar zelfs op dit tijdstip heeft de lucht een achtergrondgloed van het ijs net voorbij de horizon. Jiaggi is van oorsprong Frans. Hij kwam hier in 1976 aan met een zelfgemaakte boot, samen met een groep andere hippies, en was de enige die vergat naar huis te gaan. In plaats daarvan begon hij een toeristisch bedrijf, Blue Ice Explorer genaamd, dat, juist nu hij zelf met pensioen is, enorm goed loopt, omdat mensen gehoor geven aan de fatale aantrekkingskracht van dat verdwijnende blauwe ijs. Hij haalt zijn schouders op. Volgend jaar kopen hij en zijn Deense vriendin een kampeerwagen en willen ze terugkeren naar zijn geboortestreek, de Alpen.

Aan de kop van de fjord bereikt de zee een amfitheater van spectaculaire rotsen, uitgehouwen in een bijna perfecte cirkel. Van op de oever ziet de plantage er vreemd uit, als een vierkant van fluweel dat op de berghelling is gespeld. Binnen een kapot prikkeldraadhek ligt een hectare met recentere aanplant: lariks, witte spar, struikden en grove den. De oorspronkelijke dennen van Rosevinge staan, verwaaid en als krummholz, aan de rand van het groene vierkant, verweerd en grijs. Slechts twee lijken er nog in leven, maar hun bast is door de wind verwijderd en de resterende naalden zijn bruin met alleen aan de uiteinden nog groene plekjes. Het gras rondom is dik en sponzig en verstopt met mos. Al 120 jaar komen mensen deze vluchtelingen uit Noord-Noorwegen met een bezoekje vereren, maar nu naderen ze eindelijk, zo lijkt het, het einde van hun leven. De insecten zijn een ervan duidelijk fataal geworden. Schapen hebben aan enkele van de lagere takken geknabbeld.

In het museum van Narsarsuaq hangen foto's van gelukkiger dagen. Rosevinges fout, aldus conservator Ole, was dat hij soorten uit Noord-Noorwegen koos waarvan hij dacht dat ze uit een gelijkaardig klimaat kwamen. In feite waren de genen van de noordelijke dennen gecodeerd om veel minder daglicht en kortere seizoenen te verwachten, zodat ze niet optimaal konden profiteren van het langere groeiseizoen van Zuid-Groenland en al in de vroege herfst stopten, wanneer andere bomen nog steeds zonnebaadden.

Naast de ziekelijke dennen staat een zeer indrukwekkende lariks met geknakte, zwiepende takken die zelf meer dan honderd jaar oud lijkt te zijn. Op een metalen plaatje staat het nummer 3799. In het vierkante, door mensenhanden aangelegde bosje heerst een diepe rust. Een tapijt van naalden valt snel uiteen tot een rijke humus die een doordringende geur verspreidt. Het geluid van elk bos is anders – het complex van bladeren en naalden dat de lucht filtert tot een uniek geruis van ritselende bladeren. Dit bos klinkt als rustig golvende witte ruis.

Aan het andere einde van de plantage staat een volledig uitgeruste hut met brandhout, gereedschap, kookgerei en dekens. Het is een eenzame plek om te stranden, maar geen slechte. Het uitzicht op de fjord met ijsbergen en de witte, bevroren bergtoppen onder de paarse regenwolken, en af en toe een cruiseschip – het zou een mooi decor zijn voor het einde van de wereld.

Als ik eenmaal rond en door de hectare bos heb gelopen, is er weinig meer te zien en is het tijd om Jiaggi te wenken die in de fjord ligt aangemeerd en weer aan boord van de boot te gaan. Pas als ik achterom kijk naar het vierkant van donker wintergroen, besef ik wat er zo vreemd is aan de plantage. Er zijn bijna geen zaailingen, zelfs niet binnen het hek. Boreale soorten hebben vuur of verstoring nodig om te ontkiemen, ze hebben minerale grond nodig, geen grond bedekt met nat mos en zegge. Buiten de omheining wordt de berghelling overheerst door de laaggroeiende berk, *Betula glandulosa*, de inheemse hybride. Ik zie slechts één zaailing van een spar op een stuk kale aarde hogerop, dat erbij ligt als een litteken op een plek waar een aardverschuiving de grond heeft blootgelegd.

De tijdschaal van natuurlijke bebossing op hogere breedtegraden wordt me plotseling duidelijk, en het besef is beangstigend. Het duurt eeuwen, zo niet millennia, voor een bos vaste voet aan de grond krijgt, zelfs als de klimatologische omstandigheden gunstig zijn. De bodem, de regenval en de mate van verstoring moeten op elkaar worden afgestemd. De natuur is hier met rust gelaten en heeft besloten dat de berk hier de juiste soort is. De berk zou de grond kunnen voorbereiden – of verbranden – en zo de weg vrijmaken voor naaldbomen, maar zover is het nog niet. Hoewel de naaldbomen van de plantage, die later zijn geplant dan de dennen van Rosevinge, vooralsnog gezond lijken en welig tieren, is het ontbreken van het regeneratievermogen van de plantage eigenlijk een reden om tegen dergelijke projecten te zijn: zonder menselijk ingrijpen of verstoring zullen deze bomen zich niet uit zichzelf voortplanten. Ze zullen als relict op de heuvel blijven staan tot uiteindelijk iets anders het overneemt.

De boot draait aan het einde van de fjord, weg van de grijze steile helling en naar een majestueus zuidelijk vergezicht van donderkoppen, bergen, sneeuw, ijs en zee. De natuurlijke habitat van mossen, riet en berk houdt op bij een bepaalde hoogte en hellinghoek. Plakken perfect homogeen groen lijken uit de helling te zijn geschept. Op deze miniatuurvelden, eilanden in het bruin en grijs, kruipen tractoren onder onmogelijke hoeken rond om enorme ingepakte balen te verzamelen waarmee ze piramides van zwart plastic bouwen. De schapenboeren van de fjord slaan hooi in voor de winter, net als hun Noorse voorouders duizend jaar geleden op dezelfde velden deden. Een deel van de reden waarom er tegenwoordig zo weinig inheemse berkenbossen in Zuid-Groenland zijn, een van de argumenten voor proefaanplantingen, is dat de Vikingen ze allemaal hebben gekapt.

Op de terugweg wil Jiaggi post bezorgen. Tegenover Narsarsuaq, aan de overkant van de fjord, ligt een ouder, dichter bevolkt dorp, Qassiarsuk genaamd. Toen de Amerikanen hier in de Tweede Wereldoorlog aankwamen, trokken ze een denkbeeldige lijn door het midden van de fjord en verboden de plaatselijke bevolking om deze over te steken. Dwars op die lijn ligt nu de glanzend zwarte romp van een enorm cruiseschip onder Franse vlag. Rubberboten vervoeren passagiers door de motregen van het drijvende hotel naar de kust. Jiaggi stuurt er voorzichtig omheen en we leggen aan naast een roestige oude vrachtboot van waaruit een vorkheftruck pallets met cola, bier, toiletpapier, suiker, melkpoeder en loodgietersbenodigdheden aan het lossen is. Afgezien van de Inuit, die een tijdlang van het land leefden voordat ze naar gemakkelijker gebied overzees, in Canada, verhuisden, is Groenland nooit zelfvoorzienend geweest. Hier overleven is moeilijk, eenzaam en duur.

Huizen die er gehavend uitzien, staan wankel boven de haven. Op een binnenplaats draait een hond aan een touw rond onder de trekzalm die er aan een lijn te drogen hangt, de koppen van de vissen op stokjes. Naast een ander graast een paard aan een lijn een perfecte cirkel in het gras net boven de oever. Jiaggi verdwijnt in het café dat ook als postkantoor fungeert, terwijl ik naar het benzinestation kijk – een container met twee zelfbedieningspompen die verbonden zijn met een geldautomaat. De toeristen zijn op weg naar de ruïnes van de Noormannen op de heuvel erboven, die nu op de Werelderfgoedlijst van de UNESCO staan. Dit deel van de kust is bezaaid met kleine akkertjes van de Vikingen, omgeven door stenen en pas gemaaid gras. Een boer gehuld in een muts, sjaal en een oliejas raast me voorbij op een quad. En rondom versmelten de bergen met de zwarte wolken en verduisteren de hemel.

De laatste boerderij in het zuiden heeft de grootste, groenste velden, het resultaat van veel hard werk om de grond terug te winnen op de stenen en de toendra. Balen hooi in lichtgroen plastic worden in keurige rijen gestapeld. Een witte boerderij staat naast een blauwe en een complex van schuren, aan één kant verborgen door een ongewone en opvallende rij bomen. Het veld loopt in een zachte bocht naar beneden naar het strand, waar een auto is achtergelaten om weg te roesten. Dit was de boerderij van Brattahlid, de machtige vrouw van Erik de Rode, de eerste Vikingkolonist van Groenland, die de nederzetting stichtte in

982. Bijna een millennium later was dit de plaats waar nieuwe ontdekkingsreizigers kwamen om de schapenhouderij in Groenland te herstellen. Die pionier was Otto Friedrikssen, die hier in 1924 met zijn gezin aankwam, gesteund en aangemoedigd door de Deense regering.

Otto's kleinzoon woont nu met zijn Groenlandse vrouw in het blauwe huis. Ellen heeft vriendelijke ogen, kort, staalkleurig haar en een stijlvolle bril. In haar zwarte T-shirt en broek lijkt ze meer op een Scandinavische architecte dan op een schapenboer. Haar huis is ingericht met de gebruikelijke accenten van het Deense modernisme: licht hout en glas. De uitzondering is een tafel, gemaakt van wat lijkt op drijfhout.

'Groenlandse retro.' Ze lacht. Voordat er hout werd ingevoerd, waren Ellens voorouders aangewezen op drijfhout uit Siberië, bomen die in het ijs waren vastgevroren en vervolgens werden losgelaten door ijsbergen die langs de oostkust van Groenland naar het zuiden werden gestuwd door de Beaufort Gyre, een cyclonale stroming die weliswaar zwakker wordt, maar nog steeds tegen de wijzers van de klok rond de Noordpool draait. Het hout, voornamelijk Siberische lariks, vormde een belangrijke bron van timmerhout voor gereedschappen, ski's, tentstokken en huizen. Er spoelt nu minder drijfhout aan op de stranden van de fjorden, misschien door de houtkap in Siberië, denkt Ellen, door veranderingen in de stromingen, of doordat het zee-ijs verder weg afbreekt, waardoor het drijfhout in de Noord-Atlantische Oceaan terechtkomt in plaats van in de natuurlijke werveling van de fjorden. Misschien was dit wel de oorspronkelijke reden om zich hier te vestigen: bomen van de andere kant van de wereld die het leven op deze zeer onherbergzame plek mogelijk maken.

Ellen vertelt me het verhaal van Kaassassuk, naar wie het dorp Qassiarsuk is genoemd. Kaassassuk was een wees die 's nachts een groot stuk drijfhout uit de zee haalde terwijl iedereen sliep. De volgende ochtend kon niemand het optillen en niemand begreep hoe het drijfhout zo ver boven de waterlijn was gekomen. Ze realiseerden zich dat er een iemand onder hen moest zijn die heel sterk was, maar wisten niet dat het de wees was. Er zijn ook andere verhalen, recenter, maar van voor de komst van de Amerikanen: de grootvader van haar man vertelde haar dat hij over het water naar Narsarsuaq ging om stokken voor brandhout te halen uit de berkenbossen. Toen stond daar een ander soort bos. En ze vertelt me hoe de bomen die nu het uitzicht vanuit haar raam blokkeren, deel uitmaakten van een aanplantingsproject met exemplaren uit Alaska. Zij en haar man zetten de sparren veertig jaar geleden voor het raam waar zij ze in de gaten konden houden. Ze hadden geen idee dat de bomen het huis uiteindelijk in de schaduw zouden stellen.

Maar het is niet het gebrek aan hout dat haar nu zorgen baart, het is het tekort aan regen. Ik wijs uit het raam naar de regen die door de fjord jaagt en ze glimlacht bedroefd. 'Te laat.'

Deze zomer kwamen adviseurs van de regering met de elf schapenboeren van Qanasiassat Fjord praten over hoe zij zich kunnen aanpassen aan een warmer, droger klimaat. Het watertekort heeft ernstige gevolgen voor de hooioogst en dus voor het vermogen van de schapen om de lange winter door te komen – vandaar al die zorgvuldig verzamelde balen. Er was sprake van irrigatie met behulp van smeltwatermeren, maar zelfs die drogen nu op in de zomer. In juli heeft het maar twee dagen geregend en de hooioogst is gehalveerd.

Ellen merkte in 2006 voor het eerst iets van de klimaatverandering. De fjord bevroor vroeger altijd in de winter en dan konden ze over het water naar Narsarsuaq rijden. Maar in 2006 was dat niet het geval en sindsdien is het niet meer veilig om op het zee-ijs te rijden. De laatste drie winters is er helemaal geen sneeuw gevallen, en hun sneeuwscooters staan te roesten in de garage. Op één boerderij experimenteert men met koeien. Ellen weet niet wat ze ermee aan moet. Voor schapen ziet de toekomst er slecht uit. Ze waren van plan geweest om de boerderij door te geven aan hun zoon, maar ook hij is nu minder zeker over de toekomst.

Ellen lijkt me kalm en in staat om er wat op te vinden. Ze is tevens het hoofd van de dorpsschool in Qassiarsuk, die in 2014 werd gesloten wegens een gebrek aan leerlingen, maar onlangs weer is opengegaan met twaalf kinderen en drie onderwijzers. Pas wanneer ze over cultuur spreekt, klinken haar zorgen ook emotioneel. Zij toont me haar nationale klederdracht – een witte korte broek van zeehondenhuid, een geborduurd hemd, een rode wollen legging en witte laarzen van zeehondenhuid. Het is niet eenvoudig om deze kleding te blijven maken in de zachte winters, legt ze uit. De kleur van de zeehondenhuid wordt verkregen door deze buiten te drogen in de droge koude van de winter. Als het te mild is, wordt de huid niet wit.

'Mensen beginnen onze traditionele klederdracht van stof na te maken!' Ellen klinkt nu verontwaardigder dan tevoren. Zij wijst op de complexe bovenkant van de laarzen die eruitziet alsof deze versierd is met kralen, maar in feite zijn het kleine reepjes geverfd zeehondenleer die strak tegen elkaar zijn gelegd. 'Er zijn steeds minder mensen met dit soort vaardigheden – die kennis. Niemand weet nog hoe het heet...' Haar stem verliest aan kracht en ze laat haar handen langs haar zij zakken. Het is alsof overleven nog wel zal lukken, een technische, moderne uitdaging is die kan worden doorstaan, maar de dood van haar cultuur is onherstelbaar, onvergeeflijk. Zo eindigt de wereld dus. In duizenden kleine tragedies. Met elk uitsterven van een soort, een taal, een gewoonte, en niet met een kreet van protest, maar met een stille traan.

Groenland is opnieuw de proeftuin voor de ineenstorting van de beschaving. De Vikingkolonie ging enige tijd na 1420 ten onder. De bevolking hield er schapen, runderen en geiten en verbouwde met moeite hooi en tarwe. Op het hoogtepunt had de kolonie een bisschop, een kathedraal, twaalf kerken en driehonderd boerderijen. Men exporteerde walrusivoor en ijsbeerhuiden naar Noorwegen, en importeerde hout van de kust van Labrador in Canada. Toen het klimaat kouder werd in de Kleine IJstijd die rond 1400 begon, verhinderde het zomerijs blijkbaar dat de schepen de fjorden konden verlaten. De archeologische vondsten suggereren dat ze zonder brandhout kwamen te zitten. In minder dan 500 jaar waren ze erin geslaagd al het lage en langzaam groeiende berken- en elzenstruweel, dat duizenden jaren nodig had gehad om zich te vormen, te rooien. Maar lang voordat alle houtbronnen uitgeput waren, gingen ze ook over tot het verbranden van turf als alternatief, een nog rampzaliger keuze omdat de vorming van grond nog langer duurt dan die van hout.

Jared Diamond beschrijft in zijn boek *Ondergang* hoe een combinatie van de aantasting van het milieu en ontbossing heeft geleid tot een fatale druk op de Groenlandse kolonie.[4] Als de Noormannen de kwetsbaarheid van hun omgeving hadden ingezien en er goed mee waren omgegaan, was het misschien anders gelopen. Milieuverloedering, met name ontbossing, zo merkt Diamond op, staat centraal bij de ineenstorting van elke menselijke beschaving die we kennen.

Bluie West One was een van de vijftien bases in Groenland waarvan de Amerikaanse regering het bestaan heeft toegegeven. Er was een zestiende, Camp Century, een geheime basis onder het ijs, bedoeld als opslagplaats voor kernkoppen, zo dicht mogelijk bij Rusland. Camp Century was een plaats voor talrijke experimenten met de dynamiek van het ijs, en de bakermat van een groot deel van de moderne glaciologie. Bij één experiment boorde men anderhalve kilometer diep in het ijs tot de boor aarde en bladeren naar boven bracht. Die bevroren boorkern lag te sluimeren in een Deense universitaire vriezer tot 2020, toen analyse het oudste ooit ontdekte DNA aan het licht bracht.[5] Tussen 450 duizend en 800 duizend jaar geleden was Groenland dicht bebost met sparren, dennen en elzen met veel insecten en kevers. De gemiddelde temperatuur lag enkele graden hoger dan tegenwoordig.[6] Groenland was ontegenzeggelijk groen. En dat zal het weer zijn.

Een door de Universiteit van Kopenhagen geconstrueerd boomgrensmodel voorspelt tegen 2100 geschikte bodem- en klimaatzones voor boomgroei op alle breedtegraden in Groenland, tot aan de noordkust.[7] Dit lijkt te suggereren dat het microklimaat van Narsarsuaq, of meer in het algemeen het fjordensysteem van Tunulliarfik, dat ertoe leidde dat Erik de Rode het eiland

Groenland doopte, opnieuw een unieke klimaatniche zou kunnen worden die een veel dichtere reeks van soorten zou ondersteunen. Voor zuidelijk Groenland als geheel toonde het model klimaatanalogieën aan voor een groot deel van Noord-Amerika, Scandinavië, Siberië, Schotland, de Alpen en zelfs de Karpaten en de Oeral. Dit betekent dat Groenland, mits de bodem en het water toereikend zijn, bossen zou kunnen dragen zoals die in Duitsland of Roemenië. En, wat nog belangrijker is, het kan een toevluchtsoord zijn voor soorten die veel zuidelijker met hittestress te kampen hebben.

Het probleem met de meeste refugia is wat wetenschappers 'capaciteit' noemen. Hoelang kunnen ze als refugium dienen? Volgens de meeste prognoses zal de door de mens ontketende opwarming zo snel gaan dat gebieden die in 2100 geschikt zijn als toevluchtsoord, binnen 80 tot 100 jaar alweer ongeschikt zullen zijn naarmate de opwarming wordt versneld. Op Groenland kan dat anders zijn. Zelfs bij hogere temperaturen en met alle daarmee gepaard gaande terugkoppelingen, zal het ijs nog lang nodig hebben om te smelten. Misschien duizenden jaren, misschien honderden.

Er is nog drie miljoen vierkante kilometer ijs over, hier en daar meerdere kilometers dik. De nabijheid van de ijskap en, dat is cruciaal, het smeltwater daarvan in een valleienstelsel van microklimaten, zouden kunnen werken als een koelkast die het gebied langer relatief koel houdt, waardoor soorten een kans krijgen om te schuilen voor de droogte en de branden die voor de rest van de boreale zone worden voorspeld. De ijskap mag dan het *point of no return* gepasseerd zijn, hij heeft wel een lange staart, en die blijvende echo van ijs zal waarschijnlijk nog millennia lang de samenstelling van de nieuwe boreale bossen bepalen.

De volgende dag moet Kenneth zijn geliefde arboretum verlaten voor een afspraak in Washington DC. Hij beschouwt zichzelf als Groenlands staatsburger en zijn afkomst is te herleiden tot de vermenging van Inuit- en Deens koloniaal bloed in de loop van eeuwen. Aangezien Groenland nog steeds een provincie van Denemarken is, zij het met een eigen deelregering, heeft Kenneth een gevarieerde carrière gehad. Na zich te hebben opgewerkt in de rangen van het Deense ministerie van Buitenlandse Zaken als landbouwconsulent voor de hulporganisatie DANIDA, in Azië, is Kenneth nu viceminister van Buitenlandse Zaken van Groenland. In augustus 2019 haalt de poging van Donald Trump om Groenland te kopen alle voorpagina's. Het is niet de mogelijke rol van het eiland als reddingsboei te midden van de klimaatverandering die de belangstelling van de president heeft gewekt, maar zijn rijke minerale rijkdommen, waaronder het uranium, dat onlangs toegankelijk is geworden door het smelten van de permafrost. De VS tonen ook steeds meer belangstelling voor de heropening van enkele van hun vroegere militaire bases. Van de zestien is er nu nog maar één, Thule genaamd, naast een heilige berg waar de geesten van generaties Inuit wonen. Een landingsbaan ligt op de plaats van het Inuit-dorp Qanaq, dat onder dwang honderdvijftig kilometer naar het noorden werd verplaatst.

Ik word wakker van het geluid van de regen op mijn tent. De binnenkant is glibberig. Ik kampeer aan de voet van een puinhelling vlak bij Kenneths hut. Een telegraafpaal, een reus van een boom die ooit groeide aan de rand van de Stille Oceaan, ver van hier, ligt nu in een greppel, zijn draden verward met wilgen. De grond is een tapijt van korstmossen dat gisteren onder mijn voeten kraakte als vorst, maar nu veert als rubber. Jeneverbes en wilgenroosje strekken zich uit over de helling tot ze dunner worden waar de rotsen beginnen. In de griezelige grijze dageraad weerklinkt het eenzame '*klokklok*' van raven op de torenhoge klif erboven, een herinnering aan het feit dat er bijna geen ander vogelgezang is.

Ik loop voorzichtig de hut binnen en zie Kenneth, helemaal in het zwart, zijn zwarte tas inpakken en zwarte koffie drinken aan een ronde tafel bij het raam, onder een ijsberenvel dat aan de muur is gespijkerd. Hij praat niet graag over politiek, maar hij kan het niet laten om toch even zijn bestemming te noemen: de West Wing van het Witte Huis! Wanneer ik echter doorvraag naar Trump, wordt hij weer zwijgzaam en zijn grijsgroene ogen vernauwen zich met de berekening van de diplomaat.

'Laten we het bij de bomen houden.'

Wat voor geheime onderhandelingen hij ook voert uit naam van de overheid, het zijn waarschijnlijk de bomen die zijn meest blijvende nalatenschap zullen zijn. Samen met Poul Bjerge en Søren Ødum heeft Kenneth vrijwel zeker de vegetatie- en geologische geschiedenis van Groenland veranderd. En als het potentieel van Groenland als kritisch refugium voor boreale soorten verder wordt aangetoond, zou wel eens kunnen blijken dat hij een sleutelrol heeft gespeeld bij het bepalen van de vorm van het wereldbos dat zal ontstaan nadat onze huidige uitbarsting van milieuvandalisme voorbij is. Op een gegeven moment zal de menselijke uitstoot vertragen en tot stilstand komen. Wanneer alle methaan en koolstof die in de permafrost zijn vastgevroren, zijn vrijgekomen, de terugkoppelingen zijn uitgewerkt en het mengsel van zuurstof en kooldioxide weer is gestabiliseerd, zal de fotosynthetische machinerie die nog over is, opnieuw beginnen aan het moeizame proces van de opbouw van een bos met de beschikbare middelen die er zijn in de vorm van bodem en zaden. Hier in Zuid-Groenland zullen de gecombineerde inspanningen van Kenneth en het Amerikaanse leger bepalen wat die middelen waarschijnlijk zullen zijn.

Beneden aan de kust waaien sluiers fijne regen door de vallei. Een modderige streep ligt over de fjord. De bruisende, schuimende rivier is doortrokken met bruine aarde. Binnen de omheining van de start- en landingsbaan van het vliegveld huppelen twee grote Amerikaanse hazen over het met struikgewas begroeide grind. Kenneths schuchtere zandkleurige kop verdwijnt door de dubbele deuren van de terminal, precies op het moment waarop de voormalige glaciologen Dirk en Fazia en hun zoon Radin met Peter de boswachter terugkeren uit het zuiden. Ik sluit me bij hen aan en spring achter in hun rode truck om naar het terrein van de oude luchtmachtbasis te gaan en nog wat bomen te planten.

Vanaf de landingsbaan buigt de oude Amerikaanse weg af om

een brug over te steken en komt dan uit op een platte vlakte, bezaaid met honderden kleine bomen: Siberische lariks en Englemanspar. Dit is een favoriete plek voor bomen, het gebied waar ze zich het vrijst kunnen uitzaaien. In tegenstelling tot de fjord met zijn zegge en mos waar de naaldbomen zich nergens kunnen vestigen, is deze verstoorde stuwwal die in de jaren 1940 door Amerikaanse bulldozers werd geëgaliseerd, een ideale bodem voor zaailingen om wortel te schieten. We nemen de bazooka's en een schop en zoeken openingen in het opkomende bos waar sommige bomen al meer dan twee meter hoog zijn. Te midden van het gebarsten beton, de afwateringskanalen, de gevelde stalen masten en de omgevallen telegraafpalen die de Amerikanen hebben achtergelaten, ontspruiten scheuten. Overal waar we graven, vinden we roestige stukken machine, klinknagels uit vliegtuigen, gesmede buizen, plastic buizen en meters en meters bedrading. Op één plaats heeft een hele tros lariksen zichzelf uitgezaaid in de uiteenvallende resten van een bitumen dak. Verderop dient een asbestplaat als kwekerij voor sparren. Kenneth vond er ooit een krat met Coca-Colaflessen uit de jaren 1940. Het vreemdste schouwspel die ochtend is een gietijzeren brandkraan die er nog tussen de bomen staat. Het is een voorteken, een momentopname van de toekomst. Waar eens een miniatuurstad stond, met een ziekenhuis, een school voor zestig kinderen, vier vaste orkesten, zeven clubs en vijfduizend militairen voor wie Marlene Dietrich in 1944 nog heeft opgetreden, ligt nu, nog geen zeventig jaar later, een ontluikend bos.

De Amerikanen dronken er cocktails met het ijs van de ijsbergen die in de fjord dreven. Het ijs, in de loop van duizenden jaren gevormd onder intense druk, bruiste, kraakte en knapte in het glas. Er zijn nu echter nog maar weinig ijsbergen, en de gletsjertong is niet meer zichtbaar vanaf de voormalige basis. Die heeft zich honderden meters teruggetrokken, tot bovenin de vallei, achter een rotswand.

Toch is de dreigende aanwezigheid van het ijs overal voelbaar: in het voortdurende gebrul van de rivier, gevoed door de smeltende gletsjer, de vorm van de vallei zelf, en vooral in het licht, de heldere gloed van achter de heuvels die de hemel omkeert en de horizon lichter maakt aan de randen waar de hemelboog de ijskap raakt en het licht wordt teruggekaatst. Het ijs is Groenlands hemel en hel, zijn constante, totaliserende kracht, brenger van zowel leven als dood. Dirk en Fazia herinneren zich dat de gletsjer veel dichterbij was toen ze hier voor het eerst kwamen. En Peter herinnert zich dat hij er tientallen jaren geleden nog op heeft gelopen. Ze zijn er allemaal zeer beslist over: een bezoek aan Groenland is niet compleet zonder de gletsjer te hebben gezien.

De boomgrens is veranderd in dialoog met het ijs en hield daarbij steeds een respectvolle afstand. Overal in het ecotoon van de boomgrens bepaalt het ijs welke bomen waar kunnen groeien. Orogenese, de combinatie van tektonische beweging, ijstijd en erosie, bepaalt de geologie van de aardkorst. Naarmate de gletsjers zich verder terugtrekken, veranderen de daaruit voortvloeiende verschuivingen in het stroomgebied, de afwatering en de mineralen de bodemsamenstelling en de voedingsstoffenniveaus en maken zo dat planten, bomen en andere levensvormen die daarvan afhankelijk zijn, zich aanpassen. Het lot van het woud en dat van het ijs zijn verstrengeld in een planetaire tango die duizenden jaren duurt, hoewel de dans van dit moment voorlopig de laatste lijkt te zijn. Volgens één studie heeft een minieme toename van kooldioxide in de achttiende eeuw, aan het begin van het industriële tijdperk, van 180 tot 240 ppm, het uitbreken van de volgende ijstijd voorkomen.[8] Andere studies menen dat de volgende ijstijd over 23.000 jaar had moeten aanbreken, maar het ziet er nu naar uit dat deze zal worden uitgesteld of misschien zelfs helemaal niet doorgaat.

Ik vertrek net na zonsopgang naar de ijskap, terwijl de rozegouden gloed van de zon voor het eerst de bergtoppen in het noorden raakt. Op de Amerikaanse asfaltweg die landinwaarts naar de kop van de vallei voert, glijdt het ochtendlicht gestaag over de bergkam en langs de andere kant van de vallei naar beneden, waarbij het geel, amber en licht wintergroen van het kreupelhout van berken, jeneverbessen en wilgen dat zich op de steile helling heeft genesteld, tevoorschijn komt: de voorrand van het bos. Terwijl de weg uiteenvalt in een spoor van granieten keien, kijk ik uit naar het kenmerkende slanke symmetrische blad van de lijsterbes. In de week dat ik hier ben, heb ik alleen een *Sorbus aucuparia* uit Zweden in het arboretum gezien, en andere exemplaren uit IJsland die rond Kenneths hut zijn geplant. Kenneth zei dat de Groenlandse versie te vinden is in de bergen – de bergen die het ijs op afstand houden, boven de kleine vallei uittorenen en deze in haar vlakheid opmerkelijk en uniek maken, een naam waardig. In de taal van de Inuit betekent *narsarsuaq* dan ook 'de vlakke plaats'.

Het Engelse *rowan* is een rechtstreekse afleiding van het Noorse woord *raun*, dat 'boom' betekent, en in Schotland wordt het nog steeds zo uitgesproken. Voor de Noormannen moet het de belangrijkste boom zijn geweest en voor sommigen zelfs de enige. In hun mythologie werd de man gevormd uit een es en de vrouw uit een lijsterbes. In het Keltische Oghamschrift is de lijsterbes *luis*, en in het Welsh is het *criafol*, de 'huilende boom'. In het oud-Engels stond de lijsterbes bekend als *cwicbeam*, letterlijk, 'levende boom' of misschien zelfs 'levensboom'.[9] Voor de Kelten was de lijsterbes een poort tussen de werelden, de overgang naar de geestenwereld die men gebruikte om geesten op te roepen of inspiratie op te doen.

In de taal van de Inuit is het woord voor 'boom' *orpik*, en dat is ook gelijk het woord voor 'berk'. Dat is logisch. Voorbij de ruïnes van de Amerikaanse basis is het terrein dicht begroeid met de hybride berk, *Betula glandulosa*. De extra grote bladeren van deze boom zijn geel en lichtoranje getint, want augustus is in Groenland het begin van de herfst. Je kunt zien dat de soorten in het arboretum uit noordelijker streken stammen omdat ze dieper rood zijn – hun genetisch geheugen anticipeert op kortere dagen en dus laten ze hun bladeren eerder vallen.

De vallei versmalt tot een geul waarin de berken ongeveer zo hoog zijn als ik zelf ben. Daaronder bedekken wilg en jeneverbes de rotsen. De zon is inmiddels los van de bergen voor ons en over de rand van de vallei stroomt nu een gouden dageraad die de rotsen in vuur en vlam zet, maar tegelijk krijg ik het kouder. Het duurt even voor ik begrijp waarom: ik nader het ijs.

De wind die van de gletsjer waait is bitter en bijt in mijn gezicht. De lucht is zo schoon en fris dat ze papier zou kunnen snijden. De geur van water raakt vermengd met die van de tijm en de jeneverbes die ik onder mijn wandelschoenen verpletter. Op de top van de pas, voordat het pad afdaalt naar een vallei met gras en bloemen die naar de gletsjer leidt, komen de berken al na een paar meter nog slechts tot kniehoogte. Het ecotoon, de ecologische overgangszone, wordt verkort door de hoogte, maar ook door de aanwezigheid van het ijs. De boomgrenszone, die zich in Canada of Siberië over honderden kilometers kan uitstrekken, is op Groenland samengeperst tot enkele meters. De vallei op een steenworp afstand achter me is subarctisch, boreaal, de helling voor me die boven de tong van de gletsjer uitsteekt naar de woestenij van de ijskap erboven, is onmiskenbaar toendra: het groen, vaal en paars van lage grassen, alpiene planten, mossen en korstmossen. Ik zie wollegras, engelwortel en wilgenroosje.

Als ik afdaal in een bocht van het stroomgebied, neemt de wind af, de temperatuur stijgt iets, de bomen worden weer wat hoger en plotseling klinkt er een geluid dat ik de hele ochtend al niet had gehoord: de vogels zingen. Het is niet veel, maar een troostrijk, vertrouwd getjilp van een drietal kleine bruine vogels die wat op roodborsttapuiten lijken. Kenneth vertelde me dat de warmere temperaturen meer zwervers naar het arboretum hebben gebracht. De tapuit (*Oleanthe oleanthe*) is inmiddels een regelmatige bezoeker van Narsarsuaq. Misschien verklaart dat waarom er zo weinig Sorbus groenlandica te vinden is in het lage berkenbos van de hogere vallei. Een zaadje van de Sorbus moet de zure maag van een vogel doorstaan voordat het een kans heeft om te ontkiemen. Zou het kunnen dat de *disequilibrium dynamic* die de verspreiding van de soort beperkt, het gebrek aan zaadetende vogels in Groenland is, terwijl de door de wind bestoven berk het duidelijk veel gemakkelijker heeft? Als dat het geval is, zal de opwarming van de aarde ervoor zorgen dat meer zwervers hun weg naar het noorden vinden.

De stralende zon op de rozige kliffen en het gesteven blauw van de hemel die de hele week grotendeels verborgen is geweest, maken het tot een prachtige morgen. De geur van een weiland is zo bedwelmend dat ik hem zou willen bottelen. Het hooi is pas gemaaid: grote, met plastic beklede balen leiden de blik naar een maaidorser die midden in het werk is achtergelaten en waarvan de ruiten zijn bedekt met glinsterende dauw. Daarna loopt het pad door het weidelandschap naar een wijde bocht die door de overstromende rivier is veranderd in een reeks met elkaar verbonden geulen. De kleine bruggetjes zijn overspoeld geraakt en zorgvuldig geplaatste stapstenen liggen zichtbaar in de heldere stroom, een halve meter onder water. Voeten hebben een hoger pad uitgesneden langs de rand van de vallei, om de verdronken struiken heen, en oeverwilgen staan nu midden in de stroming. Het gebrul van de grote rivier is alomtegenwoordig. Grijs water met platen vuil ijs kronkelt rond een klif en verbreedt zich tot een schuimende rok over gelijkmatige witte granieten keien die het ijs tegenhouden en het laten dansen en duikelen tot het uiteenvalt en zich bij de stroming richting zee voegt.

De kiezelvlakte voor de gletsjer is een brede uiterwaard bedekt met stenen die op grootte zijn gesorteerd als gevolg van de wonderlijke werking van het ijs. Het gewicht van een bewegende gletsjer sorteert stenen als kogellagers, perfect naar diameter. Wanneer ik dichterbij kom, maakt het gras plaats voor mos en ganzerik – *inneruulaaraq*, 'het kleintje dat op vuur lijkt' – en ten slotte voor bleek rood en groen korstmos, gevolgd door niets dan kale rotsen en zand. De tong gaat schuil achter een rotswand en hoe hoog die is, blijkt wel uit een kolkende massa grijs water tussen de verticale muren van kale rotsen die de vallei honderden meters hoog omlijsten.

Het geluid van de rivier is oorverdovend en lijkt me iets te willen vertellen. Het is niet langer mogelijk – zo dat al ooit mogelijk was – om een omgeving in neutrale termen aan te voelen of te beschrijven. Het is onmogelijk om alleen een ruisende rivier te horen. Het is onmogelijk om niet te weten waar het water vandaan komt, waarom het in zo'n hoeveelheid en met zo'n kracht stroomt. Onmogelijk om de onuitgesproken vraag niet te horen: Wat zegt de rivier? Het is het geluid van schuld, het geluid van verwijten, van angst.

Om het ijs te kunnen zien, moet men tegenwoordig over een verraderlijk pad met behulp van touwen naar het plateau erboven klimmen. Ik klim. Na een meter of zestig zie ik de laatste wilg en de laatste jeneverbes plat tegen de grond langs het pad, ongeveer zo groot als een menselijke arm. Na nog eens zestig meter klimmen ben ik hoog boven de vallei en kijk uit over de inktzwarte zee, naar de turkooizen lucht en het grillige zwart-wit van de prachtige verticale pieken, duizelingwekkend boven de naburige fjord. Voor ons ligt het plateau, bezaaid met kristallen meren, diep, koud, verstoken van leven. Zegge en gras vormen een dunne bedekking over de rotsen. Het pad slingert zich tussen enorme rotsblokken door. Vier Canadese ganzen blijken onder één ervan te schuilen en komen hevig gakkend tevoorschijn wanneer ik al bijna op hen sta. Een minuut later landen ze op het spiegelgladde meer onder me, en doen ze de lucht rimpelen als in antwoord.

Dan daalt het pad af naar een voormalig smeltmeer dat nu een verdampt bekken van dunne modder is, begroeid met Scheuchers wollegras (*Eriophorum scheuchzeri*) – *ukaliusaq*, 'degene die op een haas lijkt'. Dankzij de piekerige bloemen, omgeven door fijne vezels, kan de plant licht opvangen en de temperatuur van haar inwendige voortplantingsorganen verhogen, waardoor ze sneller voedingsstoffen kan omzetten dan andere planten om haar heen. De Inuit aten vroeger de stengels en gebruikten haar om diarree te behandelen. Ze zal de weg vrijmaken voor andere soorten, waarvan er nu nog maar weinig zijn.

Achter de laatste bergkam wordt plotseling de volle pracht van de ijskap onthuld. Een verblindende, vuilwitte zee met zwarte piramides die eruit steken – bergen die tot aan hun nek in het ijs staan. Op de voorgrond loopt het plateau steil af boven het diep gebarsten en gespleten oppervlak van de kleine maar nog steeds prachtige gletsjer Kiattuut Sermiat. Peter vertelde dat je vroeger omhoog klom naar het ijs, maar dat het nu enkele honderden meters omlaag is tot aan het groezelige, zwart gestreepte oppervlak. Dit is de nieuwe huidziekte die het oppervlak van gletsjers teistert: roet dat van ver is komen aanwaaien en zwarte koolstof en algen die zich voeden met organische voedingsstoffen die vrijkomen door het smelten. Een donkerder oppervlak absorbeert meer zonlicht en veroorzaakt een sterkere dooi, nog een van de wrede terugkoppelingslussen die de opwarming van het Noordpoolgebied versnellen. Het ijs is als het negatief van de zee daarachter en het lijkt op een vinger van oceaan die zich vernauwt tot de monding van een fjord, en zich uitstrekt tot een weids vergezicht van een omgekeerde, bevroren oceaan, richels en dalen van golven bevlekt met donker schuim.

Tussen de rotsen en het ijs ligt een grijze poel die gevoed wordt door een gestage stroom die van het oppervlak van de gletsjer loopt, tussen de gegroefde randen. De poel rinkelt van het oplossende ijs. Aan één uiteinde verdwijnt de troebele soep in een gletsjermolen – een duistere holte onder de gletsjer – het ondergrondse geruis van het water klinkt merkwaardig verstikt. De grijze stroom verdwijnt in het duister en laat slechts een echo achter en het griezelige, onophoudelijke, dodelijke gekabbel. Er is geen geluid, behalve van het smelten, dat de immense stilte van de bergen en de ijskap vult met de kracht van een schreeuw.

Het heeft bijna de halve dag geduurd om hier te komen en het zal nog eens een halve duren om weer beneden te komen. Ik moet nu snel onderweg als ik niet in het vriesdonker wil stranden op het plateau, maar ik kan me er niet van losrukken. Van de betoverende onmetelijkheid ervan. Het mysterieuze geschenk van het leven en de belofte van vergetelheid. Mensen komen hier om de geheimen ervan te bestuderen, de wijsheid te delven, het archief van het klimaat van de planeet te raadplegen en het te zien voordat het weg is. Misschien verklaart dit de fascinatie van zovele culturen voor de koude uitersten van de aarde, van de ontdekkingsreizigers en schrijvers en vertellers van mythen en sprookjes, van sneeuwkoninginnen en Narnias. Diep vanbinnen weten we dat we het ijs nodig hebben. Zolang de mens er was, was het ijs er ook. De fascinatie komt ook voort uit de macht van dat ijs en onze onmacht ertegenover. Het staat op zich, is onvatbaar, oncontroleerbaar. Zijn kristallijne perfectie bewaart niet alleen de hele menselijke geschiedenis, maar ook onze toekomst. En wij kijken toe hoe gletsjers ons verleden en onze toekomst steeds sneller weglekken naar het warme bad van de zee. Het ijs trotseren is de dood aanschouwen.

De tango die het ijs en de bomen met elkaar dansen heeft de planeet gedurende miljoenen jaren afgekoeld. Zonder bomen om de kooldioxide in de atmosfeer te verminderen, had het ijs zich misschien nooit kunnen vormen. Het was een afname van de kooldioxide die het omslagpunt vormde voor de ijstijd in het Kwartair die miljarden planten uitroeide om ze vervolgens opnieuw geboren laten te worden gedurende de steeds 100.000 jaar durende pulsen van de ijstijden. We hebben nooit geweten dat het paradijs van de afgelopen 10.000 jaar zo kwetsbaar was. Zonder deze delicate hartslag van het ijs zou de aarde misschien nooit het vreemde evenwicht van het Holoceen hebben ontwikkeld waaruit zich zo'n buitengewone overvloed aan biodivers leven op aarde heeft ontwikkeld.

De planeet is een nauwkeurig afgesteld systeem. Een paar graden verandering in zijn baan kan een ijstijd inluiden, een paar graden temperatuurverandering kan de verspreiding van soorten veranderen, gletsjers doen smelten en oceanen doen ontstaan. In de toekomst, als het ijs weg is, zal er misschien helemaal geen boomgrens meer zijn. Naarmate de stabiele lucht- en waterstromen die samenhangen met de golfstroom, het polaire front, de poolwervel en de Beaufortgyre uiteenvallen of fluctueren, de Noordelijke IJszee volledig dooit en de Rossby-golven in de bovenste atmosfeer op hol slaan, zullen de fijne gradaties van temperatuur, hoogte en breedtegraad die voor het eerst door Alexander von Humboldt werden waargenomen, ontkoppeld raken en zullen ecologische overgangszones door elkaar beginnen te lopen. In plaats van een majestueuze, uitgestrekte zone van wouden rondom de planeet, zouden we losse clusters bos op de vreemdste plaatsen kunnen aantreffen, vluchtelingen van lang vergane grond en temperaturen, en er zouden opnieuw krokodillen aan de Noordpool te vinden zijn.

De opwarming van de aarde verstoort de meest essentiële functies van de aarde die wij en andere soorten nodig hebben om te overleven: de ademhalingscycli, de levenspulsen. Niet alleen de geologische relatie tussen ijs en boomgrens, die gedurende honderdduizenden jaren samen op en neer bewegen, maar ook de jaarlijkse fotosynthesepulsen van de seizoensgebonden productie – de zuurstofpiek in het voorjaar wanneer de bomen hun bladeren laten groeien, en de dagelijkse pieken en dalen tussen dag en nacht die de primaire chloroplastische functies van het plantenrijk regelen. Deze pulsen zijn letterlijk de hartslag van de planeet – zij voorzien onze wereld van zuurstof – maar de pieken en dalen worden vlakker, minder geprononceerd, naarmate de zuurstoffractie afneemt. Als er meer kooldioxide in de atmosfeer zit, hoeven bomen niet zo hard te werken om hun dagelijkse dosis koolstof binnen te krijgen. Ze sparen energie, ze openen minder van de huidmondjes op hun bladeren. Dat betekent dat ze minder inademen, minder transpireren en minder zuurstof uitademen.[10]

Plots krijg ik het benauwd. Onder de middagzon blinken de witte oppervlakken me schitterend, verblindend en desoriënterend tegemoet. Ik sta hier al te lang op de rand van de klip. Ik begin me duizelig te voelen, misselijk, mijn armen en benen licht van angst. Het lijkt de aankondiging van een paniekaanval, alsof ik net aan de dood ben ontsnapt. In zekere zin is dat ook zo. Uit onderzoek van Jason Box, de Amerikaanse glacioloog die ik bij het planten van de bomen ontmoette, zal blijken dat de Groenlandse ijskap in het seizoen 2019 254 miljard ton ijs heeft verloren, zeven keer zoveel als in de jaren 1990. Het smelten van de ijskappen op deze schaal was pas verwacht na 2070. En het gaat steeds sneller. Bovendien duurde het dooiseizoen in 2019 tot in oktober, en in 2020 tot in december, hetgeen de weg vrijmaakt voor een snel uiteenvallen van de ijskap.

We weten wat er aan het gebeuren is. Een ongelukkig neveneffect van de wetenschap is de illusie dat we de situatie als mens de baas zijn: het idee dat als we weten wat er gebeurt, we het ook kunnen beheersen. De ironie wil dat we dat misschien wel hadden gekund. De tragiek is dat het daarvoor nu wel te laat is. De kettingreactie is op gang gebracht. Vanaf hier zal het alleen maar sneller en sneller gaan. Jason zegt dat door de uitstoot die nu al in de atmosfeer terecht is gekomen, de zeespiegel vijf meter kan stijgen. Het is enkel de vraag hoe snel het ijs zal smelten. Opnieuw lijken de modellen de snelheid te hebben onderschat.[11] Al die verhalen en ideeën over het bevroren noorden, die zoals zoveel andere dingen in de menselijke cultuur verband houden met een stabiel klimaat, met vertrouwde soorten en regelmatige seizoenen, zullen als het licht van sterren die zelf allang dood zijn, nog jaren schijnen.

Onder mijn voeten zijn in de roodbruine rots diepe groeven uitgesleten, sporen van het onlangs voltooide geologische werk van de gletsjer. Ik heb het merkwaardige gevoel dat de tijd wordt samengedrukt. Ik sta op een geologische breuklijn, het begin van de Arctisch-gematigde overgangszone, de uiterste rand van een proces dat in planetaire termen zowat gisteren eindigde, toen Wales, Scandinavië, Siberië, Alaska en het Canadese Schild bedekt waren met ijs. In een oogwenk heeft de boomgrens het smeltende ijs naar het noorden verjaagd. Het is eigenlijk verbazingwekkend hoe snel de natuur beweegt.

Maar in de volgende oogwenk, als Groenland bebost is, als het bomeneiland Tajmyr geen eiland meer is, als er geen toendra meer is in Scandinavië of Alaska en de bossen van Noord-Amerika en Siberië verbrande prairie zijn, als er bomen staan waar ik nu sta, zullen er dan nog mensen zijn om dat te zien? Ons huidige tijdperk doet denken aan een vraag die bisschop George Berkeley in de zeventiende eeuw stelde, maar geeft er een draai aan: als er een boom in het bos groeit en er is niemand om hem te zien, is het dan echt gebeurd? Kunnen mensen zich een planeet zonder zichzelf voorstellen?

Onze huidige noodsituatie dwingt ons te herinneren wat wij tot voor kort altijd hebben geweten: dat er buiten ons een web van communicatie, zin en betekenis bestaat, een wereld van levensvormen die voortdurend kwebbelen, schreeuwen en flirten en elkaar opjagen, onverschillig over wat mens beweegt. En daar gaat een zekere troost vanuit. De uitweg uit de depressie, het verdriet en het schuldgevoel over doodlopende weg van de koolstof die we zijn ingeslagen, is de wereld zonder onszelf te beschouwen. Te weten dat de aarde, dat het leven, de evolutionaire reis zal voortzetten in al haar mysteries en wonderen. Om ons idee van tijd, en van onszelf te verruimen. Als wij onszelf zien als deel van een groter geheel, dan is het complete plaatje mooi, zinvol en respectvol, de moeite waard om misschien voor te sterven, in de veilige wetenschap dat het leven niet het tegenovergestelde is van de dood, maar een cirkel, zoals het bos ons leert, een continuüm.

Het vage gewiek van een helikopter doorbreekt het moment, een kleine rode kist die wetenschappers of toeristen de ijskap op draagt voor een glimp van de eeuwigheid in beweging. Ik begin aan de afdaling, ontzet en ontroerd, en voel me nietig. Het aanvaarden van de immense, onbetaalbare en verdwijnende ijsvoorraad van de aarde heeft me uitgeput, en ik wankel op mijn benen wanneer ik het pad afloop. De zon volgt me naar beneden. De bergen zijn scherp en fraai afgetekend in het middaglicht. De zee in de fjord weerkaatst het licht door de vallei, betoverend in haar herfstjas van goud, rood en groen. De rode, gegroefde rots maakt plaats voor grind, het pad loopt in lussen omhoog en weer omlaag over de morene voor de wijkende gletsjertong. Ik loop niet langer op grond die nog maar pas aan de lucht werd blootgesteld na duizenden jaren onder het ijs te hebben vastgezeten. Mijn schoenen veren om het mos en gras dat een plek heeft gevonden tussen het grind, het slib en de rotsen. Korstmossen beginnen de keien te ontginnen en maken zo een begin van die kostbare grond. Voor me zie ik wilgenroosje, jeneverbes, berk, en daarachter zijn de edele pieken van de naaldbomen, hun gevleugelde zaden opstijgend in de wind. Het bos zal nu snel hier zijn.

Epiloog: Denken als een bos

Llanelieu, Wales
52° 00' 01' N

Een bos is geen statisch ding, maar een voortdurend evoluerend mozaïek van soorten die op allerlei manieren met elkaar en met de rotsen, de atmosfeer en het klimaat in verband staan. De baanbrekende Russische ecoloog Soekatsjev noemde dit onderling samenhangende systeem 'biogeocoenose', levensgemeenschap. De Koyukon noemen het 'de wereld die Raaf heeft gemaakt'. De precieze werking van deze meest complexe relatie van allemaal is een mysterie waarvan we de contouren alleen maar kunnen gissen en waarvan we de uitkomst hooguit kunnen bewonderen in de vorm van de levende, ademende bossen die het leven op aarde in stand houden.

Dit boek is een poging om een glimp op te vangen van de algoritmen die in de natuur aan het werk zijn, en om eens stil te staan bij de resultaten. Het doel was niet oplossingen aan te dragen voor de crisis die de mens in de natuur heeft teweeggebracht, hoewel sommige conclusies onontkoombaar zijn. Wat we weten geeft veel aanleiding om het ergste te vrezen, en wat we niet weten laat nog ruimte voor veel hoop.

Wat me duidelijk is geworden tijdens mijn reis langs de boomgrens, is dat de opwarming van de aarde al vergevorderd is en dat de mens de omvang en de ernst van de ontketende opwarming misschien nog kan temperen, maar niet in staat zal zijn om haar te stoppen. Ook heb ik moeten vaststellen dat zelfs in de korte tijd dat ik onderzoek heb gedaan voor dit boek (2018-2021) de snelheid van de geologische veranderingen waarvan we getuige zijn, hoger ligt dan de modellen voorspelden. De wereld is in de greep van ongekende veranderingen. De planeet waarop we dachten te leven bestaat niet meer. Maar dat is oud nieuws.

De echte vraag is nu wat we met die wetenschap gaan doen. De aanvaarding van het feit dat ons milieu snel aan het veranderen is vormt een fundamentele uitdaging voor ons welvarende leven en voor westerse denkgewoonten die gebaseerd zijn op een idee (en ervaring) van vooruitgang, vrede, democratie en economische groei. De discussies in het mondiale noorden lijken gevangen te zitten tussen enerzijds steeds onrealistischer dromen over een 'klimaatneutrale' en pijnloze groene groei, en anderzijds misantropische verhalen over de apocalyps, geweld en het uitsterven van de mensheid. De geschiedenis van de mensen die langs de boomgrens wonen – en die al langer dan de meesten met de realiteit van een veranderend milieu leven – biedt echter een alternatief. Er is nog een derde verhaal, een positievere interpretatie van de relatie tussen de mens en zijn habitat, dat misschien perspectief biedt op een andere toekomst.

Bomen en mensen leven in dezelfde klimaatniche. Onze opponeerbare duimen herinneren ons er voortdurend aan dat we in bomen evolueerden en floreerden. Wij zullen altijd boswezens blijven. Gedurende de 11.000 jaar die sinds de laatste ijstijd zijn verstreken, is de mens met de bomen meegeëvolueerd. Hij heeft zich gevestigd in de habitats die door de oprukkende boomgrens zijn ontstaan en heeft die vervolgens aangepast, beheerst en beheerd, waardoor gedurende bijna die gehele periode op wereldschaal een opmerkelijk stabiele en vriendelijke leefomgeving is ontstaan. De Koyukon, de Sami, de Nganasan, de Anishinaabe zijn slechts enkele van de ontelbare inheemse volkeren van wie het wereldbeeld getuigt van onze fundamentele afhankelijkheid van het bos. Wij zijn de belangrijkste soort van het Holoceen geweest – en een geologische kracht, zeker, maar niet alleen in negatieve zin. Er is amper een bos op de planeet dat niet door de mens is verstoord, maar daardoor zijn vaak niches voor biodiversiteit ontstaan.

De Zimovs hebben vrijwel zeker gelijk als zij suggereren dat *Homo sapiens* de megafauna van Siberië heeft uitgeroeid en zo de weg vrijmaakte voor het taigawoud, maar we hebben ook de grove den naar Schotland gebracht en de balsempopulier naar het grind van de eskers aan de oevers van de Hudson Bay. We hebben de cryolithische lariksbossen van Ary Mas en de gematigde regenwouden van Wales en Schotland omgehakt, dieren geweid in de bossen, we hebben hooilanden, vennen, vlakten en heidevelden voor onszelf bestemd en het afbranden van de boreale bossen ter hand genomen, zoals de Anishinaabe van Poplar River, juist om de biodiversiteit ten bate van de mens te bevorderen in plaats van ze te vernietigen. Onze korte heerschappij als de belangrijkste soort van de planeet viel samen met het hoogtepunt van de biodiversiteit op aarde. Zoals de radicale ecoloog Ian Rappel schreef: 'Vanuit het perspectief van de biodiversiteit en de biosfeer is er niets mis met het Antropoceen. Wat er wel mis is, is de... manier waarop het nu wordt bestuurd.'[12]

Het doorbreken van het ecologisch plafond van de planeet werd slechts mogelijk gemaakt en versneld door één specifiek, recent economisch model: het industrieel kapitalisme en zijn politieke exportproduct, het kolonialisme.[13] Maar kapitalisme, de uitbuiting van hulpbronnen en arbeid om rijkdom in de handen van enkelen te concentreren, is niet noodzakelijkerwijs het beste economische model. Ons collectieve voortbestaan op deze planeet hangt er vrijwel zeker vanaf of we dit model achter ons kunnen laten. Als we de situatie overzien vanuit ons kapitalistische perspectief, worden we aangemoedigd te geloven dat er geen alternatief is en dat de crisis onze schuld is. Maar die schuld aanvaarden maakt ons niet alleen enorm machteloos, het is bovendien misplaatst.

We hebben ons economische systeem niet gekozen uit een lijst met beschikbare opties. We zijn allen in meer of mindere mate het slachtoffer van historische krachten die in de loop der eeuwen machtsstructuren hebben opgebouwd op basis van een zeer simplistisch idee van waarde. In het geval van een boom brengt alleen het hout op de markt een prijs op, niet de grond waarop hij gegroeid is of de insecten die hem bestoven hebben, de zon die hem voedde of de regen die hem heeft bevloeid. De bosgemeenschap die zoveel soorten herbergt is echter onbetaalbaar. Het kapitalisme vervreemdt en verhandelt de natuur niet alleen als producten om zo de mens in een consument te veranderen, het vervreemdt en verhandelt ons mensen zelf ook. Onze blik zelf is een product geworden. Onze aandacht is afgeleid van de biosfeer die ons in stand houdt, en deze vervreemding maakt ons in meer of mindere mate blind, doof en stom. In het perspectief van de lange geschiedenis van onze co-evolutie met het woud, is de menselijke breuk met de natuur nog maar recent. Het verhaal van het menselijk leven op aarde is ouder en genuanceerder dan de geschiedenis van het kapitalisme en – dat is het belangrijkste – nog niet af.

We worden niet onverschillig voor onze omgeving geboren. Terwijl ik dit schrijf, galmt het gejank van kettingzagen door het gemengde boslandschap van de smalle vallei Cwm Rhyd Ellyw, in de diepte achter de kerk van Llanelieu, naast mijn huis. Het is wat men noemt een plantage in oerbos, en dus hebben de autoriteiten, ondanks de aanwezigheid van enkele machtige hardhoutsoorten, de landeigenaar een vergunning verleend om het hele perceel te rooien. Alle spelers uit het boreale gebied waren er te vinden – de grove den, de berk, de lariks, de spar, de lijsterbes – en daarnaast nog verschillende andere, zoals de els, de es en Douglasspar.

Toen ik met mijn twee dochters de weg afliep om de schade te bekijken aan de plaatsen waar zij eerder nog speelden, de steen in de schaduw van een berk die zij 'het riviercafé' noemden, of de diepe poel onder een omgevallen populier 'waar de reiger woont', waren ze zo geschokt dat ze in tranen uitbarstten. De boomstammen lagen hoog opgestapeld, de lucht was zwaar van de geur van hars, de steile oevers waren bezaaid met takken en de regen vulde de diepe rupsbandsporen van de houthakkersmachines, zodat de rivier een cederrode kleur kreeg. De meisjes konden voor de eerste keer in hun korte leven de bergen zien. Ze zijn zes en vier. Ze vroegen waarom de bomen werden gekapt terwijl we de zuurstof die ze produceren en de regen die ze condenseren toch nodig hebben. Wat hen echter het meest verontrustte, en dat veroorzaakte opnieuw hevig snikken, was de bezorgdheid om de levende wezens die in het bos thuis waren geweest.

'De bomen moeten hebben gehuild.' (Een idee dat ook onder de inheemse volkeren van Canada leeft.)

'Wat als een moeder lieveheersbeestje terugkwam op haar nest en ontdekte dat de boom omgehakt was en al haar baby's weg waren?'

Ouderschap in een tijdperk van snelle klimaatverandering laat geen ruimte voor de luxe van misantropie of valse hoop. We moeten, om de woorden van de antropologe Donna Harraway van de Universiteit van Californië te parafraseren, 'bij de problemen blijven'.[14]

De bewegende boomgrens had tot mijn verbeelding gesproken na de voltooiing van mijn vorige boek over vluchtelingen in de Hoorn van Afrika. Dat was niet alleen vanuit het verlangen om na de meedogenloze hitte en het stof van de equatoriale woestijn van Kenia en Somalië eens ergens heen te gaan waar het kouder was. De Hoorn van Afrika is, net als de Sahelgordel in het algemeen, bijzonder gevoelig voor klimaatveranderingen in de oceanen en neerslagpatronen als gevolg van teleconnecties met bossen – en ontbossing – elders. De verdrijvingen en het geweld daar worden grotendeels veroorzaakt door droogte en klimaatverandering, en ik wilde schrijven over andere plaatsen waar de gevolgen van de opwarming al zichtbaar waren, waar men een glimp van de toekomst kon opvangen.

Ik besefte niet hoe relevant mijn ervaring met verslaggeving over oorlog en vluchtelingen in Afrika, over mensen die worstelen om in moeilijke omstandigheden zin en hoop te vinden, zou blijken te zijn. Slachtoffers van oorlogen of natuurrampen zijn vaak veel beter in staat op dramatische veranderingen te reageren en die te begrijpen. Tijdens een ramp wordt de sociale orde weggevaagd en worden we opnieuw aan onszelf geopenbaard. De 'mens' wordt ontketend, bevrijd van zijn gebruikelijke beperkingen, soms met barbaarse gevolgen, maar vaker met positieve effecten. Mensen zijn tot buitengewone dingen in staat. Wat ik heb geleerd in de ruïnes en de vluchtelingenkampen van Congo, Soedan, Oeganda en Somalië is dat strijd hoop voortbrengt, niet andersom. Hoop is geen inert edelmetaal dat ligt te wachten om ontdekt te worden, het is iets dat moet worden vervaardigd en geherdefinieerd in het licht van veranderende omstandigheden, steeds weer opnieuw. Wat we daarvan leren is dat wanhoop de eerste stap is op weg naar herstel. Erkennen welke schade er eerder is aangericht geeft ons kracht, zoals de ouderen van Poplar River koloniaal verdriet omzetten in een beweging die het grootste beschermde bos van Noord-Amerika veiligstelde, of zoals Thomas MacDonnell die eeuwen van overbeweiding door schapen en herten terugdraaide om een begin te maken met het herstel van het grote bos van Schotland.

Het is een burgerlijke misvatting dat 'hoop' synoniem is geworden met het redden – of bereiken – van een ideale toestand van veilige welvaart, vooral wanneer een dergelijke welvaart onverenigbaar is met de grenzen die de planeet nu eenmaal stelt aan de economische groei. Māret Buljo in Noorwegen zou moeten lachen om het idee. Hoop ligt in de gezamenlijke inspanningen, in transformatie, in zinvol werk voor het algemeen welzijn.

We staan aan de vooravond van een nieuw tijdperk in het leven van de planeet. Ten minste 2 graden opwarming is nu al onvermijdelijk – dat gaat gebeuren – hoewel sommige wetenschappers zelfs meer dan dat voorspellen, tot 4 graden 'impliciete opwarming'.[15] Vóór het einde van de eenentwintigste eeuw zal er een golf van extincties plaatsvinden, bomen zullen zich naar het noorden haasten, steppes zullen zich uitbreiden, de toendra zal samen met het Arctische zee-ijs verdwijnen, de oceanen zullen worden herschikt en steden zullen overstromen. De laatste generatie die een stabiel klimaat zal kennen, met seizoenscycli en vertrouwde soorten – en alle menselijke cultuur en tradities die op dat fundament berusten – is al geboren.

Dat is hard. Maar accepteren dat de status quo niet te herstellen is, is ook de eerste stap op weg naar actie. Plotseling is er zoveel te doen. De strijd om de schade te beperken en ons voor te bereiden op wat er komen gaat, is al begonnen. Dit is de filosofie die ten grondslag ligt aan Black Mountains College, een nieuwe modelonderwijsinstelling die ik mede heb opgericht en die gebaseerd is op hetzelfde onderzoek dat tot dit boek heeft geleid. De filosofie gaat uit van een eenvoudig inzicht van de bosschoolbeweging: dat we alleen opnieuw verbinding kunnen maken met de natuur wanneer de natuur zelf het klaslokaal is. Er wordt buiten les gegeven, en het college biedt trajecten aan voor het leren van de vaardigheden en denkwijzen die nodig zijn om de menselijke samenleving te organiseren volgens de ecologische beginselen van diversiteit, evenwicht, grenzen en symbiose. Als men meer zou leren en begrijpen hoe de boomgrens onze wereld bewoonbaar heeft gemaakt, hoe bossen regen produceren, winden aanjagen, water beheren, de oceanen bemesten, de basis vormen van veel moderne geneeskunde, de lucht zuiveren van door de mens veroorzaakte vervuiling en de atmosfeer desinfecteren, zou het veel moeilijker zijn om ze te kappen.

Meer dan van welke vorige generatie ook, zal het leven van de kinderen die deze eeuw geboren worden, afhangen van hoe het gaat met de niet-menselijke wereld. Wanneer water en voedsel schaars worden, zoals nu reeds het geval is, wanneer intercontinentale bevoorradingsketens niet langer doenlijk zijn, wanneer de industriële landbouw tot mislukken gedoemd is, zullen wij opnieuw aandachtig moeten zijn. We zullen weer terug naar het bos moeten, om wat Charles Eisenstein 'het verhaal van de scheiding' noemt, terug te draaien. En de manier waarop we dat doen is door gebruik te maken van de poort waardoor onze ziel in contact staat met de rest van de wereld: via onze zintuigen. Nieuwsgierigheid en opmerkzaamheid zijn de bescheiden maar absoluut onoverkomelijke voorwaarden voor een nieuwe relatie met de aarde. Systemen veranderen als er een cultuur is die daarom vraagt. De revolutie begint met een wandeling in het bos. Hoe heeft het ooit zover kunnen komen dat wij de namen vergaten van de levende wezens die zuurstof produceren, de lucht en het water zuiveren?

Als we deel willen uitmaken van het geheel van soorten dat samen evolueert om de komende omwenteling te overleven, moeten we die essentiële verstrengeling met andere levende wezens nieuw leven inblazen. We moeten allemaal opnieuw leren denken als een bos.

De Koyukon-jager op zoek naar een beer zal de beer geen naam geven. Hij zal het zelfs vermijden om de beer aan te kijken. De Nganasan-verteller die een verhaal vertelt over een vrouw in een chum (tent) zal de naam van dat gezinshoofd niet noemen, hij zal haar alleen 'degene die bij de deur van de chum zit' noemen. Het is een gewoonte die ook in andere inheemse culturen en mondelinge tradities voorkomt – om de namen van mensen niet te gebruiken, maar naar hen te verwijzen in termen van wie zij zijn voor de spreker: 'Hé, broer!', 'lieve schoonzus', 'leraar', 'ouder-dan-ik'. Dat is een mooie erkenning dat alle bestaan relationeel is. Geen enkel mens is herleidbaar tot één enkel zelf en bevat vele zelven, vele instanties van zijn zelf. Elk schepsel bevat mogelijkheden.

De beer een naam geven is het dier objectiveren, en dat is dus beledigend. Wij weten niet hoe de beer zichzelf noemt, noch weten we welke andere zielen of zelven het lichaam van de beer zou kunnen bevatten. Daarom is het niet noemen van de naam van de beer een teken van bescheidenheid en respect. Het niet benoemen is ook een erkenning van de onbepaaldheid – dat de aard van de beer nog niet vastligt – zijn relatie tot de jager wordt nog bepaald, een proces dat zal worden beslist door hoe de jager, en de beer, handelen. De jager zal het ook vermijden de beer aan te kijken, want zien en gezien worden is een relationele activiteit. Als je iets ruikt, lossen kleine deeltjes van datgene wat je ruikt op in je neus: het ding dat je ruikt, wordt jou. Inheemse opvattingen over zintuiglijke waarneming (en die van de moderne fenomenologie, zoals David Abram ons zo welsprekend in herinnering brengt) gaan verder dan dit wetenschappelijke feit: alle waarneming is participatie.[16] Als jij de beer ziet, dan heeft hij jou gezien, en jullie zijn beiden veranderd door dat feit.

De strikte regels en rituelen in de inheemse culturen van bosbewoners over hoe dieren en planten moeten worden bekeken, besproken, behandeld, gedood en gegeten, vloeien voort uit het feit dat het voortbestaan van de mens ten diepste verweven is met dat van andere soorten. Wanneer wij de beer eten, worden wij de beer voor zover de verzameling van soorten die leven gaf aan zijn lichaam in het onze opnieuw wordt samengesteld. In het licht van moderne wetenschappelijke studies van het spijsverteringskanaal zijn dergelijke opvattingen nog niet zo vergezocht als ze op het eerste gezicht misschien lijken. Wanneer meer dan de helft van je wortels bewoond wordt door een ander organisme of wanneer je afhankelijk bent van vliegende insecten om je bloemen te bestuiven, doe je aan gezamenlijk overleven. Alle evolutie is co-evolutie.[17]

De geduchte taboes van de Koyukon of Anishinaabe, de Sami of Nganasan zijn niet alleen een erkenning van hoe afhankelijk de mens is van natuurlijke processen, maar ook een erkenning van de enorme verantwoordelijkheid die rust op de schouders van de belangrijkste soort van de planeet. De opwarming is een gegeven, maar hoe de soorten daarop reageren is een verhaal dat nog moet worden verteld en waarin de mens een sleutelrol zal moeten spelen. Strategische ecologie zal weldra een kernelement worden van de nationale veiligheid en de weerbaarheid van een gemeenschap.

Ondersteunde migratie – soorten helpen zich te verplaatsen en aan te passen – zal een hoofddoel van het natuurbehoud worden. Wij zijn Noach met zijn ark. Wij hebben de macht om tenminste deels te bepalen wat er overleeft. De bomen die wij selecteren om te overleven, zullen millennia lang bepalend zijn voor hele bossen en ecosystemen – en ook voor de soorten die daarvan afhankelijk zijn. Het Antropoceen is nog maar net aangebroken en het zal nog lang de aarde beheersen, zelfs wanneer wij er niet meer zijn.

Het is altijd zo geweest dat het leven een morele onderneming is, dat de daad van het leven zelf een erfenis achterlaat. Als je het bos bekijkt met Keltische, Koyukon, Sami, Nganasan of Anishinaabe-ogen, zie je een wereld van meerdere zelven en zielen die met elkaar communiceren. Als wij al dit andere leven en onze afhankelijkheid ervan erkennen, worden we onherroepelijk met de vraag geconfronteerd: wat is het juiste om te doen? Het blad praat met de wind, de bloem praat met de bij, de wortels praten met de schimmels – de wereld is een chaotisch, lawaaierig oord! Wanneer we het bos in lopen, maken we de wereld met ons lichaam, met onze voeten, onze ogen, onze adem, onze verbeelding. Een miljoen willekeurige vertakkingen van de toekomst zijn mogelijk. Het bos is een zee van mogelijkheden, een oneindig experiment in co-evolutie.

Een hoopvolle toekomst is in een dergelijke definitie geen gebed om stabiliteit, om stilstand, maar een uitnodiging om deel te nemen: om te verkennen, te ervaren, te verdwalen of je weg te vinden. Het is een kans om je ware ik te verwezenlijken door het juiste te doen. Wat je nog moet doen zal je altijd meer definiëren dan wat je in het verleden hebt gedaan. Dingen kunnen niet benoemd worden omdat ze onvoltooid zijn. De evolutionaire natuur is een motor van het mysterie. Van dingen die we niet weten en niet kunnen weten. In het bos maak je deel uit van iets magisch en groots, waarin elke stap tegelijk een daad van vernietiging en van schepping, van leven is. Het is een troost dat wij altijd hebben geleefd in de ruïnes van wat voorafging en dat we er nog steeds in leven.

Wij moeten onze kinderen voorbereiden op de onzekerheid, maar niet als slachtoffers. Wij en zij zijn rentmeesters, nog steeds belast met een eeuwenoude verantwoordelijkheid. De aarde leeft en is betoverd, en handelen als deel ervan is betoveren door te leven – zien, horen, voelen, dansen – de toekomst maken met elke stap, in het volle besef dat elke beweging die je maakt, hoe groot of klein ook, ertoe doet.

Glossarium van Bomen

De volgende bladzijden bevatten beschrijvingen van de bomen die in dit boek voorkomen – de hoofdrolspelers van de hoofdstukken, en van verschillende andere veel voorkomende soorten van de boreale zone. Het zijn samenvattingen van wat ik heb geleerd van anderen die veel deskundiger zijn dan ik. Raadpleeg voor uitgebreidere informatie:

Diana Beresford-Kroeger, *Arboretum Americana* (Michigan University Press, 2003)

Diana Beresford-Kroeger, *Arboretum Borealis* (Michigan University Press, 2010)

Daniel Moerman, *Native American Ethnobotany* (Timber Press, 1998)

Nature Conservancy (nature.org)

Iain J. Davidson-Hunt, Nathan Deutsch en Andrew M. Miller, *Pimachiowin Aki Cultural Landscape Atlas* (Pimachiowin Aki Corporation, Winnipeg, 2012)

Trees for Life (treesforlife.org.uk)

Colin Tudge, *The Secret Life of Trees: How They Live and Why They Matter* (Allen Lane, 2005)

Woodland Trust (woodlandtrust.org.uk)

Alnus, els

De *Alnus glutinosa*, ook gewone els of zwarte els genoemd, is tot op een hoogte van ongeveer 500 meter een algemeen verschijnsel in het Euraziatische boreale woud. In Noord-Amerika gedijen er ook veel andere van de dertig elzensoorten. Het zijn geneeskrachtige bomen die bij de inheemse bevolking bekend staan als 'de wilg die stinkt'.

Alnus is een lid van de berkenfamilie, *Betulaceae*. Het is een waterminnende soort die vaak wordt aangetroffen in de buurt van rivieren en meren, waar zijn diepe wortels helpen de oevers te stabiliseren en de vruchtbaarheid van de bodem te verbeteren door zijn vermogen om stikstof uit de lucht vast te leggen. De els groeit snel, net als de berk. Hij vormt knoppen en bijna ronde bladeren met getande randen aan meerdere stengels en ook rechtstreeks aan de stronk. Deze knoppen en twijgen kunnen kleverig zijn, vandaar *glutinosa*.

De boom is eenhuizig, met mannelijke katjes en vrouwelijke kegelvormige bloemen die in het voorjaar bloeien voordat de bladeren uitkomen. Hij wordt bestoven door de wind. De zaden hebben luchtmembranen en ontkiemen op het wateroppervlak, waardoor ze wortel kunnen schieten op de rivieroevers waar ze aanspoelen.

De els is van cruciaal belang voor de biodiversiteit: Hij levert voedsel voor meer dan 140 insectensoorten, bladeren die in rivieren worden afgebroken, chemische stoffen die het leven in het water beschermen en wortels die een thuis bieden aan 47 verschillende mycorrhizaschimmels. Hij herbergt ook een stikstoffixerende bacterie, *Frankia alni*, die koolstof uit de boom haalt in ruil voor stikstof. Dit maakt de els tot een perfecte keuze voor het herstel van aangetaste landschappen, een pionier die de bodem bemest met stikstof, zodat andere bomen kunnen volgen. Hij werd gebruikt om door dagbouw verpest landschap te herstellen in de VS en in 1915 om de groene gordel rond Sint-Petersburg te herbebossen.

In de Keltische folklore was de els *fearn* in het Ogham-schrift, en werd hij geassocieerd met 'verbergen' en 'geheimhouding'. Elzenbossen – *carrs* – waren natte, drassige, ontoegankelijke plaatsen. Het hout blijft bijzonder goed bewaard wanneer het in water is ondergedompeld en werd daarom vaak gebruikt voor sluisdeuren en kanaalaanleg. Het werd ook gebruikt voor de houten palen waar Venetië op is gebouwd. Het is zeer goed bestand tegen vuur en wordt in bossen aangeplant als brandgang.

Betula, berk

De berkenfamilie is groot en uitgebreid en veel van de zestig soorten wereldwijd komen in het hele boreale gebied voor – van de boomgrens tot helemaal in de gematigde bossen van het zuiden. Het is bij uitstek een pionierssoort, waarvan het overvloedig op de wind verspreide zaad al na vier weken kiemt zonder dat er veel grond voor nodig is. De ruwe berk geeft de voorkeur aan zure, pas ontgonnen of verbrande gebieden waar hij, eenmaal ingeburgerd, schaduw biedt aan de jonge boompjes van andere, langer levende soorten van het bos, zoals eiken, dennen en ceders.

Zijn kenmerkende witte schors – zo vlak en fijn dat hij door sommige culturen als papier werd gebruikt – is bij de ene soort meer uitgesproken dan bij de andere. De zachte berk en de dwergberk (*Betula pubescens* en *Betula nana*) hebben een dikkere, meer gegroefde, grijze schors, die beter geschikt is voor de kou. De bladeren van de dwerg- en zachte soorten zijn ronder met een enkele rij tanden. De meeste berkenbladeren hebben aan de onderzijde huidharen, een belangrijke habitat voor insecten zoals bladluizen, die voedsel vormen voor vogels, rupsen en vlinders. De berk is een thuis voor veel vlinders en meer dan 330 soorten insecten. Zijn schimmelrelaties zijn al even uitgebreid, met een groot aantal mycorrhizapartners, en verscheidene gewone paddenstoelen zoals cantharellen, de berkenboleet en de vliegenzwam zijn van hem afhankelijk.

Het aftappen van de bomen in de lente om het voedzame sap te verzamelen was een oude gewoonte van vele culturen. In Poplar River herinneren ouderen zich *oh-chi-kah-wah-pi* – het maken van bekers van de schors om berkensap te drinken, en *no-skwa-so-wach* – het snijden van het zoete binnenste cambium om het te eten.

Het sap, de relaties met schimmels en het vermogen om aangetaste grond te herstellen zijn enkele van de vele redenen om de aanplant van berken nu aan te moedigen. De aerosolen en harsen van de boom komen zowel mens als dier in de buurt ten goede. De bladeren zijn antiseptisch, de schors kan tandbederf tegengaan en de geweekte bladeren kunnen worden gebruikt om urineweginfecties te behandelen.

Er is een legende van het inheemse Amerikaanse Odawa-volk over de man die de eerste berk werd en een Ojibwe-verhaal over hoe de berk aan zijn brandwonden kwam. Onder de Chippewa-gemeenschappen werd berkenbast gebruikt om de lichamen van de doden in te wikkelen. In de Pimachiowin Aki Atlas is sprake van Ojibwe die berkenbast gebruikten om kaarten te maken van langeafstandsroutes.

Voor de Kelten was de berk een symbool van vernieuwing en zuivering. *Beithe* was de eerste letter van het Ogham-schrift. Het Keltische feest Samhain – Halloween – werd gevierd met berkenbezems (*besom*) die het oude jaar uitvegen, en tijdens Beltane – het lentefeest – werden vuren van berken en eiken aangestoken. De boom die ook wel bekendstaat als de dame van het bos werd geassocieerd met vruchtbaarheid, vandaar het alternatief voor een kerkelijke ceremonie, een besom wedding. De Angelsaksische godin van de lente was Eostre, die ook werd gevierd in de gedaante van de berk, en van de boom werden meibomen gemaakt.

Corylus, hazelaar

De hazelaar getuigt van de menselijke relatie met het bos zoals het ooit was. Van de heggen van de Britse eilanden tot de archeologische gegevens over het leven in het Mesolithicum in Europa en Noord-Amerika blijkt duidelijk dat de mens in hoge mate afhankelijk was van de noten van de hazelaar. De hazelaar vertegenwoordigde ooit maar liefst 75 procent van het Europese bladerdak, wat tot speculaties heeft geleid dat de mens verantwoordelijk was voor de opzettelijke verspreiding van de boom. De verbrandings-, weide- en akkerbouwsystemen van de savanne lenen zich goed voor de teelt van noten, en noten zijn een rijke bron van eiwitten die kan wedijveren met vlees.

Hazelaar groeit snel en met veel stammen – takken – die ontspruiten uit een enkele basis, of stoel. Als hij met rust wordt gelaten, leeft hij niet veel langer dan honderd jaar, maar als hij regelmatig wordt gesnoeid – tot op de stronk wordt teruggekapt – kan hij bijna oneindig overleven. De bladeren lijken op die van de els en de berk, zijn rond en getand en lopen taps toe tot een punt. De hazelaar behoort eigenlijk tot de berkenfamilie, de *Betulaceae*.

De kostbare noten van de hazelaar, die zo essentieel zijn voor het leven van het bos, groeien uit de bevruchte vrouwelijke bloemen – kleine rode knoppen die aan de tak verschijnen naast de mannelijke katjes. Knaagdieren en vogels voeden zich met de knoppen, terwijl de katjes belangrijk voedsel voor insecten zijn. De katjes worden tijden de winter geproduceerd en met hars verzegeld tot de lente. De stuifmeelwolk na het smelten van de hars is een van de eerste voedingsmiddelen van de lente voor insecten die uit hun winterslaap ontwaken. De gladde schors van de boom is ook een belangrijke gastheer voor vele soorten korstmossen.

Haessel komt van het Angelsaksische woord voor 'kap', het kapje of mutsje dat de noot draagt. De Kelten noemden de hazelaar *Coll* en schreven er wijsheid aan toe. In de Keltische mythologie groeiden er negen heilige hazelaars rond een poel en lieten ze noten in het water lieten vallen die door een zalm werden gegeten. De vlekken op zalmen kwamen overeen met het aantal noten dat ze hadden gegeten. Twijgen van de hazelaar worden gebruikt als wichelroede, terwijl de rook van brandende noten deel uitmaakte van een oud en krachtig Keltisch ritueel om de toekomst te voorspellen.

In een wereld die met voedselcrises wordt geconfronteerd, kunnen de noten van de hazelaar opnieuw een essentieel onderdeel worden van het menselijk dieet.

Juniperus, jeneverbes

Jeneverbes is het tapijt van het boreale gebied. De boom, die in Schotland soms *mountian yew*, bergtaxus, wordt genoemd, is een kruiper, blijft dicht bij de grond en doet in veel opzichten niet aan een boom denken. Het is de wijdst verspreide groenblijvende conifeer ter wereld, die voorkomt van Japan tot Europa en Afrika en in Noord- en Midden-Amerika. Er zijn vele varianten in de boreale zone en een zestigtal soorten wereldwijd, allen leden van de medicinale familie die *Cuppressaceae* wordt genoemd.

De lichtpaarse bes van de vrouwelijke plant is een specerij die wordt gebruikt als smaakmaker voor vlees en jenever, maar was ook een geneeskrachtig ingrediënt. Hij komt tevoorschijn uit een huls van korte, stekelige, bladachtige schubben die hittebestendig en waterafstotend zijn en giftige stoffen bevatten om dieren te ontmoedigen ze op te eten. De wasachtige schubben bevorderen op drie manieren het ecologisch welzijn: ze werpen schaduw op de grond, waardoor de bodemvochtigheid behouden blijft, ze beperken de bodemerosie, ze concentreren geneeskrachtige harsen voor vogels en voor de gezondheid van de bodem en de atmosfeer in het algemeen.

De vogels van het boreale gebied, met name de kramsvogel en de beflijster, die de jeneverbes eten, lijken van cruciaal belang te zijn voor de ontkieming ervan. De bes blijft tot wel drie jaar aan de plant hangen. Met zijn ondoordringbare omhulsel heeft het zaadje de groeven nodig die ontstaan wanneer het door de maag van een vogel gaat, om te kunnen ontkiemen. De planten en de vogels hebben elkaar nodig.

De harsachtige takken van de jeneverbes hebben altijd een heilige rol gespeeld, en de rook van hun verbranding is een integraal onderdeel van veel inheemse ceremonies. Voor inheemse Amerikaanse stammen is jeneverbes een symbool van bescherming. De inheemsen van de prairie zoals de Cheyenne en de Dakota hingen takken van jeneverbesstruiken aan hun tipi's om ze te beschermen tegen stormen. De harsen zijn antiviraal en gezondheidsbevorderend en helpen bij ademhalingsproblemen. Volgens de Keltische folklore kan jeneverbes ook helpen bij het opwekken van samentrekkingen van de baarmoeder om een bevalling op gang te brengen.

Hoewel de jeneverbes over de hele wereld voorkomt, gaat hij op bepaalde plaatsen snel achteruit en heeft hij bijzondere bescherming nodig. De boom houdt niet van schaduw, en de medicijnen in de boom hebben zonlicht nodig om geactiveerd te worden en vrij te komen. Het zou goed zijn om jeneverbessen te planten rond scholen, kinderdagverblijven, verzorgingstehuizen en ziekenhuizen.

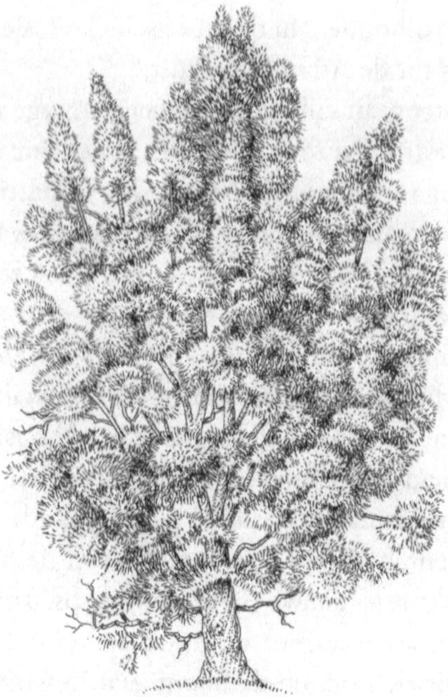

Larix, lariks

De lariks, in Noord-Amerika bekend als tamarack, is een buitenbeentje, een bladverliezende conifeer. Er zijn wereldwijd slechts negen soorten lariksen, waarvan de meeste voorkomen in Siberië en de binnenlanden van Eurazië. *Larix laricina* is de tamarack van Canada en Alaska, ook wel Amerikaanse lariks genoemd. *Larix gmelinii* en *sibirica*, die langer en eleganter zijn dan de in hun groei geremde volhouders in de Siberische kou, sieren de bossen van de Rockies tot de Atlantische kust.

Lariks en water gaan samen, niet alleen vanwege zijn vermogen om grondwaterstromen te reguleren en water van vloeibaar naar ijs en weer terug te transformeren met de gymnastiekoefeningen van zijn cellen, maar ook vanwege de manier waarop hij zich voortplant. Het stuifmeel van de lariks verplaatst zich, net als dat van andere naaldbomen, in het water. Het zaad zwemt net als menselijk sperma de stuifmeelbuis in om de eicel te bevruchten.

Het bladverliesmechanisme van de lariks maakt hem tot de meest ongewone conifeer. De productie van abscisinezuur is wat hem onderscheidt. Dit hormoon stimuleert het terugtrekken van chlorofyl uit de naalden van de boom, waardoor deze oranje of bruin verkleuren. Een verdere daling van de herfsttemperatuur veroorzaakt een nieuwe toevloed van abscisinezuur die het bladweefsel aantast waarmee de naald aan de tak is bevestigd. Bladafval hoopt zich op, en de boom gaat in winterrust. In het voorjaar worden de bomen weer actief en ademen kooldioxide in dat ze gebruiken om bladeren te produceren die vervolgens vallen. Met dit proces worden megatonnen koolstof vastgelegd en opgeslagen omdat de schaduw van de bomen de bosbodem afkoelt, de schimmelactiviteit vertraagt, de verdamping vermindert en de ontbinding afremt.

Voor de inheemse volkeren van Siberië was de lariks de boom des levens die centraal stond in al hun mythologie en heilige rituelen. Bij de volkeren van Noord-Amerika en Europa werd de tamarack gewaardeerd om zijn wortels, die werden gebruikt om kano's van berkenbast in elkaar te naaien en zelfs om de dekken en rompen van grote zeilschepen te verbinden. In waterputten werden pijpen gebruikt die gemaakt waren van rechte tamarack-stammen – die bestand zijn tegen verrotting.

De lariks is een van de meest effectieve bomen voor de vastlegging van kooldioxide en de regulering van het grondwater en zal dus van vitaal belang zijn voor strategische benaderingen van de ecologie.

Picea, spar

Volgens Diana Beresford-Kroeger is de spar het werkpaard van het wereldbos. Er zijn 45 soorten, maar de twee belangrijkste zijn de witte spar en de zwarte spar, die het grootste deel van de subarctische atmosfeer 'schoonwassen'.

Picea glauca is de witte versie, ook bekend als Canadese spar, weidespar, kattenspar of, voor het Chipewyan-volk, grote broer. *Picea mariana* is de zwarte, ook wel oostelijke, veen-, moeras- of dubbelspar genoemd.

Beide hebben de stevige groene naalden die eigenlijk bladeren zijn die strak zijn opgerold tot een buisje en spiraalvormig zijn gerangschikt rond de tak. Hun stammen zijn lang en recht, hoewel noordelijke exemplaren en zwarte sparren die altijd met hun wortels in het water staan in het muskeg, soms onvolgroeid zijn. Naalden, schors, wortels en kegels zijn allemaal rijk aan gom en harsen die zowel een geneeskrachtige als een pyrotechnische waarde hebben. De traagst groeiende bomen in de meest marginale habitats zijn het rijkst aan geneesmiddelen.

Het superdonkere mesofyl van de spar kan fotosynthetiseren onder extreme omstandigheden en haalt het maximale uit moeilijke uithoeken van de planeet. Zijn donkere bladeren absorberen straling en plegen fotosynthese, waardoor de planeet tweemaal wordt gekoeld omdat wordt voorkomen dat langgolvige straling terugkeert in de atmosfeer om vervolgens te worden gevangen door broeikasgassen.

In de Noord-Amerikaanse mythologie hebben sparren een wisselende betekenis. Voor zuidwestelijke stammen zijn ze symbolen van de hemel. In een Hopi-mythe was de spar een medicijnman die zichzelf in een boom veranderde. In de mythe van de Pima-overstroming overleefden een vader en moeder van het Pima-volk de zondvloed door te drijven in een bol sparrenhars. En er is een Iroquois-legende over een meisje dat gered werd van heksen door de geest van de spar.

Bij de Anishinaabe wordt de spar *ka-wa-tik* genoemd, en de kegels van jonge bomen werden gekookt om diarree te behandelen. De wortels van de spar, *wahtup*, werden in water zacht gemaakt en gebruikt om berkenbast samen te binden voor kano's en als strikken voor konijnen.

Uit sparrenhout gewonnen gom, pek, harsen en oliën kunnen worden gebruikt in plaats van op aardolie gebaseerde producten. Er wachten nog genoeg alternatieve toepassingen om ontdekt te worden, als we maar wat moeite doen en geduld hebben.

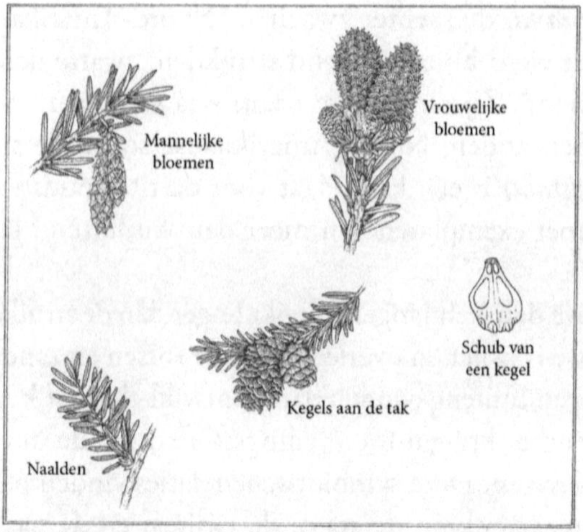
Vrouwelijke
bloemen
Mannelijke
bloemen
Schub van
een kegel
Kegels aan de tak
Naalden

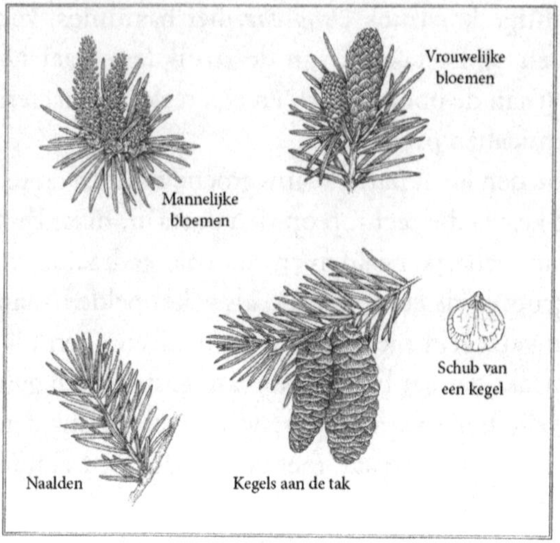
Vrouwelijke
bloemen
Mannelijke
bloemen
Schub van
een kegel
Naalden
Kegels aan de tak

Pinus, spar

Pinus sylvestris, de grove den, is de vertegenwoordiger bij uitstek van de dennenfamilie in Eurazië, terwijl zijn tweelingbroer, *Pinus banksiana*, de scepter zwaait in Noord-Amerika. Door de kolonisten werd hij afwisselend struikden, zwarte den en grijze den genoemd. Zijn indiaanse naam was *kohe*, een Athapsakan-woord. Een andere Noord-Amerikaanse soort, de stoppelden (*Pinus aristata*) is een kandidaat voor de titel 'oudste boom ter wereld', met exemplaren van meer dan vijfduizend jaar oud in Californië.

De grove den leeft langer en reikt hoger dan de struikden, maar deze laatste is taaier en overleeft op kale rotsen en zandgrond, en hij heeft een buitengewone relatie ontwikkeld met korstmossen om toegang te krijgen tot voedingsstoffen die de dunne grond niet kan leveren. Deze symbiotische relaties vinden plaats op de wortels, maar ook op de stam, de twijgen en de naalden. Het schilderachtige korstmos *Usnaceae*, het baardmos, kan worden aangetroffen op de takken van de struikden, waar het stikstof opvangt en aan de boom levert, en een reeks antibacteriële zuren en biochemicaliën produceert.

De grove den heeft paren blauwgroene naalden en rechte symmetrische kegels die rechtop op de tak staan, maar de struikden heeft stompe scherpe naalden en een paar gedraaide vrouwelijke kegels tegenover elkaar op de tak, als gekoppelde bananen. Deze kegels zijn verzegeld met gom en gaan alleen open bij vuur. De hars die maakt dat het brandhout van de struikden gewaardeerd wordt om zijn hoge warmteopbrengst, betekent ook dat een dode den maar langzaam vergaat, met takken die tot wel honderd jaar kunnen blijven liggen.

Noord-Amerika is rijk aan dennen van allerlei soorten, meer dan honderd, en de inheemse volkeren van het continent hadden er een breed scala van medicinale toepassingen voor. De naalden, hars en gom zijn antiseptisch en antibacterieel. Verschillende delen van de boom werden verbrand, geweekt of gekookt om aandoeningen van de luchtwegen te verhelpen. De Cayuga verzamelden dennenknopen – waarin het medicijn het sterkst geconcentreerd was – en wonnen het merg om tuberculose te behandelen.

Voor de stammen van de Great Lakes zijn dennenbomen een symbool van harmonie met de natuur. De Iroquois verbrandden naalden van de witte den (*Pinus strobus*) om geesten uit te drijven en vrede te zoeken, terwijl afgevallen takken werden verbrand en de rook werd gebruikt om de ogen te 'wassen' van iemand die een dode had gezien. In Siberië waren de dennenbossen rond de oevers van het Baikalmeer heilig voor de Boerjat. In het Verenigd Koninkrijk werden grove dennen van oudsher gebruikt als markeringspunten in het landschap, om grenzen en doorgangsrechten aan te geven. De oude Egyptenaren begroeven een beeld van de god Osiris in een uitgeholde pijnboom.

Terwijl de grove den en de witte den beide kwetsbaar zijn voor droogte, lijkt de struikden zeer goed overweg te kunnen met seizoensgebonden watertekorten. Gezien zijn enorme verspreidingsgebied in Noord-Amerika, dat zich uitstrekt over 1600 kilometer ten zuiden van de poolcirkel, zou het een kandidaat kunnen zijn voor toekomstige bossen met zijn brede klimaatniche.

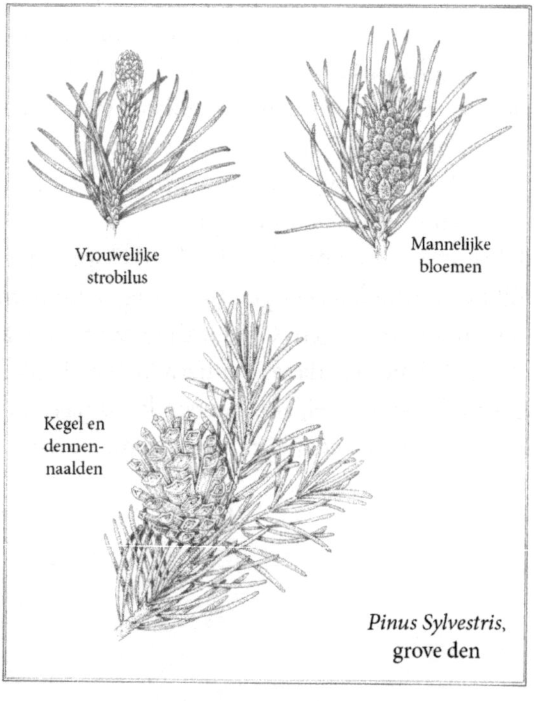
Vrouwelijke
strobilus
Mannelijke
bloemen
Kegel en
dennen-
naalden
Pinus Sylvestris,
grove den

Populus, esp, populier

De esp of populier is een van de wijdst verspreide bomen ter wereld, van de poolcirkel tot Noord-Afrika en in het boreale gebied tot aan Japan. Net als de berk is het een pionierssoort die na de laatste ijstijd als een van de eersten het noordelijk halfrond heeft gekoloniseerd. Het is een snelgroeiende plant die zich na verstoring of brand krachtig vernieuwt.

De schors is glad en grijs, de bladeren klein en rond. Ze hebben een unieke aanpassing aan de basis van de bladstengel, waar ze afplatten en zeer buigzaam en toch sterk zijn, zodat ze kunnen meedraaien en fladderen in de wind, wat aanleiding geeft tot de naam ratelpopulier – *Populus tremuloides*. Volgens de Ieren trilde hij van de emotie. Wanneer ze voor het eerst verschijnen zijn de bladeren koperachtig bruin, daarna vullen ze zich met chlorofyl en worden ze groen, voordat ze in de herfst weer geel worden. Het ratelen van de bladeren weerkaatst het licht rond de boom en verdeelt de biochemicaliën in het blad.

Populieren zijn een belangrijke bron van medicijnen voor mens en dier. Vlinders komen erop af vanwege de salicylaten en mineralen zoals zink en magnesium. Door de lage zuurgraad van de schors komen er korstmossen op voor die alleen op populieren groeien. De mens kan de binnenste schors, die naar meloen smaakt, eten, en de buitenste schors wordt gebruikt voor de behandeling van van alles, van diabetes, hartkwalen en geslachtsziekten tot maagpijn. De bladeren kunnen de pijn van bijen- en wespensteken verzachten, en de witte peridermis van de schors kan worden verzameld en als poeder worden aangebracht om het bloeden te stelpen.

De bloemen van de populier produceren in het voorjaar lange draden met donzige zaden, vergelijkbaar met katoen, vandaar de Engelse soortnaam *cottonwood*. De zaden worden zelden gebruikt, en de boom geeft er de voorkeur aan zich vegetatief voort te planten, zichzelf te klonen. Grote opstanden van populieren zoals in Poplar River zijn waarschijnlijk één enkel organisme van duizenden jaren oud. De Anishinaabe gebruikten populier voor het roken van voedsel en huiden en voor rookfakkels om muggen op afstand te houden.

In Griekse mythen stond hij bekend als de schildboom, die fysieke en spirituele bescherming bood. De Gaelic naam van de boom is *critheann*, en de Highlanders dachten dat de boom magisch was, verbonden met het rijk der feeën. Daarom rustte er een taboe op het gebruik ervan voor de bouw.

Wereldwijd lijkt de populier te lijden onder hittestress. Aan beide zijden van de Atlantische Oceaan, zo merkt Diana Beresford-Kroeger op, heeft de *Populus tremuloides* echter mutaties voortgebracht met triploïden – drie sets chromosomen in plaats van de normale twee – die de kans zouden kunnen bieden om meer veerkrachtige exemplaren te kweken.

Populus balsamifera, balsempopulier

De balsempopulier is een andere *cottonwood* van de wilgenfamilie, de *Saliaceae*, met wolken pluis die elk voorjaar door de vrouwelijke bomen worden losgelaten. Net als andere populieren heeft de balsempopulier de gewoonte zich vegetatief te vernieuwen door ondergronds uitlopers uit te zenden tot over een afstand van veertig meter van de moederboom. Hij lijkt op de populier met zijn rechte grijze stam, maar hoewel die glad is bij jonge boompjes, zal deze na verloop van tijd scheuren en barsten in diepe groeven. De bladeren zijn langer, groener en enigszins hartvormig, veel groter dan die van zijn neef.

De 'balsem' in de naam komt van de rijke oleohars die in de knoppen en bladeren van de boom zit. Dit is het medicijnkastje van de boom, en de reden van een van zijn bijnamen, de balsem van Gilead. Deze hars is geconcentreerd vanwege de voorkeur van de boom voor de moeilijke habitat van de boomgrenszone. Waar weinig hardhoutsoorten kunnen overleven, gedijt de balsempopulier goed. Hij verdraagt de kou en wordt tot dertig meter hoog en twee meter in diameter. Hij komt nooit voor in krummholz, de gedrongen vorm, maar groeit altijd alleen maar recht en hoog.

Hoewel hij wereldwijd voorkomt, vormt hij buiten Noord-Amerika geen grote opstanden. Het was een belangrijke boom voor de inheemse bevolking, die hem de *bam*, *bamtree* of *hackmatack* noemde en die de hars gebruikte voor de behandeling van een hele reeks ziekten, waaronder kanker, hoge bloeddruk en hartkwalen. De olie van de boom is een geneesmiddel dat door de inheemse Amerikanen in veel verschillende behandelingen wordt gebruikt, en het hout heeft geneeskrachtige, antibacteriële eigenschappen en wordt daarom gebruikt voor tandenstokers en eetstokjes. De Westerse geneeskunde heeft haar achterstand nog niet ingehaald en het medicinale potentieel van de balsempopulier nog niet volledig onderzocht.

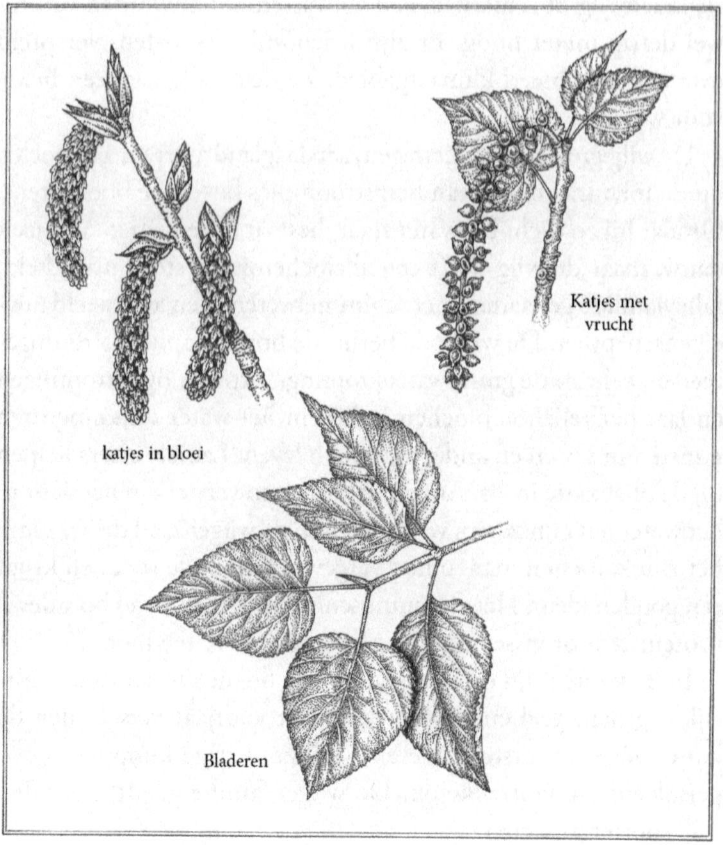
katjes in bloei
Katjes met
vrucht
Bladeren

Salix, wilg

De wilg is nog zo'n pionierssoort die voorkomt voorbij de boomgrens en de overgang naar de toendra markeert. Als geoorde wilg of boswilg kan hij groeien als struik, kruipend langs de grond, of als kraakwilg of schietwilg een volwassen boom worden van tot wel dertig meter hoog. Er zijn driehonderd soorten, verspreid over een zeer breed klimaatgebied. Ze delen allemaal een liefde voor water.

De wilg groei aan waterwegen, aan laaglandrivieren, aan poelen op de toendra en ook aan bergstroompjes boven de boomgrens. Omdat hij zo dicht bij water staat, bestaat er een risico op meeldauw, maar de wilg heeft een allelochemische stof ontwikkeld, salicylanilide genaamd, met schimmelwerende en antimeeldauweigenschappen. De wilg beschermt de bovenloop van stroomgebieden, beheert de grondwaterstroming, vertraagt overstromingen en laat herstellende biochemicaliën in het water vrijkomen ten gunste van vissen en ander aquatisch leven. Labiele esters helpen bij de oliefixatie in vis. Andere salicylzuren versterken het licht in het water ten gunste van waterplanten, en wilgenzaad drijft, zodra het zijn katoenen manen heeft afgeworpen, in de rivier en krijgt een gouden kleur. Het zijn minuscule voedselpakketjes boordevol proteïnen voor vissen die het geluk hebben ze te vinden.

In de winter zijn de kale takken van de meeste soorten kleurrijk – groen, geel en rood – en in het voorjaar verschijnen de katjes vóór de eerste bladeren – dikke, harige knoppen, goed geïsoleerd en aantrekkelijk. De wilgenfamilie voedt meer dan 450 soorten insecten.

De katjes zijn een van de eerste bronnen van stuifmeel voor hommels. Bijen zoeken de wilgen op om toegang te krijgen tot hun geneeskrachtige stuifmeel en nectar, die antibiotische eigenschappen hebben. Vlinders zijn ook afhankelijk van wilgen voor biochemicaliën voor chelatie van de metalen die ze nodig hebben voor hun spectaculaire kleuren. Metalen zijn de elektronenkern in de kleur van hun vleugels.

Wilgen zijn essentieel voor schone en gezonde stroomgebieden, maar ook voor een gezonde insectenpopulatie. Nu bestuivers worstelen met de opwarming van de aarde, zal het planten van meer wilgen hen helpen. De meeste soorten kunnen groeien uit een stek die in de grond is gestoken. Wilgenzaden beginnen 36 uur na het ontkiemen te groeien en stoppen niet meer: ze behoren tot de snelst groeiende bomen van het bos.

De jonge scheuten zijn altijd gebruikt voor manden en om mee te weven, en het volwassen hout is goed voor allerlei dingen, waaronder meubels, karrewielen, cricketbats en klompen. De Ojibwe maken hun zweethutten van wilg en de medicinale toepassingen variëren van pijnbestrijding en het bestrijden van ontstekingen tot het verlichten van constipatie en het gebruik als antibioticum. Op de twijgen van de wilg werd al gekauwd voordat de werkzame stof aspirine eruit werd geïsoleerd en aan de wereld werd verkocht.

Sorbus, lijsterbes

Overal in het boreale gebied is de lijsterbes in de lente een vertrouwd beeld met zijn witte bloemen en in de herfst zijn oogst van trossen rode bessen. Hij is een lid van de rozenfamilie, de *Rosaceae*, en de symmetrische getande bladeren lijken op die van de es, waardoor de andere naam, *mountain ash*, 'berg-es', is ontstaan. *Sorbus aucuparia* is de gewone Europese vorm, *S. americana* en *S. decora* zijn de Noord-Amerikaanse varianten. De Groenlandse variant, *Sorbus groenlandica*, is een ondersoort op zich.

De *Sorbus* zijn snelgroeiende pioniers van het bos die zich gemakkelijk vestigen op de onwaarschijnlijkste plaatsen en daarom een belangrijk lid zijn van de boreale club, met zoveel nuttige relaties met schimmels en korstmossen dat alleen de hazelaar er nog meer heeft. Zijn bloemen hebben in de lente een sterke zoete geur die aantrekkelijk is voor bestuivers en voedsel biedt aan allerlei insecten die zelf weer een prooi vormen voor de trekvogels die na een lange winter terugkeren. De lijsterbes is het vangnet van het boreale gebied en slaagt erin stuifmeel en nectar te produceren ongeacht verstoringen in het weerpatroon.

In de herfst doen de vogels zich weer tegoed aan de rode bessen van de *Sorbus*, alvorens naar het zuiden te vliegen. Het rood van de lijsterbes is de voorbode van de winter. De vogels verspreiden op hun beurt de zaden. Er zitten er acht in elke rode bolvrucht. Het taaie omhulsel van het zaad kost wat moeite om af te breken, hetzij in het spijsverteringskanaal van een dier, hetzij door de inwerking van het weer. Zaden kunnen nog verscheidene jaren nadat ze zijn geproduceerd, ontkiemen.

Ook de mens kan lijsterbessen eten, en ze werden vaak ingemaakt om bij vlees te eten. In de Schotse Hooglanden bestond er een taboe op het gebruik van alle delen van de boom behalve de bessen, en een strikt taboe op het snijden van het hout met een mes. Lijsterbessen werden geplant in de buurt van huizen om bescherming te bieden, en werden geassocieerd met het feeënrijk. De kleine vijfpuntige ster van de bes is een pentagram, een oud beschermend symbool. In Scandinavië werden runen geschreven op lijsterbeshout om te worden gebruikt voor waarzeggerij.

De bladeren van de lijsterbes zijn zilverachtig aan de onderzijde. Ze weerkaatsen het licht en kunnen het opstijgende vocht uit de bodem vasthouden en opvangen. De wortelmassa spreidt zich uit en kan vochttekorten in de winter en de zomer overleven. Daarom is de lijsterbes een goede boom om aan te planten om klimaatverandering te matigen.

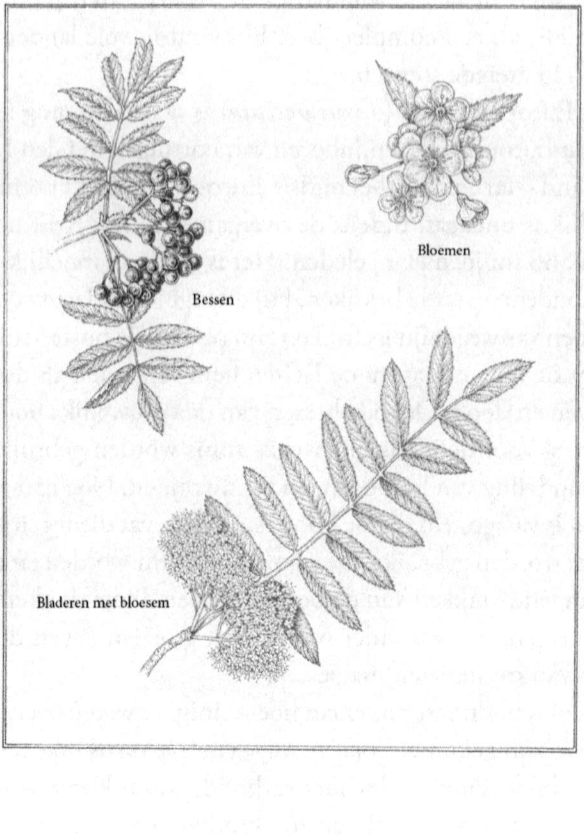
Bloemen
Bessen
Bladeren met bloesem

Taxus, taxus

De taxus is een curiositeit. Het is een conifeer die dol is op karige bodems in een nat klimaat. Hij komt voor van het Verenigd Koninkrijk en over heel Europa tot in bergachtige gebieden in Noord-Afrika, Iran en de Kaukasus, maar toch wordt hij alleen aangetroffen in kleine populaties of als afzonderlijke bomen, bijna nooit als een compleet bos. Hij staat in vele landen op de lijst van bedreigde soorten.

Eén Europese taxus (*Taxus baccata*) is de oudste nog levende boom in Europa – de Venijnboom van Fortingall in Glen Lyon in Schotland – en Taxus is het oudste Europese geslacht bomen, dat kennelijk is ontstaan tijdens de overgang van het Krijt naar het Tertiair, 66 miljoen jaar geleden. Het is dan ook moeilijk om de taxus zonder respect te bekijken. Hij dwingt je aandacht voor hem te hebben vanwege zijn leeftijd en zijn potentiële onsterfelijkheid. Dit was de reden waarom de Kelten hem vereerden als de boom van leven en dood. De rode bessen van de vrouwelijke boom zijn zeer giftig voor de mens, hoewel ze soms worden gebruikt voor de behandeling van hoofdpijn en zenuwpijnen. Nog niet zo lang geleden is vastgesteld dat de boom stoffen bevat die tegen kanker kunnen worden gebruikt. De stam kan enorm worden en de laag overhangende takken van de boom, die een dikke donkere schaduw vormen en waaronder weinig kan groeien, geven de taxus een air van mysterie en magie.

De taxus herinnert ons eraan hoe weinig we weten over bomen en hoe ze zijn gekomen waar ze nu staan. De taxus lijkt een relict te zijn – hij was ooit veel wijder verbreid – maar klimaatveranderingen in het verleden hebben zijn huidige verspreiding bepaald, waardoor hij beperkt is tot refugia. Er zijn aanwijzingen dat ijsschommelingen in het Neogeen (34 tot 35 miljoen jaar geleden) de verspreiding van de taxus hebben aangetast, en dat de schommelingen van de talrijke ijstijden in het Kwartair, met inbegrip van de laatste ijstijd, de populaties verder uiteen hebben geslagen.[1]

Het verspreidingsvermogen van de taxus is gering. De kleine

groene zaadknoppen die de rode bessen worden wanneer ze met stuifmeel bevrucht worden, bevinden zich tussen de bladsteel en de stengels van de bladeren. De platte, naaldachtige bladeren hebben aan de onderzijde grijze en gele banden en zijn spiraalvormig aan de tak bevestigd, hoewel ze door een draaiing aan de basis in rijen lijken te staan. De taxus verspreidt zijn zaad niet ver en groeit niet gemakkelijk uit dat zaad, omdat hij een vochtig, voedselrijk microklimaat nodig heeft en een andere laagblijvende plant, vaak jeneverbes, om de zaailingen tegen planteneters te beschermen. Taxus zal op verstoorde plaatsen hardhout verdringen om nieuw bos te vormen, maar als hij eenmaal in een gemengd bos is geveld, zal hij moeite hebben om zich te verjongen.

De overblijfselen van de taxus stammen uit een fase van het bos voor de mens er was. Zijn huidige verspreiding is het resultaat van een klimaat dat zich tegen hem heeft gekeerd en de vochtige nevels van het Plioceen heeft verloren, alsook van latere kap door de mens. In dat opzicht is hij niet alleen een geestverschijning uit het verleden, maar ook het spook van het toekomstige bos.

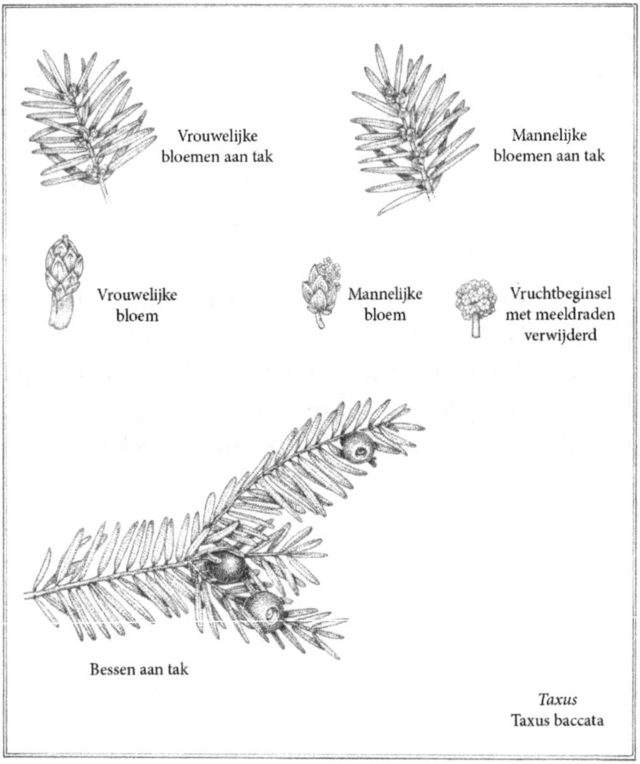
Vrouwelijke bloemen aan tak
Mannelijke bloemen aan tak
Vrouwelijke bloem
Mannelijke bloem
Vruchtbeginsel met meeldraden verwijderd
Bessen aan tak
Taxus
Taxus baccata

Noten

Proloog

1 Thomas Berry, The Dream of the Earth (Sierra Club, 1988).

1. Het zombiebos

1 Ron Summers, Abernethy Forest: The History and Ecology of a Scottish Pinewood (RSPB, 2018).

2 Ibid.

3 Oliver Rackham, Trees and Woodland in the British Landscape (Phoenix, 1976).

4 Rob Wilson et al., 'Reconstructing Holocene Climate from Tree Rings: The potential for a long chronology from the Scottish Highlands', The Holocene, 22, 3-11, 2019. Zie ook Miloš Rydval et al., 'Spatial reconstruction of Scottish summer temperatures from tree rings', International Journal of Climatology 37:3, 2017.

5 Jurata Buchovska en Darius Danusevicius, 'Post glacial migration of Scots pine', Baltic Forestry, 2019.

6 Garrett Hardin, 'The Tragedy of the Commons', Science 162:3859, 1243-48, 13 december 1968. Hardins argument was dat men er niet op kan

vertrouwen dat mensen zich gematigd gedragen in hun omgang met de meent. De volledige uitdrukking die hij gebruikte was 'the tragedy of freedom in the commons', de tragedie van de vrijheid op de meent, en in het artikel worden manieren besproken waarop de mens kan worden gedwongen zich terughoudend op te stellen en gemeenschappelijke ruimten niet te overexploiteren of te vervuilen. Hoewel dit een relevant argument is voor het huidige beheer van natuurlijke hulpbronnen, is het geen bruikbare verklaring voor het verleden en evenmin een rigoureus engagement met inheemse praktijken. Dat kon echter niet voorkomen dat Hardins artikel wel op die manier werd gelezen. Zie George Monbiot, 'The Tragedy of Enclosure', Scientific American, januari 1994.

7 John Prebble, *The Highland Clearances* (Penguin, 1969).

8 Arthur Mitchell (ed.), 'Geographical Collections', 2 in Professor T.C. Smout, *History of the Native Woodlands of Scotland 1500 - 1920* (Edinburgh University Press, 2008).

9 Jim Crumley, *The Great Wood: The Ancient Forest of Caledon* (Birlinn, 2011).

10 Vladimir Gavrikov and Pavel Grabarnik et al., 'Trunk-Top Relations in a Siberian Pine Forest', *Biometrical Journal* 35, 1993.

11 Diana Beresford- Kroeger, *The Global Forest: 40 Ways Trees Can Save Us* (Particular Books, 2011).

12 Rackham, *Trees and Woodland.*

13 Eurostat database, ec.europa.eu.

14 Leif Kullman, 'A Recent and Distinct Pine (Pinus sylvestris L.) Reproduction Upsurge at the Treeline in the Swedish Scandes', *International Journal of Research in Geography* 4, 2018.

15 Leif Kullman, 'Recent Treeline Shift in the Kebnekaise Mountains, Northern Sweden', International Journal of Current Research 10:01, 2018.

16 Summers, *Abernethy Forest.*

17 Ibid.

18 Fiona Harvey, 'London to have climate similar to Barcelona by 2050', *Guardian,* 10 juli 2019.

19 Summers, *Abernethy Forest.*

20 Bob Berwyn, 'Many Overheated Forests May Soon Release More Carbon Than They Absorb', *Inside Climate News*,13 januari 2019.

2. De rendieren achterna

1 *Last Yoik in Sami Forests?*Greenpeace, 2005. Een film die de strijd tegen het kappen van Finlands oerbossen documenteert.
2 Persoonlijke mededeling van Diana Beresford- Kroeger.
3 Diana Beresford-Kroeger, *Arboretum Borealis* (Michigan University Press, 2010).
4 Abrahm Lustgarten, 'How Russia Wins the Climate Crisis', *New York Times*,9 december 2020.

3. De Slapende Beer

1 Anton Tsjechov, *De reis naar Sachalin.*(Atlas, 2004).
2 Anatoly Abaimov et al., 'Variability and ecology of Siberian larch species', Swedish University of Agricultural Sciences, Department of Siviculture, Report 43, 1998.
3 Bob Berwyn, 'When Autumn Leaves Begin to Fall – As the Climate Warms, Leaves on Some Trees are Dying Earlier', *Inside Climate News*, 26 november 2020.
4 Berwyn, 'Many Overheated Forests...'
5 Elena Parfenova, Nadezhda Tchebakova en Amber Soja, 'Assessing landscape potential for human sustainability and "attractiveness" across Asian Russia in a warmer 21st century', *Environmental Research Letters* 14:6, 2019.
6 Lustgarten, 'How Russia Wins...'
7 Ibid.
8 Oliver Milman, 'Global heating pushes tropical regions towards limits of human livability', *Guardian*,8 maart 2021.
9 Gabriel Popkin, 'Some tropical forests show surprising resilience as temperatures rise', *National Geographic*, 19 november 2020.
10 A.A. Popov, *The Nganasan:The Material Culture of the Tavgi Samoyeds*,Routledge Uralic and Altaic Series 56, Routledge, 1966.
11 Piers Vitebsky, *The Reindeer People: Living with Animals and Spirits in Siberia* (Mariner Books,2005).

12 Peter Wadhams, *A Farewell to Ice* (Penguin, 2015).
13 Svetlana Skarbo, 'Weather swings in Siberia as extreme heat is followed by June snow, tornadoes and floods', *Siberian Times*, 9 juni 2020.
14 *Shaman*, Lennart Mari. A documentaire uit 1977, uitgekomen in 1997, https://www.youtube.com/watch?v=2ZlOPkIbR5o.
15 Eugene Helimski, 'Nganasan Shamanistic Tradition: Observations and Hypotheses,' paper gepresenteerd tijdens de conferentie 'Shamanhood: The Endangered Languages of Ritual' in het Centre for Advanced Study, Oslo juni 1999.
16 W. Gareth Rees et al., 'Is subarctic forest advance able to keep pace with climate change?' *Global Change Biology* 26:4, april 2020.
17 Dr. Zac Labe van de Universiteit van Colorado, geïnterviewd door Jeff Berardelli, 'Temperatures in the Arctic are astonishingly warmer than they should be', *CBS News*, 23 november 2020.
18 Tsjechov, *De reis naar Sachalin.*
19 Craig Welch, 'Exclusive: Some Arctic Ground No Longer Freezing – Even in Winter', *National Geographic*,20 augustus 2018.
20 S. Zimov et al., 'Permafrost and the global carbon budget', *Science* 312:5780, 16 juli 2006.
21 University of Copenhagen, 'Arctic Permafrost Releases More Carbon Dioxide than Previously Believed', phys.org, 9 februari 2021.

4. De grens

1 Charles Wohlforth, *The Whale and the Supercomputer* (Farrar, Straus & Giroux, 2004) vertelt het verhaal van zijn onderzoek en de debatten die dat losmaakte.
2 Ken Tape, 'Tundra be dammed: Beaver colonization of the Arctic', *Global Change Biology* 24:10, oktober 2018; Ben M. Jones et al., 'Increase in beaver dams controls surface water and thermokarst dynamics in an Arctic tundra region, Baldwin Peninsula, northwestern Alaska', *Environmental Research Letters* 15, 2020.
3 Seth Kantner, *Shopping for Porcupine* (Milkweed Editions, 2008).
4 Anna Terskaia, Roman Dial en Patrick Sullivan, 'Pathways of tundra encroachment by trees and tall shrubs in the western Brooks Range of Alaska', *Ecography* 43, 2020.

5 Merlin Sheldrake, *Entangled Life (*Bodley Head, 2020).
6 S.W. Simard et al., 'Net transfer of carbon between ectomycorrhizal tree species in the field', *Nature* 388, 1997; Ferris Jaber, 'The Social Life of Forests', *New York Times Magazine*, december 2020.
7 'Satellites reveal a browning forest', NASA Earth Observatory, 18 april 2006.
8 'Land Ecosystems Are Becoming Less Efficient at Absorbing CO2', NASA Earth Observatory, 18 december 2020.
9 Kate Willett, 'Investigating climate change's "humidity paradox"', *Carbon Brief*, 1 december 2020.
10 Max Martin, 'Add atmospheric drying – and potential lower crop yields – to climate change toll', *Toronto Star*,12 maart 2021.
11 T.J. Brodribb et al., 'Hanging by a thread? Forests and Drought', *Science* 368:6488, 17 april 2020.
12 Jim Robbins, 'The Rapid and Startling Decline of World's Vast Boreal Forests', *Yale Environment* 360, 12 oktober 2015.
13 Ibid.
14 Fred Pearce, *A Trillion Trees* (Granta, 2021).
15 Ibid.
16 David Ellison et al., 'Trees, Forests and Water: Cool Insights for a Hot World', *Global Environmental Change* 43, 2017.
17 A.M. Makarieva and V. G. Gorshkov, 'Biotic pump of atmospheric moisture as driver of the hydrological cycle on land', *Hydrological Earth System Science* 11, 2007.
18 Ibid.
19 Roger Pielke en Piers Vidale, 'The Boreal Forest and the Polar Front', *Journal of Geophysical Research* 100:D12, 1995.
20 Makarieva en Gorshkov, 'Biotic pump of atmospheric moisture...'
21 Fred Pearce, 'A Controversial Russian Theory Claims Forests Don't Just Make Rain – They Make Wind', *Science*, 18 juni 2020.
22 Kyle Redilla, Sarah T. Pearl et al., 'Wind Climatology for Alaska: Historical and Future', *Atmospheric and Climate Sciences* 9:4, oktober 2019.
23 Richard K. Nelson, *Make Prayers to the Raven: A Koyukon View of the Northern Forest* (University of Chicago Press, 1983).

24 'Project Jukebox', University of Alaska Fairbanks Oral History Program. Zie https://jukebox.uaf.edu/site7/interviews/3623 voor de interviews met Attla.

25 *Make Prayers to the Raven*, KUAC Radio, Fairbanks. Documentaireserie beschikbaar op YouTube.

26 World Wildlife Fund for Nature and Huslia Tribal Council, *Witnessing Climate Change in Alaska*, 2005. Een door studenten samengestelde reeks radioprogramma's met interviews van inwoners van Huslia is beschikbaar op https:// wwf.panda.org/discover/knowledge_hub/where_we_work/arctic/ what_we_do/ climate/climatewitness2/huslia/radio_programmes/.

27 Juliet Eilperin, 'As Alaska warms, one village's fight over oil and development', *Washington Post*, 14 december 2019.

28 Beresford- Kroeger, *Arboretum Borealis.*

29 Ibid.

30 Dieter Kotte et al. (eds), *International Handbook of Forest Therapy* (Cambridge Scholars, 2019).

31 Sabrina Shankman, 'What Has Trump Done to Alaska? Not as Much as He Wanted', *Inside Climate News*, 30 augustus 2020.

5. Het bos in de zee

1 Diana Beresford-Kroeger, *To Speak for the Trees: My Life's Journey from Ancient Celtic Wisdom to a Healing Vision of the Forest* (Penguin, 2019).

2 Ibid.

3 John Laird Farrar, *Trees in Canada* (Fitzhenry and Whiteside, 2017).

4 Beresford- Kroeger, *To Speak for the Trees*;zie ook Katsuhiko Matsunaga et al., 'The role of terrestrial humic substances on the shift of kelp community to crustose coralline algae community of the southern Hokkaido Island in the Japan Sea', *Journal of Experimental Marine Biology and Ecology 241, 1999.*

5 Charles C. Mann, *1493: How Europe's Discovery of the Americas Revolutionized Trade, Ecology and Life on Earth* (Granta, 2011).

6 Tracy Glynn, 'Canada is under-reporting deforestation, carbon debt from clearcutting: Wildlands League', *NB Media Coop*, 15 januari 2020;

Frederick Beaudry, 'An Update on Deforestation in Canada', treehugger.com, 31 januari 2019.

7 De brandcycli en de culturele geografie van de Anishinaabe worden gedetailleerd beschreven in Iain J. Davidson-H unt, Nathan Deutsch en Andrew M. Miller, *Pimachiowin Aki Cultural Landscape Atlas: Land That Gives Life* (Pimachiowin Aki Corporation, 2012).

8 David Lindenmayer en Chloe Sato, 'Hidden collapse is driven by fire and logging in a socioecological forest ecosystem', *Proceedings of the National Academy of Sciences of the USA* 115:20, 2018.

9 Robin Wall Kimmerer, *Braiding Sweetgrass* (Milkweed, 2013).

10 *Pimachiowin Aki Cultural Landscape Atlas* is een uitgebreide uitleg van de geologie van Lake Agassiz.

11 Columbia University, 'Northern peatlands may contain twice as much carbon as previously thought', phys.org, 21 oktober 2019.

6. Een laatste tango met het ijs

1 Wadhams, *AFarewell to Ice*.

2 C. Rahbek et al., 'Humboldt's enigma: What causes global patterns of mountain biodiversity?' *Science* 365:6458, september 2019.

3 Richard T. Corlett and David A. Westcott, 'Will plant movements keep up with climate change?' *Trends in Ecology and Evolution* 28:8, 2013.

4 Jared Diamond, *Ondergang: waarom zijn sommige beschavingen verdwenen en hoe kan de onze haar ondergang voorkomen* (Spectrum, 2013).

5 Andrew Christ en Paul Bierman, 'Ancient leaves preserved under a mile of Greenland's ice – and lost in a freezer for years – hold lessons about climate change', *Conversation*, 15 maart 2021.

6 Ker Than, 'Ancient Greenland Was Actually Green', *Livescience*, 5 juli 2007.

7 Signe Normand et al., 'A Greener Greenland?: Climatic potential and long-term constraints on future expansions of trees and shrubs', *Philosophical Transactions of the Royal Society* 368:1624, 2013.

8 Peter Branner, 'The Terrifying Warning Lurking in the Earth's Ancient Rock Record – Our climate models could be missing something big', *Atlantic*, maart 2021.

9 Max Adams, *The Wisdom of Trees* (Head of Zeus, 2014).
10 Ellison et al., 'Trees, Forests and Water...'
11 Aslak Grinsted and Jens Hesselbjerg Christensen, 'The transient sensitivity of sea level rise', *Ocean Science* 17, 2021.
12 Ian Rappel, 'Habitable Earth: Biodiversity, Society and Rewilding', *International Socialism,* april 2021.
13 Ibid.
14 Donna Harraway, *Staying with the Trouble: Making Kin in the Chuthulucene* (Duke University Press, 2016).
15 James Hansen, *Storms of my Grandchildren* (Bloomsbury, 2009); James Hansen et al., 'Young people's burden: Requirement of negative CO2 emissions', *Earth System Dynamics* 8, 2017; David Wadsell, 'Climate Dynamics: Facing the Harsh Realities of Now, Climate Sensitivity, Target Temperature and the Carbon Budget: Guidelines for Strategic Action', presentatie van het Apollo-Gaia Project, september 2015.
16 David Abram, *The Spell of the Sensuous* (Vintage, 1997).
17 'Collaborative survival', gezamenlijk overleven, is een term van Anna Tsing in *De paddenstoel aan het einde van de wereld* (Octavo, 2021)

Epiloog: Denken als een bos

1 P.A. Thomas and A. Polwart, '*Taxus baccata* ', *Journal of Ecology* 91, 2003.

Dankbetuigingen

Hartelijk dank aan mijn genereuze gastheren en gastvrouwen, vrienden op zoveel plaatsen die me met nieuwe ogen hebben leren kijken: in Schotland, Thomas MacDonnell, Margaret Bennett, Rob Wilson, Fiona Holmes en Trees for Life, Mark Hancock en Cairngorms Connect; in Finnmark, Hallgeir Strifeldt, Tor Havard Sund, Māret Buljo, Inge-Marie Gaup Eira, Issát H. Eira, Berit Utsi, Niillas Mihkkael, Māarija Eira, Sara-Irene Haetta, Thomas Myrnes Nygård; in Rusland, Elena Kukofskaja, Nadezjda Tjebakova, Aleksandr Bondarev, Sophy Roberts, Ko van Huissteden, Sander Veraverbeke, Djazda en Maria Yevstappi, Misha en Anna Chuperin, Anatoly Gavrilov, Nikolai Zimov, Nikolai Kozak en Nikolai Baronofsky; in Alaska, Pat Lambert, Adam Weymouth, Ken Tape, Seth Kantner, Roman Dial, Patrick Sullivan, Rebecca Hewitt, Brendan Rogers, John Gaedeke, Carl Burgett; in Canada, Diana en Christian Beresford-Kroeger, Sophia en Ray Rabliauskas en iedereen in Poplar River, LeeAnn Fishback, Steven Mamet, Dave Daley; in Groenland, Kenneth Høegh, Ellen Friedrikssen, Dirk van As, Faezeh M. Nick, Peter Friis Møler, Jason Box en iedereen bij Greenland Trees, en aan Jennifer Cartwright die me veel leerde over refugia.

Dank aan het geweldige team in Londen en New York dat het project vanaf het begin heeft gesteund: Sophie Lambert, Anna Stein, Bea Hemming en Elisabeth Dyssegaard. Aan Jonny Donovan, wiens gezelschap en enthousiasme me op weg hielpen in Noorwegen. Aan vroege lezers en kritische vrienden Jay Griffiths, Tom Bullough, Diana Beresford-Kroeger, Elfie Rawlence, Simon Rawlence en Zanna Jeffries. Dank aan de bomen die hun leven gaven voor dit boek. Aan mijn vrouw Louise en dochters Daphne en Cissy, die mij minder hebben gezien dan zou hebben gemoeten. En ten slotte aan Brigid Hogan, die opdracht gaf voor de prachtige illustraties door Lizzie Harper. De tekeningen zijn opgedragen aan de nagedachtenis van haar broer en mijn schoonvader, Patrick Hogan, een boom van een man die tijdens de pandemie is overleden, terwijl dit boek werd geschreven.

Register